ALSO BY SEYMOUR BRITCHKY

The Restaurants of New York

THE LUTÈCE
COOKBOOK

THE

LUTÈCE

COOKBOOK

by

André Soltner

with Seymour Britchky

Illustrations by Henry Kibel

Alfred A. Knopf   NEW YORK   1995

THIS IS A BORZOI BOOK
PUBLISHED BY ALFRED A. KNOPF, INC.

Library of Congress Cataloging-in-Publication Data
Soltner, André, [date]
The Lutèce cookbook / by André Soltner, with Seymour Britchky. — 1st ed.
p.   cm.
Includes index.
ISBN 0-679-42273-0
1. Cookery, French. 2. Lutèce (Restaurant : New York, N.Y.)
I. Britchky, Seymour. II. Title.
TX719.S63   1995
641.5′09747′1—dc20

Manufactured in the United States of America

First Edition

To my mother, Eugénie Soltner—called Mimi—
who taught me the love of cooking

and

To my wife, Simone, who for more than thirty years,
during good times and bad times—in the extremely
difficult restaurant world—was my equal and my
support in all things and in every way

and

To all spouses who live in the shadow of well-known
cooks—today's star chefs owe more of their success
to these unknown partners than the world can know

Contents

THE LUTÈCE
COOKBOOK

INTRODUCTION

~•❧•~

Lutèce and André Soltner

A world traveler with a keen eye, strolling Manhattan's East 50th Street, may well be struck by, even look twice at, the pale-gray façade of No. 249, for on this otherwise ordinary midtown block, here is a gray unlike the ashy tones that are much of visible New York. There is warmth in this gray, which, in different lights, is a hint of ocher, or pink, or cream. If the traveler's eye is truly sharp, he may even recognize that what caught his attention was four stories of *pierre de Paris,* the building stone of Paris, and that these blocks of it apparently came to the New World with their own supply of that city's gold-and-silver light.

All of which is only in part an illusion, for No. 249 is the site of Lutèce, which is not only a French restaurant on Manhattan Island but an outpost of Paris itself. And when, twenty years into the restaurant's storied life, its chef and proprietor, André Soltner, undertook proverbially to engrave in stone the establishment's unique status, he sent to France for several tons of real stone with which to do the job. Today, the slender building, demurely set a few feet back from its building line, seems to look out on this street with a coquettish smile, as if confident that occasional passers-by will respond with smiles of their own when they realize that they have chanced upon a bit of Paris in New York.

A low iron fence banked with planters of ivy stands six feet forward of No. 249, and in bad weather a rolled-up awning the full twenty-foot width of the building is unfurled to shelter the space between the greenery and the façade. At the curb, a young linden tree—its boughs, in season, a fresh minty green—reaches as high as the top of the second story. The vertical oblong of the building is repeated, in small, in its slender windows. A few steps down to the entrance, a plaque to the right of the door announces, brass letters on black, LUTÈCE.

The restaurant is installed in what long ago was the residence of its first and former owner, one André Surmain. Over the years, the lower two

floors of what was then an entirely private town house have been transfig-
ured into a place of quite public accommodation that, today, is at once
familiar and legendary.

One enters Lutèce to a tiny foyer off which, to the right, a barroom of
fancifully minuscule proportions is tucked away. Its space, under a three-
globe chandelier, is occupied almost entirely by a short pewter bar, of
Parisian provenance, and a handful of small round marble-topped tables
surrounded by Paris café chairs. The walls of this apple-green den are
adorned with a whimsical collection of art and mementos, dominant
among them a misty mural (by the muralist Jean Pagès) of a Paris street
scene in which the house (now museum) of the nineteenth-century French
painter Eugène Delacroix figures importantly. Lest you lose your way, to
the right of the mural hangs a bona fide Paris street sign, white letters
on indigo blue, of the depicted thoroughfare: PLACE DE FURSTENBERG,
6° ARR.
  It is the minor miracle of this tiny but essential corner of Lutèce that
it accommodates with aplomb a bewilderingly intricate traffic of diverse
comings and goings—early arrivers congregating and sipping aperitifs
while they wait for tables, waiters ordering and picking up drinks from the
bar, guests checking and retrieving coats, others being greeted or good-
byed by various members of the staff—with, often, much gay ceremony.
When, inevitably, the clusters of guests and help become enmeshed, the
civility and good humor that this place seems to confer on all within its
rooms make of the scene a complex, mannerly, collision-free choreogra-
phy, a dance of courteous deferral.
  At the back of this ground floor are two of the restaurant's four dining
rooms. One is led to them through a long dark-wood corridor—furnished
with floor-to-ceiling racks of wine—that is hung with many of the count-
less awards and honors that Lutèce, and its proprietor, André Soltner, have
earned over three decades. Adjacent to this strait, visible through a long
horizontal window, is a glistening kitchen, in it a host of bustling figures
in tall *toques blanches,* often among them Soltner himself, who smiles out
sunnily and waves—and sometimes exits from the kitchen into the corridor—to greet passing guests he knows on sight.
  A dozen steps farther, then a couple down, and you are in the first

dining room. Perhaps because this square space with a table in each corner is the smallest of the restaurant's four dining rooms, a cachet of especial desirability has always attached to tables here. Like all the dining rooms this one is in a way fantastical. Its misty gray-green walls are adorned with a painted-on trelliswork that—intertwined with trailing vines that at one point "grow" across the ceiling—frames the vaporous ground of hazy green. What with the flagstones underfoot, and the soft light, it takes but a small effort of mind to imagine that, here in a woods adjacent to a grand country house, one is in a glade to which a stone walk was laid long ago. *Such* a nice place for a picnic.

Continue along the flagstones back toward that imagined country house, and you come upon its garden—which is to say, this restaurant's fabled "Garden." Here is the room most people think of when they think of Lutèce, though it is in fact the last of the dining rooms to have been put in final form. Once, when Lutèce was new, the Garden was actually out of doors, open to the sky, usable only in fine weather. (In those days, the first owner, André Surmain, tried to stretch the outdoor season by installing heat lamps on tall poles among the tables. But, as the ground underfoot was uninsulated, and as the lamps could not be fine-tuned, more than one patron found himself suffering from the polar discomforts of cold feet and fevered brow.) In time, Surmain installed a roof; some years later Soltner insulated the ground under the flagstones; today the Garden is clement always.

The roof Surmain installed is a vaulted translucent ceiling lined with pale-green blinds through which, by day, the light of the New York sky is filtered, throwing a luminous incandescence over the fairyland that is this fabled retreat; at night the illumination is a soft-glowing pink, which seems to radiate from pink walls that, behind a creamy lattice, bracket the room down its long sides. The lattice is punctuated at intervals by short columns of whited brick, each of which supports a palm in a shiny, copper-trimmed brass pot. The snowy tables, surrounded by commodious wicker chairs, are set, as are the tables throughout Lutèce, with gleaming crystal, glinting flatware, white plates, and, on every table, pink or red roses in a slender silver vase.

Still, as if perversely clinging to a past best forgotten, the Garden seems occasionally to betray a continuing taste for traffic with the elements. As recently as the late 1980s, patrons experienced one of the more dramatic reminders of the room's alfresco origins. On a night when New York was enjoying one of its cleansing cloudbursts, and just when Lutèce was enjoying the height of its dinner hour, all at once it was observed by those present that, from the ground up the Garden was filling with water—water that was coursing down its walls. Soltner, urgently summoned from the kitchen, got the picture, ran out of the restaurant and around the block, had himself buzzed into an apartment building with access to the back yard (by pressing the bells of all the apartments), invaded the yard, clambered up the fire escape ladder of a building next to Lutèce, and—by now wet to the skin—reached to remove the child's ball that had somehow got stuck in the rain gutter.

The pool drained, the flagstones were mopped, diners who had fled to dry ground in other parts of Lutèce returned to their tables. (Patrons at two of the tables never fled at all, just removed their shoes, rolled up their trousers, ate and drank throughout the irregularity.) Within minutes, all who had fled were back in their chairs. No one had left the restaurant. To this day, a number of those who were present that night stop to remind Soltner of his memorable flash flood whenever they return to Lutèce in search, presumably, of further adventure.

As the rooms downstairs seem like faraway places, those a flight up exist in a long-lost time, when traditional adornment and luxury were permitted to hearten and delight.

Lutèce is neither clamorous nor ever hushed, but it does have a quiet corner, the five-table Petit Salon, the smaller of the two cushily carpeted upstairs rooms. Le Petit Salon faces south, and at lunchtime the high-ceilinged space is flooded with the light that pours through the gauzy curtains hanging in its tall windows. The windows are hung as well with blue-and-ivory drapes that match the room's Toile-de-Jouy wallpaper, the details of its manorial pattern a fantasy of statuary, farm animals, peasants at their tasks, noblemen at their sports. The dominant piece at the center of the room is a handsome old copper distilling vessel that André Surmain persuaded the proprietors of the Hôtel de la Poste, in Beaune, to sell. Fresh flowers, a huge burst of them, sprout from the vessel's top, glow in the light of the crystal chandelier that hangs just above them, quicken this cushy room with their color and warmth.

Gobelin tapestries are not commonplace fixtures in New York eating places, but Le Grand Salon, the last of the dining rooms, is dominated by a genuine example, an intricately woven hunting scene that was presented to Lutèce by Miguel Aleman, a former president of Mexico who was a Lutèce stockholder in the restaurant's first years. The tapestry has hung here from the start, and from time to time knowledgeable guests—presumably to relieve André Soltner of the burden of its ownership—have made modest offers for it.

The walls of the room that houses this imposing work have been surfaced with a padded fabric—its airy design a web of stylized florets and horns of plenty in muted earth tones—that is at once cozy and smart. What with its carved fireplace, mementos on the mantle, and framed paintings on the walls, Le Grand Salon is the homiest of the Lutèce dining rooms. In part, this is so because when Lutèce became entirely his own, André Soltner appointed it with reminders of his past. He asked his parents to send from Alsace two paintings with which he had more or less grown up, oils by a friend of the family. The smaller of them is a still-life of game and wild mushrooms that hung in the Soltner family's house. The larger is of the Three Musketeers, and it was made for the wood-paneled office of Soltner's late cabinetmaker father. Here the paintings keep company with two old florals that have hung on these walls from the first, both of them latterly cleaned and restored by an expert who recognized one as a Florentine relic of no little value.

A rooster (the bird-emblem of France) stands on the mantel—not a stuffed rooster, but a piece that seems to encapsulate Lutèce, for the whimsical bird is an artful assemblage of knives, forks, and spoons. The Soltners spotted it in Paris years ago, and saw at once that it belonged in Lutèce. It shares this ledge with a silver trophy awarded to Soltner at the Alsatian Regional Council for the First Festival of International Gastronomy in Colmar; and with a cylindrical glass vase of flowers, which are reflected in the large framed mirror just over the fireplace. This room, too, is overhung with a crystal chandelier—here it conveys not so much grandeur as the stately grace of an earlier time. By day the chandelier's glittery light is supplemented by a bit of daylight that enters through the glass transom of folding doors opening onto a tiny terrace—on which, when Lutèce was young, lunch was served at a pair of small tables under the sky.

Such are the visible parts of a mise-en-scène to which knowing New Yorkers, and well-advised visitors from fifty states and a hundred nations, have for a third of a century repaired: to eat and drink, certainly, but to indulge as well, if only for the duration of lunch or dinner, in a disappearing way of life.

It has been said that of New York restaurants in its class, only Lutèce is not tailored to its time or place, does not address itself to the received tastes of a fickle public, does not indiscriminately flatter. It is, rather, the repository of the gracious ways of our inherited past, those courtly manners—cordial, gay, and at ease—that honor preeminently the shared human moment. No one is immune. All who enter come under the spell. Lutèce has the power to civilize.

Of course such an establishment appeals principally to those who need no such influence. For all its renown, it is at heart a neighborhood restaurant, albeit serving an extended community. Of eating places usually mentioned in the same breath as Lutèce, most are restaurants in which fame and fashion are on parade, where any number of those present are on hand because of who else may be present. But the guests at Lutèce are, mostly, neither on display nor agape. This is a public place, to be sure, but very much one for private pleasure, host to those whose preferences about where to eat are matters of taste, not calculation. Lutèce is that rarest of restaurants, one in which you find yourself surrounded by patrons at the other tables whom, you infer from appearances, you would not mind having at your own.

None of which is to suggest that the century's most brilliant luminaries have shunned Lutèce. In fact its autograph book is replete with fond greetings and rave reviews from the likes of such domestic and imported artists as Judy Collins and Itzak Perlman, Douglas Fairbanks, Jr., and Claudette Colbert, Balanchine and Noguchi, Jean Pierre Aumont and Jeanne Moreau. Diana Ross and Mick Jagger have signed the book, as have Lionel Hampton and Frank Sinatra, Cosby and Gleason, Ono and Lennon. But then, so have Lindbergh and Cousteau, General Dayan and General Gavin, Mantle and Pelé, Prince Rainier and Giscard d'Estaing, Elie Wiesel and Christiaan Barnard ("with sincere gratitude from the bottom of my transplanted heart").

Through the restaurant's rooms have passed William Paley and Pearl Bailey, Dore Shary and Hugh Carey, winners of the Oscar and winners of the Nobel Prize, American Wimbledon champions, Russian chess champions, and French ski champions, as well as champion eccentrics: Groucho Marx wore his beret throughout dinner, and Vladimir Horowitz, having presumably forgotten his—and despite Mrs. Horowitz's remonstrations—put his menu where his beret belonged. To mention only those presidential aspirants whose names begin with "M," Senators Mondale, Muskie, McGovern, and McCarthy (Eugene) all apparently thought that their political chances could only be furthered by an appearance here. Mayors have eaten at Lutèce, senators and governors of two dozen states, ambassadors to and emissaries from countries on every continent, prime ministers, Secretaries General of the United Nations, Secretaries of State, and, regularly for many years, a former President of all the states.

When circumstances require it, Lutèce reaches out to those who will not, or cannot, come in: as Katharine Houghton Hepburn shuns the New York restaurant scene, Soltner decided to send out, for her pleasure, his famous escargots, the Hepburn town house being only a couple of blocks away—her thank-you note, on letterhead that is complete with the unfamiliar middle name, is a Lutèce memento tucked into the autograph book; when James Levine, Artistic Director and Principal Conductor of the Metropolitan Opera, cannot get away from the opera house for his Lutèce lunch, Soltner has been known to ship a nicely roasted young chicken straight from the oven to Lincoln Center; and though Jacqueline Kennedy shunned New York restaurants not at all (and came often to Lutèce), when she moved to the city in the 1960s, and gave a party for her friends in her new apartment, the man preparing the food in her kitchen was André Soltner—who was overseen at his tasks by two young children seated near him, side by side, on the kitchen counter.

The decades-long appeal to the good and the great is really acclaim for André Soltner—who, it is often aptly said, *is* Lutèce. But it was not always so. Though Lutèce is now and forever identified with Soltner—an Alsatian by birth, a French chef by training, an American by adoption—the André who founded it, André Surmain, the French-sounding name notwithstanding, was a New Yorker, an airline caterer by profession, who had taken a French name to go with his ambitions. Though the East Side town house in which he started the restaurant in 1961 was then the house he lived in (it had been the site of a cooking school he ran with James Beard), his search for a chef took him beyond the boundaries of the five boroughs, ranged as far as Paris, where, on a tip, Surmain ate one day at the restaurant Chez Hansi.

Surmain liked his lunch and sent his compliments to the chef. When the young chef came out to thank his admirer, Surmain suggested they meet privately. The meeting took place, and Surmain offered the chef ninety-five dollars a week (equivalent to what he was earning at Chez Hansi) to take charge of the kitchen in his new Manhattan restaurant—which, he confidently explained, was going to be the best restaurant in America. The unencumbered and game young man had, as a child, listened with fascination to his grandfather's stories about escapades in America, including tales—probably tall—of adventures among American Indians, and other tales—quite true—of the family bakery in Reno, Nevada. His curiosity about the New World had been on hold ever since, but now it was piqued, and he accepted the offer on the spot. The young man was of course the twenty-seven-year-old André Soltner—who, on that day, had no idea he was saying yes to his destiny.

He also had no idea whom he was dealing with. When Soltner arrived in New York he found that he was but one of three men who had been lured to Lutèce with a promise of the top job. And though at Soltner's insistence the matter was promptly straightened out, Soltner getting the appointment, André Surmain's ploy served as André Soltner's real introduction to his new boss, the dawning of what he was soon to learn well: that no two more disparate characters had ever entered, eyes open, into a voluntary professional marriage. Surmain was artful, Soltner direct. Surmain was imperious, Soltner all charm. Surmain was a businessman, Soltner a workman.

During the early years, when Surmain was sole proprietor, he set his dining room captains a lordly example that they never matched, though they tried. At times his high-handedness took an amusing turn. To a patron who complained about the absence of valet parking, Surmain, raising himself to his full height, answered, "Sir, our guests come with their chauffeurs." (This was long before the restaurant had any reputation at all.) Another, for complaining that the only celebrity in the house was Salvador Dali, was merely ejected, no explanation. Surmain turned people away for what he deemed inappropriate clothing, on occasion scornfully declined to accept payment from those who found any fault with his restaurant (their money was not good enough for his bank account), and set prices for his food and wine with, apparently, one purpose in mind: that they be the highest prices in town, if possible the highest on earth. "But we are only soup merchants," Soltner would say during their frequent disagreements—which was not how Surmain saw it at all.

Still, even as differences simmered behind the scenes, the kitchen was gaining an international reputation. Lutèce was seven years old when, in 1968, Soltner's talents were commended at the highest level of professional recognition. That year he was honored with a French chef's most sought-after distinction. Until then, no chef working outside of France had been granted the august title Meilleur Ouvrier de France.

Eventually, Soltner's down-to-earth way would become the Lutèce way, for when he agreed to come to New York, it had been with the understanding that one day he would become a partner. In 1965 Surmain was held to his promise, and Soltner bought a thirty-percent share. (When necessary, Soltner held Surmain to his promises by explaining that he would leave if they were not kept.) After several more years of amicable discord, André Soltner bought the remaining seventy percent. And while the friendship of the two men, now untroubled by policy disagreements, continues to the present, the singularity of Lutèce dates from that year— 1972.

Soltner instituted many changes. Perhaps most notably (and indeed most noticeably), he began to make a practice of spending much time in the dining room, all smiles and accessibility and sweet reason, talking amicably to his customers, which constituted an immediate good-bye to the hauteur, high seriousness, and attendant discomforts that were the old Lutèce. Hospitality, cordiality, ease—even jollity!—took their place, all of them the inexorable effect of the new chef-proprietor's beaming benevolence. Where André Soltner goes, as if by magic, contentment follows. The patience, good will, and evident pleasure with which he fraternizes— answering questions, listening to jokes, taking orders, suggesting bottles of wine, recounting cautionary tales of a restaurateur's unpredictable life, indulging almost any culinary whim (and nonculinary whims within reason)—are in their sum a thing apart. Soltner's manner transformed

Lutèce overnight. And, overnight, a restaurant that had been struggling to survive caught on.

Still, the buyout had drained Soltner's savings, he needed cash for working capital, and in this connection, to students of Soltner's way with the world, it is instructive to observe how he handled that early difficulty: He determined the location of the nearest bank (in which he had never set foot), pulled an overcoat over his chef's clothes, and walked there. An hour later he had a $40,000 line of credit from a banker who had never heard of him before that day. No references, no balance sheets, no financial projections. Reporters were not present for the transaction, but it is safe to assume that Soltner cast some of the very spells with which he has charmed mankind ever since.

André Soltner was born in the small town of Thann, in Alsace, on November 20, 1932, the second son of a cabinetmaker. Had he been the first son, he would today be a cabinetmaker himself. But in those days, in that part of the world, the tradition of primogeniture was still strong, and André's older brother was natural heir to the family enterprise. Moreover, though the young man wanted to take up the family profession just the same—he had spent many enjoyable hours in his father's shop—his mother objected, saying only that she was against the brothers both being cabinetmakers. André did not then ask her why—nor has he ever. Instead (as he tells the story in English today), he agreeably announced, "OK, I be a chef."

It was not a surprising choice, for just as he had spent time in his father's shop, he had put in many hours, from the age of around six, watching his mother at work in her kitchen, helping her, and at the same time learning to prepare in her way the home cooking on which he was brought up—the kind of food that he reveres today as much as the classic French cookery on which his reputation was built.

Soltner was fifteen years old when he decided to become a chef, which was about a year later than normal, in that era, for moving on from school to a professional apprenticeship. But his first language at home had been Alsatian, his first at school had been French, during the German occupation he was taught in German, after that again in French—as a result of which educational disorder André's parents decided that an extra year of French-language schooling was called for. It was therefore on behalf of a comparatively mature teenager that André's father addressed inquiries to the principal hotels and restaurants of the region in search of a place for his aspiring son.

An opening was found in Colmar—capital city of Haut-Rhin, one of the two departments that comprise Alsace—and André began a trial apprenticeship at La Maison des Têtes, then the city's most prestigious restaurant. But it was only about a month later, at five o'clock one morning (everyone else was still asleep), that André packed his belongings, tiptoed past the ground-floor apartment in which his boss slept, threw his suitcase over the locked gate that guarded the entrance to the restaurant, and, like a prisoner slipping out of jail, climbed the barrier to freedom. Carrying his suitcase, he walked to the railroad station and took the first train home.

As André explains it now, he had been raised by nice people, had enjoyed a normal life, was not ready for the likes of the barbarian at La Maison des Têtes, who worked his apprentices as if they were delinquents and slaves from seven in the morning to eleven at night (from which their relief was a single day off every *other* week).

"That's it. No more," he announced to his parents when, still outraged, he arrived home unexpected. But he was referring only to the job in Colmar, not to his culinary ambitions, which he did not intend to abandon.

By chance, at just that time another establishment to which his father had written—the Hôtel du Parc, in the city of Mulhouse—responded to the earlier inquiry, asked if the young man was still interested. And so it was that only days later André had a new place. There then began one of the most thoroughgoing culinary educations ever imparted and absorbed.

All such apprenticeships begin with a two- or three-month trial, at the end of which time, if both parties agree, the novice signs a contract to serve a full term. Soltner remembers clearly the day he signed (for the required three years), and the words with which the chef—André's new boss—greeted the event when the ink was dry: "Now," the man said, "you belong to me."

The speaker was René Simon—not a famous chef (the celebrity chef had not yet been invented), but an excellent one, and something of a legend. He was, in fact, so thoroughgoing a French cook that, it was told of him, he quite naturally prepared the wedding dinner after his own wedding—then removed his apron and sat down to eat it with his new wife and their families. In time André became a favorite of Simon, and the chef became in effect the young man's second father. In later years, and for as long thereafter as Simon lived, when Soltner returned to France he never failed to visit his old mentor.

As it happened, the two took the same day off, and when Simon was feeling remorseful about having applied, in his impatience with André, a bit of corporal punishment he would sometimes make a gesture of redress. "Bubbi [the name by which André was always called at the Hôtel du Parc], Thursday you have lunch with me," Simon would announce, and of course there was no arguing with the master over such an invitation/command. So the young apprentice would remain in Mulhouse and bicycle the eight kilometers to Simon's house for lunch, though he would have preferred a trip to Thann to see his family.

Simon was thoroughly schooled in the rules of classic French cooking as they had been set down by Auguste Escoffier. He was also a hard worker, a stickler, and occasionally a hot-tempered disciplinarian. Soltner recalls being dazed and knocked almost off his feet by a double sirloin to the back of the neck: he had mistaken a veal chop for a pork chop. A half-pail of nine-sided boiled potatoes would be angrily thrown out because boiled potatoes had to be cut eight-sided. Today at Lutèce, though the rules are stringent, they are never arbitrary—still, Soltner looks back nostalgically to the days of his old teacher's unwavering tutelage.

The Hôtel du Parc carried three apprentices—each year one apprentice graduated, each year another was signed on. And every two or three months the apprentices would move from one kitchen station to the next, in a rotation that continued throughout the term of service. The apprentice assisted the garde-manger (cold food, the boning of meat, etc.), then worked for the pastry chef, then for the saucier (sauces), then the entremetier (soups, vegetables, eggs), and so on; at the end of the cycle he started again. For one who was eager to take it all in, it was a complete course in French cooking. "When you came out," Soltner says now, "you were a good cook."

One of the regular turns was given over to preparing two meals a day for the hotel's entire staff of eighty, and as members of the staff were most certainly not fed the same food as the guests, the apprentice learned, in addition to high-class cooking, what Soltner refers to as "basic cooking—hamburgers, tripe, dishes like that."

The work was from early morning until nine at night, a different apprentice working an hour or two later each night to make certain the fires were out, the ovens cleaned, everything in its place. (The apprentices had a few hours off each afternoon, but on two days of the week these periods were given over to the schooling that was a required part of an apprentice's education.) It was arduous, even backbreaking work. But today, of those days, Soltner insists, "I liked it, I loved it, I *wanted* it—and I was happy!" Asked how he could nurture his intimate feelings for food while working so long and so hard, Soltner says, "It was the guy [Simon], he was a good guy, he fed us well, he treated us well. And he *wanted* to teach me."

Soltner remembers the thrill of learning and of getting things right. He recalls the first time he was allowed to make the pastries for a vol-au-vent, the moment when, after the pastries had baked awhile (and here, when telling the story, his voice falls to a whisper), he opened the oven door to check on them—and they had *grown*. When the pastries at last came out of the oven, and when everyone saw that they had puffed up perfectly, Simon complimented him grandly: "Look what Bubbi did!" he proclaimed for all to hear—and now, forty-five years later, Soltner says, "You could give me a million dollars today, I would not feel as good!"

The Hôtel du Parc kept Soltner on for a few months after his apprenticeship (during this time he was paid an actual salary, not the pittance apprentices earned), pending the two days of competitive final exams that an apprentice must pass to earn his Certificat d'Aptitude Professionnelle. On the first day the apprentice is tested for cooking, on the second for his knowledge of theory. Soltner is still a little proud of the fact that on both days he earned the highest score in the region of Haut-Rhin.

It is customary for an apprentice to move on once his training is completed, so after passing his exams Soltner left the Hôtel du Parc and took his first job as a journeyman, four months as assistant saucier at the luxurious beachfront Hôtel Royal in the chic Normandy resort of Deauville—where, each year, during the feverishly busy six-week heart of the summer season, international high society is drawn to world-class horse racing, the fashionable beach, the casinos at night.

After one winter in a kitchen close to home, at the Hôtel Europe in the town of St. Louis, the fledgling chef went to work in Switzerland, at the Palace Hôtel in Pontresina, not far from St. Moritz. In those days Pontresina was a summer resort only, and Soltner worked there two summers. In between he signed up for a winter job, also in the Swiss Alps, at the Hôtel Acker, in Wildhaus. What he signed, however, was a contract in which he promised that, for as long as he worked at the Hôtel Acker, he would not—ski. The management did not wish to lose its help to broken limbs. Soltner, however, was an enthusiastic skier, and, having signed, never intended to comply. He was, after all, twenty years old, and close at hand was the greatest skiing on earth. In fact, during his months at the Acker he skied every chance he got, on his free time between meals and on his days off. But, ironically, it was while he was back in Alsace visiting his family that the Hôtel Acker lost its cook to the dangerous game.

High in the Vosges Mountains, in freezing weather, early in the morning at the very start of a day's skiing, Soltner fractured his leg. A bad break, he was in severe pain, he imagined the marrow leaking out of his bone, he thought he would die. There were no roads, and in those days no helicopters to rescue the injured. But he was with friends. It took them seven hours to bring him, on a sled fashioned of four skis, through the deep snow down to the valley. Soltner spent weeks in the hospital, spent all his savings on medical care (having broken his contract, his Swiss health insurance was worthless), spent the rest of his life never again setting foot in the Hôtel Acker.

He returned the following summer to Pontresina, but then Soltner (still young, and once again in good health) was drafted into the French army. Had he suffered his army service to follow the normal, crushing course of the normal military stint, Soltner, being a chef, would have done his time in an army kitchen, a prospect he was determined to avoid. Called before an examining board of eight army officers at the start of his tour of duty, the young recruit was asked to confirm, by answering yes, the information in his file: name, date of birth, place of birth, etc. To everything he answered yes—until he was asked if, as the documents showed, he was a chef. No, said Soltner, he was not a chef. Not a chef? What was he? He was a cabinetmaker.

Much consternation among the officers. Are you sure? The young man was sure. The voices of the officers were rising now. If, as you say, you are a cabinetmaker, why do all these papers say you are a chef? The young man did not know. The officers looked at Soltner with the look—suspicious, scornful—that officers have always reserved for troublemakers. But Soltner stuck to his story. Eventually the captains and colonels, nonplussed and not a little angry, crossed out "chef" and wrote in "cabinetmaker." From there to the Twenty-Seventh Regiment of the Infanterie Alpine— the French Ski Patrol, exactly the assignment the avid young skier wanted—was surely an easy road for one so nervy.

Soltner did not long to give two years of his life to the military, but he does recall his service with some nostalgia. He seems proud to have been one of thirty men chosen to represent his battalion in a competition for the French Army ski championship. To get ready, the team was sent to Val d'Isère, where, though the skiing was fabulous, the competition among battalions was fierce, the training hell. In the final event—fifty kilometers of skiing, mostly cross-country—each soldier carried a seventy-pound pack, and a rifle. For a team to qualify, all thirty members had to complete the course, no matter what. Even an injured or disabled man had somehow to be carried or dragged to the finish.

Soltner still skis, and even competes whenever he gets a chance—but without a pack, and unarmed.

The army, however, was only an interlude.

In France in the 1950s to succeed as a chef, it was well, if not quite essential, to make a reputation in Paris. So when his army days were over, Soltner, with the help of his old mentor, René Simon, got a job at a place in the Sixth Arrondissement, Chez Hansi, an Alsatian restaurant that at that time was still owned by Alsatians.

Paris, it turned out, was something else. Soltner's training and early experience had been at the comparatively sedate tempo of the French provinces and the Swiss Alps, so he was almost stupefied to discover the mad pace at which the kitchen of a busy Parisian brasserie operates, the pace of, say, the floor of the Bourse during a panic. He had thought of himself as not only a good cook, but a good worker. Yet when he showed up for work at Chez Hansi, and was immediately put on the line—he could not do it. He could not keep up. "These Parisians," he thought, "they fly." He noticed that, unlike himself, these Parisians wore "these blue French slippers," in which, as he reports it now, "They walked three times faster than I could run in my shoes." By the third day, Soltner, too, was wearing "these blue French slippers"—and performing at the headlong velocity.

"Chez Hansi was a very good school for me," he says today. "Talent is one thing, but if you cannot 'get it out,' the people complain that your service is no good." At Chez Hansi, the ingredients were good, the cooking was good (classic French cooking as well as brasserie dishes and Alsatian food), and the volume was often more than good: as many as 200 lunches and 300 dinners on a busy day. So Soltner learned a lot—even about cooking, but especially about organization: how to "get it out." Lutèce does not operate at the pace of Chez Hansi, but, though it is a fact rarely noted amid all else that is written about Lutèce, the service never lags. For which there are two explanations: "First," says Soltner, "I never forgot what I learned. And second, for myself, it drives me crazy when I am in a restaurant and the food doesn't come, and doesn't come—and doesn't come."

He started at Chez Hansi as chef tournant, the cook who replaces the other cooks on their days off, so that one day he was pastry chef, the next day sauce chef, etc. Presently, he was made second in command, sous-chef; and then chef, in charge of a kitchen staff of seventeen in a large, thriving Paris restaurant, at age twenty-seven.

Had Soltner remained in Paris he surely, in time, would have had a restaurant there of his own. But even before New York called, Soltner's Paris career was in doubt. At one point, unhappy with his earnings at Chez Hansi, he accepted a job at higher pay in the town of Luc-sur-Mer, in Normandy. Much distress at Chez Hansi, but finally the restaurant agreed to match the better offer. Soltner retracted his resignation, which left him in a tight spot with his connections in Luc-sur-Mer. So, with typical bravura, he sent—a ringer!, one Jean-Paul Bucher, another alumnus of the Hôtel du Parc, and a former assistant to Soltner at Chez Hansi.

In Luc-sur-Mer, Bucher identified himself as Soltner—and no one was the wiser. A few days later, the impostor revealed his true identity, and was kept on anyway. (Today, Bucher is the most successful restaurateur in France, stock in his company is traded on the Bourse, he is the millionaire proprietor of almost every famous brasserie in Paris—La Coupole, Brasserie Flo, Chez Julien, etc.—and others as far away as Tokyo. He has always wanted a brasserie in New York, too, but only in partnership with Soltner—who, however, is otherwise engaged.)

Finally, of course, the fateful day arrived, André Surmain had lunch at Chez Hansi, and Paris lost Soltner to New York.

In the intervening three decades and more, over one and a half million guests have shown up for lunch or dinner at Lutèce. Some of them, on their first visit, arrive in a state of trepidation, expect to be treated with the superciliousness that often obtains in restaurants of international repute. And though that was what they might well have encountered during the reign of the restaurant's first owner, nowadays you are received at Lutèce as civilly as at the local restaurant where you have been doing dinner once a week forever.

At Lutèce, you are not, for example, *evaluated* by a tuxedoed maître whose job it is to choose a table for you according to the style or apparent cost of your clothes; or the degree of worldly urbanity implied by your bearing; or the familiarity, via the media, of your face. In fact, you are not greeted by a maître at all, but, usually, by Simone Soltner, André Soltner's wife of more than thirty years, whose manner to almost anyone who enters Lutèce is, remarkably, that of one cordial human being to another. As to where you are seated, that has to do mainly with your own preference, which means that Madame Soltner may well ask whether you prefer to sit upstairs or down; that if you do not know the difference and wish to be shown around, you need only say the word; that if the first table you are offered is not to your taste, you will be shown others if others are available; that if you are but an ordinary citizen, and the table you choose happens to be right next to one occupied by a political potentate, television star, or gossip column luminary, no problem, the table is yours just the same, for Madame Soltner becomes painfully hard of hearing whenever a class distinction snaps its fingers for attention.

You are served by a dining room staff in black and white. The waiters are distinguishable from the captains by their long white aprons. And their deliberate, businesslike demeanor is exactly the style Soltner wants—"Just do your work," he tells them. "Be friendly, but don't chat"—for to Soltner the best service is an unobtrusive pampering that leaves guests with nothing to concern themselves about but themselves.

The three charming and knowledgeable Lutèce captains, on the other hand, may well engage in colloquies with you, for it is their job to explain both the special dishes of the day and the dishes on the printed menu (many long-time customers never see the printed menu, are interested only in the dishes of the day); to take your order (unless Soltner gets to you himself); to discuss with you the choice of a bottle of wine (unless you prefer to choose from the broad list unaided); and to see to it that during your stay any impromptu wishes are heard and addressed. If it looks to you as if the captains' attentions are divided equitably among the tables, rather than allotted disproportionately to people they know well, that is all part of what makes Lutèce a most democratic of aristocratic restaurants.

To its patrons Lutèce seems to function effortlessly, as if it were driven by a carefully built, lovingly maintained spring-wound mechanism. Actually, no Swiss movement powers the place, any more than any computer governs it. And though André Soltner loves a good machine (is the first to buy one if it works better than what it will displace), most of the practices that go into the operation of his restaurant are manual and arduous and time-consuming.

Accordingly, there is only a hint of light in the sky, the birds in these East 50th Street trees have only just begun to sing, and a man sweeping the sidewalk of an ivied apartment building across the street from Lutèce is the only other visible figure on the block—it is, in short, 5:30 a.m.— when the first two members of the kitchen staff show up, singly, for work.

Actually, they do not so much show up as, the dim hour notwithstanding, burst upon the premises bright-eyed and prancing, as if from energizing warmups, and with a world to conquer. Whichever of them shows up first admits himself with a key and throws the switches—burglar alarm, fans, lights—and sets going the first of the many pots of (strong, bracing) coffee that the staff and a stream of visitors will drink through the morning. Within minutes, the two are in their kitchen clothes and at their posts, one in the restaurant's main floor kitchen, the other in the downstairs "prep" kitchen. So while the city is asleep, and before the rest of the staff starts arriving, these gentlemen are in feverish motion, and have working, typically, simultaneously, the beginnings of a few gallons of pea soup, of two dozen tartes flambées (to be distributed gratis by the slice to guests awaiting their dinners), a dozen whole soufflés glacées (to fill but a fraction of the hundreds of orders of this amazing dessert served each week), a boeuf à la mode, a sauce Périgourdine and a sauce Bordelaise, fifteen crèmes caramel, the apples for a fifteen-inch tarte Lutèce, more. (If a visitor disappears for, say, twenty minutes, and then returns, he finds under way almost a whole new cast of dishes.) When these two men are not stirring or tasting or testing or checking by eye, they are adding a little something here, something else there, chopping vegetables by hand (at a timed 250 strokes per minute), or pushing sauces through strainers with a quickness and vigor that approaches violence; or they are, incredibly, wiping down and washing up counters and cabinets, putting supplies and equipment in order as they go along—creating the impression that the Lutèce kitchens are in a perpetual state of being made neater and cleaner and more functional than they ever were before.

The main floor kitchen is that intricate assemblage—of ovens and broilers and burners—that you see through an interior window when you walk the wood-paneled corridor to the ground-floor dining rooms; while the basement prep kitchen, a vast floor-through workplace, the underpinning of the Lutèce operation, is almost never seen by the public at all—down here, chores that in other restaurants are performed in cramped corners stolen from closet-size kitchens are carried out in a space that dwarfs many a public dining room.

White-tiled, brightly lit, and gleaming, this subterranean hive is populous and humming by 7 a.m. In it there are any number of large ovens and a giant ice cream machine, a walk-in refrigerator the size of a second bedroom, an electric stockpot as big as a washing machine, and an electric mixer with the proportions of a small airplane engine; a pastry roller that was acquired in France in 1965—it is so rare that its twin waits in storage in case the working one breaks down; a Robot-Coupe food processor that is much like other food processors except that its metal bowl holds fifteen quarts (Soltner found the thirty-quart model beyond his needs).

Slicing, boning, kneading, chopping, stirring, straining are done on a hundred feet of counter space (refrigerated compartments underneath), utilizing supplies and equipment stored on as many yards of steel shelving both in and out of refrigerators: oil in huge cans, liquors and milder potions in outsize bottles, vinegars and flours, salt and pepper, scores of dozens of eggs and as many pounds of butter, parchment paper and aluminum foil and plastic film in log-size rolls, giant copper pots with massive steel handles, huge strainers and big stainless-steel colanders, food scales—including an old balancing scale with brass counterweights—buckets of wooden spoons and spatulas, whisks and knives: altogether, more than the eye can take in.

A few hours into the morning, and all of Lutèce is abuzz. And starting at around 9:30, when André Soltner descends from his top floor apartment for the start of his fifteen-hour day, he is both in charge, issuing the occasional direct order, and just another member of the crew, working with his staff much as they work with one another—except that he is called to the telephone at, it seems, regular ten-minute intervals. The Lutèce kitchen phones, however, are fitted with long wires, so Soltner can check some shallots here, add garlic there, shake a pan, and chew a carrot for tenderness (having plucked it with his fingers from the boiling water), all while he converses with a customer or supplier or fellow restaurateur, and, at the same time, answers with a word or gesture the questions that members of his crew now and again come forward to pose.

Whether Soltner is present or not, this kitchen is unlike *all other restaurant kitchens:* no backbiting, no griping, no temper tantrums, no stubborn defense of turf. Civility reigns. All hands mingle at close range, keep moving, do not collide, as if choreographed. Nor is this decorum an enforced discipline. It is, rather, the culture of Lutèce, so thoroughly a part of the place that only an outsider notes it. Here is life as it was before the hypersensitive ego was allowed out.

By the time Soltner arrives fish are being gutted, lobsters cracked, chickens dismembered; pears are being cored and peeled and poached for the day's duck; the pea soup is done and a fish soup is under way; a side of salmon that has been curing under a carpet of parsley is being cut in thin slices that are then layered between glistening sheets of oiled paper. Move too quickly among the innumerable and heady scents that fill the air in the various precincts of these kitchens, and you bedazzle your sense of smell.

In the small downstairs dining room, a worker sits at a table polishing the silverware that lies before him in a great mound. At around ten, the waiters and captains begin to arrive. Doors and windows are opened to air the rooms. The chairs—downstairs they are in stacks, upstairs they are upside down on the tables—are put in their places. By the time the silver polisher has done his job, when his cloths are black and the silver is gleaming, two layers of snowy linen are spread on each table (the first larger than the second, so that it shows like a long skirt under a short one), and the tables are set with napkins, china, crystal—and that polished silver.

Outside, from trucks that often line the curb, cases are carried across the sidewalk to be delivered into the barroom. Presently the traffic does a ninety-degree turn, begins to move up and down the street as some of the cases are carried (young members of the kitchen staff do the heavy lifting) to the air-conditioned wine cellar that Lutèce maintains in the basement of an apartment building a few doors west, while on trips back the restaurant's own stocks are replenished from the cellar. There are 40,000 bottles of wine in that cellar, with around 500 bottles of the most popular wines usually on hand in the restaurant itself. Most of those who come to Lutèce, even those who frequent it, have no idea that when they order a wine that is even a little rare it must be fetched from a densely stocked vault up the block.

Said vault is a cozy, low-ceilinged place with two "streets"—they assuredly cannot be called thoroughfares—the street sign over one reading BURGUNDY, over the other, BORDEAUX. The sides of these streets are shelves upon shelves of reclining bottles. Historic empties, standing up, are stored here as well, some marked with the names of the eminents who drank them. A double magnum of 1959 Lafite, for example, was enjoyed in 1976 by a group that included Frank Sinatra and Walter Mondale. Another such was drunk by drinkers unknown in 1989 (by which time the wine probably tasted even better than when imbibed by the baritone and the future Vice President). And just as there is a standing giant jeroboam bottle, empty, that once was filled with Léoville-Poyferré of 1934 (the one great Bordeaux year of the 1930s), so there exists a full one lying down, patiently waiting for its buyer. Wander about this room for a while, and then examine your feelings—you will find that you have grown not only wistful but thirsty.

At around midmorning tall brown bags of rolls arrive from the baker. Most of them will be spread with the butter that, at about the same time, shows up in thirty-six–pound cartons, along with several boxes of eggs (thirty dozen to the box), thirty quarts of milk, ten quarts of heavy cream, and a package the size of a shoebox of crème fraîche. All of them will eventually leave by the door through which they entered, albeit hidden on the way out within the tastefully fed frames of this restaurant's contented clientele.

To this orderly commotion, throughout the day, come the visitors, some by appointment, others unannounced. Many of course are selling their wares, though often they are more interested in attaining to the rank "Purveyor to Lutèce" than in any mere profit the connection might afford. But, almost alone among restaurateurs, Soltner regularly receives another kind of visitor, for in the restaurant world his is one of the names that occur to those who want advice, answers, help of any kind.

Today is no exception. This morning Soltner receives by appointment the owner and the chef of a restaurant in San Francisco. The two gentlemen contemplate buying what in the Lutèce kitchen is called a "combi" oven, Lutèce being one of the first restaurants in this country, if not the very first, to use one. These glass-walled ovens will of course roast dry, but they will also steam themselves up, creating a moist roasting environment for those things that must be kept juicy. Lutèce now has two such, and Soltner, standing before one of them, delivers a ten-minute lecture on its installation, operation, and advantages, with specific reference to dishes that benefit especially from its features. He does not know these guests well, but he gives them all the time in the world. He seems to feel that there exists a natural fraternity of America's, and the world's, cooks and restaurateurs. He acts accordingly—and thereby helps to make it so.

Half an hour before the restaurant opens for lunch, the kitchen staff, some standing at their posts, take an informal meal, the likes of sautéed meat, noodles, green salad, to which everyone helps himself, though there are those who pass up this menu for idiosyncratic assemblages they put together from what else is on hand. One cannot help but observe that the drinks taken with these repasts comprise a veritable index of beverages one is meant never to think of in the same breath as French food: tap water, iced tea, milk, Coca-Cola. The prime heretic is Soltner himself, who, seated on a chair that is too low for the work counter on which he has his plate, assuages his thirst with iced coffee. His somewhat ungainly lunch is taken just inside the door to the main floor kitchen, which is to say, next to the telephone, and throughout the meal Soltner is interrupted by its ringing—and by visits from his dining room captains, who during this break stop by to take down information on the specials of the day, which Soltner provides in detail.

The curtain goes up officially at noon, though it is often a few minutes before then that the first arrivals are led past the kitchen to tables in the Garden. The show is about to begin, but all is calm. The casual staff lunch segues into the patrons' more formal one with a gradual, effortless quickening of tempo. The waiters begin showing up at the kitchen window with orders, the tall white hats—Soltner's among them—begin bobbing as the cooks shift into the pounding and carving, the dipping and flouring, the broiling and sautéing, the myriad small operations that, under the onlooker's eye, coalesce magically into carefully arranged just-done dishes—which are then conveyed to the dining rooms by deft carriers in formals.

To anyone who has observed restaurants from a vantage other than the customer's, what is most striking about this operation is the almost dreamlike quiet in which it is carried out. But this is a businesslike decorum, not a solemn one. There is no shouting at all, no more talking than necessary, and yet no one appears constrained. Cooks do not bark at waiters (a major miracle in a restaurant kitchen), nor do waiters at busboys, nor does Soltner at anybody (though he has from time to time been known to make his displeasure vividly clear). As he does many times a day, at the beginning of the lunch hour Soltner puts on a clean apron, for now that his audience is on hand he will be making frequent sorties into the dining rooms, and it takes no time at all for a working cook's apron to lose its presentability. Early on he heads out—quite unnecessarily—to reassure himself that the rooms are properly set up; then to greet and personally take the orders from customers he knows well; then to talk to people who have simply asked to meet him; then, later, to encourage those who have declined dessert to have "just a little."

No one enjoys Lutèce more than those who eat here all the time. And at lunchtime, more so than at night, Lutèce is a repair for those to whom the place is a habit, a cherished routine. They fall into this sanctuary as if into a shelter from their cares, even when the very topic of conversation is exactly that: their cares, and how to deal with them. These regulars are the knowing. They know that, whatever the problem, Lutèce may well be half the solution, a setting in which sweet reason will at last take root. The power of good food, good wine, and the gracious surroundings of Lutèce is such that even fractious opponents in time achieve compromise here.

Lutèce lures the mind from its wraths. Come to Lutèce to work out a problem, and you are suddenly unable quite to recall what the fuss was all about. The sights and sounds are at once calming and vivifying. Listen, and you hear the murmur of civil discourse among the tasteful. Look, and you see yourself surrounded by the contented. Close your eyes, breathe deep, and you imagine that life is, contrary to rumor, fair. After lunch at Lutèce, either you hate to go back to the office, or you go back to do more than ever. The spirit touches even Soltner himself, and sometimes, at the end of the lunch hour, when almost everyone has left, he will sit at one of the few remaining occupied tables to chat with late-lingering guests he knows well, to share in the grace he cultivates.

In the kitchens, the end of lunch flows smoothly into preparations for dinner, but Soltner usually spends his early afternoons making and fielding phone calls, signing checks in the third-floor office, and, of course, receiving visitors.

This afternoon's first caller is a young Englishman who wants to take Soltner's picture for a book of photographs he hopes to publish of eminent New Yorkers where they work. He is an ambitious beginner with no reputation, but for Soltner it is no more than a common courtesy to show him through the restaurant in search of the right setting; and, when the barroom is finally chosen, to permit him to throw open the curtained windows for more light, move the tables and chairs and the bottles on their shelves, and generally set up a small disturbance as he sets up his equipment. Soltner cheerfully poses sitting and then standing, moves an inch this way and an inch that, smiles and then does not, and so on during the half-hour session. At the end Soltner pours the stranger a Cognac and wishes him good luck.

Later in the afternoon, when Soltner has just eased himself back into the comfort and familiarity of his kitchen, another visitor is announced, this one unscheduled, a cook looking for a job.

Anywhere else, word would be sent out, no openings, and that would be that. But here Soltner himself goes out front to talk directly to all such seekers—on this occasion a boyish Frenchman with whom he has a cup of coffee while giving him the bad news. The two chat for a while about the cook's training and experience, and Soltner suggests restaurants where he may have better luck, people to whom he should talk. To the young man the interview is bittersweet, for after a ten-minute chat with this very plausible—or quite implausible—boss, the young cook's interest in working at Lutèce is keener than it had been when he first dropped by on an outside chance.

At around five in the afternoon, in Le Petit Salon, a table—awash in the light that falls through the tall window under which it stands—has been set for two (sometimes, when there will be guests, for three or four). This is respite, when Simone and André Soltner privately enjoy the pastime they professionally advance. The menu is chosen by the proprietor, the early, quiet dinner is served by a member of the dining room staff, and lasts about an hour. At six, Lutèce is open again to the public.

If, of the two-act play that is Lutèce, lunch is an Apollonian Act I— gracious, cordial, serene—then dinner is, if never quite a Bacchic, then a Dionysian Act II—merry, convivial, gay. It is as if those who come for lunch come with an agenda, while at dinner only pleasure occupies every mind; as if what is accomplished by day is celebrated at night. The daytime crowd is all confidence and poise. At night, those who flow through the front door are eager, even giddy, with anticipation.

Lutèce, well into the busy dinner hour, from a vantage just at the entrance to the barroom: A chorus of laughter audible from the Garden is almost boisterous, a reminder that, as Soltner puts it, Lutèce is "not a church," and that those who come expecting to attend a solemn rite presided over by a solemn guru are sometimes disappointed to find only "a chef who can walk." The stairway to the upstairs dining rooms endures an intrepid tramping of guests and staff (among them, sometimes, on his rounds, the "chef who can walk"), the traffic unhurried but intense. The kitchen, seen through the long horizontal window, is a little smoky, as in an impressionistic haze—as if one is seeing through time, back into the old world in which this classical kitchen exists. The workers in the white hats are moving now to a rapid, irregular, almost hectic beat. Their eyes are down, on the unseen work counter before them; or their heads are turned to the dishes in the stoves and broilers behind them; or they are squinting at the slips of paper pinned over the window. Only occasionally do they look directly at the captains and waiters who come by to deliver both those slips of paper and the many spoken requests that, together, determine the cooks' every move. Yet every so often, when a dish just done *must* be served at once—a soufflé, say—a cook will look up, collar whatever waiter is within arm's reach, plant the dish in his hands, and tell him where to take it—and off it goes.

Only Soltner pays much attention to the parade that passes in two directions through the corridor before him, always ready to step out of the kitchen, disengage a group of new arrivals he knows well from Madame Soltner's care, announce, "I go with you," and show them to their table himself, the guests and their host chatting as they go—a conversation that, as the group takes its seats, becomes a discussion of drinks, the special dishes of the night, wine. (Thus does Soltner make efficiency of necessity, for these are some of the many patrons who prefer to discuss their dinner with no one but Soltner himself; within a few minutes he has shown them to their table, has settled with them on what they will eat and drink, and, having left them in a state of cosseted, contented expectation, returns to the kitchen—to visit them at least one more time, to be sure, before the evening is done.)

Stick for stick, Lutèce at night is Lutèce by day, all the pieces in the same places. But at the dinner hour they are seen by so-called artificial light, unsupplemented by the natural article, which makes for a dramatic transformation. By night the airy daytime rooms are more formal, more sparkling, more intimate. Even casual dinners take on ceremony, everyone present is romanticized at least a little, even dries get a little high.

When work in the kitchen is mostly done, when the trays of cookies and sweets are being offered among the tables, Soltner goes visiting, upstairs and down.

To watch him approach a table is to observe in action a fusion of the diffident and the secure. He stands tall, even leans back a little, as if to make clear that he is poised to depart, but at the same time his smile and his inquisitive look declare that he would be delighted to stay. Soltner's is not a shaky ego—he is able and willing to imagine (as innumerable restaurateurs are not) that certain folk, out to dinner, prefer the fraternity of their chosen company to the charms of their host. Which is why at Lutèce you never see what elsewhere you see so unmistakably—guests politely talking to their host while cordially wishing he would get very lost. Soltner has the touch. You see him depart from one table after the exchange of only the most cursory formalities, while at another he will linger—tell half a dozen stories, answer as many questions—until the good will palpably overflows. Ask him how he developed this talent for reading peoples' moods, and he says, "This is an instinct. You cannot learn it." Well, you could try.

By the time Soltner has done his rounds, most of the staff are gone for the night. Of those who remain, a few do the final cleaning up, so that when Soltner is back in the kitchen, it is being rubbed and scrubbed around him. Soon the wooden counters look as though they have been sanded, the metal stoves and cabinets and sinks as if just burnished.

Back at his station just inside the main-floor kitchen door, he begins the preparations for a series of phone calls he will make before the night is over. He reads through a batch of white slips of paper, on each a note about a unique item for the following day: a cake ("Happy Birthday Mom") that will be required for a group of six; special dishes requested in advance by guests who know that such things are possible; the particulars of the fixed menu ordered in advance by the host for a group of sixteen, who will have Le Petit Salon all to themselves. ("Of course," says Soltner, "when someone does not want what everyone is having, no problem—we make him something else.")

He looks at the next day's lunch reservations, makes an educated guess about how many more will call in the morning, decides how much food to order for the lunchtime *plat du jour;* he studies the individual names, looking for those whose habits and preferences he knows—and he begins to think, there and then, about what he will offer them. He peruses the dinner reservations, makes another set of educated guesses. All the while, as the few remaining guests trail out through the passageway before him, he looks up from his papers, smiles, says good night again.

He picks a roll from what remains of the evening's bread supply, cuts it in half, and, the halves in his hand, descends to the silence and calm of the downstairs kitchen—which, inactive since late afternoon, is utterly still. Before anything else, he looks into the giant electric stockpot, in which thirty gallons of fond de veau—the cardinal juice of French cookery—simmer at an almost imperceptible boil. He judges the simmer to be a bit slow, turns up the heat. (The simmer will go on through the night, the thirty gallons will eventually be five of a stout concentrate—that essence, in turn, to become a critical element in any number of profound sauces.)

But it has been a long day. An intermission is due. Soltner enters his room-size refrigerator, emerges with a length of hard sausage and a brick of sweet butter. He butters his roll, on his ancient slicing machine cuts half a dozen slices from the sausage, builds a sandwich, lifts himself up onto a wooden counter, and, sandwich in fist, a glass of water at his side, sups in the manner of a day laborer on a quarter-hour break. "I need this quiet time," he says as he starts to eat, and this room—feverishly busy twelve hours of the day but dead silent now—is the ideal place, the calm center of his province.

At around midnight, sandwich dispatched, notebook in hand, Soltner goes exploring in his big refrigerator. There are hundreds of individual items in here, meat and seafood and poultry, fruits and vegetables, butter and eggs. There is even, ingeniously, a kind of icebox *within* this icebox, the so-called fish file, a stainless-steel chest of four steel drawers in which, each day, the seafood received is, after its preliminary preparation—cleaning, boning, etc.—filed by type and strewn with ice cubes, so that the fish file is always several degrees colder (though above freezing) than the refrigerator itself. Soltner looks through what little seafood is left at the end of the day, makes notes, moves on to veal, racks of lamb, guinea hens, rabbits, sweetbreads, foie gras, more—those foods that (unlike, say, flour or oil or vinegar) must be ordered very carefully, so that on the one hand the item does not run out, and, on the other, is not around so long that it cannot be used.

Orders for foodstuffs have been placed all day long—by calls to suppliers from Soltner himself and from members of his staff. But now begin those calls that are made, weirdly, into a kind of void. Armed with the knowledge of how full is his reservation book, and how full is his refrigerator, Soltner, over and over, speed-dials, pauses, and then talks—to answering machines. Ten pounds of salmon in fillets, four chickens of four pounds each, two pounds of sea scallops and so many lobsters, so much bread and so much foie gras and so many ducklings—dozens of items all told. All of this is for delivery in the early morning. And though some of the calls reach the live people who run the businesses that function by night to service restaurants by day (Soltner chats for a few minutes with these waking workers, many of whom he has dealt with for decades), mostly it is by way of acts of telephonic faith that these crucial orders are placed. Sure enough, when early morning finally rolls around, just what the doctor ordered will start rolling in.

French news is broadcast on American cable television each night at seven o'clock, and André Soltner's VCR records it. Six hours later, Soltner is ready to watch it before going to bed. "It relaxes me," he says, as he starts upstairs . . .

That, however, is but one possible ending, weary veteran retiring for the night. Other Soltners, other endings—for example, the Saturday night ending, when Simone and André put sleep on hold, fasten their seatbelts, and head north to their country house. Especially when there is snow on the mountains, Soltner is eager to get upstate fast, sleep fast, and get onto the slopes when the sun is barely above the horizon. Once, in his haste, a Soltner somewhat younger than he is at this writing was doing 100 miles per hour on the New York State Thruway at two in the morning. He took his exit so fast that the unseen police car behind him, running without lights, overshot the exit, had to make a fast U-turn—then speed south on the deserted northbound side of the New York State Thruway—to land its prey. Brought before a sleepy judge, Soltner pleaded guilty, and put himself at the mercy of the court.

"Ten days," said the judge. (Long, long pause.) "Or fifty dollars."

Soltner was on the slopes at dawn.

—*Seymour Britchky*

Les Grands-Parents

Emilie Weber and Pierre Kurtz

*Marie Meyer and Eugène Soltner
and their children*

Mama and Papa Soltner

*The future chef starts his
apprenticeship—age fourteen*

*André as a soldier
in the ski patrol*

*And on his scooter
in Wildhaus*

*André dining
with his parents*

*And in Paris
with his Chez Hansi brigades
(1956)*

The chef cooks at his country home in Hunter, New York

André and his wife, Simone, prepare for friends

AUTHOR'S PREFACE

❧

My earliest memories are of my mother's kitchen in our house in the small town of Thann, in Alsace, where I was born. I spent many hours in that kitchen while my mother was cooking, a young boy trying to help his mother, and trying to do the things she did.

As I grew up, I sometimes tried to do even better than she did. But in a way, to this day, I never succeeded, because when my mother cooked for her family—for my father, for my brother and me, and years later for my young sister—what she did was more than the work of cooking. It was an expression of love. And when we sat down together and ate the food she made, it was a fulfillment of that love. The food my mother cooked every day was part of what made us a family every day. That is where my strong feelings for food began.

Later I became an apprentice and then a chef, but before that I was already a kind of apprentice in my mother's kitchen, where I learned to do almost everything she could do. In that early "apprenticeship" I became interested in food and cooking, and starting then I always wanted to do more and learn more. And of course there were people to help me.

I remember, for example, that next door to us in Thann lived an old man. He was a barber. But he was also the expert in our town on mushrooms. He liked to go in the woods looking for them.

Naturally I wanted to go with him, and when I was maybe ten or eleven years old I asked him if I could. He said yes, and after that he always said yes when I asked him.

He watched me, he explained to me what was what, where the mushrooms grew, how to find them, which ones were good, and which ones were not. By the time I was fourteen, I was good at hunting mushrooms, maybe even as good as the man next door who taught me.

When I hunted mushrooms by myself and brought a few pounds of them home to my mother, she would use them to make a mushroom omelette for the family. To have my mother cook the food that I brought home, and then for everyone to sit together around the family table to eat it! For me it was a communion.

I never forget a camping trip of a few days that I made when I was a boy scout. The other boys and I found a huge number of black trumpet mushrooms. We filled a big basket with them. Of course, I was in charge of the cooking, and that night, at our campsite, I cooked the mushrooms in oil in a pan over a fire.

Mushrooms that are just picked have a taste that you never find in mushrooms that are even a few days old. Today I still have in my mouth the taste of those black trumpets.

I still go out hunting for mushrooms. Usually on Sunday afternoon, my wife and I look for them in the woods near our house in the country. (My wife also learned how to find mushrooms when she was a child.) We know where the girolles grow, and sometimes we also find cèpes, even a few morilles. I cook them at home, as my mother did.

Because my mother liked to make many different kinds of chestnut desserts, I would go out in the fall to pick chestnuts for her. It was not far to go, a fifteen-minute walk outside of town to where they grew. In our house, to store the chestnuts, we had a wooden case that my father built. The chestnuts were buried in sand in this case, and that way they would keep for two or three months.

On the cold mornings, we would put warm roasted chestnuts in our pockets, wrapped in paper, and we would eat them while we walked to school. At night my mother roasted chestnuts and put them on the family table, under a blanket to keep them warm. We sat around the table and talked, and we would reach under the blanket for the warm chestnuts.

Alone or with friends I gathered and caught other things too—trout, which we caught by hand (we took watercress from the same streams), and frogs for frogs' legs. Sometimes we did more than we should, taking grapes from private vineyards. (In French this is *chapardage*—small-time poaching.)

Naturally we would also go hunting for berries—huckleberries, raspberries, wild strawberries—and also wild cherries, depending on the time of year. The cherries were in the woods quite near our house, and the raspberries and strawberries were in the valley, a trip of half a day. But to get the wonderful huckleberries, we had to hike in the Vosges Mountains. We would go very far, to where the shepherds would go for the whole summer with their flocks. At night we would find farmers who would let us sleep in their barns with the farm animals. We brought food with us, but sometimes we would also buy extra food from the farmer whose barn we slept in. After two or three days, when our pails were full, we would make the long walk back home.

The fruit I brought home my mother would make into tarts. But there would always be a big amount left over, and the extra fruit she made into preserves, jams and jellies, enough to last for the whole year, and I would help her.

In 1946, after the war was over, when it was possible again to travel, my mother went to visit relatives in the Périgord, taking with her my baby sister. Because of what I had learned in her kitchen, my mother could leave to me the feeding of her husband and her older son.

For four weeks, I shopped in the market every morning. And every day for lunch and dinner I served a first course, a main course, and a dessert (which was more than we usually ate, because I did not keep myself on so strict a budget as my mother). I loved it. My father and my older brother, they loved it too. I was thirteen.

My wish to cook for others, and for my food to be appreciated, is a wish to do what my mother did, a wish to be for others what she was for us. The possibility that my cooking will please people, and that they will be pleased with me because of it, is what always excited me about being a chef.

When I was fifteen, I became for three years an apprentice in the kitchen of the Hôtel du Parc, in Mulhouse, a city not far from our town. Each week on my day off I would go home to visit my family. One of those visits I remember very well.

In the hotel kitchen, I had finally learned to make an omelette. Really, I must have made a thousand of them before I could do it right. But when I went home on my day off, and made omelettes for my family, they all said, No, my mother's omelette was better.

They were right. My mother's omelette *was* better, because it was made with love, love for us. In my mother's omelette, and in all the things my mother made, there was something that was part of us. We knew the taste of her food the same way we knew each other.

For me to be an apprentice at the Hôtel du Parc was a good education, because it taught me how to cook. But no education can teach someone to cook the way my mother cooked, to prepare food with the feeling for the people closest to her that was always in her heart when she cooked. That cannot be learned in a hotel kitchen or in a restaurant kitchen. It can only be learned by one loved one from another.

I was around sixteen years old, still an apprentice, the first time I had a chance to cook for people outside my family. In those days, the kitchen of the Hôtel du Parc closed for dinner at nine o'clock. On this night it was my turn to work late, to clean up the kitchen and close it down properly. I was still working at ten o'clock when the owner of the hotel—the big boss—came in with a dozen of his friends. They had been out for the day hunting.

No one was around except me, and everything was put away. He asked me, Could I give his friends something to eat? "Of course," I told him. "I will cook for them." (It was my chance!) He was very skeptical that I could do it, but he let me go ahead.

There was a trout tank in the kitchen with live trout in it, so I made for them truite au bleu. Then I made médaillons de veau aux champignons. They raved about the food. The big boss praised me.

The next day I was called into his office together with the chef. He told the chef what a good job I did, and he raised my salary from 1,500 francs a month to 3,000 francs a month. That was from $3 to $6, nothing to nothing, but it was a fortune compared to what the other apprentices were making. Still, to me that did not matter. What mattered to me was that I gave pleasure, the people were pleased with me.

Always I worked long hours—as an apprentice, then as a chef, then as proprietor and chef of Lutèce. But even when I work hard, I do not afterwards run away from food and cooking. They are part of my life always, the life I began when I was a boy and a young man.

So, for example, just as my mother made preserves of the fruit I picked, to this day I too make preserves. To do it is my way of life. Not to do it would be unnatural for me. Then to eat in the morning for breakfast the preserves I make myself, that is a special joy. I give jars of these preserves to my friends, I give them sometimes to customers. I could give someone a very expensive present, but when I give a jar of my own preserves—sometimes people are overwhelmed.

In this same way, I make my own cider. Every year, usually on Election Day, I go to a farm near my house in the Catskill Mountains where they squeeze apples to make juice. These people make a special juice for me, with no preservative in it, and they fill ten big glass water jugs with this juice, and I let this juice ferment at home. In two weeks it starts to bubble. Then, a month later, around Christmas time, the cider is ready. I put it in old champagne bottles, and I cork it with a small corking machine.

This cider making I started with two friends—for the pleasure of it, as with everything I do with food. One of these friends was from Normandy, where a lot of cider is made, and he knew best how it is done. We even applied for a license to make cider. (This was not necessary, but we were enjoying ourselves.) Then these friends moved away from the Catskills, so now I do it alone, and it is still fun for me. I had labels printed up: CIDRE LUTÈCE. This cider is not the best in the world—that comes from Normandy—but it is good. The license still hangs on the wall in my cellar.

Even when I was a young man in Paris, where I worked a long day at the restaurant Chez Hansi, and lived in a small room with only a hot plate to cook on, I often cooked on my day off. On that hot plate I prepared special dishes for my wife in the days when I was courting her. Today, I still do the cooking at home. And sometimes, just as in Paris, I make special dishes for my wife. After all these years, it is still a way to make the marriage good. In a way, I do the same thing for my customers. I cook for them, I pamper them, and they come back.

When I start to cook something, I already have in my mouth, and in my mind, the taste of what I am cooking. It is like a dream, a dream of what the food is going to be.

It was like that from the beginning, from when I was a boy. It is, I think, the gift of cooking. And when I cook for others, my delight is to believe that what I am tasting and what I am dreaming is exactly what they will soon be tasting and enjoying. This is what connects me, so closely, to the people who come to Lutèce.

For me, to have a restaurant without that experience, a restaurant just as a business, would mean nothing—because you cannot cook for a huge crowd and also feel that you are cooking for people. To have, instead of Lutèce, a very big restaurant, or two restaurants, or a chain of restaurants (which many people have suggested to me), where I would not be able to feel and see for myself the pleasure I give, would be the opposite of why I cook.

I have always cooked to give pleasure and joy and to make a closeness between the people I cook for and myself. That is what I tried to do more than forty years ago when I cooked for my father and my brother, and it is what I did that night at the Hôtel du Parc, and when I cooked for my wife in Paris, and when I cook for her today. It is what I have tried to do every day for more than thirty years at Lutèce.

In all those years, I was never away from Lutèce for sickness. But that record of good health cannot go on forever, and Lutèce must have someone to step in if I am sick or injured. The time came for me to make new plans for the restaurant.

That is why I have recently sold a majority interest in Lutèce. Now, if I must be out of the picture, there are people to take my place. Lutèce will continue, and forty-two employees (who have worked for me for ten years, twenty years, even longer) and their families, to whom I have a responsibility, are not in danger that their lives will be disrupted.

In front of Lutèce in the early days with André Surmain

The Upstairs Room

The Downstairs Room

Later . . .
Lutèce in New York

Pierre Autret, in charge of
the wine cellar a few doors
west of Lutèce

André in the Lutèce kitchen

Dining with Simone and his niece

André the celebrity

with James Beard

with Julia Child

with Jim Villas

with Mayor Koch

WINE AT LUTÈCE

At Lutèce we have, I think, a good wine list—it has won many awards—and I am proud that in our cellar are many of the greatest wines in the world from the best vintages. But Lutèce is not a restaurant where people come to drink Château Latour from six different years, or four or five different great Burgundies from the same year, or something like that. There are a few small groups who have such dinners at Lutèce—I have the wines available, and I am glad that they can enjoy them at my restaurant. But most of my customers come to Lutèce for the food more than for the wine. And for me also, maybe because I am a chef, food is first.

But in the early 1960s, when Lutèce was new and was owned by André Surmain, he wanted to build up a wine cellar of old wines, rare French wines. In those days you could still do it. The wines were expensive, but the cost was not yet so high that you had to charge impossible prices. Later you could not build up such a cellar starting with nothing, but he was able to do it because he started early enough.

By the time I took over in 1972, it was already too late to add very much of that kind of wine to what we already had, because wines from the nineteenth century and wines from the first part of the twentieth century almost could not be bought anymore—except by people who did not care about the cost. The prices did not have anything to do with what these wines were worth, but only with how much money people would pay for them. Still, there were quite a number of such bottles in our cellar in 1972, and even today I have many of them. And now that Lutèce is no longer a young restaurant, much of the wine that we bought when it just came on the market, and of which we have good stocks, is hard to find.

It is my business of course to sell these bottles, and if possible to sell them before they grow *too* old. And yet when people order one of the very old bottles, I sometimes try to discourage them, because I do not want them to be disappointed.

I explain to them that if they buy one of these old wines, it is at their own risk, that there is no sending back such a bottle. Many people believe that the older a wine is, the better it is, so I feel I have to tell them that this bottle of wine or that one is maybe very interesting, but in their old age many great wines are not at their best anymore. Such wines may be good to drink, but other wines in the cellar are better and also cheaper.

It is my policy to be careful this way, because sometimes people expect miracles from these old bottles. It is true that these wines are sometimes very good, even superb—but usually they are not miracles. I prefer that when people drink wine with my food, they do not get less than what they expect.

I myself never recommend expensive wine. My captains never do either. And when a customer is given the wine list at Lutèce, he is also handed a wine card on which two dozen inexpensive wines are listed. Many people do not look further than this card for their bottle.

When we do sell an expensive wine, it is always to someone who chooses his own bottle from the list. And when a customer asks me to choose a wine for him, and if it is someone I do not know, I do not go higher than $45 or $50, and the wine is always something I myself would want. Only for a customer I know very well—someone who I know spends hundreds of dollars when he picks his own bottle—then maybe I will go as high as $100.

Although the expensive old wine is not what I try hard to sell, the old bottles are the ones that I still remember selling years later.

Soon after I took over Lutèce I recall that a man called up to make a reservation for lunch. At the same time, he asked me to open one of these very old bottles in advance—I do not remember which wine it was, but the price was $750. I did not want to open such a bottle just because someone I did not know asked me on the telephone to do it, so I told him I would be happy to open the bottle if he would first send over $750 to the restaurant, and I explained to him why. He agreed, and fifteen minutes later a limousine came to Lutèce, and the chauffeur got out and came inside, and he gave me $750 in cash for the bottle. Later of course the man came with his friends and they drank this wine with their lunch.

Today this is a funny story to me, because this man's name was well known in New York. He was someone who could easily pay for such a bottle, and he was someone who would not make a reservation and then not show up. But his name did not mean anything to me then. Of course, he had been to Lutèce before—that is how he knew we had that bottle. After that he became a very good customer. Naturally I did not again ask him to send money in advance.

Of all the old wines that Surmain bought, a case of 1890 Château Lafite was the one that attracted the most attention, I think because it was a very famous château, and also because it was from the nineteenth century. When I took over Lutèce in 1972, we still had ten of the original twelve bottles. It took me twenty years to sell those ten bottles, and some of the sales I still recall.

I remember when one of my captains came to me in the kitchen one night and told me that a very young couple just ordered a bottle of the 1890 Lafite. He knew I would want to know it before he opened the wine. I told him to try to talk them out of it—because they were so young. I especially did not want to take a chance on selling a $1,200 bottle of wine to youngsters. It would be like taking advantage of them—or it could look that way.

The captain came back in a few minutes and said, No luck, this is the wine they want. So I told him I would take care of it, and I went out myself and explained to them that I could not guarantee the wine, that it might be no good. Then I said to this young couple that the 1961 Lafite was better—perfect wine, I could guarantee it—and it was half the price. I did no better than the captain. In fact worse, because the young man said that now he wanted to have both wines, the 1890 *and* the 1961, to compare them. I gave up. They bought them both, and they drank them both. I do not know which one they liked better.

Another time three gentlemen ordered a bottle, and again I explained that they were taking a chance. They took the wine anyway, and drank it. Then they ordered another bottle of the same thing! That to me was really crazy. How much more can you learn about 1890 Lafite? And we have thousands of other bottles in the cellar.

When I sold the next-to-last bottle—it was at that time $1,800 on the list—then I had the problem that someone would some day buy the last one, and there would be no more. I did not want to sell the last bottle. I was proud to have it, and I wanted to keep it on my list. So I made the price $5,000. No one will buy it for so much money, that was what I thought.

About two years after I made the price $5,000, the American distributor for Château Lafite sent a letter to people saying that the cellar master from Lafite was coming to America with his equipment, and that anyone with old bottles of Lafite could have them recorked.

The way it works, when a bottle is opened to be recorked a very small amount of the wine is poured out and tasted. If the wine is good, the small amount of wine is replaced with wine of Château Lafite that the cellar master has with him for this purpose. He replaces the poured-off wine with wine of the same year, or the closest year possible. Then a new cork is put in and a new cap is put on top. But if the wine is not good, Lafite does not put on a new cap, and the wine cannot be sold.

I brought eighty bottles of Lafite to the office in the Seagram Building where the Château was doing this work. I had bottles from 1914, 1918, 1934, 1943, 1945, 1947, 1949, 1950, 1952, 1953, 1954, 1955, 1958, and 1959. I also had with me the bottle from 1890, which I left for last. The cellar master was there with two assistants, we spent the whole morning opening and tasting and recorking the wines from 1914 to 1959. It was very interesting—I was very lucky, and I did not lose one bottle.

But then it was time to open the 1890, and I was not so sure I should do it. I just wanted to keep the wine on my list. But I could not do that if it was not good and could not be sold. We held the bottle up to the light and looked at it. We knew that the last bottle I sold was good—but from the same case one bottle can be good, the next one bad. Also we saw that this bottle had a lot of sediment in it. And so on. But finally the cellar master said I should take a chance, the wine looked OK to him, and I went ahead and told him to open it. I was nervous, but the wine was good.

Not long afterwards, a man ordered that bottle for $5,000. He was at Lutèce with his family, I suppose it was an important family occasion. The $5,000 did not mean that much to me. I just wanted to keep the bottle, and I tried to talk him out of it. But no way. He and his family drank the wine, and he took the empty bottle home with him, and that was the end of that.

Lutèce is a French restaurant, in some ways a typical French restaurant. But because I am an Alsatian, in a small way Lutèce is also an Alsatian restaurant, and in addition to classic French food I always offer one or two

Alsatian specialties. So it should be no surprise that no restaurant in America sells more Alsatian wine than Lutèce. Alsatian wine is our one wine specialty.

I believe very much in Alsatian wine. I like Alsatian wines because they are light, and because they are good. And I like to offer them because many people in America still do not know them, though they are becoming more popular. These wines are fine with all the food served at Lutèce—but they are exceptional with the Alsatian dishes.

I introduced many customers to Alsatian wines. Some of them, after they try these wines, never drink anything else at Lutèce.

I remember an evening when former President Nixon was at Lutèce. That night he was a guest at someone else's table. When I came to take the order, the host asked Mr. Nixon what he wanted to eat and drink, and he said that, as usual, he would leave the choices to me.

First we decided on the food, and then I suggested that the group drink Alsatian Tokay. Mr. Nixon said no, he did not want a sweet wine. I explained to him that Alsatian Tokay was not like other Tokays (such as Hungarian Tokay), that it was not sweet. So Alsatian Tokay is what they drank.

The next day I received a telephone call from an assistant to Mr. Nixon. She said that he wanted to know how to buy two cases of this Alsatian Tokay. I told her that in the United States the wine was sold only at Lutèce, and that there was nowhere else to buy it. But later I made an arrangement so that two cases could be shipped to him. After that night, whenever he came to Lutèce he always drank my Alsatian Tokay.

A few years later, when I was visiting Alsace, a parcel of the vineyard where this Tokay is made was dedicated to me with a stone marker. At this ceremony I was able to present to the winegrower a letter from Richard Nixon praising his wine.

For many years at Lutèce I served nothing but French wine (including Alsatian wine). That was Surmain's policy when he opened Lutèce, and I thought it was right. But in addition to being a Frenchman and an Alsatian, I am also an American. For years, many people asked me about American wines, and some people criticized me for not having them. So finally I decided to add some of them to my list.

And who drinks these American wines? The French. Most of my customers of course are American, and mostly they drink French wine. But when my countrymen (and also other Europeans) come to Lutèce—a French restaurant in America—many of them think, Now is the time and this is the place to try American wines. So far they have been happy with them.

French wine, Alsatian wine, American wine—wine is the perfect drink with Lutèce food, whether you have it at Lutèce or prepare it at home from the recipes in *The Lutèce Cookbook*. The wine does not have to be expensive. It only has to be good.

INGREDIENTS

❧

Ingredients at Lutèce

If you wish to cook successfully, ingredients are the most important thing. They are more important even than a talent for cooking. If you have good ingredients, it is hard to spoil them, hard to make bad food from them. But to make good food from bad ingredients, that is impossible.

For survival, frozen and canned foods will serve the purpose. But we do not cook just to feed ourselves, just to survive. For the kind of cooking that we try to do at Lutèce, cooking that does more than just keep you alive, cooking that gives pleasure and joy, you must have good ingredients.

So when I am asked, which I often am, What is your secret?, the answer is, I have no secret—except that the secret of all good cooking is good ingredients, which is really no secret at all. It is true for a chef cooking in a restaurant, and it is true for someone cooking at home.

When I first came to America, there were already many French chefs here who came before me. Most of them were making good food, but many of them complained because they wanted everything to be the way it was in France. Some of them complained about the flour, or about the meat, or the seafood, or the vegetables—almost everything.

It was true that many things were different here. And in those days a few things—for example, most American veal, or the herbs that you could only get dried, not fresh—were not good enough in this country at that time. But most American products were as good as the French, only different. The French cook had to adapt to the differences. It was really not so hard.

Today there is almost nothing I cannot do with American ingredients as well as I can do it with French ingredients. It is important for Americans to understand that when it comes to ingredients they are not at a disadvantage. The results in America may be a little different, but they are just as good.

Many people believe that for a chef to buy good ingredients, he must get up early in the morning and go to the market himself. People who know that I work a long day sometimes ask me, How do you manage to go to the market? The answer is, I never go to the market.

A chef has a choice—either to cook or to go to the market. There is no way a chef can work in his restaurant until late at night, then be at the market at four o'clock in the morning, and then work another full day at the restaurant. It is true that when I worked in France I sometimes went to the market, and I would come back to the restaurant at ten o'clock or eleven o'clock in the morning—and that was really too late. To prepare lunch, you should start earlier than that.

I do not like to criticize my colleagues, but I think that some of the chefs who go to the market early in the morning are interested in public relations—to have their pictures in magazines and in newspapers buying at the market before the sun is out, so everybody will think they get up early in the morning to buy the best ingredients for their restaurant.

In my opinion, the companies who buy at the market and then sell to me, and to other restaurants, have the pick of the best, because they buy for fifty restaurants, or a hundred restaurants, or more. These wholesalers control more business than any chef, and they have the most influence with the people who sell at the market. When I buy from wholesalers, I do not sacrifice quality. In fact, I think I get the best quality.

So when you hear that the real chefs get up at three o'clock in the morning and go to the fish market or the vegetable market or the meat market, it is a little bit exaggerated. Most chefs do not do it.

Of course, to be sure that I get the best quality from my suppliers, I deal with them a certain way. I pay my bills on time, always. I do not argue about prices unless they are really too high. And when someone sends me something that is not good, which sometimes happens, I do not take it. Sometimes I call a supplier into Lutèce to show him that what he sent me is not acceptable.

There are many advantages in working this way with good suppliers for many years. For example, when there are unusual things at the market—game, or a not-so-common fish, or certain vegetables that are hard to get—these people will buy them for me even if I did not order them. They know that if something is unusual, and good, I want it. Very often, I make these things into special dishes of the day even when I do not know, almost until the last minute, that I am going to serve them. So it is really useful to get along well with suppliers.

Over the years I also made connections with producers who sell me things directly. Some of them are farmers near my house in the Catskill Mountains, and others are farmers in different parts of the country. They sell me wild mushrooms, all kinds of berries, some of my greens, turnips, apples, peaches, and other fruits. The people who send me shallots, for example, are onion growers in Walla Walla, Washington, who are old friends now. Years ago, when they were having trouble producing shallots successfully, I suggested to them that they should go to Brittany, and learn from the farmers there, which they did. Now, every week or ten days, I get a shipment of wonderful American shallots from Walla Walla. In addition to these people who supply me with American products, there are others who fly fresh seafood and game into New York from all parts of the world, and I buy from them too.

In a way, all these suppliers are as important to Lutèce as the people who work in the restaurant. I try to treat them all well, and they all do a very good job for me.

Ingredients at Home

If a busy chef cannot go to the markets early every morning, the person who takes care of a house and a family, or who has a job, also cannot do it. But you can buy excellent ingredients from stores, though sometimes to get the best you have to pay more—as I do when I buy for Lutèce.

For most things, the important word is "fresh." And what you buy should be fresh not only when you buy it, but when you use it—so you should only buy what you will need for one or two days. Of course I am not talking about sugar or salt or flour—these things last a long time. But vegetables, meat, poultry, fish, and shellfish should be bought fresh, and kept refrigerated, and used as soon as possible.

DAIRY PRODUCTS   The dairy products I cook with at Lutèce—milk, cream, butter—are the same products (except for crème fraîche) that anybody can buy in American supermarkets or grocery stores. If these things are fresh, they are excellent. Fortunately, with all dairy products you can tell what is freshest by the date stamped on the package. Dairy products lose freshness not only in stores, but in the refrigerator at home, so you should buy only what you will use soon. When you are in doubt, you can tell the freshness of these things by smelling them.

EGGS   Eggs have to be as fresh as possible. It is easy to tell, after you open it, if an egg is fresh—the yellow stands up, and the white is gelatinous and holds a shape. If that is not what you see when you break open your eggs, you should find another place to buy them, or you should not store them at home for so long, or both.

At Lutèce we use large eggs, and when recipes in this book call for eggs, large eggs are meant unless another size is specified.

FISH   It is always better to buy a whole fish than to buy the fish in fillets or steaks. When you buy the whole fish you can see with your eyes whether or not it is fresh. After you find a whole fish that looks good to you, then you can have your dealer fillet it for you.

When you look at a whole fish you should look for a fish that is slick, but even this can fool you, because the fish dealer can wash a fish so that the skin shines almost as if it is fresh. So you must also look at the eye, which should be bright and clear. If the eye is not bright, the fish is not fresh. And you should look at the gills, which must be red, not brown.

Finally, smell the fish. A fish does not have to smell very much for you to know that it is not fresh. A fresh fish always smells fresh.

FLOUR   I use all-purpose flour almost all the time, and that is what you should use when you prepare the recipes in this book, except of course where the recipe calls for special flour—whole wheat, rye, etc.

For puff pastry I use what in France is called "farine sans corps"—flour without body—because pastry made with this kind of flour will not shrink. This flour is sold in America under the brand name Wondra, it is called "quick-mixing" or "quick-dissolving" flour, and it is sold almost everywhere. I also find that it is a better flour for dusting—lightly coating—and we use it for that at Lutèce. But at home it is really not necessary to dust with one kind of flour instead of another.

Note: In most of the recipes for pastries or breads, the quantity of flour is given by weight. That is the best, most accurate way of measuring flour, and it is a good idea to have a food scale for this purpose.

GARLIC Where garlic is listed as an ingredient in this book, I usually say "green germ removed." This "green germ" is a small center piece of each clove that I usually cut out because of its bitterness. When you buy garlic, look for bulbs that are firm—not soft, and not brittle.

HERBS More and more, all kinds of fresh herbs are available in this country. In this book, in a few places where a recipe calls for herbs, I do say that dried herbs can be substituted for fresh ones, but this is always a compromise. Fresh herbs are best.

If you have a small piece of land, or even a window box, it is possible to have such things as parsley and chives always on hand. Some people who do not grow anything else grow herbs in boxes or pots in their kitchen windows.

There is one herb, tarragon, that is sold preserved in vinegar. This preserved tarragon is better than dried tarragon, but you have to be a little careful where you use it—you cannot put it in recipes where the taste of the vinegar would be wrong in the dish.

An exception to the rule of dried herbs is the bay leaf. In practice, almost always the dried bay leaf is used. Dried thyme is also an acceptable substitute for the fresh herb.

Note: **Bouquet garni:** Many of the recipes in *The Lutèce Cookbook* call for a bouquet garni—a few herbs tied together with a string and added to the pot. In some of these recipes the herbs are listed. Otherwise, your bouquet garni should be made of:

8 to 10 sprigs fresh parsley   1 bay leaf
2 sprigs fresh thyme

MEAT You cannot eat meat as soon as it is slaughtered. It has to rest for some time. But for me the aging of meat for tenderness is overdone in this country. I prefer meat that is fresh.

When meat is aged a long time, of course it becomes very tender. But at the same time it loses flavor and it loses juiciness. So when I buy meat it may need two or three days of aging, but I prefer to control that myself.

When meat is delivered to Lutèce, I expect it to be red—inside and out—not brown. And I expect it to be juicy, not dry. And those are the things that you should look for, too. This applies to all meat.

When I buy baby lamb, for example, it was slaughtered the day before. I age it myself—just for a day or two—before serving it.

The same rule applies to rabbits, and even to venison—which years ago people used to age much too long. Some people still do. I handle venison like any other meat; my venison has good flavor when it reaches the table—and still it is not tough.

OIL   The recipes in this book call most of the time for peanut oil as the basic cooking oil—it is easy to get, and it will serve you very well in these recipes. But over the years I have used a few different kinds of oil at Lutèce, all of them mild. We have used peanut oil, a combination of 90 percent peanut oil and 10 percent olive oil, and recently I have tried grape seed oil. The last one, grape seed oil, I like because it has a very natural taste, and because you can heat it to a higher temperature than other oils before it will smoke. The three oils—peanut, peanut with a small amount of olive oil, and grape seed oil—may be used interchangeably.

In certain parts of France, olive oil is the basic cooking oil, and I use it in some recipes in this book. But the taste of olive oil is most of the time too strong for my cooking. Even when I do use it I use only a very refined French oil, which is milder than most of the olive oils from Italy or Spain or other countries.

POULTRY   When you buy chickens or ducks or turkeys you must get the freshest birds possible. Frozen birds are not acceptable. Chickens, especially, have not as much taste nowadays as the chickens we ate one generation ago. So chickens especially, when they are not fresh, should be avoided. Fortunately, chicken is not very expensive, compared to other poultry and to meat, so it is worthwhile to pay a little more to the butcher shops and specialty stores that have fresh chickens. Sometimes you can also find fresh birds in farmers' markets, and even in some supermarkets that carry local products. For Lutèce, when I can get them, I prefer to buy free-range chickens, chickens that are not penned up while they mature. These chickens always have better flavor than other birds.

SHELLFISH   Lobsters, crabs, oysters, clams, mussels—all these, when we buy them for Lutèce, they are alive. When any of these things come into the restaurant not alive, we do not take them. And they must stay alive until we prepare them, otherwise we do not use them. Even though it is possible to keep shellfish alive in a refrigerator for a day or two, at Lutèce we order shellfish every day.

At home, it is just as important that you buy live shellfish, and that they be still alive until you cook them. The best thing is to buy shellfish the day you are going to prepare it. Lobsters and crabs are at their peak when they are active, but they are still good as long as they are still alive. A bad smell always means that the lobsters or crabs can no longer be used.

For oysters, clams, and mussels the shells should be closed tight. If a shell is open, that oyster or clam or mussel is dead, and you must throw it away. Also, if you can open a mussel by pushing the top and bottom of the shell in opposite directions between your fingers, that mussel is bad. (Sometimes you will find that such mussels are filled with sand, not with the meat of a mussel.) All mussels should be tested this way.

Scallops are the one type of shellfish that you buy already shelled, because that is how they are almost always sold in this country. But like all shellfish, if they have an odor, they are no longer good to eat.

Shrimp should be fresh, not frozen. It is too bad that fresh shrimp are hard to find, but lately they are beginning to show up in some fish markets and in specialty stores. For the best results, it is a good idea not to make shrimp dishes unless you find a source for fresh shrimp—sometimes a fish dealer can order them for you.

Frogs' legs are also very hard to find fresh. But, like fresh shrimp, fresh frogs' legs can sometimes be located, and some dealers will order them for you.

STOCKS   Many of the recipes in this book call for stocks—Fond Blanc de Volaille, Fond de Veau, Fumet de Poisson, etc. At Lutèce we make all of these stocks ourselves, but I know that not everyone will want to do the same thing at home. For some recipes, it would take more time to make the stock than to make the dish.

But if you do want to make stocks at home, it is a good idea, when you deal with your butcher, to be sure that you get the backs and necks when you buy chickens or other birds, and the bones when you buy meats. These things can be frozen until it is time to make your stock.

Note: In many places in this book (but not all places), where I list stock as an ingredient I give plain water as an alternative. To use stock is always better. But if you make the dish well you will still get a very good result even if you use water instead. For an even better result, you can do what I do when I cook at home without a stock: I use bouillon cubes. This will be shocking to many people, but the bouillon cubes that are sold under the brand name Knorr, which come from Switzerland, are excellent (there may also be other good brands); they are very valuable to the cook at home who has not much time. They are not as good as a real stock, but they are better than plain water. They make a good dish even better, as long as they are used *with restraint.*

VEGETABLES   Because I am Alsatian, I sometimes say that I am from "asparagus country." In Alsace, we produce and eat a great amount of asparagus. When you order this vegetable in a restaurant in Alsace you expect that it was picked the same morning. In New York it is probably impossible to get any vegetable as fresh as that in a restaurant. (It is probably impossible also in Paris.) But certain vegetables are like flowers—they are at their peak when they are just cut.

Of course the freshest vegetables—the ones with the best flavor—are picked ripe from the cook's own garden. Every year my wife and I grow vegetables in our small garden near our house in the Catskill Mountains. But it would be a big mistake to think that a garden is necessary for having good vegetables. I often buy excellent produce at roadside stands on country roads. And the farmers' markets that are now more and more common in cities and towns are also good places to find fresh produce.

But you will probably buy most of your vegetables from supermarkets, greengrocers, and specialty stores, and in all of these places you can find good things. It is important to look for vegetables that are firm and ripe and not discolored, and to look for leaves that are not wilted and have not started to turn brown or to fade.

If the vegetable you are going to cook will be a vegetable garnish, it is sometimes a good idea to change your mind about what garnish to use if another vegetable looks better in the store where you are shopping.

Nowadays it is possible, because of cold storage, and because things can be shipped quickly across the country, to buy almost any vegetable at any time of the year. Vegetables shipped across the country or even shipped from one country to another can be very good. But as a rule, produce is the best when it is local and when it is in season.

VINEGAR   In France red wine vinegar is what most people use for most things. Of course it is a matter of taste, but for me red wine vinegar is too strong. Except for that, I really am not too particular about vinegar. At home—but never at Lutèce—I sometimes use Chinese rice vinegar, and it is fine. But if you want a result as close as possible to what we get at Lutèce, buy what we use at the restaurant—French tarragon vinegar. There are good brands available in specialty shops, and even some supermarkets carry one or two kinds. Naturally, if a recipe in this book asks for a different kind of vinegar—balsamic vinegar, for example—that is the kind to use.

WINE FOR COOKING   In some restaurants you see dishes called, for example, Coq au Chambertin—but never is a chicken cooked in real Chambertin anymore, because Chambertin wine is much too expensive. It would be better to call such a dish Coq au Vin or Coq au Vin Rouge or something like that, because otherwise the public in a small way is being cheated.

At Lutèce I cook mainly with dry white wine, usually a Chardonnay, from California. But when I make dishes like Matelote de Poissons au Riesling or Coq Sauté au Riesling I make them with real Riesling— Riesling from Alsace—because that is my professional responsibility. At home, of course, if you use instead a dry American or a dry French wine, or a different Alsatian wine than Riesling, the results you get with this substitute wine will still be very good, but the taste of the dish will be a little bit different from the authentic preparation.

Whatever you cook, when you pick the wine to cook with never use wine that has gone bad. You can cook only with wine that is good enough to drink.

Some Hard-to-Find Ingredients

CRÈME FRAÎCHE   Today I use American commercial crème fraîche, and I am satisfied with it. Thirty years ago there was no such thing, and I did without.

The best French crème fraîche comes from Normandy, where, because of the soil and because of the grass, the dairy products have almost unbelievably high fat content, so high that you cannot use Normandy cream for whipping cream—it is *too* rich. American crème fraîche is not the equal of the crème fraîche from Normandy, but it is good, and I have learned to make up for the lower fat content. Here in this book, when one of the recipes calls for crème fraîche, use American crème fraîche—as I do—and you will get a good result.

The real problem with American crème fraîche is finding it. A restaurant, of course, can get it through wholesalers, but supermarkets and regular grocery stores almost never carry it. You usually have to look in specialty shops. You may also be able to order it from a cooperative grocer who deals with a wholesaler who carries it.

I do not recommend the method that some people use to make imitation "crème fraîche" from buttermilk. Such "crème fraîche" is really unacceptable, because the flavor is wrong and because the fat content is wrong for French cooking.

ORGAN MEATS   Sweetbreads and kidneys and brains are as common in America as in any other country—because the slaughtered animals here have the same organs as everywhere else. But organ meats very often do not reach American butcher shops, because Americans eat very little of these things. Specialty butcher shops sometimes carry them, and many butchers will get them for you. Just be sure to make clear that what you want are *fresh* organ meats.

PORK SKIN   Your butcher may have this available. If not, he should be able to get it for you.

SEA URCHINS   Most American fish stores do not carry sea urchins, but usually a dealer can get them for you if you order in advance. Like all seafood, they must be absolutely fresh.

SORREL   In Europe this leafy vegetable is very common, and it is also very delicious. But in America you usually have to look for it in ethnic markets or farmers' markets. If you have it in Lutèce any time between the middle of April and the end of October, that sorrel comes from my garden near my house in the Catskill Mountains.

TRUFFLES   Every year, usually in January, I buy for the restaurant forty or fifty pounds of fresh truffles, enough for the whole year. Some I use soon after I buy them. The rest I cook in white wine, and put them up in jars, and use them as I need them. They are excellent that way.

But if you look for fresh truffles in stores, even when they are in season, you will find them only in certain specialty shops. The rest of the year you must use canned truffles, which also you will have to look for in specialty shops and fancy grocery stores. But if you get a good brand, they can be fine, very much like the ones I prepare for future use in Lutèce.

WILD MUSHROOMS   In French restaurants in New York, when I first came to this country, on all the menus there was listed Médaillons de Veau aux Girolles. (Girolles are the mushrooms that in English are called chanterelles.) I did not put this dish on the Lutèce menu, partly because there were no fresh girolles in America, as far as I knew. All the restaurants used canned girolles from Germany.

Years later, a man came to see me at Lutèce. He wanted to sell me fresh American girolles, from Oregon. I asked him how come it was that all of a sudden there were fresh girolles in America when before that there were always none. It could not be, I told him, that they appeared overnight. He explained to me that there were always fresh girolles in America, but that there was no market for them. So all American girolles were shipped to Germany, where they were canned. Then they were sent back to America.

Today, it is still not so easy to find fresh wild mushrooms in this country. You see them sometimes in supermarkets, but mostly you have to look in farmers' markets and in specialty shops. Of course the problem is made a little easier because you can usually substitute one kind of wild mushroom for another—or even, if it is necessary, cultivated mushrooms (champignons) for wild ones—and still have a good result. Also, some wild mushrooms are sold dried. We never use these at Lutèce, but they are an acceptable substitute for fresh wild mushrooms if nothing else is available—these dried wild mushrooms, of course, can also be combined with fresh champignons.

KITCHEN EQUIPMENT

❧❧❧

APPLIANCES One summer, when Lutèce was still a new restaurant, while I was on vacation in France I visited the restaurant of Paul Bocuse. After lunch, Bocuse took me into his kitchen and showed me what he called his "new toy." He put some parsley in this toy, and *whooosh!*—in two seconds this parsley was chopped parsley. Right away, I bought one of these new toys.

This toy was a Robot-Coupe food processor, and Lutèce was the first restaurant in America to have any kind of food processor in the kitchen. Much later, in the 1970s, the Robot-Coupe started to be sold in America as the Cuisinart.

At the beginning, the people who made these Robot-Coupes did not have anybody to sell for them in this country. And because I was cooking in New York, and using their machine, they came to my partner and to me and they asked us if we wanted to be the exclusive distributors in America of the Robot-Coupe.

My partner, André Surmain, was very much a businessman, and he wanted to do it. But I was a cook first, only after that was I a businessman, and I was afraid that this new business would be trouble, and that it would get in the way of taking good care of Lutèce. So we did not do it. Afterwards, years later, Surmain would sometimes remind me that we missed a big chance.

I do not regret that I never sold food processors, but I am glad I bought them, because with the food processor many jobs that used to be very hard work, and took a long time, are now easy to do. Every recipe in this book can be done by hand. But there are some recipes that many people would never even try if all the steps had to be done only by hand. So I recommend that if you are going to buy only one electric appliance for cooking, it should be the food processor.

The other electric appliances I recommend are the mixer, the blender, and the hand blender. All of these make work in the kitchen easier, and there are some jobs for the mixer and for the two kinds of blender that cannot be done as well with the food processor. I recommend the hand blender especially (these have been available for a long time, but only lately have they become popular). With this appliance you can do the work of a blender in almost any container. I use all of these machines in the kitchen of Lutèce, and I use all of them at home.

COOKWARE   When it comes to pots and pans, I do not use aluminum anymore, because it discolors certain foods. At Lutèce we cook in copper that is lined with stainless steel, nothing else. These copper-and-steel pots and pans conduct heat very well, they are strong, and they last a long time. I also use this copper lined with steel at home, and in a home kitchen it should last forever.

But there is one thing I do like to do at home that I cannot do in Lutèce, and that is to cook in nonstick pots and pans. (We tried them at Lutèce, but with all of the heavy restaurant use, the nonstick surfaces came off, and we had to replace these pots all the time.) The only disadvantage to nonstick cooking is that in some dishes making a good sauce requires that the cooking juices stick to the surface, and caramelize a little, and this does not happen on nonstick surfaces.

I also like to cook in cocottes (in English, casseroles) of enameled cast iron. But, believe it or not, this cast iron is breakable, and in Lutèce from time to time our cast-iron cocottes broke. At home they can last indefinitely.

Whatever kind of cookware you use, do not start out by buying these big sets of all sizes of pots and pans. Start with a few pieces, and then buy what you need, when you need it, one piece at a time. This way you will not find yourself with pots and pans you never use.

Eventually, if you cook regularly, you will probably end up with two or three sizes of skillet (frying pan, sauté pan), three or four saucepans, one or two soup kettles, one or two baking dishes, one or two terrines, a roasting pan, and one or two cocottes (covered casseroles). For cooking at home, it is always a good idea to buy utensils that have metal or heat-proof handles, so that the same piece can be used on top of the stove and also in the oven. And it is also practical to have pots and pans that come with fitting lids.

CUTLERY   As with all kitchen equipment, you do not need a large collection of knives. You need a large knife for chopping, a small one for peeling vegetables, and one or two knives of an in-between size (which can be used for boning if you do not have a special boning knife). These are the basic knives, and it is possible to get along very well with nothing else. All of them should be made of carbon steel, and you should have what is called a "steel" for sharpening them—knives of carbon steel are easy to sharpen, and they take a very sharp edge.

You will also find it is useful to have a serrated knife for cutting bread, and these are always made of stainless steel. A cleaver is useful too, for cutting through bones and—using the side of the cleaver—for flattening meat.

You can work with knives on a work counter that is already in place, but a cutting board is practical to have because you can put it anywhere. It is helpful to have a small butcher block (we have one at Lutèce), but I manage without one at home.

In addition to the kitchen equipment that comes under the three headings—APPLIANCES, COOKWARE, CUTLERY—there are many, many other items that kitchens accumulate over the years. Of course you can go out and buy every one of them right away (I list a few dozen of them below, under MISCELLANEOUS), but it is better to add each item to your kitchen when you need it, otherwise you will end up with many gadgets that you never use at all.

MISCELLANEOUS   I give here a list of many of these other pieces of kitchen equipment (and also supplies). It is not a complete list of all the things that can go in a kitchen, but these are items that are mentioned often in this book.

You do not need everything on this list to start cooking from *The Lutèce Cookbook,* and for many of these things you can use something else instead. But if there was a kitchen that had all the equipment on this list, you could make almost every recipe in this book in that kitchen. There are some things that almost every kitchen *will* need, and these are marked with an asterisk (*).

*aluminum foil

baking sheets

*bowls—several, large and small

bread pans

candy thermometer

cheesecloth

*colanders

deep fryer

double boiler (bain-marie)

flan rings

food mill

food scale—especially for measuring flour by weight

*forks—large ones, for picking up large pieces of meat

*four-sided grater

funnel

gratin dishes

ice cream maker

ladle—especially for removing fat from the surface of cooking liquids

*measuring cups

*measuring spoons

meat grinder

parchment paper

pastry bag

pastry brushes—for applying glazes and egg wash

pâté molds

*pepper mill

pie pans

*plastic wrap

ramekins

*rolling pins

*sieves and strainers—a fine sieve (in French, *tamis*), and a small and a large strainer

*skimmer—for removing foam from the surface of cooking liquids

*slotted spoons

soufflé molds

*spoons—large ones

spring-form cake pan

*vegetable peeler

vegetable steamer

wire racks

*wire whisks

*wooden spoons and spatulas

Cooking from
The Lutèce Cookbook

꧁꧂

LUTÈCE FOOD TODAY   This is mostly a book of classic French cuisine and Alsatian home cooking. I learned these kinds of cooking when I was very young. But in the more than forty years that I have been cooking professionally, there were trends and movements, even fads, away from traditional cooking, and some of these new ideas influenced a little the way I cook. Especially, there was "nouvelle cuisine," which you do not hear so much about anymore. Many people criticized nouvelle cuisine, but I never said that it was not good.

The best things about nouvelle cuisine are that you cook "à point," which means, "to the perfect point"—not overcooking and not undercooking; and you have to use first-class ingredients. In nouvelle cuisine you cannot hide careless cooking and poor ingredients under heavy sauces.

But really, nouvelle cuisine was not so nouvelle, not so new. In classic French cooking—in all good cooking—you avoid extremes and you use only good ingredients. This is the way I was taught, and it is the way I work.

What happened to nouvelle cuisine is that many people took it to extremes. To avoid overcooking they served food that was almost raw. They combined foods that did not go together. They served tiny, tiny portions—on big, big plates. Eventually people turned against it.

Yet how I cook today *is* influenced by nouvelle cuisine—a little—because when it was around it caused me to try new things. What I liked I kept. Still, this is a book of classic French cuisine and Alsatian home cooking.

THE RECIPES   When I cook, I almost never make a dish exactly the same way that I made it before, or even exactly the way that I give the recipe for it here in *The Lutèce Cookbook*. The only exceptions are when I am making pastry or bread, which always have to be done exactly in the correct proportions.

Even when I make something that I have cooked hundreds of times in my life, I change it, so that in a small way, or in a not-so-small way, I make an old familiar dish into something that it never exactly was before.

Sometimes I change the amount I use of this ingredient or that one. Or I substitute a new ingredient for the regular one. Or I just add something that I usually do not include—maybe a different herb, or a vegetable that happens to be very good at this particular time of the year, and that I am sure will create a good variation.

Once in a while, I change a dish in several ways. I am making the same dish, but this time the sauce is lighter, and the flavoring is milder, and maybe I do not brown the meat (or the fish, or the poultry, or whatever) quite as much as usual, so that altogether the dish has a new personality. It is different from the original in the same way, for example, that two versions of the same traditional dish are different from one family to another, or from one restaurant to another. Still, they are the same dish.

The person who cooks at home can do the same thing. And if you cook at all often, and if you enjoy cooking, almost automatically you will want to experiment this way. You will think that maybe it is a good idea to change this or that, and then you will do it, and you will see how it works. Eventually, you will become more confident. You will find that even though you start out with printed recipes, you make these recipes into your own dishes.

After all, that is how cooking came to be what it is. It grew from primitive cooking into the thousands and thousands of different dishes that ordinary people and talented cooks and professional chefs prepare.

Usually, the best way to approach a recipe is to cook it exactly the way it is written—the first time you try it. Then you know the starting point. (Every recipe, in this book or in any cookbook, is a starting point.) Maybe you will like some of my dishes exactly this way. Maybe you will think of how others can be improved. And, if you are experienced in cooking, you may even want to change some recipes the first time you do them. Either way, not only do you have my permission, you have my encouragement.

COOKING FOR SPECIAL DIETS   Most of the recipes in this book can be traced back to classic French cooking, and some of them are still close to the originals. So it is not surprising that cream and butter and eggs are used in many recipes—sometimes in what will seem like large amounts to people who are used to diet-conscious cooking.

At Lutèce, we often have guests who ask us to follow their diets when we cook for them. For vegetarians we make complete vegetarian lunches and dinners. For people who want us to cook for them with no butter or cream, or no eggs, or with very little salt, or without alcohol or sugar—we are prepared, and we oblige. But it is something of a problem when they also want their food to be the same as Lutèce food—we do the best we know how, we get as close as we can, but when food is changed this way, something is lost.

Once in a while, when someone asks me to cook according to his or her diet, I go ahead and describe the special dishes of the day anyway. These are often very tasty old-style dishes of home cooking, and sometimes the dieters try them (they go off their diets), and they *love* them. As far as I can see, there are no bad effects. My own feeling is that the best way to eat is a little of everything in a balanced way. That is how I myself eat. And I think that you can eat very healthfully that way in Lutèce.

But I do know that some people, for health reasons, must be careful. To them I say, yes, you can cut down on the butter and cream and eggs, etc. But just as I always use these ingredients only in moderation, they should also be cut back only in moderation. Eliminating them completely will often ruin a recipe; the food that results will not give pleasure. So alter the recipes according to your needs, but alter them in moderation. Leave room for pleasure.

THE MENUS   Because cooking is my life, this book is the story of my life. The recipes come from all the times of my life, from when I was a child in my mother's kitchen in a small town, until I became the chef and the owner of a well-known restaurant in a big city.

But it is mostly a cookbook, and because it is also a restaurant cookbook, in addition to the recipes I have included also more than twenty menus. With these short menus I introduce the main recipe chapters of the book.

All of these menus are, in a way, souvenirs of my life. They are groups of dishes that, in different places, at various times, I have eaten with my family or friends; or they are dishes that I prepared in the hotel or restaurant kitchens where I cooked.

I want to say here that not every one of these menus is what people today would call a balanced diet! In some of the menus not all of these "food groups" are included. But every menu represents for me some of my history, and of course I cannot change my history—and really I do not want to.

I hope that the people who read this book, and cook from it, will be interested from time to time to prepare complete meals of these menus. It would mean to me that people will be cooking and eating and enjoying food in exactly the same way that I have cooked food and eaten it and enjoyed it myself.

SOUP

*A typical dinner of dishes my mother
prepared in her kitchen when I was a boy
in the 1930s and 1940s*

Soupe de Semoule de Ma Mère (PAGE 99)

Tarte aux Pommes de Terre (PAGE 227)

Mousse au Chocolat (PAGE 451)

*A dinner of dishes prepared with foodstuffs
that I gathered in the countryside
when I was a boy in the 1930s and 1940s*

Soupe de Grenouilles (PAGE 95)

Médaillons de Veau aux Champignons (PAGE 316)
(alternate preparation with wild mushrooms)

Tarte aux Myrtilles (PAGE 472)

MY COUNTRY HOUSE is in Hunter, New York, which is skiing country. Near our house we have a neighbor who used to have a dog, a beautiful Labrador retriever named Sammy.

In the skiing season, Sammy liked to run up on Hunter Mountain, where the skiing was. On the mountain, Sammy would stand always in the same place, and he would follow, turning his head, each skier who went by. He would stay there all day, until it got dark, watching all the skiers.

One day, when I was in Hunter, Sammy took a walk from his house, which was about two hundred yards away, to our house for a visit. He was a very friendly dog. When I have a guest, I offer him hospitality, and I decided that I would make for Sammy some soup. So, with some bones and vegetables and other things, I made soup, which Sammy ate, and enjoyed very much.

After that, when I was at my house, Sammy would not go to the mountain. Instead, he would visit me. As soon as my car drove up, he would run to our house. And he would follow after me the whole day. All because of my soup.

I tell this story to introduce this chapter on soup, food that has a very basic appeal, so basic that it appeals even to dogs.

Here at the very beginning of the recipe part of this book, I offer two menus from the early part of my life. Both of these menus begin with soup.

Bouillon de Boeuf
aux Quenelles à la Moëlle

BEEF BROTH WITH MARROW DUMPLINGS

This is a dish made every day in Alsatian homes, but you will find it nowhere else in France. It is the marrow dumplings, especially, that make it different from all other kinds of boiled beef broth.

My mother made a Bouillon de Boeuf every Saturday, and that day we ate the beef with broth. But she always made enough broth so that on Sunday she could cook rice in it, and on Sunday we had rice soup.

Note: This recipe calls not only for a marrow bone, but also for raw marrow, which you can get from your butcher.

Serves 6

The Beef Broth

3 pounds beef with bones (ribs, shins), or oxtails

1 marrow bone

1 medium onion, cut in half

2 cloves

2 medium carrots, trimmed, peeled, and washed

1 white turnip, peeled and washed

½ small green cabbage, washed

1 tomato

1 leek, washed

1 stalk celery, peeled and washed

2 garlic cloves, unpeeled

1 bouquet garni (page 55)

1 teaspoon salt

pepper, fresh ground

The Quenelles

4 ounces beef marrow

3 ounces (approximately ¾ cup) dry bread crumbs

1 ounce (approximately 2 tablespoons) semolina

1 large egg

1 pinch grated nutmeg

1 tablespoon chopped parsley

½ teaspoon salt

pepper, fresh ground

flour for forming the quenelles

The Beef Broth

1. Put the beef and the marrow bone in a pot. Add water to cover, plus half an inch more. Over high heat, bring to the boil. Reduce the heat to low, and cook slowly, uncovered, for 1 hour. From time to time, skim off the foam and grease.

2. In a skillet, using no oil or fat, brown the onion halves on the flat sides until they are almost black. Stud each onion half with 1 of the cloves.

3. Add the carrots, turnip, cabbage, the whole tomato, leek, celery, and onion halves (studded with the cloves) to the pot. Tie the garlic and the bouquet garni in a piece of cheesecloth, and add them to the pot. Add the salt and pepper. Continue to cook slowly for another 1½ hours, covered, but with an opening for steam to escape.

The Quenelles

4. Put all the ingredients listed under *The Quenelles* (except the flour) in a food processor, and process—until they form a paste. *Do not over-process—it takes only a few seconds.*

5. Dust your hands with flour, and form the marrow paste into quenelles—balls the size of marbles.

6. Put the quenelles in a pot, together with 2 cups of the beef broth, and simmer them very gently. *Do not boil rapidly, or the quenelles will fall apart.* The quenelles are ready when they float to the surface—about 10 minutes.

Assembling the Quenelles and the Bouillon

7. Pour the main portion of the beef broth through a fine sieve. Taste the bouillon, and add salt and/or pepper if necessary. With a slotted spoon, remove the quenelles from the broth they cooked in and add them to the bouillon. (Discard the broth in which the quenelles were cooked, or re-serve it for another soup.) Serve hot.

Note: The boiled meat and vegetables may be served as a main course after the soup, garnished with Sauce Raifort (page 523).

Consommé Madrilène

TOMATO-FLAVORED CONSOMMÉ

This is a dish I prepared often during my apprenticeship, and I continue to serve it at Lutèce—cold in the summer, hot in the winter.

Because it requires so many steps, it makes no sense to prepare it for fewer than 10 people, but it is a great light soup for large parties.

Serves 10

The Stock

2 pounds chicken bones

2 pounds beef bones, preferably beef shin bones

2 large carrots, trimmed, peeled, washed, and chopped coarse

1 leek (the white part only—set aside the green leaves), washed and chopped coarse

½ stalk celery, peeled, washed, and chopped coarse

1 medium onion, peeled, studded with 2 cloves

1 medium onion, unpeeled, cut in half, the flat sides browned in a skillet until almost black (*use no oil or butter*)

1 bouquet garni (page 55)

2 garlic cloves, peeled, green germs removed

1 teaspoon salt

pepper, fresh ground

Clarifying the Stock

1 pound raw chicken legs, coarse ground; OR 1 pound lean beef, ground

1 leek (the green part only—which was set aside during the preparation of the stock)

2 carrots, trimmed, peeled, washed, and chopped coarse

½ stalk celery, peeled, washed, and chopped coarse

1 tomato, chopped coarse

2 sprigs fresh tarragon, or ½ teaspoon dried tarragon (*do not* use tarragon preserved in vinegar)

½ teaspoon fresh thyme, or ¼ teaspoon dried thyme

½ teaspoon pepper, fresh ground

4 egg whites

To Flavor the Consommé

3 medium tomatoes, ripe
chopped chervil

The Stock

1. Put the chicken bones, beef bones, and 5 quarts of water in a large pot. Bring to the boil, and boil over medium heat for 2 to 3 minutes. Skim the foam from the top of the water.

2. Add the remaining ingredients listed under *The Stock,* and bring to the boil again, and again skim the foam from the top of the water. Cook slowly for 2½ to 3 hours, partly covered, skimming the surface 2 or 3 more times during the cooking. Strain through a cheesecloth or a fine sieve. Let cool.

3. When the stock has cooled, remove all the fat that has risen to the top.

Clarifying the Stock

4. Put the ground chicken [legs] (or ground beef) in a large pot. Add all the other ingredients listed under *Clarifying the Stock.* Add the stock. Stir everything together, mashing and crushing the solid ingredients. Put over medium heat and bring to the boil, stirring gently and often to prevent the egg whites from sinking to the bottom of the pot and burning.

5. When the stock comes to the boil, stop stirring. Cook gently, uncovered, for 45 minutes. The liquid should cook a little more actively than at a simmer. Taste, and add salt and pepper if desired.

6. Pass the liquid through a wet cloth and let it stand in a bowl for a few minutes. Remove all the fat that rises to the surface. (At Lutèce, every last bit of fat is removed by skimming the surface of the broth with paper towels.) To remove the fat more easily, chill the stock, then remove the fat, and then reheat it.

To Flavor the Consommé

7. Cut a conical plug from the stem end of each tomato and discard. Blanch the tomatoes in boiling water for 10 seconds, drain them under cold water, and peel off the skins. Cut the tomatoes in half horizontally, squeeze out and discard the juice and seeds, and chop the pulp in ¼-inch cubes.

Consommé Madrilène continued

8. In a pan, gently cook the tomatoes for 3 or 4 minutes. *(Do not use oil or butter.)* Add the tomatoes to the clarified consommé.

Serving the Consommé

9. Serve hot or cold, sprinkled with the chopped chervil. (When cold, the soup jells slightly.)

❦

Crème d'Avocat à la Ciboulette

CREAM OF AVOCADO SOUP, WITH CHIVES

I never saw an avocado until I came to America in 1961. But from the beginning I was very much interested in preparing things from this side of the ocean, and right away I saw that the avocado was a wonderful food.

By coincidence, at just about the time I came to America, avocados came to France. So when I went back to France for a visit in 1962, I saw avocados where I never saw them before.

I do not remember where I found this avocado soup—I may have learned it from one of the American cooks who came to work for me, or it may even have been in a magazine or newspaper—but now I make it my own way, and it helps very well to serve the need we have at Lutèce for good cold soups during the hot summers in New York.

Note: Do not prepare this soup more than 1 hour in advance, because the avocado darkens, and the soup loses its attractive green color.

Serves 4

1 thin slice bread
1 tablespoon unsalted butter
2 ripe avocados
2 cups Fond Blanc de Volaille
    (page 512)

salt
pepper, fresh ground
1 dash Tabasco sauce
½ cup heavy cream
1 teaspoon chopped chives

1. Cut the bread in ¼-inch cubes. In a skillet, melt the butter over medium heat. Sauté the cubes of bread in the butter until they are golden brown. Set aside.

2. Peel and pit the avocados. Cut the meat of ½ of one avocado in ¼-inch cubes. Set aside.

3. Put all the remaining avocado meat in a food processor. Add the Fond Blanc de Volaille, salt and pepper to taste, and Tabasco. Process for 1 to 2 minutes, until the mixture is thoroughly blended and smooth. Add the cream and process for a moment longer.

4. Pass the mixture through a sieve into a bowl. Add the cubes of avocado. Refrigerate.

5. Serve cold, in soup bowls, with the chives and croutons sprinkled on top.

~᠊ᘒᕽᡃ~

Crème de Merlan

CREAM OF WHITING

This is a delicious soup and—because whiting is an inexpensive fish, and very easy to get at any time of the year—a useful one.

Serves 4

3 medium whitings
4 tablespoons (½ stick) unsalted
    butter
2 leeks (the white part only),
    washed and sliced
1 cup (approximately ½ pound)
    mushrooms, washed and
    sliced

½ cup dry white wine
salt
cayenne pepper
1½ quarts Fumet de Poisson
    (page 513), or water (see *Note*
    on page 58)
3 slices white bread
¼ cup heavy cream

1. Wash and eviscerate the whitings, and remove the gills. Cut the fish in small pieces—8 to 10 pieces per fish, including the heads and tails.

2. In a large sauté pan, melt 2 tablespoons of the butter. Add the leeks and mushrooms, and sauté them over medium heat, *without browning*, for 5 minutes. Add the wine, salt, cayenne pepper, and Fumet de Poisson (or

Crème de Merlan (continued)

water). Bring the pot to the boil over high heat, and cook over high heat for 30 minutes.

3. Cut the bread in ⅜-inch cubes. Melt the remaining 2 tablespoons of butter in a skillet. Sauté the bread in the butter until the croutons are golden brown. Set aside.

4. Press the contents of the sauté pan very firmly through a fine sieve, so that little is left behind but the bones. Stir in the cream, and bring to the boil. Serve hot, with the croutons.

Crème de Moules aux Quenelles à la Moëlle

CREAM OF MUSSEL SOUP WITH MARROW DUMPLINGS

Although mussels are not Alsatian (Alsace does not border on the sea), my father was crazy about them, so my mother made mussel soup. But when she made it, she made it the Alsatian way, with marrow dumplings, which is *very* Alsatian.

This is a dish very close to the heart of my family.   *Serves 6*

The Quenelles

4 ounces beef marrow (obtainable from butchers)

½ cup dry bread crumbs

1 tablespoon uncooked cream of wheat

1 tablespoon chopped parsley and chervil, mixed

2 egg yolks

salt

pepper, fresh ground

1 pinch grated nutmeg

1 quart Fond Blanc de Volaille (page 512), or water (see *Note* on page 58)

The Mussels and the Finished Soup

2 pounds mussels

5 tablespoons (⅝ stick) unsalted butter

3 shallots, peeled and chopped

⅓ cup dry white wine

1½ quarts Fond Blanc de
    Volaille (page 512), or water
    (see *Note* on page 58)
1 cup heavy cream

6 egg yolks
salt
pepper, fresh ground
1 tablespoon chopped chives

The Quenelles

1. In a small bowl, using a fork, puree the marrow. Stir in the bread crumbs, cream of wheat, mixed parsley and chervil, and the egg yolks. Add salt, pepper, and the nutmeg. Mix thoroughly.

2. Roll dollops of the mixture between the fingers of one hand and the palm of the other to form ¾-inch-long egg-shaped ovals (quenelles).

3. Put the Fond Blanc de Volaille (or water) in a large saucepan and bring it to the boil. Add the quenelles, return to the boil, and simmer for 10 minutes.

The Mussels and the Finished Soup

4. Squeeze each mussel in your hand, pushing the top and bottom of the shell in opposite directions, and discard those that open. Scrub the mussels to remove the beards, and wash them in 2 or 3 changes of water.

5. In a pot, melt the butter, and sauté the shallots for about 30 seconds. Add the mussels to the pot, and cook, covered, until they open—about 3 minutes. Add the wine, bring to the boil, and cook until the mussels are done—about 2 minutes more. Remove 12 mussels from the pot and set them aside for a garnish. (Use the remaining mussels for another purpose.)

6. Strain the liquid from the pot into a saucepan. Add the Fond Blanc de Volaille (or water), bring to the boiling point, and keep hot.

7. In a double boiler, over lightly simmering water, whisk together the cream and egg yolks, whisking constantly until the mixture is frothy. Still whisking constantly, slowly add the hot liquid. Continue to cook until slightly thickened. *Do not boil.* Strain through a fine sieve. Add salt and pepper to taste.

8. Put the quenelles and the reserved mussels in a soup tureen, and pour the soup over them. Serve hot, sprinkled with the chopped chives.

Bisque de Crevettes

SHRIMP BISQUE

It is not easy to make this soup at home the same way we make it at Lutèce, because we always make it with fresh shrimp, which we usually get from Alaska. But sometimes there are no fresh shrimp to be had, even for us. When that happens, we do not make Shrimp Bisque.

You should have the same policy. If there are no fresh shrimp at the fish markets, do not try to make this soup.   *Serves 6*

24 medium shrimp, fresh
2 ounces (a scant ½ cup) all-
    purpose flour
3 tablespoons (⅜ stick) unsalted
    butter, at room temperature
2 tablespoons peanut oil
¾ cup diced carrots
¾ cup diced onions
½ cup diced celery
2 sprigs fresh thyme
1 bay leaf
2 garlic cloves, peeled, green
    germs removed

½ cup tomato puree
1 pinch saffron
¼ cup Cognac
1 cup dry white wine
2 quarts Fumet de Poisson
    (page 513), or water (see
    Note on page 58)
salt
cayenne pepper
½ cup heavy cream

1. Separate the tails and bodies of the shrimp. Remove the meats from the tails, and set them aside. Put the heads and the shells of the tails in a food processor and process until coarsely crushed—a few seconds.

2. Make a beurre manié by mashing together the flour and 2 table-spoons of the butter. Set aside.

3. In a large pot, heat the oil over high heat. When the oil is very hot, add the crushed shells and the heads of the shrimp—*but not the meats*—and sauté vigorously for 4 minutes, still over high heat. Add the carrots, onions, celery, thyme, bay leaf, and garlic, and continue to sauté for 3 more minutes.

4. Add the tomato puree and saffron. Add the Cognac, and set it aflame. When the flame has subsided, add the wine, Fumet de Poisson (or water), salt, and cayenne pepper to taste. Cover, and cook gently for 1 hour.

5. Pass the contents of the pot through a fine sieve, pushing hard, so that everything but the shells passes through. Rinse the pot of any solids. Then return this liquid to the pot.

6. Away from the heat, vigorously stir the beurre manié into the liquid. Return the pot to the heat, and, while stirring, bring it to the boil and cook gently for 15 minutes. Still over heat, whisk in the cream. Pass the bisque through a fine sieve again.

7. Cut the meat of the shrimp into small pieces, and sauté it in the remaining butter for 2 minutes. The meat may then be stirred into the soup or sprinkled over the individual servings. Serve hot.

Minestrone des Grisons

MINESTRONE WITH PEARL BARLEY

Grisons is the canton of Switzerland near the border of Italy. When I was a young chef, I worked in Switzerland during the summer seasons of 1952 and 1953 in the Palace Hôtel in the town of Pontresina.

In those days, Pontresina was a summer resort—the people on their vacations came for the hiking and the mountain climbing and the fantastic scenery, all of which I enjoyed too. Today Pontresina is also a ski resort, like St. Moritz, which is very near.

The kitchen where I worked was well run, we had the best ingredients. The cooking was mostly classic French, but it was there that I learned to make this soup, which is not French at all. And though it is called Minestrone, it is not really Italian either—you will never find pearl barley in Italian Minestrone. This soup is Swiss, and it is the pearl barley that makes it so.

Serves 6

Minestrone des Grisons (continued)

1 large tomato	salt
2 tablespoons olive oil	pepper, fresh ground
½ cup chopped carrots, in pieces about ⅛″ × ⅜″ × ⅜″	½ cup chopped cabbage, in pieces about ⅛″ × ⅜″ × ⅜″
½ cup chopped onions, in pieces about ⅛″ × ⅜″ × ⅜″	1 cup chopped potatoes
½ cup chopped celery, in pieces about ⅛″ × ⅜″ × ⅜″	½ cup pearl barley, washed in cold water, drained
½ cup chopped leeks (the white part only), in pieces about ⅛″ × ⅜″ × ⅜″	1 tablespoon chopped parsley
	1 tablespoon chopped basil
1½ quarts Fond Blanc de Volaille (page 512), or water (see *Note* on page 58)	1 garlic clove, peeled, green germ removed
	3 ounces smoked bacon, chopped coarse
	¼ cup grated Parmesan cheese

1. Cut a conical plug from the stem end of the tomato and discard. Blanch the tomato in boiling water for 10 seconds, drain it under cold water, and peel off the skin. Cut the tomato in half, squeeze out and discard the juice and seeds, and chop the pulp in ¼-inch cubes.

2. In a large saucepan, heat the olive oil. Add the carrots, onions, celery, and leeks, and sauté until they are golden brown. Add the Fond Blanc de Volaille (or water), salt, and pepper. Bring to the boil and cook slowly for 20 minutes. Add the cabbage, potatoes, pearl barley, and tomato. Cook slowly for 45 minutes.

3. Mash together in a mortar (or process in a food processor) the parsley, basil, garlic, and bacon until they form a paste. Over heat, whisk this paste into the soup.

4. Serve hot, with the grated cheese.

Gazpacho

Certainly this is not French food, but for hot summers Lutèce has to make many cold soups, and Gazpacho is a good one.

Originally Gazpacho was a tomato and cucumber salad—how it became a soup, I do not know. There are many, many ways to make it, but this method is excellent—people tell me all the time that they never have Gazpacho in Spanish restaurants that is as good as this one.

At Lutèce, we make Gazpacho with fresh tomatoes. But if you make it with canned tomatoes, you will get just as good a result—or better. Sometimes (but only very rarely) a canned product is better than the fresh one, and tomatoes are canned when they are at the peak of their ripeness, when they are riper than almost any tomatoes you can buy in a store.

Serves 6

The Soup

5 medium tomatoes, or two 14-ounce cans solid plum tomatoes, chopped
¼ cup olive oil (plus 1 tablespoon if you use fresh tomatoes)
2 slices white bread

1 tablespoon vinegar (tarragon vinegar preferred)
2 garlic cloves, peeled, green germs removed
salt
pepper, fresh ground
1 pinch cayenne pepper

The Garnishes

1 small red pepper, seeds and stem removed, chopped
1 small green pepper, seeds and stem removed, chopped

¼ cup chopped onion
2 slices white bread, crusts removed, cut in cubes

The Soup

1. Cut a conical plug from the stem end of each tomato and discard. Blanch the tomatoes in boiling water for 10 seconds, drain them under cold water, peel off the skins, and chop them.

2. In a skillet, heat the 1 tablespoon of olive oil. Sauté the tomatoes for 8 minutes. (If you use canned tomatoes, omit this step, and use the entire contents of the cans, including the liquid.)

3. Soak the bread in 1 cup of water. Put the tomatoes, ¼ cup of olive oil, the bread, vinegar, garlic, salt and pepper to taste, and cayenne pepper in a blender. Blend for 10 minutes. Pass through a fine sieve.

4. Put the soup in a bowl. Put 4 ice cubes in the soup. Refrigerate until very cold. Serve with the garnishes.

Gazpacho aux Huîtres

GAZPACHO WITH OYSTERS

This is a nice variation on basic Gazpacho, in which the cold soup is enhanced with oysters.   *Serves 6*

24 oysters, fresh   1 recipe Gazpacho (page 84)

1. Open the oysters and remove the meats from the shells, being careful to keep all the oyster liquid. Filter this liquid through a cloth into a saucepan.

2. Add the oysters to the liquid, bring the liquid to the boil, and poach the oysters for 30 seconds. Set the oysters aside, in the liquid, to cool.

3. When the oysters are cool, add them to the Gazpacho *without the liquid.*

❧

Potage au Potiron

PUMPKIN SOUP SERVED IN A PUMPKIN

Note: It is nice to serve this soup in the pumpkin shell, and that is the way we serve it at Lutèce. But of course you may serve it from any soup tureen, or in cups.

Serves 6

1 ripe pumpkin, 8 to 10 inches in diameter

¼ pound (1 stick) unsalted butter

1 medium onion, peeled and chopped

⅔ cup dry white wine

2 small white turnips, peeled and sliced

1 carrot, trimmed, peeled, washed, and sliced

1 large potato, peeled, washed, and cut in 6 to 8 pieces

approximately 5 cups Fond Blanc de Volaille (page 512), or water (enough to cover— see Step 3) (see *Note* on page 58)

salt
pepper, fresh ground
1 10-inch length of a narrow
    baguette (French bread), or

2 small rolls, in thin slices,
    crusts removed
½ cup heavy cream

1. Cut the top off the pumpkin so that it can serve as a lid—the lid should be at least 5 inches across. With a large spoon, scoop out and discard all the seeds and stringy material.

2. Scrape out all the pumpkin meat, being careful not to break through the shell. There should be about 6 cups of pumpkin meat. Set aside the hollow pumpkin and its lid in a warm place.

3. In a large pot, heat 2 tablespoons of the butter over medium heat. Add the onion and sauté, stirring often, until softened—about 5 to 6 minutes. Add the wine and simmer for 1 minute. Add the turnips, carrot, pumpkin meat, potato, and enough Fond Blanc de Volaille (or water) barely to cover. Season lightly with salt and pepper, and bring to the boil, covered.

4. While the soup is coming to the boil, heat 3 tablespoons of butter in a large skillet over medium heat. Add half the bread slices and toss them constantly in the butter until lightly browned—about 5 minutes. When the pot has come to the boil, add these browned croutons to it. Boil the soup gently, covered, for 1 hour.

5. While the soup is cooking, sauté the remainder of the bread slices in the remaining butter. Set these croutons aside.

6. When the soup has cooked, puree it in a food processor or blender until it is smooth, working in batches if necessary. Put the soup in a clean saucepan, stir in the cream, and bring to a simmer. Taste for seasoning, and add salt and pepper if necessary.

7. Pour the soup into the reserved pumpkin shell, and serve it hot from the pumpkin shell. Serve the reserved croutons separately, with the soup.

Potage Crème St. Germain

SPLIT PEA SOUP

Serves 6 to 8

½ pound split peas

4 tablespoons (½ stick) unsalted
  butter

2 ounces smoked bacon, diced

1 medium white onion, peeled
  and sliced

1 leek (the white part only),
  washed, cut in ¼-inch slices

1 carrot, trimmed, peeled,
  washed, cut in ¼-inch pieces

1 garlic clove, peeled and
  crushed

1½ quarts Fond Blanc de
  Volaille (page 512), or water
  (see *Note* on page 58)

1 bouquet garni (page 55)

salt

pepper, fresh ground

3 slices white bread, crusts removed, cut in ¼-inch cubes

½ cup heavy cream

½ tablespoon chervil leaves

1. Wash the split peas in several changes of cold water. Then soak them in cold water for 2 hours. Drain and set aside.

2. In a large saucepan, melt 2 tablespoons of the butter. Add the bacon, and sauté over medium heat for 4 minutes. Add the onion, leek, carrot, and garlic, and sauté over low heat for 3 more minutes.

3. Add the split peas, the Fond Blanc de Volaille (or water), bouquet garni, salt, and pepper to taste. Bring to the boil, and simmer over low heat, covered, for 1½ hours.

4. While the soup is simmering, melt the remaining 2 tablespoons of butter in a skillet, and sauté the diced bread until these croutons are golden brown. Drain the croutons on a paper towel and set aside.

5. When the soup has cooked, remove the bouquet garni, puree the soup in a food processor (about 2 minutes), and pass it through a fine sieve. Return the soup to its pot, and bring it to a simmer. Stir in the cream. Taste and add salt and pepper if necessary. Sprinkle with the chervil, and serve hot with the croutons.

Potage Cressonière aux Huîtres

WATERCRESS SOUP WITH OYSTERS

There is nothing in classic French cooking anything like this soup. You could say it is nouvelle cuisine, but who knows what that is exactly?

In fact, you almost never hear about nouvelle cuisine anymore, though it has left some wonderful things behind. This delicious combination—oysters and watercress—is the kind of thing that nouvelle cuisine inspired.

Serves 4

4 tablespoons (½ stick) unsalted butter
1 leek (the white part only), washed and chopped fine
1 medium white onion, peeled and chopped fine
¾ pound potatoes, peeled, cut in pieces, and washed in cold water
1 bunch watercress, stems removed, cut once or twice

3 cups Fond Blanc de Volaille (page 512)
2 cups Fumet de Poisson (page 513)
salt
pepper, fresh ground
16 oysters
½ cup heavy cream
1 ample teaspoon chopped chervil

1. In a saucepan, melt the butter. Add the leek and onion. Sauté gently—but do not brown—for 2 minutes. Add the potatoes, watercress, Fond Blanc de Volaille, Fumet de Poisson, salt, and pepper to taste. Cook gently for 30 minutes.

2. Open the oysters. Put the meats and liquid in a small skillet. Bring the liquid to the boil, and poach gently for 30 seconds.

3. Remove the oysters from the juice. Filter the liquid through a cheesecloth. Return the oysters to their liquid. Set aside.

4. When the soup has cooked for 30 minutes, pass it

through a food mill or process it in a food processor until it is blended. Bring it back to the boil. Stir in the cream.

5. Add the oysters and their liquid. Heat, but do not boil. Serve hot, sprinkled with the chervil.

⁓ ❧ ⁓

Potage Maigre aux Racines

ROOT VEGETABLE SOUP

This is a recipe not so much for a soup as for a cooking broth. In this broth we cook a julienne or brunoise of vegetables, individual vegetables, rice, semolina, many things. The result is much better, much tastier, than if we were to cook these things just in salted water.

So unless a customer asks us for it—usually somebody who is on a diet—we do not serve this soup at the restaurant. But it is an important part of Lutèce cooking, and if you take the trouble to prepare it, it can be an important part of home cooking too.   *Serves 6*

1 cup lentils	1½ cups diced carrots
salt	½ cup diced leeks
pepper, fresh ground	1 cup diced white onions
2 tablespoons (¼ stick) unsalted	½ cup diced celery
butter	1 ounce parsley sprigs

1. Thoroughly wash the lentils under cold running water. Cook them slowly for 45 minutes in 2 quarts of water, with salt and pepper. Then let the lentils rest for at least 5 minutes, away from heat.

2. Pour the liquid through cheesecloth, and set it aside. Discard the lentils.

Note: Do not press the lentils against the cloth, or the liquid will become cloudy.

3. Melt the butter in a pot, and gently sauté the carrots, leeks, onions, and celery until they are golden brown. Add the reserved liquid and the parsley. Taste for seasoning, add salt and pepper if necessary, bring to the boil, and cook very gently for 1 hour.

4. Line a colander with a moistened cloth napkin—*not cheesecloth*—and pour the soup through it.

⮜⭑⮞

Pot au Feu du Pêcheur

FISH SOUP

At one time I had a cook in my kitchen by the name of Jean-Jacques Le Saout, who worked at Lutèce when the restaurant was new. He was from Brittany, and after a number of years at Lutèce he went back there to open his own restaurant—La Cotriade, in Pléneuf-Val-André—which has been a great success.

Before he came to Lutèce, this man had cooked at one of the most famous restaurants in all of Brittany, the seafood restaurant Chez Mélanie, in Riec-sur-Belon, the town that the famous Belon oysters come from.

At Chez Mélanie he learned to make this soup. At Lutèce he taught it to me.   *Serves 4*

½ pound carrots, trimmed, peeled, washed, and cut in sticks 1½″ × ¼″ × ¼″

½ pound celery, peeled, washed, and cut in sticks 1½″ × ¼″ × ¼″

2 small potatoes, peeled and cut in half

salt

½ pound string beans, trimmed and broken in half

1 pound mussels

½ cup dry white wine

½ pound fillets of sole

½ pound fillets of codfish

½ pound fillets of bass

½ pound fillets of snapper

1¼ quarts Soupe de Poisson (page 100)

1 tablespoon chopped parsley

Pot au Feu du Pêcheur (continued)

1. Put the carrots, celery, and potatoes in a pot of salted water to cover. Bring to the boil, and cook over medium heat for 2 minutes. Add the string beans and continue cooking for 10 more minutes. The vegetables should be a little firm. Drain.

2. Squeeze each mussel in your hand, pushing the top and bottom of the shell in opposite directions, and discard those that open. Scrub the mussels to remove the beards, and wash them in 2 or 3 changes of water. Put them in a saucepan with the white wine. Bring to the boil, and cook them until they open—about 3 minutes. Remove the mussels from the shells and set them aside.

3. Cut the fish so that there are 4 portions of each type. Arrange the fish in the bottom of a large skillet. Add the vegetables and cover with the Soupe de Poisson. Bring gently to the boil, which will take about 8 to 10 minutes. Lower the heat and cook slowly for 8 minutes more.

4. Add the mussels and cook for 1 more minute. Serve hot in 4 soup bowls, sprinkled with the chopped parsley.

Soupe à la Bière

BEER SOUP

This winter soup is Alsatian, but you can make it with a light-colored beer from anywhere. *Serves 6*

10 tablespoons (1¼ sticks) un-salted butter	4 cups light-colored beer
6 slices French bread, cut thin	1 pinch sugar
¼ cup all-purpose flour	1 pinch grated nutmeg
4 cups Fond Blanc de Volaille (page 512)	salt
	pepper, fresh ground
	1 cup heavy cream

1. In a skillet, melt ½ of the butter. Fry the slices of bread in the butter until they are golden brown. Set aside and keep warm.

2. In a large pot, melt the remaining butter. Stir in the flour and cook until golden brown. Gradually whisk in the Fond Blanc de Volaille and the beer and bring to the boil. Add the sugar and nutmeg, and salt and pepper to taste. Simmer for 20 minutes.

3. Lower the heat under the pot, and stir in the cream. Pass through a fine sieve.

4. Put the bread in the bottom of a soup tureen. Pour the soup over the bread, and serve very hot.

Soupe à l'Oignon Gratinée

ONION SOUP GRATINÉE

Do not think for a minute that this is the notorious soup you get in Paris workingmen's cafés at five o'clock in the morning. Only the name is the same.

In those soups the onions are sautéed until they are black, and the soup is dark and bitter. Some people like it that way—which I can never understand.   *Serves 6*

4 tablespoons (½ stick) unsalted
    butter
½ pound onions, peeled and
    chopped
2 tablespoons all-purpose flour
2 cups dry white wine
6 cups Fond Blanc de Volaille

(page 512), or water (see *Note*
    on page 58)
1 teaspoon salt
pepper, fresh ground
4 ounces French bread, sliced
3 ounces grated Swiss cheese
    (Emmental or Gruyère)

1. In a pot, melt 1 tablespoon of the butter. Add the onions, and sauté them until they are golden brown.

2. Add the flour, and cook over medium heat, stirring, for 3 more minutes. Add the wine, bring to the boil, and cook for another 3 minutes. Add the Fond Blanc de Volaille (or water), salt, and pepper, and bring to the boil. Simmer for 30 minutes.

Soupe à l'Oignon Gratinée (continued)

3. While the soup is simmering, melt the remaining 3 tablespoons of butter in a skillet. Sauté the bread until it is golden brown on both sides.

4. Preheat the oven to 450°.

5. Stir ¼ of the bread and ¼ of the cheese into the soup, and simmer the soup for 10 more minutes.

6. Pour the soup into an ovenproof tureen or into ovenproof serving bowls. Top the soup with the remaining bread and then with the remaining cheese.

7. Put the soup in the preheated oven, and bake until the cheese is nicely browned—6 to 8 minutes.

Soupe aux Amandes

ALMOND SOUP

My memory is not clear about this soup, but I know that it is connected to the great chef Jean Troisgros, who is now dead.

Either I had this soup, or something like it, in his restaurant in France, or else it is something he and I came up with when he visited me in New York at Lutèce, which he did many times. Anyway, it was a long time ago.

Whenever I make this soup, I remember Jean Troisgros.

Serves 4

6 ounces shelled almonds,
    peeled
3 hardboiled eggs (page 119),
    yolks only
3 cups heavy cream

1 quart Fond Blanc de Volaille
    (page 512), heated
2 egg yolks
salt
pepper, fresh ground

1. Put the almonds and the yolks of the hardboiled eggs in a food processor, and process until you have a smooth paste.

2. In a pot, combine the paste and 1½ cups of the cream. Add the heated Fond Blanc de Volaille. Bring to the boil, and simmer for 5 minutes.

3. In another pot—not over heat—stir together the 2 egg yolks and the remaining 1½ cups of cream. When the soup has cooked, pour it over this egg-yolk-and-cream mixture, and whisk over medium heat for 2 minutes. *Do not boil.* Add salt and pepper to taste. Serve hot.

Note: At Lutèce the soup is sprinkled with a few peeled, slivered almonds that have been lightly toasted in the oven or under the broiler.

༺ঌ৸ৎ༻

Soupe de Grenouilles

SOUP OF FROGS' LEGS

When I was a child, mostly in the spring and fall, I used to go fishing for frogs—in the River Thur, and in the little streams and at the edges of the ponds nearby.

My friends and I would go out carrying hazelnut sticks on which we tied a string. To the end of the string we tied a bent pin and a tiny piece of red cloth. The frogs would bite the cloth, and that was how we caught them.

We would take the frogs home, and our mothers would prepare with the legs wonderful Alsatian dishes like this one. *Serves 6*

2 tablespoons (¼ stick) unsalted butter
3 shallots, peeled and chopped
24 frogs' legs (the legs of 24 frogs)
½ cup dry white wine
1½ quarts Fond Blanc de Volaille (page 512), or water (see *Note* on page 58)

1 teaspoon salt
pepper, fresh ground
1 pinch grated nutmeg
1 scant tablespoon arrowroot
1 cup heavy cream
1 bunch watercress (about 4 ounces), washed, stems removed
4 egg yolks

1. In a large pot melt the butter. Add the shallots, and gently sauté them. *Do not brown.* Add the frogs' legs and continue gently sautéing for 2 minutes. Add the wine, the Fond Blanc de Volaille (or water), salt,

Soupe de Grenouilles (continued)

pepper, and nutmeg, and simmer until the legs are tender—about 10 minutes. (The larger the frogs' legs, the longer they will have to cook.)

2. Remove the frogs' legs from the pot. Remove the meat from the bones, and set aside the bones. Cut the meat in small pieces, and set aside the meat.

3. Return the bones to the pot. Bring the liquid (bouillon) to the boil and simmer, uncovered, for 10 minutes.

4. In a small bowl, whisk together the arrowroot and ½ of the cream, whisk this mixture into the simmering bouillon, and cook for 20 minutes more. Pass this bouillon through a fine sieve into a pot.

5. Bring a pot of water to the boil, add the watercress, and cook for 3 minutes. In a colander, rinse the watercress under cold running water. Drain, and set aside.

6. In a small pot, over low heat, whisk together the remaining cream and the egg yolks until the mixture is frothy. Whisk this mixture into the bouillon. Over low heat, bring the bouillon almost to the boil, but *do not boil.* Taste, and add salt and pepper if necessary. Pass the bouillon through a fine sieve.

7. Add the meat of the frogs' legs and the watercress to the bouillon. Serve hot in soup bowls.

~~※~~

Soupe de Clams

CLAM CHOWDER

This is the first real American dish I ever tasted.

When I first came as a young man to America, there was a respected old French restaurant called La Toque Blanche on the next block from Lutèce, and one of the owners of that restaurant—Ernest Luthring-shauser—adopted me, became like my uncle. He used to invite my wife and me to his country house on Long Island, and sometimes he would take me out fishing for clams. From the clams we brought back to his house, he made this clam chowder.

La Toque Blanche is gone now, and Ernest Luthringshauser is gone also, but we continue to visit his wife—my wife and I still call her Tante Jeanne—at her Long Island house, and she comes regularly with her family to Lutèce on her birthday.

I still serve clam chowder from time to time at the restaurant, and I even prepare it at home. Whenever and wherever I make it, I do it according to my old friend's recipe, which I learned more than thirty years ago. *Serves 6*

24 clams (large cherrystones, or what are available)
2 tablespoons (¼ stick) unsalted butter
1 cup diced onions
½ cup diced carrots
½ cup diced celery
½ cup diced leeks (the white part only)
2 garlic cloves, peeled, green germs removed, and chopped fine
½ cup peeled, seeded, and chopped tomato

1 bay leaf
1 sprig thyme
2 quarts Fond Blanc de Volaille (page 512), or water (see *Note* on page 58)
1 pound potatoes, peeled, washed, cut in small dice
½ cup heavy cream
1 dash Tabasco sauce
salt
pepper, fresh ground
1 tablespoon chopped parsley

1. Wash and open the clams. Set aside their liquid. Chop the clam meats and set them aside.

2. In a large pot, melt the butter. Add the onions, carrots, celery, and leeks, and gently sauté for 5 minutes. *Do not brown.* Add the garlic, tomato, bay leaf, thyme, Fond Blanc de Volaille (or water), and the liquid from the clams. Bring to the boil, and cook gently for 15 minutes. Add the potatoes and cook gently for 15 more minutes.

3. Add the chopped clams, cream, Tabasco sauce, salt and pepper to taste, and bring quickly to the boil. When the soup has come to the boil, *immediately* turn off the heat. (If permitted to continue cooking, the clams will become tough.) Serve hot, sprinkled with the chopped parsley.

Soupe de Lentilles à l'Alsacienne

LENTIL SOUP

Today, in French restaurants in France, you almost do not find this kind of soup—or any kind of soup—on the menus anymore. But earthy, peasant soups like this one are still very much a big part of French home cooking.

A dinner of this soup, with maybe a little charcuterie or some cheese, and a salad, is a complete evening meal.   *Serves 4*

1 cup lentils
1 tablespoon butter
2 tablespoons olive oil
3 strips smoked bacon, diced
1 white onion, peeled, sliced
    thin
1 carrot, trimmed, peeled,
    washed, and sliced thin
1 small white turnip, peeled,
    washed, and sliced thin
½ stalk celery, peeled, washed,
    and sliced thin

1 bay leaf
1 sprig thyme
½ garlic clove, peeled, halved,
    green germ removed,
    mashed
1½ quarts Fond Blanc de
    Volaille (page 512), or water
    (see *Note* on page 58)
salt
pepper, fresh ground
1 whole duckling skin; or 2
    slices of bread, crusts
    removed, cut in small cubes
½ tablespoon vinegar
½ cup heavy cream (optional)

1. Wash the lentils in 2 or 3 changes of cold water. Refrigerate them in water overnight.
2. In a pot, melt the butter with the olive oil. Sauté the bacon for 2 minutes. Add the onion, carrot, turnip, and celery, and simmer over low heat, stirring from time to time, until the vegetables are golden brown—about 8 minutes more.
3. Drain the lentils and add them to the pot. Add the

bay leaf, thyme, garlic, Fond Blanc de Volaille (or water), a little salt, and pepper. Bring to the boil, and simmer, covered, for about 1¼ hours, until the lentils are thoroughly cooked.

4. While the soup is cooking, cut the duckling skin in small pieces, and sauté them in a hot heavy-bottomed skillet until they are browned and crisp. Drain off all fat. (If bread is used instead, make croutons by sautéing the cubes of bread in butter until they are golden brown.)

5. When the soup is done, stir in the vinegar, and then the heavy cream (if used). Taste, and add salt and pepper if necessary. Serve hot, with the pieces of duckling skin (or croutons) sprinkled on top.

Soupe de Semoule de Ma Mère

ROASTED SEMOLINA SOUP

Semolina is basically durum wheat flour, but coarse-ground.
From this flour my mother made this soup when I was a child. I hated it. My mother had a hard time getting me to swallow it. The way she made it, it was lumpy, and I hated those little lumps.

Later I came to like semolina soup very much, enough to serve it now and then at Lutèce—but with no lumps.   *Serves 4*

2 tablespoons (¼ stick) unsalted butter
½ cup semolina
2 ounces smoked bacon, cut in small pieces
¼ cup carrot, trimmed, peeled, washed, and chopped fine
¼ cup celery, peeled, washed, and chopped fine
¼ cup leek (the white part only), washed and chopped fine
¼ cup onion, peeled and chopped fine
6 cups Fond Blanc de Volaille (page 512), or water (see *Note* on page 58)
salt
½ cup heavy cream

1. In a skillet, melt 1 tablespoon of the butter, then add the semolina. Cook over low heat, stirring, until the semolina is uniformly golden brown—about 5 minutes.

Soupe de Semoule (continued)

2. In a saucepan, melt the remaining 1 tablespoon of butter. Add the bacon, and sauté for 3 minutes over medium heat. Add the carrot, celery, leek, and onion, and sauté for 3 minutes more. *Do not let the vegetables brown.*

3. Add the semolina to the vegetables. Add the Fond Blanc de Volaille (or water), and salt to taste. Bring to the boil, and simmer gently, covered, for 40 minutes. Stir in the cream, cook 2 minutes more, and serve hot.

Soupe de Poisson

PROVENÇALE FISH SOUP

Every day at Lutèce, at lunch and dinner, this soup is available on the menu, as it has been for more than twenty years. We change the printed menu from time to time, but this dish is so popular that it has a permanent place.

Provençale Fish Soup is not at all like the food I grew up with—nothing about it is Alsatian—but it is popular with me, too.

My wife and I sit down to dinner every afternoon at five o'clock—an hour before the first customers arrive—and every week or two we begin our dinner with this wonderful soup. *Serves 6*

2 codfish heads, or 6 whiting heads

1 whiting, 12 to 16 ounces, or 2 small whitings

5 tablespoons (almost ⅓ cup) olive oil

1 medium onion, peeled, cut in large pieces

½ head fresh fennel (the knob only), cut in large pieces

1 medium tomato, ripe, cut in quarters

1 tablespoon tomato puree

½ head garlic, unpeeled (broken in half—do not cut through the cloves)

1 pinch saffron

salt

1 pinch cayenne pepper

½ cup dry white wine

pepper, fresh ground
1 bouquet garni (page 55), tied in
   a piece of cheesecloth

12 slices French bread
1 garlic clove, peeled

1. Cut the codfish heads in half and wash them under cold running water.

2. Eviscerate the whiting, and remove the gills. Wash it, and cut it into 5 or 6 pieces, including the head and tail.

3. In a large pot, heat 4 tablespoons of the olive oil. Add the whiting, the codfish heads, the onion, and the fennel. Sauté over medium heat, without browning, for 5 minutes.

4. Add the tomato, tomato puree, the half head of garlic, saffron, a little salt, cayenne pepper, and wine to the pot. Bring to the boil, and cook for 5 minutes.

5. Add 2 quarts of water to the pot, salt and pepper to taste, and the bouquet garni. Bring to a rolling boil over high heat and boil vigorously for 40 minutes, uncovered. Taste, and add salt and pepper if necessary.

6. Pass the contents of the pot through a fine sieve, pushing very firmly, so that nothing is left behind but the bones.

7. Lightly brush each slice of bread with the remaining olive oil. Toast the bread under the broiler or in a hot oven. With the clove of garlic, rub each slice of the toasted bread. Serve this toast with the soup.

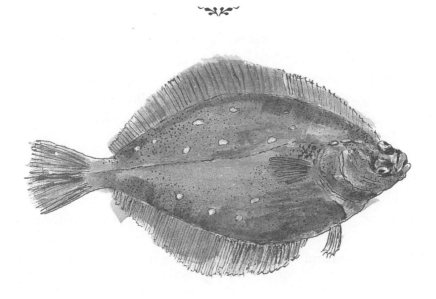

Soupe Glacée à l'Oseille

SORREL SOUP

When I worked as a young man for two summer seasons in Switzerland, my job in the kitchen was what is called "entremetier," which means I was in charge of soups and vegetables. That is when I learned to make this soup.

At Lutèce, I sometimes make it just because the weather in summer seems to call for it. Or I make it when I feel like it. Or I make it when someone who had it before calls me up and asks me in advance to prepare it for him again.

Like most of the dishes that are not on our printed menu, we have Soupe Glacée à l'Oseille only three or four times a year, not because it is not good, or not well liked—it is good *and* well liked—but because it is more interesting for the people who cook the food, and more interesting for the people who eat at Lutèce often, if what we cook is always changing.

That is why, very often, customers will say to me, "André, I don't know how you do it. I have been eating here for years, and I never have the same thing twice."

Serves 4

5 ounces sorrel, washed, stems removed	salt
1 tablespoon unsalted butter	pepper, fresh ground
1½ quarts Fond Blanc de Volaille (page 512), or water (see *Note* on page 58)	1 pinch paprika
	3 egg yolks
	½ cup heavy cream

1. With a sharp knife, cut the sorrel leaves into threadlike strands.

2. Melt the butter in a saucepan, add the sorrel, and cook it over medium heat for 4 minutes. Remove and set aside ¼ of this sorrel for a garnish.

3. Bring the Fond Blanc de Volaille (or water) to the boil and add it

to the saucepan. Add salt and pepper to taste, and the paprika, and cook slowly for 10 minutes.

4. In a bowl, mix together the egg yolks and cream. Whisk this mixture into the soup. Bring up the heat of the soup, but *do not boil.* Pass the soup through a food mill, or process it in a blender or food processor for 2 minutes.

5. Cool over ice or in the refrigerator. Serve cold, garnished with the reserved sorrel.

APPETIZERS

A typical fish and shellfish dinner at Lutèce

Tartare de Saumon (PAGE 129)

Homard au Beurre d'Escargot (PAGE 270)

Oranges (ou Pamplemousses) Glacées
au Sabayon (PAGE 453)

Lunch at Lutèce today—spring

Coquilles St. Jacques Marinées
aux Épinards et Aneth (PAGE 112)

Poussin Poché aux Petits Légumes,
Sauce Suprême (PAGE 304)

Tarte à la Rhubarbe (PAGE 465)

COLD SEAFOOD APPETIZERS

THOUGH I LIKE SEAFOOD very much, for myself I prefer to have seafood as a first course, and then something else—chicken, or beef, or veal, and so on—for my main course.

But for many people, seafood is almost their whole way of life, and for them I suggest this seafood dinner of Lutèce dishes—starting, of course, with one of the cold seafood appetizers from this chapter.

With another one of these cold seafood appetizers, I introduce this springtime lunch that you could have at Lutèce today. The main course is made with spring vegetables, and the dessert with a springtime fruit.

Of course if you cannot get to Lutèce, this is not a difficult lunch to prepare at home.

Ballottine de Sole Sauce Émeraude

BALLOTTINE OF SOLE WITH SALMON
AND MOUSSELINE OF SOLE

I first made this dish for a television program. It was in the 1960s, the television crew came to Lutèce, and they filmed me in the restaurant kitchen while I worked on this ballottine.

I made the dish mainly for the television people, as something that I thought it would be good to film. But it was also very good to eat, so good that now and then I still make it for my customers.

Ballottine de Sole (continued)

Note: A ballottine is a dish of fish (or meat, or fowl) that is rolled into a bundle and then cooked.

Serves 8

The Ballottine

2 pounds whole fillets of sole, the larger the better, skin removed

salt

2 recipes Mousseline de Poisson (page 527), prepared with sole

½ pound fillet of salmon, cut in fingers

1 bay leaf

2 sprigs thyme

The Sauce Émeraude

1 ample tablespoon parsley, chopped fine

1 ample tablespoon spinach, chopped fine

1 ample tablespoon watercress, chopped fine

1½ cups Mayonnaise (page 515), prepared with a pinch of cayenne

The Ballottine

1. Wet a clean kitchen towel, squeeze out all the excess moisture, and spread it on a work surface. Spread a piece of parchment paper of the same size over the towel. Arrange the whole fillets of sole over the paper. The length of the fillets should be parallel to the short side of the towel, and the fillets should be made to fit close together, without spaces between them, and with a border around the fish on all four sides.

2. Season the fillets with salt, and spread the Mousseline evenly over them.

3. Arrange the fingers of salmon on the Mousseline, in a row parallel to a short side of the towel, in such a way that when the ballottine is rolled up, the salmon will form a core from one end of the ballottine to the other.

4. Starting at the end near which the salmon fingers are placed, firmly roll the fillets and Mousseline (with the fingers of salmon inside), into a cylinder. Use the towel and paper to hold everything together as you roll,

but do not roll the towel or parchment paper into the ballottine. When the ballottine is all rolled up, the towel and the parchment paper are wrapped around the *outside* of the ballottine.

5. With twine, firmly tie the ballottine (with the towel and parchment paper still wrapped around it) in 3 places—one near each end, and one in the middle.

6. Put the ballottine in a large pot and cover it with salted water. Add the bay leaf and thyme. Bring to the boil, and gently simmer for 30 minutes. Remove the ballottine from the water, and cut the strings. With your hands, and with the towel and the paper still wrapped around it, roll the ballottine tighter. Tie it with 3 strings again. Let it cool for 2 hours in its liquid. Then refrigerate overnight.

The Sauce Émeraude

7. Wrap the parsley, spinach, and watercress in a kitchen towel. Twist the towel until all the juices are extracted. Add the juices to the Mayonnaise. Serve the ballottine cold, in slices, with this sauce.

Brioche aux Trois Poissons

THREE FISH IN BRIOCHE PASTRY

Here is a favorite dish of James Levine, the Artistic Director and also the Principal Conductor of the Metropolitan Opera.

He very often comes late to lunch, after his morning rehearsals, and by that time he has a wonderful appetite. He starts with a double order of this Brioche aux Trois Poissons. *Serves 8 to 10*

Brioche aux Trois Poissons (continued)

½ pound fillets of salmon
½ pound fillets of sole
½ pound fillets of bass
salt
pepper, fresh ground
juice of 1 lemon
3 shallots, peeled and chopped
1 ample tablespoon chopped
　parsley
1 ample teaspoon chopped
　tarragon
1 ample teaspoon chopped
　chervil

1 recipe Mousseline de Poisson
　(page 527), prepared with
　pike, or another white fish
unsalted butter for buttering the
　pâté mold
1½ pounds Pâte à Brioche (page
　534)
1 egg, beaten with a little cold
　water
¾ cup Sauce Cresson (page 156)

1. Cut the salmon, sole, and bass in ½-inch cubes, and put them in a bowl. Add the salt, pepper, lemon juice, shallots, parsley, tarragon, and chervil. Toss. Let the fish marinate for 5 minutes.

2. Stir the Mousseline into the marinated fish.

3. Heavily butter a 2-quart metal pâté mold, and line it with parchment paper.

4. Roll out ¾ of the Pâte à Brioche, and line the pâté mold with it. The pastry should overhang the edge of the mold by ½ inch.

5. Fill the pastry-lined mold with the fish mixture. Fold the overhanging pastry over the top. Brush the exposed pastry with the beaten egg.

6. Roll out the remaining pastry to the size of the top of the mold. Put this pastry on top, brush it with the beaten egg, and let it rise in a warm place for 25 minutes. (It will rise only a little.)

7. Preheat the oven to 325°.

8. Put the filled mold in the preheated oven for 1 hour. Remove it from the oven and let it cool. Refrigerate overnight.

9. Serve at room temperature, with the Sauce Cresson.

Note: When you cut the filled brioche into slices, you will find a gap between the pastry top and the fish. At Lutèce, we pour the Sauce Cresson into this space.

Clams Barigoule

CLAMS IN BROTH, WITH VEGETABLES

Dishes with the word "barigoule" come from the south of France, from Provence, and they usually include artichokes.

This barigoule is a variation, a way of fitting a non-Provençale food—the cherrystone clams—to a Provençale way of cooking.   *Serves 6*

30 cherrystone clams

1½ cups dry white wine

1 cauliflower, very small, washed, green leaves removed, cut in small florets

18 small baby artichokes

1 lemon, cut in half

5 tablespoons (almost ⅓ cup) olive oil

2 young carrots, trimmed, peeled, washed, and cut in ⅛-inch disks

1 small white onion, peeled and cut in rings

6 garlic cloves, peeled, halved, green germs removed

1 bay leaf

1 sprig thyme

salt

pepper, fresh ground

1 tablespoon chopped parsley

1. Open the clams, and empty the meats and juice into a bowl. Discard the shells. Shake the bowl so that any sand in the clams is released and sinks to the bottom of the bowl.

2. With a fork, lift the clams out of their juice one at a time, and put them in a saucepan. Filter the juice through a cloth napkin, and add it to the saucepan. Add ½ cup of the white wine.

3. Bring to the boil, but *do not let the clams cook*. As soon as the liquid comes to the boil, remove the saucepan from the heat and set it aside.

4. Blanch the cauliflower in boiling salted water for 5 minutes. Drain.

5. With a serrated knife, or a very sharp knife, trim ½ inch from the top of each artichoke. Discard the cut-off tops. Remove and discard the 2 outer layers of artichoke leaves. With a vegetable peeler, trim the bottoms

Clams Barigoule (continued)

of the artichokes. Rub the bottom of each artichoke with the exposed part of the halved lemon (to prevent discoloration).

6. Slightly pry open the top of each artichoke, and pull out the strawlike material—the choke—that may be found in some of them.

7. In a saucepan, heat the olive oil. Add the carrots, onion, and garlic. Sauté until barely browned—around 4 minutes. Add the remaining 1 cup of wine, 1 cup of water, the bay leaf, thyme, and salt and pepper to taste. Bring to the boil. Add the artichokes, return to the boil, cover, and cook for 12 minutes. Add the cauliflower, and cook, covered, 4 minutes more. Strain the clam juice over the vegetables, and cook 1 minute more.

8. Turn off the heat. Add the clams—but do not cook them.

Note: This dish is best served in soup plates or deep bowls. It may be served hot as soon as it is ready; or it may be refrigerated and served cold.

❦

Coquilles St. Jacques Marinées aux Épinards et Aneth

MARINATED SCALLOPS WITH SPINACH AND DILL

When a customer says to me, "I just want to start with a salad," I feel that I have to give him something more than just a salad.

This is a salad, but it is more than a salad. So the customer is happy, and I am happy. *Serves 4*

The Vinaigrette

2 tablespoons olive oil
2 tablespoons peanut oil
1½ tablespoons tarragon
   vinegar

1 teaspoon Dijon mustard
salt
1 pinch cayenne pepper

The Salad

1 small ripe avocado
12 large sea scallops, very fresh
1 pound leaf spinach, stems re-
    moved

1 scant teaspoon cracked pepper
1 small bunch dill, in sprigs

The Vinaigrette

1. Whisk together all the ingredients listed under *The Vinaigrette*.

The Salad

2. Peel the avocado and remove the seed. Chop the avocado in fine dice.

Note: This step should not be performed more than 1 hour before the dish is served, or the avocado will discolor.

3. With a sharp knife, cut each scallop in thin slices. Arrange the slices on a plate.

4. Using ¼ of the vinaigrette, brush the slices of scallop with the vinaigrette, first one side, then the other. Let the scallops marinate this way for 10 minutes.

5. Thoroughly wash the spinach, dry it in a towel, and toss it with the remainder of the vinaigrette. Spread the leaves of spinach on 4 plates.

6. Arrange the slices of scallop decoratively on the spinach; sprinkle them with the diced avocado and cracked pepper. Arrange the sprigs of dill on top.

᠃᠊ᢌᠯᡭ᠊᠃

Effeuillée de Flétan
aux Noix sur Salade d'Endives

HALIBUT AND WALNUTS ON ENDIVES SALAD

Some years ago, all of a sudden, everybody wanted to eat light. We had to come up with a great many dishes to satisfy this demand.

People are not eating that way so much anymore, but from that light style of eating many good dishes came about, like this one.   *Serves 4*

4 ounces shelled walnuts
1 tomato
1 pound fillets of halibut
1 small head of Boston lettuce,
   separated into leaves,
   washed, and dried
3 tablespoons Vinaigrette (page 525)

1 tablespoon shallots, peeled and
   chopped fine
3 medium endives, washed, and
   cut in 1-inch lengths
1 scant tablespoon chives,
   chopped fine

1. Preheat the oven to 350°.
2. Arrange the walnuts on a baking sheet, and put them in the preheated oven for 10 minutes. Remove the walnuts from the oven, rub them between your fingers to remove their skins, and break them into pieces—about 4 or 5 pieces per walnut half. Set them aside.
3. Cut a conical plug from the stem end of the tomato and discard. Blanch the tomato in boiling water for 10 seconds, drain it under cold water, and peel off the skin. Cut the tomato in half, squeeze out and discard the juice and seeds, and chop the pulp in ¼-inch cubes.
4. In a steamer, steam the halibut for 10 minutes. Remove any remaining skin or bones. Break the fish into the flakes into which it naturally falls. Set the fish aside to cool to room temperature.

Note: If a steamer is not available, put the halibut in a pot of water, bring it to the boil, and simmer for 10 minutes.

5. In a bowl, toss the leaves of Boston lettuce with 1 tablespoon of the Vinaigrette. Arrange the leaves on 4 plates.
6. In a bowl, gently toss the halibut, shallots, endives, and the remaining 2 tablespoons of Vinaigrette. Arrange this mixture on the leaves of lettuce. Sprinkle with the chopped tomatoes, walnuts, and chives.

Crabe au Coulis d'Avocat

CRABMEAT WITH AVOCADO PUREE

Serves 4

4 medium tomatoes, ripe
½ pound cooked crabmeat
2 shallots, peeled and chopped
   fine
2 tablespoons Mayonnaise (page
   515)
salt

pepper, fresh ground
1 small ripe avocado
½ cup plain natural yogurt
5 drops Tabasco sauce
1 ample teaspoon chopped
   parsley

1. Cut a conical plug from the stem end of each tomato, making as small a hole as possible, and discard. Blanch the tomatoes in boiling water for 10 seconds, then drain them under cold water, and peel off the skins. Cut a lid from the smooth bottom of each tomato (opposite the stem end) and set the lids aside. With a melon scoop, or with a small spoon, carefully remove the pulp and seeds from the tomatoes, leaving a neat shell.

2. In a bowl, mix the crabmeat, shallots, and Mayonnaise. Season with salt and pepper to taste. Fill the tomato shells with this mixture, and cover them with their lids.

3. Peel the avocado, cut it in half, remove and discard the pit, and cut the meat in pieces. Put the pieces in a food processor. Add the yogurt, and salt and pepper to taste. Process until the mixture is smooth, with no solid pieces remaining—about 3 to 4 minutes. Add the Tabasco, and turn the processor on for a few seconds more to mix it in.

Note: Do not prepare the avocado more than 1 hour in advance. Otherwise it will lose its attractive green color.

4. Put equal amounts of the avocado-and-yogurt mixture on the center of 4 plates.

Crabse au Coulis d'Avocat (continued)

Put a stuffed tomato on the mixture on each plate. Sprinkle with the chopped parsley, and serve.

~~✺~~

Huîtres Pochées en Gelée

POACHED OYSTERS IN JELLY

Note: This recipe calls for seaweed for the presentation, but if seaweed is unavailable, watercress or any other green may be used instead. If you use a green, skip Step 5, and substitute the green for the seaweed in Step 9.

Serves 4

24 oysters
1 cup dry white wine
juice of ½ lemon
salt
pepper, fresh ground
1 scant tablespoon (or 1 enve-
    lope) powdered gelatin
½ pound seaweed (for presenta-
    tion)
2 tablespoons (¼ stick) unsalted
    butter

2 medium carrots, trimmed,
    peeled, washed, and cut in
    very fine strips
1 leek (the white part only),
    washed, and cut in very fine
    strips
3 celery stalks (or 1 small knob
    celery), peeled, washed, and
    cut in very fine strips
8 sprigs cilantro, chopped fine

1. Open the oysters, and remove the meats from the shells, taking care to keep the liquid. Retain the 24 bottom halves of the shells, wash them, and set them aside.

2. Strain the liquid through a very fine sieve into a small pan. Add the wine and lemon juice to the liquid, very little salt, and pepper.

3. Bring the liquid to the boil, and add the oysters. After 10 seconds, remove the oysters, and put them on paper towels. Continue to cook the liquid for 5 minutes, to reduce it.

4. While the liquid is reducing, dilute the gelatin in 2 or 3 tablespoons of cold water. Add this to the boiling liquid, and continue to simmer for 2 minutes more. Let the liquid cool.

5. Blanch the seaweed in boiling water for 2 minutes, to give it a nice green color. Chill the seaweed in ice water. Drain and set aside.

Note: At Lutèce an inedible seaweed is used. When boiled and chilled, it turns an attractive green color.

6. Prepare a julienne of the vegetables as follows: In a sauté pan, melt the butter. Add the carrots, leek, celery, and salt and pepper to taste. Stew, covered, over low heat, stirring occasionally, until the vegetables are soft— about 12 minutes. *The vegetables must not brown.* Set aside and let cool.

7. Arrange the reserved oyster shells on a plate. Put equal amounts of the vegetables in the half-shells. Then put a poached oyster on the vegetables in each shell.

8. Lower the cooled liquid, in its pan, into ice water to chill it, stirring it constantly. When the liquid becomes syrupy, but before it becomes thick, stir in the cilantro. Spoon some of this jelly over each of the oysters, using it all up. Refrigerate.

9. Arrange the seaweed on 4 plates. Arrange 6 of the oysters on the seaweed on each of the plates.

⌒⋙⋘⌒

Mille Feuilles de Saumon Fumé

MOUSSE OF SMOKED SALMON IN PUFF PASTRY

This is really a Napoleon, and it looks exactly like one of our dessert Napoleons.

I suggest that you make it with Eastern Nova Scotia smoked salmon. If that is not available, any smoked salmon will do, but for reasons of color the Scottish and Norwegian smoked salmons are not as nice as the other kinds.

I usually make this Mille Feuilles when one of my regular customers calls me up and asks me to do it for him. When the day comes around, since I am making it anyway, that day it is a special for the whole restaurant. *Serves 6*

10 ounces smoked salmon, East-
    ern Nova Scotia preferred
juice of 1 small lemon
white pepper, fresh ground
1¼ cups heavy cream
½ pound Feuilletage Spécial
    (page 532), or Feuilletage
    Rapide (page 531)
1 egg beaten with a little cold
    water

1 cup sour cream
2 tablespoons shallots chopped
    fine
1 tablespoon chives chopped
    fine
salt
pepper, fresh ground
sprigs of parsley for the garnish

1. Process the smoked salmon in a food processor until it is pureed— about 1 to 1½ minutes. Add the lemon juice and pepper, and process a few seconds longer to blend them in. Refrigerate until chilled.

2. Whip the cream until it forms soft peaks, fold it into the salmon puree, and then push this mousse through a fine sieve.

3. Roll out the Feuilletage to a sheet ⅛ inch thick and at least 12 inches wide. Prick the pastry all over with a fork. Put the pastry on a large baking sheet, and refrigerate it for at least 30 minutes (or put it in the freezer for 10 minutes).

4. Preheat the oven to 350°.

5. Remove the pastry from the refrigerator and put it in the preheated oven for 15 minutes. Remove the pastry from the oven, brush it with the beaten egg, and put it back in the oven for 5 minutes more. The pastry should be golden brown and flaky—if it is not, bake it a little more. Re- move the pastry from the oven, and cut it into 3 equal strips, each around 4 inches wide.

6. Spread ½ of the smoked salmon mousse evenly on a strip of pastry. Put a second strip of pastry on top, and spread it with the remainder of the mousse. Cover with the last layer of pastry, the glazed side up. Cut in 6 equal slices.

7. Prepare a sour cream fines herbes as follows: In a bowl, mix to-

gether the sour cream, shallots, and chives. Add salt and pepper to taste.

8. Garnish the Mille Feuilles with the sprigs of parsley, and serve with the sour cream fines herbes.

~᠕~

Oeuf Surprise au Caviar

ENRICHED EGG WITH BLACK CAVIAR

This is a very impressive first course. You can use any caviar, according to your budget—even red caviar is fine.   *Serves 4*

4 large eggs
½ cup sour cream
2 shallots, peeled and chopped
    fine
1 tablespoon vodka
6 ounces black caviar

pepper, fresh ground
salt
2 slices Pain de Campagne (page
    541), plain or toasted, cut in
    strips

1. Cook the eggs in salted boiling water for 8 minutes. Cool thoroughly under cold water—around 8 to 10 minutes.

2. With an egg cutter or a sharp serrated knife, cut ¾ inch off the small end of the eggs. Empty the eggs with a small demitasse spoon, and set aside the large part of each shell intact. Chop the contents of 2 of the eggs. (Use the contents of the other 2 eggs for another purpose.)

3. Set the reserved shells in 4 egg holders; or embed each of them in a cup of coarse salt, the salt extending ¼ of the way up the height of the egg shell.

4. Mix together the chopped eggs, sour cream, shallots, vodka, ¼ of the caviar, pepper, and a very small amount of salt.

5. Put equal amounts of the mixture in the 4 egg shells. Top with the remainder of the caviar. Serve with the strips of Pain de Campagne.

~᠕~

Oursins en Gelée de Champagne

SEA URCHINS IN CHAMPAGNE JELLY

It is too bad that in America sea urchins are hard to get. You have to deal with a good fish market that will order special things for you.

For Lutèce I often get sea urchins from Japanese suppliers (though what they supply to me are American sea urchins). It is really because of the Japanese that sea urchins are beginning to become known at all in this country. Slowly Americans are starting to like them. Twenty years ago, I could not sell an order of sea urchins in a month, but today I know that when I offer them I will sell at least a few orders.

In France, sea urchins have been common and popular for centuries, but this way of making them is modern. The recipe *looks* complicated, and it is true that there are many steps, and that they take time. But each step is easy to do.

Note: This recipe calls for seaweed for the presentation, but if seaweed is unavailable, watercress or any other green may be used instead. If you use a green, skip Step 7, and substitute the green for the seaweed in Step 16.

Serves 4

The Gelée de Champagne

¾ cup Fumet de Poisson (page 513), or Fond Blanc de Volaille (page 512)
salt
pepper, fresh ground

1 egg white
1 scant tablespoon (or 1 envelope) powdered gelatin
½ cup Champagne (or another white wine)

The Sea Urchins and Seaweed

3 dozen sea urchins
1 pound seaweed (for presentation)

The Chaud-Froid of Sea Urchin

1½ tablespoons unsalted butter
1½ tablespoons all-purpose flour
1 cup Fumet de Poisson (page
    513), or Fond Blanc de
    Volaille (page 512)
salt

pepper, fresh ground
½ tablespoon (or ½ envelope)
    gelatin
¾ cup heavy cream
12 of the sea urchins set aside in
    Step 6

The Final Assembly

⅓ cup Fumet de Poisson (page
    513), or Fond Blanc de
    Volaille (page 512)
1 cup chaud-froid of sea urchin
    (prepared in Steps 8 through
    12)

2 tablespoons chervil leaves
1 cup of the gelée de
    Champagne (prepared in
    Steps 1 through 3)

The Gelée de Champagne

1. In a sauté pan, warm the ¾ cup of Fumet de Poisson (or Fond Blanc de Volaille) and add salt and pepper to taste. Beat the egg white until stiff, and stir it into the warmed liquid. Dissolve the gelatin in a small amount of cold water, and stir it in.

2. Constantly stirring, bring the liquid to the boil, and immediately lower the heat. Let the liquid simmer—without stirring—for about 5 minutes.

3. Turn off the heat, cover the pan, and let it rest for 5 minutes. Pass the liquid through a sieve lined with a wet cloth. Stir in the Champagne (or another white wine) and let cool.

The Sea Urchins and Seaweed

4. With a towel hold a sea urchin in your hand. Using a knife, scrape the pins from the surface of each sea urchin shell until the shells are smooth. (This step is optional. But at Lutèce, we do carefully strip the shells.)

5. Insert a blade of a scissors into the soft round top of each sea urchin. Cut the soft top away, leaving a circular hole about 1½ inches in diameter.

Oursins en Gelée de Champagne (continued)

6. With a demitasse spoon, *being careful not to break the sacs,* remove the yellow-orange roes and set them aside. Discard everything else in the shell. Thoroughly rinse 24 of the shells, and drain them, upside down, on paper towels. (The remaining 12 shells may be discarded.)

7. Blanch the seaweed in boiling water for 2 minutes, to give it a nice green color. Chill the seaweed in ice water. Drain and set aside.

Note: At Lutèce an inedible seaweed is used. When boiled and chilled, it turns an attractive green color.

The Chaud-Froid of Sea Urchin

8. In a saucepan, melt the butter. Whisk in the flour, and cook gently for 1 minute. *Do not brown.* Remove the saucepan from the heat.

9. Warm the 1 cup of Fumet de Poisson (or Fond Blanc de Volaille), and add it to the saucepan. Bring to the boil, stirring constantly. Then cook for about 10 minutes, stirring from time to time to prevent burning. Add salt and pepper to taste.

10. Dissolve the gelatin in the cream, stir the cream into the saucepan, and return it to the boil. Cook slowly for 4 minutes.

11. Add 12 of the reserved sea urchin roes. Bring to the boil, and immediately turn off the heat. Pass the contents of the saucepan through a fine sieve, using pressure to push the sea urchins through.

12. Put equal amounts of the chaud-froid in the 24 shells, and let it cool in the shells at room temperature until it is somewhat gelatinous.

The Final Assembly

13. In a saucepan, bring the ⅓ cup of Fumet de Poisson (or Fond Blanc de Volaille) to the boil. Gently add the remaining 24 reserved sea urchin roes. Immediately remove the saucepan from the heat. *The liquid must not boil after the roes have been added.*

14. Let the roes stand for 3 to 4 minutes in the liquid. Then, very gently, remove them from the liquid, being careful not to break them. Drain the roes on paper towels.

15. Put 1 sea urchin roe on top of the chaud-froid in each of the 24 shells. Sprinkle them with the chervil.

16. Lower the container of gelée de Champagne into ice water until it begins to become gelatinous. Then distribute this gelée de Champagne among the shells, to cover the roes. Refrigerate.

Note: Remove the shells from the refrigerator 10 minutes before serving. To serve, put equal amounts of the seaweed on 4 plates. Put 6 of the shells on the seaweed on each plate.

~~❧~~

Pantin de Filet d'Anguille au Vert

PÂTÉ OF EEL

A "pantin" is a pâté that is not made in a mold. When a pantin is finished, it looks a little bit like a loaf of bread. This one is wrapped in crêpes and then in pastry.

In the part of northern France where this dish comes from, a housewife makes this pantin with as many different greens as possible. She is proud if she finds even as many as ten different greens to combine with the eel. In this recipe I use five greens, but you may add any other green herbs that you like.

Note: The recipe calls for a mousseline of pike, but sole or tilefish may be substituted for the pike.

Serves 8

The Crêpes

¾ cup all-purpose flour
1 pinch salt
1 egg
½ cup milk

½ tablespoon unsalted butter
1 teaspoon chopped parsley
1 tablespoon peanut oil

Pantin de Filet d'Anguille (continued)

Preparing the Pantin

4 pounds eel, skinned, eviscerated, and filleted—bones
  saved
1 tablespoon unsalted butter
½ pound sorrel, washed, stems
  removed, sliced coarse
½ pound spinach, washed, stems
  removed, sliced coarse
2 tablespoons chopped parsley
1 tablespoon chopped chives
1 teaspoon chopped tarragon

1 recipe Mousseline de Poisson
  (page 527), prepared with
  pike (or sole, or tilefish)
1 recipe Pâte Brisée (page 537)
1 egg, beaten with a little cold
  water
1 cup Gelée (page 514), prepared
  with the eel bones, and refrigerated (or prepare a
  Gelée with commercial aspic
  jelly powder)

The Crêpes

1. Put the flour and salt in a bowl. Whisk in the egg. Then, whisking
constantly, slowly add the milk. Whisk until this batter is homogeneous.

2. Melt the ½ tablespoon of butter and mix it into the batter. Stir in
the chopped parsley. (At this point, if there is time, it is well to let the batter rest for 10 minutes.)

3. Brush the bottom of a skillet, approximately 8 inches in diameter,
with the oil. Heat the skillet, and prepare 3 crêpes as follows: Add enough
of the batter to coat the bottom of the skillet; cook until the crêpe that
forms is golden brown on one side; turn the crêpe and cook it until it is
golden brown on the other side. Remove the crêpe from the skillet and set
it aside. Prepare the second and third crêpes the same way, oiling the skillet again if necessary.

Preparing the Pantin

4. Cut the eel in pieces 4 inches long. Bring 2 quarts of water to the
boil, add the eel, return to the boil, and cook for 3 minutes. Cool the eel
under cold running water and then drain it. Carefully scrape away all of
the black second skin. Remove all remaining small bones from the eel
(ideally with needle-nose pliers).

5. In a saucepan (not of aluminum), heat the 1 tablespoon of butter.
Add the sorrel and spinach and cook over high heat for about 4 minutes,

until all the moisture has been cooked off. Turn off the heat, and stir in the parsley, chives, and tarragon.

6. Arrange 2 of the crêpes on a work surface, one crêpe overlapping the other by a few inches. Spread some of the mousseline in a rectangle across the overlap of the 2 crêpes. With this layer of mousseline as the bottom, build up a loaf by adding additional layers—first of the eel, then the greens, then more of the mousseline, continuing until all 3 have been used up. The top layer should be of mousseline.

7. Bring the exposed edges of the crêpes over the layered loaf. Cut the third crêpe in half and finish the package with these 2 crêpe halves.

8. Roll out the Pâte Brisée to a rectangle about ⅛ inch thick. The rectangle should be large enough to enclose the loaf. Put the loaf on the rectangle of pastry, and brush the exposed border of the pastry with some of the beaten egg. Bring up the exposed edges of the pastry to form a package again. Where the edges of the pastry come together, seal them well. The loaf must be entirely sealed within the pastry.

9. Butter a pastry sheet and put the pantin on it. Brush the top and sides of the loaf with the beaten egg. With a sharp knife, cut a hole ¾ of an inch in diameter in the top of the pastry, *and in the crêpe just under it.* Form a tube of parchment paper and insert it, like a chimney, in the hole. Refrigerate for at least 30 minutes.

10. Preheat the oven to 350°.

11. Bake the pantin for 1¼ hours in the preheated oven. Remove the parchment paper tube, let the pantin cool, and refrigerate it again.

12. Remove the Gelée from the refrigerator in time for it almost to become liquid before performing Step 13. If the Gelée liquefies, chill it, in its container, in ice water, to thicken it a little before you continue.

13. When the pantin has been thoroughly chilled, insert a funnel in the hole and pour the cold Gelée through it. The Gelée should spread over and around the loaf that is encased within the crêpe and the pastry. (During the baking, a space will form between the meat and the crêpe; it is into this space that the Gelée should flow.) Refrigerate overnight. Remove from the refrigerator 30 minutes before serving. Serve sliced.

Note: At Lutèce, we usually garnish the pantin with a green salad. It may in addition be served with Mayonnaise (page 515), or with Mayonnaise au Gingembre et Curry (page 516).

Salade de Moules aux Haricots Verts

MUSSEL SALAD WITH GREEN BEANS

Serves 4

salt	4 shallots, peeled and chopped
1 pound string beans, trimmed	fine
1 tomato	¼ cup dry white wine
1½ pounds mussels	¼ cup Vinaigrette (page 525)
1 tablespoon unsalted butter	1 tablespoon chopped parsley

1. Bring 2 quarts of salted water to the boil, add the string beans, and cook until tender—about 4 minutes. Drain the beans and plunge them into ice water to cool them. Drain them again and set them aside.

2. Cut a conical plug from the stem end of the tomato and discard. Blanch the tomato in boiling water for 10 seconds, drain it under cold water, and peel off the skin. Cut the tomato in half, squeeze out and discard the juice and seeds, and chop the pulp in ¼-inch cubes.

3. Squeeze each mussel in your hand, pushing the top and bottom of the shell in opposite directions, and discard those that open. Scrub the mussels to remove the beards, and wash them in 2 or 3 changes of water.

4. In a large pot, melt the butter. Add half the chopped shallots and sauté them lightly for 2 minutes. Add the mussels and the wine, and cook, covered, over high heat until the mussels open—about 3 minutes.

4. Remove the mussels from the shells. Remove the small tough membrane from each of the mussel meats. In a bowl, mix the string beans, mussels, diced tomato, and the remainder of the shallots with the Vinaigrette.

5. Serve sprinkled with the chopped parsley.

Sardines en Eschabèche

MARINATED SARDINES

Here is a wonderful dish that is very inexpensive to prepare. The sixteen sardines called for should weigh about a pound. Sometimes, when I want to make this dish at home, I find beautiful sardines in an American supermarket for less than a dollar a pound.

Note: You may notice that the bones are not removed from the sardines—that is because they are soft and edible.

Serves 4

16 fresh sardines
1 ample tablespoon flour
½ cup peanut oil
1 medium onion, peeled and
   sliced thin
1 carrot, trimmed, peeled,
   washed, and sliced thin
4 garlic cloves, peeled, halved,
   green germs removed

3 tablespoons vinegar
1 bay leaf
2 sprigs thyme
½ teaspoon salt
pepper, fresh ground
1 pinch cayenne pepper
1 tablespoon chopped parsley

1. Scale the sardines, and remove the heads. Eviscerate the sardines through the opening at the head end, and remove the gills. Wash the sardines thoroughly under cold running water, and dry them on paper towels. Roll them in the flour.

2. In a skillet, heat half (¼ cup) of the oil. Add the sardines, and sauté over medium heat until they are golden brown—about 1 minute on each side. Put the sardines, side by side, in one layer, in a deep nonmetallic dish or pan. Discard the oil from the skillet.

3. Add the remaining ¼ cup of oil to the skillet, and heat it. Add the onion, carrot, and garlic, and sauté gently for about 5 minutes—until the vegetables are very lightly browned.

Sardines en Eschabèche (continued)

4. Add the vinegar and 1 tablespoon of water to the skillet. Add the bay leaf, thyme, salt, pepper, and cayenne pepper. Bring to the boil, and cook gently for 5 minutes. While the contents of the skillet are still cooking, pour them over the sardines. Set aside and let cool.

5. Cover the sardines and their marinade with parchment paper, and refrigerate for 2 days. Remove from the refrigerator 1 hour before serving. Serve the sardines in the marinade, sprinkled with the chopped parsley.

Note: Serve with Pain de Campagne (page 541).

Saumon Mariné
sur Salade de Concombres

COLD MARINATED SALMON ON CUCUMBER SALAD

For some reason, European customers at Lutèce especially like this dish—which has always been on our menu. Americans enjoy it too—for them it is something like gravlax.   *Serves 8*

The First Step

1 fillet of salmon, about 2½ pounds, skin removed	¼ cup chopped dill
1½ tablespoons salt	½ tablespoon white pepper, coarse ground
½ tablespoon sugar	½ cup olive oil

The Next Steps, 12 Hours Later

2 medium cucumbers, peeled	salt
2 tablespoons Vinaigrette (page 525)	pepper, fresh ground
1 tablespoon crème fraîche	4 small bunches of dill, for the garnish

The First Step

1. Remove all the bones from the salmon, and arrange the salmon on a dish. In a small bowl, mix together the salt, sugar, chopped dill, pepper, and olive oil, and coat the salmon with this mixture. Refrigerate, covered, for 12 hours. From time to time spoon the liquid that is produced over the salmon.

The Next Steps, 12 Hours Later

2. Cut the peeled cucumbers in half lengthwise. With a spoon, scrape out the seeds and discard them. Slice the cucumbers thin.

3. In a small bowl, combine the Vinaigrette and the crème fraîche. Whisk in salt and pepper to taste. Moisten the cucumber slices with this dressing.

4. Cut the salmon in very thin slices and serve it on the cucumber salad, garnished with the sprigs of dill.

~✖~

Tartare de Saumon

SALMON TARTARE

I was already working in America, but the first time I ever saw this dish I was in Paris, in the Brasserie Flo. I think that the Brasserie Flo made it exactly like beef tartare—what is usually called steak tartare—except that they made it with salmon instead of beef.

When I came back to New York, I tried it that way. Then I tried adding to the raw salmon some smoked salmon, which I first steamed a little—and I liked very much better that result. All the other ingredients are what you find in most steak tartare recipes. *Serves 8*

Tartare de Saumon (continued)

1½ pounds fillet of salmon, skin
    removed; small bones, if any,
    removed
4 ounces smoked salmon
½ teaspoon salt
pepper, fresh ground
¼ cup olive oil, French light
    olive oil preferred
2 egg yolks
8 drops Tabasco sauce

½ cup chopped onions
½ pound lettuce, or another
    salad green
1 hardboiled egg (page 119),
    chopped
3 cornichons (small French
    pickles or gherkins),
    chopped
2 tablespoons chopped parsley

1. Put the fillet of salmon in a food processor, and process in short bursts until the salmon is chopped coarse. Transfer the salmon to a bowl.

2. In a vegetable steamer, steam the 4 ounces of smoked salmon for 3 minutes, covered. Flake the smoked salmon into small pieces, and add it to the bowl.

3. With a wooden spoon, gently mix the smoked salmon and the fresh salmon. Then gently mix in the salt, pepper, oil, egg yolks, Tabasco, and ½ of the chopped onions.

4. Arrange the lettuce leaves on 8 plates. Put equal amounts of the salmon mixture at the center of the lettuce on each of the plates. Garnish with the remaining chopped onions, and with the chopped hardboiled egg, cornichons, and parsley.

Note: This dish may also be served as an *amuse-bouche* on triangles of buttered toast.

Caution: This recipe uses raw egg yolks, so there is a risk of salmonella contamination. Please use only farm-fresh eggs that have been kept refrigerated. This precaution notwithstanding, you prepare this recipe at your own risk.

Terrine de Crevettes aux Légumes

TERRINE OF SHRIMP WITH VEGETABLES

In the earliest days of Lutèce we often served dishes like this. In those days, such terrines were very much in style, but now they no longer are. We had it on the printed menu back then, but today I only make it from time to time. In this case, I followed the fashion.   Serves 6

12 young string beans, washed
    and trimmed
4 fine young carrots, trimmed,
    peeled, and washed
6 small asparagus
14 ounces pike meat (or sole, or
    tilefish), uncooked
8 ounces shrimp, uncooked,
    shells removed

3 eggs
salt
pepper, fresh ground
2 cups heavy cream, very cold
unsalted butter for buttering the
    terrine

1. Cook the string beans in boiling salted water for 5 minutes. Cool immediately in ice water, and drain.

2. Cook the carrots in boiling salted water for 12 minutes. Cool immediately in ice water, and drain.

3. Cook the asparagus in boiling salted water for 7 minutes. Cool immediately in ice water, and drain.

4. Puree the pike (or sole, or tilefish) and half the shrimp in a food processor for about 2 minutes. With the processor still running, add the eggs, salt and pepper to taste, and process until smooth—about 1 more minute. Add the cream last, all at once, let the processor run for only a few seconds, and then quickly turn it off. *Do not overprocess.*

5. Cook the remainder of the shrimp in salted water for 1½ minutes.

6. Preheat the oven to 225°.

7. Butter a 1½-quart terrine. Line it with parchment paper. Coat the bottom and sides of the lined terrine with the processed mixture (the

Terrine de Crevettes aux Légumes (continued)

mousseline). Add a layer of the vegetables, then a layer of the mousseline. Add a layer of shrimp, then another layer of the mousseline. Continue in this way until all the vegetables, shrimp, and mousseline have been used up. The top layer should be of mousseline. Cover the terrine with aluminum foil or with a tight-fitting lid.

8. In the preheated oven, set the terrine in a pan of hot water, the water reaching about ⅔ the way up the side of the terrine. Cook in the oven for 1 hour. The water should not quite boil.

Note: At Lutèce the terrine is served hot with a Sauce Homard à la Crème (page 522) or with a Beurre Blanc (page 505). The sauce may be prepared while the terrine is in the oven.

The terrine may also be served cold, with Mayonnaise (page 515). To serve it cold, let it cool to room temperature after Step 8, then refrigerate it overnight. Remove the terrine from the refrigerator ½ hour before serving.

Terrine de Homard

TERRINE OF LOBSTER

Serves 12

½ pound young string beans, washed and trimmed

salt

1 pound young carrots, trimmed, peeled, and washed

5 quarts Court Bouillon (page 507)

3 lobsters, about 1½ pounds each

1½ recipes Mousseline de Poisson (page 527), prepared with pike (or sole, or tilefish), and with a pinch of cayenne pepper

unsalted butter, for buttering the terrine and the aluminum foil

1. Cook the string beans in boiling salted water for 5 minutes. Cool immediately in ice water, and drain.

2. Cook the carrots in boiling salted water for 12 minutes. Cool immediately in ice water, and drain.

3. Bring the Court Bouillon to the boil. Put the lobsters, whole, in the Court Bouillon, return to the boil, and cook for 8 minutes. Let the lobsters cool in the Court Bouillon until they reach room temperature.

4. Remove the lobster meat from the tails and claws, taking care to keep the meat of the tails in one piece. Remove the dark vein from each tail. Save the tomalley and any coral.

5. Cut the claw meat into small pieces. In a bowl, mix together the claw meat, the tomalley, any coral, all small pieces of lobster meat (but not the tails), and the Mousseline of pike (or sole, or tilefish).

6. Preheat the oven to 225°.

7. Butter a 1½-quart terrine. Line it with parchment paper. Coat the bottom and sides of the lined terrine with the Mousseline.

8. Fill the terrine with layers: first a layer of string beans, then a layer of carrots (the vegetables parallel to the length of the terrine), then a layer of the Mousseline, and so on. When the terrine is almost half full, lay in the tail meats of the lobsters (the tails parallel to the length of the terrine). Then fill the terrine with additional layers of the string beans, carrots, and Mousseline. The top layer should be of Mousseline.

9. Cover the top of the terrine with buttered aluminum foil. The foil should reach part way down the outside of the terrine and should form a good seal with it.

10. Set the terrine in a pan of hot water in the preheated oven. The water should reach ⅔ of the way up the side of the terrine. Cook in the oven for 1 hour. The water should not quite boil.

11. Remove the terrine from the oven, let it cool to room temperature, and refrigerate it overnight. Remove from the refrigerator ½ hour before serving.

Note: Serve sliced, on a green salad. Mayonnaise au Gingembre et Curry (page 516) is an excellent cold sauce for this terrine.

Terrine de Saumon
Fumé aux Épinards

SMOKED SALMON TERRINE WITH SPINACH

At a big gathering of chefs at the Watergate, in Washington, I was served an *amuse-bouche* prepared by the well-known chef there—Jean-Louis Palladin. It was a mousse of salmon and spinach on toast.

I liked the combination of salmon with spinach, and I thought that I would try to come up with something of my own using the same ingredients.

The very first time I tried out this dish in the Lutèce kitchen, my result was almost exactly what I imagined in my mind it would be. I served it that same day to my customers.

This terrine is easy to make, it is delicious, and it can be made a day or two in advance.

Serves 6

1 pound spinach, stems removed	1 tablespoon Worcestershire
salt	sauce
½ pound (2 sticks) unsalted but-	½ teaspoon Tabasco sauce
ter, at room temperature,	1 pound smoked salmon, cut in
plus butter for buttering the	thin slices
terrine	

1. Wash the spinach in 3 changes of cold water, and drain it. Put it in 3 quarts of boiling salted water (not in an aluminum pot), and cook vigorously over high heat for 4 minutes. Plunge the spinach in ice water to cool it. Drain. Press the excess water out of the spinach by forming it into a ball in your hands and squeezing it.

2. Put the spinach, butter, Worcestershire sauce, and Tabasco in a food processor. Process until you have a smooth paste.

Note: This paste should be prepared with the ingredients at room temperature, because if the paste is too cold, it tends to separate. If it does separate, add a tablespoon of hot water, and process again until it is blended.

3. Butter the bottom and sides of a 1½-quart terrine mold. Then line the mold with parchment paper.

4. Fill the mold with layers of the thin-sliced salmon alternating with ¼-inch layers of the spinach. The bottom and top layers should be of salmon.

5. Refrigerate for at least 3 hours before serving. (The dish may be prepared a day or two in advance.)

6. To remove the terrine from its mold, invert it over a serving plate. If necessary, slip a knife between the parchment paper and the mold, or lower the mold into hot water for a few moments before inverting it.

7. Cut the terrine in ¼-inch slices with a knife that is dipped in hot water before each cut.

8. Serve on a green salad with toast.

Note: At Lutèce the terrine is served with toasted Pain de Campagne (page 541), but it may be served with any toasted white bread.

Terrine de Saumon Mousse de Brochet

TERRINE OF SALMON WITH MOUSSE OF PIKE

Serves 10 to 12

The Mousse

13 tablespoons (1⅝ sticks) unsalted butter, plus butter for buttering the plate

1¾ teaspoons salt

⅗ cup (½ cup, plus 1½ tablespoons) all-purpose flour, sifted

½ pound fillet of pike (or sole, or tilefish), skin removed

1 pinch pepper, fresh ground

1 pinch grated nutmeg

1 egg

2 egg yolks

Assembling the Terrine

2 pounds fillet of salmon, skin removed, in ¼-inch slices

3½ ounces Cognac

1¾ ounces port

salt

¼ cup shelled pistachio nuts

6 slices fatback, sliced very thin

1 truffle, cut in strips (optional)

The Mousse

1. In a saucepan, bring to the boil 5 ounces of water, 2 tablespoons of the butter, and ¼ teaspoon of salt. When the water boils, stir in all the flour. Mix well over high heat until the mixture no longer clings to the sides of the saucepan, but falls away.

2. Butter a plate, spread this mixture over it, cover it with wax paper or plastic wrap, and let the mixture cool to room temperature.

3. In a food processor, process the pike (or sole, or tilefish) with 1½ teaspoons of salt, the pepper, and the nutmeg. Set aside.

4. In a food processor, process the mixture prepared in Step 2 until it is smooth. Add the processed fish, the remaining 11 tablespoons of butter, the egg, and the egg yolks. Process until thoroughly blended and smooth.

Assembling the Terrine

5. Moisten the salmon with the Cognac and port. Add salt.

6. Put the pistachio nuts in a small saucepan of water, and bring the water to the boil. Remove the nuts from the water, peel them, and mix them into the mousse.

7. Preheat the oven to 225°.

8. Line a terrine with the slices of fatback. Fill the terrine with alternate layers of the mousse and the slices of salmon, with the strips of truffle (if used) halfway up. The bottom and top layers should be of mousse. Cover with fatback, and tamp the terrine down so that it is firmly packed. Cover the terrine with its lid or with aluminum foil.

9. Set the terrine in a pan of hot water, and cook for 2 hours in the preheated oven. Cool to room temperature, and then refrigerate. Remove from the refrigerator ½ hour before serving.

Note: Serve with Mayonnaise (page 515) to which chopped parsley and/or other chopped herbs have been added.

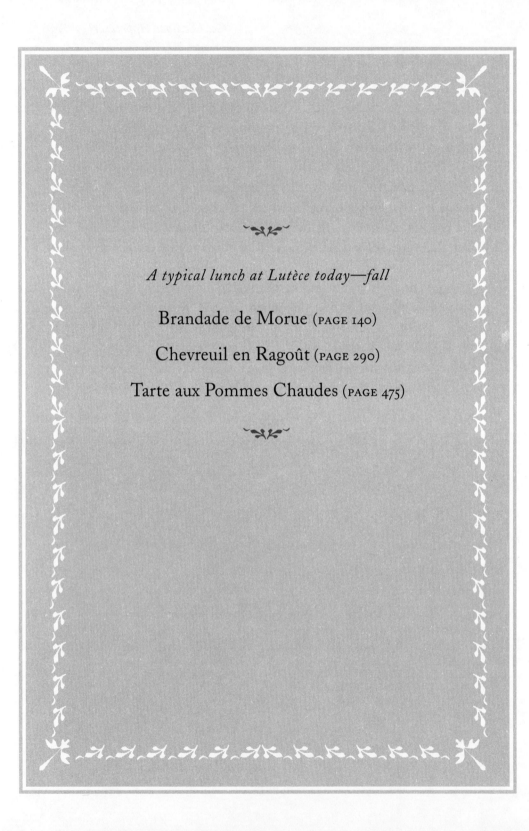

A typical lunch at Lutèce today—fall

Brandade de Morue (page 140)

Chevreuil en Ragoût (page 290)

Tarte aux Pommes Chaudes (page 475)

HOT SEAFOOD APPETIZERS

WHEN THE FIRST cold weather comes, in the fall, people start to think about hot food, and about food that has vigorous flavor. So in this menu of dishes that we often serve at Lutèce in the fall, I start with one of the hot seafood appetizers in this chapter, Brandade de Morue, a tasty paste of salted cod flavored with garlic.

Beignets de St. Jacques au Coulis de Tomates

SCALLOP FRITTERS WITH COULIS OF TOMATO

It is not on the Lutèce menu, but often I make this dish as a special appetizer for lunch. It is a simple dish, everybody likes it, and I have no idea where I learned it. *Serves 2*

4 large sea scallops
½ tablespoon chopped parsley
1 teaspoon chopped shallots
juice of ½ lemon
1 quart oil for deep frying
1 leek (the white part and a little of the green), washed, and

cut in thin strips 2 inches long
½ cup Coulis de Tomates (page 506)
½ recipe Pâte à Frire (page 536)
salt

Beignets de St. Jacques (continued)

1. Cut the scallops in half, to form 8 disks. Put them on a plate, and add the parsley, shallots, and lemon juice. Turn the scallops a few times in those ingredients to coat them, and refrigerate for 15 minutes.

2. In a deep fryer, heat the oil to 375°.

3. Fry the strips of leek until golden brown and crisp—about 3 minutes. Remove the leeks from the oil with a wire skimmer, and set them aside on a paper towel.

4. In a saucepan, warm the Coulis de Tomates.

5. One by one, dip the scallops in the Pâte à Frire, and plunge them into the hot oil. When the scallops rise to the surface, turn them with a fork so that they brown on all sides. When they have browned, drain them on paper towels, and sprinkle them with salt.

6. Pour the coulis onto 2 plates. Arrange 4 of the beignets on each plate. Arrange the fried julienne of leeks over the beignets.

Brandade de Morue

MOUSSE OF SALTED CODFISH

In almost all versions of this dish, the codfish is stretched with potatoes, which is an economy.

But in Lutèce I do not save money at the expense of a dish, so I always make my Brandade de Morue this way, without potatoes. I like the stronger fish flavor.   *Serves 4*

1 pound salted fillets of codfish, as white as possible

1 cup plus 1½ tablespoons olive oil

1 cup milk

2 garlic cloves, peeled and cracked

1 bay leaf

1 sprig thyme

a scant ¼ teaspoon white pepper, fresh ground

4 slices French bread, about ¼ inch thick, crusts removed

salt (if necessary)

1. Desalt the codfish by soaking it in cold water for 24 hours. Change the water 3 times during the 24-hour period.

2. In a saucepan, combine 1 cup of the olive oil, the milk, garlic, bay leaf, thyme, and pepper. Bring to the boil and keep hot, covered, over a very low flame.

3. Cut the bread into ¾-inch squares. In a skillet, heat the remaining 1½ tablespoons of olive oil and sauté the bread until golden brown. Set aside.

4. Cut each codfish fillet into several large pieces. Steam the fish in a steamer for 15 minutes. Remove any remaining skin and bones.

Note: If you do not have a steamer, put the cod in a pot of unsalted water instead, bring to the boil, and simmer for 15 minutes.

5. Put the fish—while it is still as hot as possible—in a food processor. Remove the bay leaf and thyme from the saucepan, and add the liquid to the processor. Process at once, until you have a smooth puree—about 2 minutes. *Do not overprocess.* Taste and, if necessary, add salt—usually, salt is not needed. The brandade should be fluffy and light in color.

6. Serve hot, surrounded by the croutons prepared in Step 3.

Calamares Farcis

STUFFED SQUID

When we bought a new steamer for the Lutèce kitchen, I thought I should come up with recipes that would put it to good use. That is how these Calamares Farcis were born.

Except that it is a time-consuming recipe, it is not a hard dish to make. And it is nothing at all like the many stuffed squid dishes you find in cuisines other than French.

Serves 6

The Broth

1 bay leaf
10 sprigs parsley
1 clove
2 sprigs fresh thyme, or ½ tea-
    spoon dried thyme
2 carrots, trimmed, peeled,
    washed, and cut in ⅛-inch
    slices
4 small white onions, peeled, cut
    in ⅛-inch slices

4 stalks of celery, peeled,
    washed, and cut in ⅛-inch
    slices
1 tablespoon vinegar
1 thread saffron
½ teaspoon pepper, fresh ground
salt
1 garlic clove, peeled, green
    germ removed, chopped
2 cups dry white wine

Preparing the Squid

1 tablespoon unsalted butter
1 cup mixed vegetables—celery,
    carrots, the white of a leek—
    all chopped fine
15 black olives, pitted and
    chopped

6 squid, 6 to 8 ounces each
salt
¼ recipe Mousseline de Poisson
    (page 527), prepared with
    pike, or whiting

The Final Assembly

1 tablespoon chopped cilantro,
    or parsley

The Broth

1. Prepare a broth as follows: Put 2 quarts of cold water in a large saucepan. Tie the bay leaf, parsley, clove, and thyme in a piece of cheesecloth and add them to the water. Add the carrots, onions, celery, vinegar, saffron, pepper, salt, garlic, and wine. Bring to the boil and simmer for 3 minutes. Do not remove the vegetables. Set aside and keep warm.

Preparing the Squid

2. In a sauté pan, melt the butter. Add the cup of mixed vegetables and the chopped olives. Sauté gently until cooked. *Do not brown.* Set aside.

3. Clean the squid by removing the black ink bag and the cranial cartilage. Remove the tentacles by pulling them off. Rinse the bodies and tentacles under cold running water.

4. Put the squid and the tentacles in a steamer and steam, covered, until tender—about 40 minutes.

Note: The squid will be more tender if they are steamed, but if you do not have a steamer, they may instead be poached in salted water, covered, until tender—about 40 minutes.

5. Mix together the sautéed vegetables and olives with the Mousseline of pike or whiting. Put this mixture in a pastry bag, and pack the squids three-quarters full with the mixture. Close the ends of the squids and secure each with a toothpick.

6. Put the stuffed squid and the tentacles in a pot. Cover with the reserved broth (and vegetables). Bring to the boil, and simmer very slowly for 25 minutes.

7. Remove the squid from the pot, remove and discard the toothpicks, and, with a sharp knife, cut each squid in half lengthwise. Put the two halves of each squid on a plate, with some of the tentacles.

The Final Assembly

8. Spoon the broth and its vegetables over the squid. Sprinkle with the chopped cilantro (or parsley), and serve.

Chausson aux Crabes
Sauce Béarnaise

CRABMEAT TURNOVERS

Serves 6

½ pound fillets of pike (or sole, or whiting), cleaned and trimmed

1 egg

½ teaspoon salt

¼ teaspoon white pepper, fresh ground

1 cup heavy cream, very cold

4 ounces crabmeat, all bones and cartilage removed

1 tablespoon chopped parsley

flour for flouring the work surface

1 pound Feuilletage Rapide (page 531)

1 egg beaten with a little cold water

1. Cut the pike (or sole, or whiting) in small pieces, and put it in a food processor. Add the egg, salt, and pepper, and process until the fish is pureed—about 30 seconds.

2. Add the cream (which must be very cold), and process again until the cream is thoroughly absorbed and a smooth mousse is formed—about 1 minute.

3. Put the mousse in a bowl and, with a spatula, stir in the crabmeat and parsley. Refrigerate.

4. Flour a work surface, and roll out the Feuilletage Rapide to a sheet ⅛ inch thick. Cut 6 circles, each 6 inches in diameter, from the pastry.

5. With a rolling pin, roll each circle into an oval shape 8 inches long. Brush the beaten egg around the edges of each oval, so that when they are folded, they will stick together.

6. Put ⅙ of the fish-crabmeat mixture at a point on the oval's long axis 2 inches from one end of the oval.

7. Fold the other half of the oval over the crabmeat mixture. Seal the edges of the top to the bottom of the ovals by gently pressing down with your fingertips. Working along the sealed edge of each turnover,

with the back of a fork crimp the edge by pushing it toward the crabmeat. This pinches the pastry and forms a kind of wall of pastry around the crabmeat.

8. Put the turnovers on a baking sheet, brush them all over with the beaten egg, and make a decorative design on each turnover, using the tines of a fork. Refrigerate for at least 20 minutes.

9. Preheat the oven to 375°.

10. Bake the turnovers in the preheated oven for 15 minutes. Serve warm, with Sauce Béarnaise (page 522), or with a green salad.

Chou Farci aux Grenouilles

FROGS' LEGS IN CABBAGE

This is not a traditional Alsatian dish, but the Alsatian influence is obvious—in the cabbage and in the frogs' legs, both of which are very big in Alsatian cooking.

In this dish the ingredients are down to earth, but the preparation is elaborate. You do sometimes find dishes like this one in the fancier Alsatian restaurants, but I myself never made it until I came to New York.

Some people like the dish because it is a way of eating frogs' legs without bothering with the bones.

Serves 4

Chou Farci aux Grenouilles (continued)

The Stuffed Cabbage

1 small head Savoy cabbage
salt
3 tablespoons (⅜ stick) unsalted
    butter
24 frogs' legs (the legs of 24
    frogs)
2 shallots, peeled and chopped
¾ cup dry white wine

½ cup Fond Blanc de Volaille
    (page 512), or water (see *Note*
    on page 58)
pepper, fresh ground
1¼ cups sliced mushrooms
½ tablespoon all-purpose flour
½ cup heavy cream
1 egg yolk

The Braising

unsalted butter for buttering the
    baking dish and the parch-
    ment paper
2 carrots, trimmed, peeled,
    washed, and cut in thin disks
1 medium onion, peeled and
    sliced
2 sprigs thyme

1 bay leaf
½ cup dry white wine
½ cup Fond Blanc de Volaille
    (page 512), or water (see *Note*
    on page 58)
salt
pepper, fresh ground

The Stuffed Cabbage

1. Separate the cabbage leaves without breaking them. Set aside 8 of the largest leaves. Slice the remaining leaves in ⅛-inch strips. You should have about 1 cup of the strips.

2. In a large pot, bring salted water to the boil, and blanch all the cabbage—the large leaves as well as the strips—for 5 minutes. Cool the cabbage under cold running water, and then drain it. Set aside separately the leaves and the strips.

3. Melt 1 tablespoon of the butter in a skillet. Add the frogs' legs, and sauté them over medium heat for 3 minutes. *The frogs' legs should brown only very lightly.*

4. Add the shallots, wine, Fond Blanc de Volaille (or water), and salt and pepper to taste, and bring to a light boil. Cook gently for 3 minutes. Drain the contents of the skillet in a colander, but retain this liquid.

5. Return the liquid to the skillet, and boil it until you have reduced it to ¼ of its volume.

6. Separate the meat of the frogs' legs from the bones.

7. Melt 1 tablespoon of the butter in another skillet. Sauté the mushrooms until all the liquid from the mushrooms is cooked off. Add the meat of the frogs' legs to this skillet. Set aside.

8. In a saucepan, melt the remaining 1 tablespoon of butter. Whisk in the flour, and cook over medium heat for 1 minute. Remove the saucepan from the heat and add the reduced liquid (Step 5). Return the saucepan to the heat, bring the liquid to the boil, and cook, stirring constantly, for 3 minutes.

9. In a small bowl, mix together the cream and egg yolk. Add this to the saucepan, return to the boil, and *immediately* remove from the heat. Strain this sauce over the frogs' legs and mushrooms. Toss and let cool.

10. Put the reserved cabbage leaves on a work surface. Cut the tough center rib from each leaf, leaving a slit. Put ⅛ of the frogs' legs-and-mushroom combination on each leaf, and form each leaf into a neat package around the filling.

The Braising

11. Preheat the oven to 375°.

12. Choose a baking dish in which the packages will fit closely, and butter it. Form a bed of the carrots, onion, and the reserved cabbage strips on the bottom of the baking dish. Add the thyme and bay leaf. Put the eight packages on the vegetables. Add the wine, Fond Blanc de Volaille (or water), salt, and pepper.

13. Cover the baking dish with buttered parchment paper, and put it in the preheated oven for 25 minutes. Lift the parchment paper, and baste the tops of the packages every 5 minutes during this cooking.

14. At the end of the 25 minutes most of the liquid will be gone, and what remains of it will be syrupy. Serve on 4 plates, with the vegetables and liquid from the baking dish.

Grenouilles Sautées Provençale

FROGS' LEGS PROVENÇALE

No dish is more typical of Provençale cuisine than this one. Of course it must be made only with fresh frogs' legs. *Serves 2*

18 to 24 frogs' legs (the legs of
    18 to 24 frogs)
flour for coating the frogs' legs
salt
pepper, fresh ground
1 tablespoon peanut oil
1 tablespoon unsalted butter
2 shallots, peeled and chopped
    fine

1 garlic clove, peeled, green
    germ removed, and chopped
    fine
1 tablespoon lemon juice
2 tablespoons Fond de Veau
    (page 510) (optional)
1 tablespoon chopped parsley

1. Put the frogs' legs in a bowl with enough flour to coat them. Toss the frogs' legs with the flour until they are well coated. Shake them free of excess flour, and season them with salt and pepper.

2. In a skillet, heat the oil and sauté the frogs' legs over high heat until they are nicely browned—5 to 8 minutes.

3. Holding the frogs' legs in the pan with a lid, pour off the oil from the pan (or tilt the pan, and soak up the oil with a paper towel). Still over high heat, add the butter to the pan, and melt it. Add the shallots and garlic, and sauté for a few seconds. Add the lemon juice and the Fond de Veau (if used).

4. Serve hot, sprinkled with the chopped parsley.

Huîtres Glacées sur Julienne de Poireaux

POACHED OYSTERS ON LEEKS

The combination of oysters and leeks is very old, but it was not until the 1970s and the 1980s that it became popular. There was a time when every French chef was cooking oysters with leeks, each chef in a slightly different way. I began serving this dish at Lutèce more than twenty years ago.

The combination is less popular with other chefs now—the fashion is over—but I go on making it from time to time, just like before, as long as I can get good oysters.

Note: This recipe calls for seaweed for the presentation, but if seaweed is unavailable, watercress or any other green may be used instead. If you use a green instead, omit Step 1, and substitute the green for the seaweed in Step 8.

Serves 4

salt
1 pound seaweed (for
    presentation)
1½ cups heavy cream
1 tablespoon unsalted butter
1½ cups leeks (the white part
    only), washed, cut in strips
    2″ × ¹⁄₁₆″ × ¹⁄₁₆″

pepper, fresh ground
24 oysters
¼ cup dry white wine
juice of ½ lemon
1 pinch cayenne pepper

1. Salt 2 quarts of water and bring it to the boil. Plunge the seaweed into the boiling water, and boil for 2 minutes. Cool the seaweed in ice water, and set it aside.

Huîtres Glacées (continued)

Note: At Lutèce an inedible seaweed is used. When boiled and chilled, it turns an attractive green color.

2. Whip ¼ cup of the cream until stiff. Refrigerate.

3. Melt the butter in a sauté pan. Add the julienne of leeks and a moderate amount of salt and pepper. Sauté, without browning, over low heat until tender—about 8 minutes.

4. Open the oysters and keep all of their juice. Wash the bottom half-shells and set them aside. Pass the juice through a sieve and put it in a saucepan. Add the white wine, lemon juice, and cayenne pepper. Quickly bring the liquid to the boil.

5. Add the oysters and cook for 15 seconds. Immediately remove the oysters with a slotted spoon, and set them aside.

6. Over high heat, reduce the cooking liquid to ¼ of its volume. Add the remaining 1¼ cups of cream, and cook over medium heat until the sauce becomes velvety. Pass this sauce through a fine sieve. Then mix it with the whipped cream.

7. Preheat the broiler.

8. Arrange the seaweed on 4 plates. Put 6 half-shells on each plate, and put equal portions of the leeks in the half-shells. Add an oyster to each half-shell. Spoon the sauce over the oysters.

9. Put the plates under the broiler until the oysters are golden brown—about 1 minute.

Oeufs d'Alose à l'Oseille

SHAD ROE WITH SORREL SAUCE

There are shad in France, and shad roe, but they are very rare. I myself never saw French shad, and I never prepared shad roe until I came to America. To me it is an American dish.

So it is always a big surprise when, every year in the spring, during the shad roe season, people tell me that they never had shad roe better than at Lutèce.

We do not do anything so very special, either—and maybe that is the reason. This is a simple dish. And of course the shad roe we use is absolutely fresh.   *Serves 4 (serves 2 as a main course)*

3 tablespoons (⅜ stick) unsalted
    butter
1 pound sorrel, washed, stems
    removed, cut in fine strips
salt
pepper, fresh ground

1 pinch sugar
½ cup heavy cream
2 pairs shad roe
1 tablespoon milk
flour for dusting the shad roe

1. In a skillet melt ½ the butter. Add the sorrel, salt and pepper to taste, and the sugar, and cook over medium heat until the liquid is completely evaporated. Add the cream and cook until the sauce thickens—about 6 minutes. Set aside and keep warm.

2. Moisten the pairs of shad roe with the milk. Dust them with flour and with salt and pepper. In a skillet, heat the remaining 1½ tablespoons of the butter. Add the shad roe. Cook slowly, over low heat, about 6 minutes on each side.

Note: The roe must not be overcooked—when done correctly it remains a little pink at the center.

3. Put the roe on warm plates, and spoon the sorrel sauce around it.

Note: The roe is crisped a little when it is sautéed. To preserve the crispness, put the sauce around the roe, not directly on it.

Pétoncles Brunoise

BAY SCALLOPS WITH FINE-MINCED VEGETABLES

There are bay scallops in France, but they are unusual. I never did them until I came to this country—where of course they are common and very popular.

The first time I cooked them—it was this recipe—they were a big flop. I had no experience with bay scallops then, and I overcooked them, which is easy to do. You have to do them very fast.

I remember that disaster as if it was yesterday—and it was thirty years ago. Some things I forget, but not my mistakes.

Serves 4

1 pound bay scallops
1 tomato
4 tablespoons (½ stick) unsalted
 butter
1 tablespoon chopped shallots,
 peeled and chopped fine
1 carrot, trimmed, peeled,
 washed, and cut in ⅛-inch
 cubes
2 celery stalks, peeled, washed,
 and cut in ⅛-inch cubes

½ cup dry white wine
salt
pepper, fresh ground
5 threads saffron
½ cup heavy cream
½ tablespoon chervil leaves, or
 Italian parsley leaves,
 chopped

1. Remove and discard the rubbery membrane that is attached to each scallop. Wash the scallops under cold water and drain them.

2. Cut a conical plug from the stem end of the tomato and discard. Blanch the tomato in boiling water for 10 seconds, drain it under cold water, and peel off the skin. Cut the tomato in half, squeeze out and discard the juice and seeds, and chop the pulp in ¼-inch cubes.

3. In a saucepan, heat 1 tablespoon of the butter. Add the shallots, carrot, and celery, and sauté over medium heat for 3 minutes. *Do not brown.* Add the wine, salt, pepper, and saffron. Cook until the liquid is reduced by ½.

4. Add the cream, and cook until the sauce begins to thicken a little—about 4 minutes. Add the chopped tomato and 2 tablespoons of the butter. Bring to the boil and boil vigorously for 1 minute. Add salt and pepper to taste.

5. In a skillet, melt the remaining 1 tablespoon of butter over high heat. Add the scallops, and sauté, still over high heat, for 2 minutes. *Do not overcook.* Add the sauce prepared in Step 4, bring to the boil, and immediately remove the skillet from the heat. Serve in soup plates, sprinkled with the chervil (or Italian parsley).

Quenelles de Brochet

PIKE DUMPLINGS

Not many years ago, making these quenelles at home was an adventure, so French housewives often bought their quenelles pre-prepared by the charcutier. There were even restaurants that bought their quenelles ready made.

But ever since food processors, this famous dish became easy to make even at home.

Note: If you use a Sauce Béchamel in Step 12, you may use either Béchamel I or Béchamel II, but at Lutèce, Sauce Béchamel II is preferred.

Serves 8 (16 quenelles)

The Panade

1½ cups milk
3 tablespoons (⅜ stick) unsalted
    butter
4 ounces (1 scant cup) all-
    purpose flour, sifted

1 egg
1 egg yolk

Quenelles de Brochet (continued)

The Quenelles, the Sauce, and the Final Baking

1 pound skinless fillet of pike
10 ounces (2½ sticks) unsalted
    butter at room temperature,
    plus butter for buttering the
    plate
½ teaspoon salt
¼ teaspoon white pepper, fresh
    ground
1 pinch grated nutmeg
6 eggs

4 egg whites
¾ cup heavy cream, cold
3 cups Sauce Homard à la
    Crème (page 522), or
    Sauce Béchamel, Method II
    (page 518)
½ cup grated Swiss cheese
    (Emmental or Gruyère)

The Panade

1. In a heavy-bottomed saucepan, bring to the boil the milk and butter. Remove the saucepan from the heat, add all the flour at once, and mix with a wooden spoon until thoroughly blended.

2. Put the saucepan over high heat, and cook—stirring constantly with a wooden spoon to prevent burning—until the mixture is dry, about 3 minutes. When ready, the mixture is a thick paste, and the bottom of the panade, where it is in contact with the saucepan, is white.

3. Add the egg and the egg yolk, and, stirring constantly, cook for 1 more minute. Remove the panade from the heat, and let it cool to room temperature.

The Quenelles, the Sauce, and the Final Baking

4. When the panade has cooled, cut the pike into chunks, put the chunks in a food processor, and process for about 30 seconds. Add the panade, the 10 ounces of softened butter, the salt, pepper, and nutmeg, and process until the mixture is smooth—about 1½ minutes. *Do not overprocess.*

5. Add the 6 whole eggs, 2 at a time, and process each time until the mixture is smooth—about 1 minute each time. Then add all the egg whites and process again until smooth—about 1 minute or a little more. *Do not overprocess, or the mixture will become warm.*

6. Add the cream, and process for 1 more minute. The mixture should be very smooth after this step.

7. Put the mixture in a bowl, and chill it by lowering the bowl into ice water. (Chilling in ice water is best, but the mixture may also be covered with paper and refrigerated for at least 1 hour.)

8. In a large pot, bring salted water almost to the boil. With a spoon, mold the quenelles into egg-shaped dumplings, and lower them into the water. Let them cook for about 10 minutes in water that is barely moving, not quite simmering.

9. With a slotted spoon, remove the quenelles from the water and drain them on a cloth napkin.

Note: The preparation may be interrupted at this point, the quenelles wrapped in plastic wrap and refrigerated overnight.

10. Prepare either the Sauce Homard à la Crème or the Sauce Béchamel II.

11. Preheat the oven to 350°.

12. Butter well an earthenware plate. Arrange the quenelles side by side on the plate. Pour the Sauce Homard à la Crème, or the Sauce Béchamel II, over the quenelles. Sprinkle the quenelles with the grated Swiss cheese, and put them in the preheated oven for 15 minutes—the quenelles will double in size. Serve immediately, while the quenelles are puffed and light.

❧

Saumon (ou Bass) en Croûte

SALMON (OR BASS), WITH MOUSSELINE OF PIKE,
IN PASTRY

I first saw this dish at Paul Bocuse, in Lyon. Bocuse makes it with loup, a fish you usually cannot get in New York, so I substitute salmon, sometimes bass.

At first I would make it only for four people eating together, and they had to order it in advance. But now there is so much demand for it that I have it always available. I serve it at room temperature at lunch, hot for dinner. *Serves 12*

The Fish Baked en Croûte

1 salmon (or bass), 4½ to 5 pounds, head and tail removed
1 teaspoon chopped tarragon
1½ teaspoons chopped parsley
2 recipes Mousseline de Poisson (page 527), prepared with

pike (or sole, or tilefish), and with the juice of ½ lemon
2 pounds Feuilletage Rapide (page 531)

The Sauce, When Served Hot

1 cup Sauce Choron (page 521)

The Sauce (Sauce Cresson), When Served at Room Temperature

1 cup Mayonnaise (page 515)
½ bunch watercress

The Fish Baked en Croûte

1. Poach the salmon (or bass) in boiling water for 30 seconds. Put it on a dry cloth and remove the skin. Split the fish lengthwise into halves and remove all the bones.

2. Spread one half of the fish with the chopped tarragon, the chopped parsley, and then the Mousseline. Put the other half of the fish on top.

3. Preheat the oven to 350°.

4. Roll out the Feuilletage Rapide into a rectangle somewhat longer than the fish and a little more than twice as wide. Cut it in half lengthwise. Put the fish on one of the rectangles of pastry, cover it with the other, and seal it within the 2 layers of pastry by pinching the 2 layers together around the edges. Trim the pastry to the shape of the fish. You may simulate fish scales on the top pastry by making indentations with the metal nozzle of a pastry bag.

5. Bake in the preheated oven for 40 minutes.

Note: At Lutèce, this dish is served either hot or at room temperature.

The Sauce (Sauce Choron), When Served Hot

6. Prepare the Sauce Choron while the fish is in the oven.

The Sauce (Sauce Cresson), When Served at Room Temperature

7. Put the Mayonnaise and watercress in a food processor, and process for 1 minute. (The Sauce Cresson is prepared either in advance, or while the fish is in the oven and then cooling.)

~☙~

Saumon Glacé à la Mousse de Moutarde

SALMON GLAZED WITH MOUSSE OF MUSTARD

For years this has been a favorite dish at Lutèce. It is easy to make and takes very little time.

The recipe is one that I have given to many of my customers. They do it at home, and they agree that it is easy to do, and easy to do well.

Serves 4 (serves 2 as a main course)

½ pound fillet of salmon, in 1
  piece, skin removed
1 tablespoon unsalted butter
pepper, fresh ground
⅔ cup heavy cream
2 scant tablespoons moutarde
  de Meaux (whole-grain
  mustard)

1 egg yolk
1 teaspoon lemon juice
¼ teaspoon salt

1. Cut the salmon in thin slices. Flatten the slices between 2 sheets of oiled parchment paper, striking them with the side of a cleaver or broad-bladed knife. The slices should be about ¼ inch thick—where they are thicker, use the cleaver or knife to reduce them to ¼ inch.

Saumon Glacé à la Mousse de Moutarde (continued)

2. Butter the center portions of 4 flameproof plates (two 12-inch plates if served as a main course). Sprinkle the buttered portion of the plates with ground pepper, and arrange the slices of salmon on the buttered portions of the plates.

3. Preheat the broiler. (If heating the broiler does not automatically heat the oven, also preheat the oven to 400°.)

4. To prepare the mousse of mustard: In a bowl, whip the cream—do not overwhip; the cream should not be stiff. In another bowl, combine the mustard, egg yolk, lemon juice, salt, and pepper. With a spatula gently fold this mixture and the whipped cream together.

5. Cover the salmon with the mousse—the salmon should be completely hidden under it. Put the plates under the broiler until the mousse is golden brown—about 2 minutes.

6. Turn off the broiler. Put the salmon in the preheated oven for 2 minutes more. *Do not overcook.* Serve immediately.

❧

Saumon Rôti

ROAST SALMON

This is no example of classic French cooking. I got the idea for this dish from a recipe in a magazine. It is delicious, and I am always successful with it. It is especially popular with people who want to avoid cream and butter.   *Serves 4 (serves 2 as a main course)*

½ pound mixed salad greens—
   mesclun, mâche, or watercress, or a mixture of them,
   or whatever greens are available
1 pound fillet of salmon, in 1
   piece, skin on

salt
pepper, fresh ground
3 tablespoons peanut oil, plus oil
   for oiling the skillet
1 tablespoon vinegar
4 drops sesame oil
juice of ½ lemon

2 shallots, peeled and chopped
  fine
2 tablespoons herbs (chives,
  parsley, or chervil, or a mixture of 2 or 3 of them),
  washed and chopped fine
½ teaspoon coarse salt

1. Wash and dry the salad greens, and set them aside in a bowl.

2. Cut the salmon into 4 serving pieces. With a very sharp knife, score the skin in a diamond pattern. *Cut all the way through the skin, but not into the meat.* Season the salmon with salt and pepper to taste.

3. Preheat the oven to 375°.

4. Brush a very small amount of the peanut oil on the bottom of an ovenproof nonstick skillet, and heat it. Put the salmon in the skillet, skin down, and cook on top of the stove, over medium-high heat, until the skin is golden brown and crisp—about 5 minutes.

5. Turn the salmon over, and transfer the pan with the salmon to the preheated oven for 1½ minutes.

6. In a small bowl, whisk together the remaining peanut oil, vinegar, sesame oil, lemon juice, shallots, herbs, salt, and pepper. Add this dressing to the reserved salad greens, and toss.

7. Arrange the salad on 4 plates. Arrange the 4 pieces of salmon on the salads, skin up. Sprinkle the salmon with the coarse salt.

Note: Larger portions of the Saumon Rôti serve very well as a light main course. As a main course at Lutèce, the salmon is garnished with vegetables and served with Sauce Béarnaise (page 522).

Soft-Shell Crabs Amandine

SOFT-SHELL CRABS WITH ALMONDS

Soft-shell crabs are one of many foods that were new to me when I came to this country. But I have completely adopted them.

We start serving them at Lutèce in early spring, when they first appear. At that time there is a lot of excitement about the first soft-shells of the season.

We go on serving them almost every day for around six weeks. Then the crabs start to get bigger, and are not as good. (It is also when the excitement dies down.) Then we do not do them again until the next spring.

Note: You should make this dish with live crabs. But if Step 1 is done for you in advance by a fish dealer, cook the crabs no more than 1½ hours after they are pre-prepared.

Serves 4

8 soft-shell crabs

salt

pepper, fresh ground

melted unsalted butter for buttering the crabs

flour for dusting the crabs

2 tablespoons peanut oil

4 tablespoons (½ stick) unsalted butter

3 shallots, peeled and chopped fine

½ cup dry white wine

1 cup heavy cream

½ cup slivered almonds

¼ cup Italian parsley, chopped coarse

1. Wash the crabs under cold running water. Remove the lungs, and remove the black skin from the back. Trim off the serrated edges of the soft shells with a scissors.

2. Preheat the oven to 375°.

3. Season the crabs with salt and pepper. Brush them with the melted butter, and dust them with flour. Heat the oil in a skillet, and sauté the crabs on both sides, over medium heat, until nicely browned—about 3 minutes on each side.

4. Butter a baking pan with 2 tablespoons of the butter. Sprinkle the chopped shallots in the pan. Put the crabs in the pan, side by side, and add the wine. Bring to the boil, add the cream, and put the baking pan in the preheated oven for 10 minutes.

5. While the crabs are in the oven, melt the remaining 2 tablespoons of butter in a skillet. Sauté the almonds in the butter until they are golden brown.

6. Remove the baking pan from the oven and put the crabs on 4 plates. Spoon the sauce from the baking pan over the crabs. Sprinkle the crabs with the almonds and parsley.

Soufflé aux Fruits de Mer

SEAFOOD SOUFFLÉ

Americans are surprised when I tell them that you do not find this dish in restaurants in France. Soufflés are French food, for sure, but they are much more popular in America than in France.

Dessert soufflés in particular are popular in America, and that is what I made a lot of at first in Lutèce. When I saw how much people liked them, I started to make appetizer soufflés too.

Soufflés are the kind of dish people expect at Lutèce. I am very often asked to make them. And I am always happy to do it.

Note: At Lutèce, this soufflé is served with Sauce Homard à la Crème (page 522), which should be prepared in advance.

Serves 6

unsalted butter for buttering the mold(s)

flour for flouring the mold(s)

¾ cup Sauce Béchamel, Method I or II (page 517 or page 518), warm and well seasoned

½ pound lobster meat, uncooked (½ pound fillet of sole may be substituted), pureed in a food processor

3 egg yolks

¼ cup cooked lobster meat, cut in ¼-inch cubes

¼ cup scallops, blanched for 10 seconds in boiling water and cut in ¼-inch cubes

¼ cup shrimp, cooked for 1 minute in boiling water and cut in ¼-inch cubes

¼ cup raw mushrooms, cut in ¼-inch cubes

salt

pepper, fresh ground

4 egg whites of large eggs (or 3 from extra-large eggs)

1. Butter the inside of one 6-cup soufflé mold, or six 1-cup molds. Flour the coating of butter, and shake out any excess flour.

2. Combine the Sauce Béchamel and the pureed lobster (or sole).

Beat in the 3 egg yolks. Then stir in the cubed lobster meat, scallops, shrimp, and mushrooms. Taste for seasoning, and add salt and pepper if necessary.

3. Preheat the oven to 325°.

4. Beat the egg whites until stiff. With a spatula, gently fold the egg whites into the seafood mixture. *Do not overwork.*

5. Put the soufflé mixture into the mold (or molds), and bake in the preheated oven: in the large mold for 20 to 25 minutes, or in the small molds for about 15 minutes.

Note: When done, the tops should be golden brown. The large soufflé should rise about 1½ inches above its mold, the small soufflés about 1 inch above theirs.

Soufflé d'Oursins
Sauce Échalotes

SEA URCHIN SOUFFLÉ WITH SHALLOT SAUCE

When it is done at home, this dish makes a big impression on guests. It is just a soufflé, and if you are used to making soufflés, this one will give you no problem. But serving it in the sea urchin shells is always a knockout. It is even a knockout at Lutèce. *Serves 4*

The Soufflé

18 sea urchins	salt
½ cup milk	pepper, fresh ground
3 tablespoons (⅜ stick) unsalted butter	2 egg yolks
1 tablespoon all-purpose flour	1 pinch cayenne pepper
	2 egg whites

The Sauce

3 tablespoons (⅜ stick) unsalted butter	⅓ cup dry white wine
3 shallots, peeled and chopped	salt
	pepper, fresh ground

The Soufflé

1. With a towel, hold each sea urchin in your hand. With a knife, scrape the pins from the surface of each sea urchin shell until the shells are smooth.

2. Insert a blade of a pair of scissors into the soft round top of each sea urchin. Cut the soft top away, leaving a circular hole about 1½ inches in diameter.

3. With a demitasse spoon, scoop out the yellow-orange roe sacs and set them aside. *To prevent the roe from mixing with other things in the shell, be careful not to break the sacs.* Discard everything else in the shell. Thoroughly rinse 16 of the shells, and drain them, upside down, on paper towels. (The remaining 2 shells are not used.)

4. Heat the milk and keep it hot.

5. In a heavy-bottomed saucepan, melt 1 tablespoon of the butter over medium heat, and mix in the flour. Cook for 2 minutes. *Do not brown.*

6. Remove the saucepan from the heat, and whisk in the hot milk, stirring until the mixture is smooth. Return the saucepan to the heat and, stirring constantly, bring to the boil. Cook slowly for about 5 minutes, still stirring. Stir in the salt and pepper to taste.

7. Still over heat, whisk in the egg yolks, and cook for 1 more minute, stirring constantly to prevent sticking. Remove from the heat.

8. With a wooden spoon, gently stir in the sea urchin roes (at this point it is no longer necessary to prevent the sacs from breaking) and the pinch of cayenne.

9. Preheat the oven to 250°.

10. Whip the egg whites, and gently fold them in.

11. With a brush, butter the insides of the sea urchin shells with the remaining 2 tablespoons of butter. Fill the shells to the rim with the mixture. Bake in the preheated oven for 10 minutes.

The Sauce

12. While the soufflés are baking, heat 1 tablespoon of the butter in a small pan. Sauté the shallots for 1 minute. Add the wine. Bring to the boil over high heat, and boil vigorously for 2 minutes.

13. Add the remaining 2 tablespoons of butter. Add salt and pepper to taste. Bring to the boil over high heat, and boil vigorously until the butter is blended in—about 1 to 2 minutes.

Note: Arrange 4 of the shells on each of 4 plates. Serve the sauce separately.

A typical dinner in a first-class Alsatian restaurant

Crème de Moules aux Quenelles à la Moëlle
(PAGE 80)

Pâté de Caille (PAGE 171)

Bacheofe (PAGE 378)

Soufflé au Kirsch (PAGE 458)

TERRINES AND PÂTÉS

AS AN ALSATIAN, I suggest that some day you go to Alsace on vacation. I suggest also that when you are there you go to one of the first-class restaurants, and have a dinner of Alsatian food—like the dishes that make up the menu that introduces this chapter.

If you do not find exactly these four dishes in one restaurant on the night you are there, when you get back from your vacation you can prepare this dinner yourself, at home. One of these four courses, Pâté de Caille, is an Alsatian game dish from this chapter of Terrines and Pâtés.

Mousse de Canard (ou Pigeon) au Genièvre

DUCK MOUSSE (OR PIGEON MOUSSE) WITH JUNIPER BERRIES

If you have this Mousse de Canard in Lutèce in September or October, the juniper berries that you find in it were picked by my wife and me near our house in upstate New York. In the years when they are very plentiful, we get a lot of them, and then we use them through the whole winter.

This recipe is really not mine; I got it from the great chef Jean Troisgros. He made his mousse with grives (thrushes), but you cannot get thrushes in America, so I make it with duck or pigeon.   *Serves 10*

1 duckling, about 5 pounds, or 4 pigeons (or squabs), about 1 to 1¼ pounds each	1 tablespoon salt
½ pound chicken livers	pepper, fresh ground
1 cup duck fat (preferred), or lard	6 juniper berries
	3 ounces dry white wine

1. Cut up the duckling (or pigeons), with the bones. Grind the bird(s), bones included, with the chicken livers in a meat grinder, using the fine blade.

Note: At Lutèce this step is done with a food processor, but if you use a processor at home the blade may be damaged by the bones.

2. Preheat the oven to 250°.

3. Add ⅓ of the duck fat (or lard) to the ground meat. Add the salt, pepper, and juniper berries. Work this mixture with a wooden spoon until it is smooth.

4. Put the mixture in an ovenproof saucepan. Put the saucepan, covered, in a larger pan of hot water, and place it in the preheated oven for 30 minutes.

5. Remove the mixture from the oven, thoroughly stir in the wine, and return the mixture to the oven, still covered and still in the pan of hot water, for another 15 minutes.

6. Remove the mixture from the oven, and push it through a fine sieve. Let it cool.

7. In a saucepan, warm the remaining ⅔ cup of fat (or lard) until soft. Put the fat in a food processor, add the meat mixture, and process until thoroughly combined. Pack this mousse in a bowl, cover it with plastic wrap, and refrigerate overnight. Take the mousse from the refrigerator ½ hour before serving. Serve with toast.

Note: To store the mousse for future use, seal the top with a layer of fat or lard before refrigerating.

Pâté en Croûte Alsacienne

ALSATIAN PÂTÉ IN PASTRY

Many small Alsatian restaurants and cafés serve this pâté as their specialty, their only dish. With bread, a salad, and a glass of Riesling, it makes a delightful light dinner. *Serves 8 to 10*

The First Day

1 pound fresh ham
½ pound lean veal
¼ pound pork belly (pork fat)
2 tablespoons lard
4 shallots, peeled and chopped fine

½ cup dry white wine
½ teaspoon Quatre Épices (page 528)
1½ teaspoons salt
¼ teaspoon pepper, fresh ground
3 tablespoons Madeira

The Second Day

1 egg
3 tablespoons heavy cream
salt
pepper, fresh ground
flour for dusting
1¼ pounds Pâte à Pâté (page 536), or Pâte Brisée (page 537)
unsalted butter for buttering the mold

6 slices fatback, ⅛ inch thick
2 truffles (optional)
1 egg beaten with a little cold water
1 cup Gelée (page 514), or prepare a jelly with commercial aspic jelly powder

The First Day

1. Cut ½ of the ham, ⅔ of the veal, and ½ of the pork belly into strips, and put the strips in a bowl. Cut the remaining ham, veal, and pork belly in chunks, and put them in a second bowl.

2. Melt the lard in a saucepan over medium heat. Add the shallots, sauté them for 30 seconds, add the white wine, bring it to the boil, and

Pâté en Croûte Alsacienne (continued)

immediately remove the saucepan from the heat. Set it aside and let it cool to room temperature. When the liquid has cooled to room temperature, add ½ of it to each bowl.

3. Add ½ of the Quatre Épices, salt, pepper, and Madeira to each bowl. Cover both bowls with plastic wrap. Refrigerate both bowls overnight.

The Second Day

4. Pass the contents of the second bowl (the bowl with the chunks, *not the strips*) through a meat grinder, using the medium blade. Then pass them through the meat grinder a second time, again using the medium blade. Mix the unbeaten egg and the cream into this ground meat and fat. Add a little salt and pepper.

5. Dust a work surface with the flour, and roll out ⅔ of the Pâte à Pâté (or Pâte Brisée) to a sheet ⅛ inch thick. Butter a rectangular 9-inch metal pâté mold. Line the mold with the rolled-out pastry—the pastry should overhang the edges of the mold by ½ inch.

6. Line the mold again—within the pastry—with 5 slices of fatback, setting aside 1 slice of fatback for the top.

7. Fill the mold with alternating layers of, first, the ground meat mixture and then the strips. Be sure that the bottom layer and the top layer are of the ground meat mixture.

Note: If you use the optional truffles, cut them in long pieces, and, when the pâté is ½ built up, arrange the pieces of truffle in a long row down the center. Then resume filling the mold.

8. Fold the overhanging edges of pastry over the top. Brush the folded-over pastry with the beaten egg. Roll out the remainder of the pastry to a sheet ⅛ inch thick that will fit the top. Cover the top with this pastry, and press the edges of this pastry to the exposed rim of pastry that was brushed with the beaten egg, so that the 2 pastries adhere. Then brush the top with the beaten egg, and, with the tines of a fork, make a decorative pattern on the top pastry.

9. Cut a hole about ¾ of an inch in diameter in the middle of the top pastry. Insert a chimney formed of a strip of parchment paper or alu-

minum foil in this hole. The chimney should extend down through the pastry, but not into the meat. Refrigerate for at least 1 hour.

10. Preheat the oven to 350°.

11. Bake the pâté, with its chimney in place, in the preheated oven for 50 minutes, until the pastry is golden brown. Let the pâté cool—first at room temperature, then in the refrigerator, for at least 3 hours.

12. Melt the Gelée (or prepared jelly). Then cool it again by lowering its container into ice water, *but do not let it congeal.* The Gelée must be cooler than room temperature, but it must still be liquid.

13. Remove the chimney. Through a funnel, pour the liquid into the pâté so that it flows into the space between the meat and the pastry. Refrigerate overnight. Serve the next day, but remove the pâté from the refrigerator ½ hour before serving.

Note: The pâté may be kept in the refrigerator for several days.

~§~

Pâté de Caille

PÂTÉ OF QUAIL

Long ago, when Lutèce was new, there was a quail farm on Long Island, and that farm supplied us with beautiful quails. Even though the farm is gone now, I continue to make quail dishes for the restaurant. But when the farm was still selling to me those wonderful birds, I was always looking for new ways to use them.

One year, when I was on my vacation in France, I was as usual in Paris for part of the time. And when I am in Paris, I always go to Mora, a store that sells all kinds of kitchen equipment. In Mora, or in any store like that, I get excited, and I buy this and I buy that, and I take things home and start to play with them.

That year in Mora I saw some pâté forms—they are really small oval or circular metal collars three or four inches across—that interested me. I bought them, and took them to New York, and started thinking of things to do with them. That was when I began making this dish in Lutèce in those forms.

In the end, you really do not need the forms to make a Pâté de Caille. Here is how to do it with only a pastry sheet.

Note: Steps 1 and 2 (the opening and boning of the quails) may be done for you in advance by your butcher.

Serves 4

Preparing the Quails
4 quails

The Stuffing

¼ pound fresh unsmoked bacon (preferred), cut in ½-inch cubes, or smoked bacon blanched for a few minutes in boiling water

1 sprig thyme, or a pinch of dried thyme

¼ pound fresh foie gras (preferred), or calf's liver, cut in ½-inch cubes

¼ pound lean veal, cut in ½-inch cubes

the livers and hearts of the quails

2 shallots, peeled and chopped

1 tablespoon Cognac

1 scant teaspoon salt

pepper, fresh ground

Stuffing and Roasting the Quails; Assembling the Pâté

salt

pepper, fresh ground

4 slices fatback (approximately 6″ × 4″), sliced thin

¾ pound Pâte à Pâté (page 536), or Pâte Brisée (page 537)

1 teaspoon peanut oil

1 egg beaten with a little cold water

1 cup dry white wine

2 teaspoons powdered gelatin

1 tablespoon Madeira

Preparing the Quails

1. With a sharp knife, cut through the backs of the quails—through the bone—so that the birds may be opened. (The incisions extend from the head end of the birds to the rear.) *Do not cut the quails in half.* Keep

the livers and hearts (which are usually packed inside), and set them aside.

2. Carve out the bones of the birds, including the leg bones, and set them aside.

The Stuffing

3. In a sauté pan, over medium heat, sauté the bacon with the thyme for about 3 minutes. Add the foie gras (or calf's liver) and the veal. Sauté for 4 to 5 minutes more. Add the reserved hearts and livers (if you wish, cut them in pieces) and the shallots, and sauté briefly, no more than 1 minute. Add the Cognac, and set it aflame.

4. When the flame subsides, discard the thyme sprig. Pass the contents of the pan through a meat grinder, using the fine blade. (Or put the contents in a food processor and process briefly—1 minute should be enough. *Do not overwork.*) Add the salt and pepper.

Stuffing and Roasting the Quails; Assembling the Pâté

5. Lightly salt and pepper the boned birds inside and out. Stuff each bird with about 1 tablespoon of the stuffing. (This step should use up about ½ of the stuffing.) Close the birds. Wrap each bird in 1 slice of the fatback.

6. Divide the Pâte à Pâté (or Pâte Brisée) in half. Roll out each half to a square ⅛ inch thick. (If the pastry has been evenly divided, the squares will be the same size.)

7. Oil a baking sheet and put 1 of the squares on the baking sheet. Brush the edges of this square with a little of the beaten egg. Put the 4 birds on the square of pastry. The birds should be arranged in 2 parallel head-to-head pairs, with some space between the 2 pairs. Pack the remainder of the stuffing between and around the birds.

8. Put the other square of pastry over the birds, the edges of the top pastry directly over the edges of the bottom pastry. Press the edges of the top pastry to the edges of the bottom pastry, so that they hold together all around. Trim the pastry so that the edges of the top and bottom pastry match. Brush the remainder of the beaten egg across the top. Engrave a pattern with the tines of a fork into the top pastry.

9. With a sharp knife, cut a hole, ¾ inch in diameter, in the center of the top sheet of pastry. Roll a 1½-inch strip of aluminum foil or parch-

Pâté de Caille (continued)

ment paper into a chimney 1½ inches long, and insert the chimney in the hole. The chimney should touch the stuffing, but must not pierce it. After the pâté is assembled, refrigerate it for at least 2 hours.

10. During the last 15 minutes of Step 9, preheat the oven to 325°.

11. Bake the pâté on the pastry sheet in the preheated oven for 1¼ hours. The pâté is ready when the top is golden brown. (If it starts to color too soon, lower the heat.) Remove the pâté from the oven. When it has cooled to room temperature, refrigerate it for at least ½ hour.

12. Meanwhile, break the reserved bones in pieces. Put them in a saucepan. Add 1 cup of water, the white wine, a little salt, and pepper. Bring to the boil, and reduce the liquid to ⅓ its original volume. Pass this liquid through a fine sieve and return it to the saucepan.

13. Dissolve the 2 teaspoons of gelatin in the Madeira, and stir the Madeira into the saucepan. Bring to the boil. Then set the saucepan in a container of ice water. Remove it from the ice water when the liquid just begins to thicken, but before it jells.

14. Remove the chimney from the pâté. Through a funnel, pour the slightly thickened liquid into the pâté. Refrigerate for at least 2 more hours before serving.

Note: To serve, cut the pâté into 4 quarters, so that each serving includes an entire bird. The pâté may also be cut from edge to edge in slices that cut through the birds.

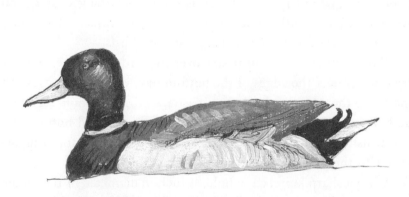

Rillettes de Porc
(ou Lapin, ou Canard)

BASIC PORK PASTE (OR RABBIT OR DUCK PASTE)

This is basically a cold pork spread. I love it on toasted country bread, and that is how we serve it at Lutèce. But I vary the style of the rillettes, sometimes substituting duckling or rabbit for some of the pork.

Rillettes de Porc is a good dish to make at home, because it keeps for weeks. In the old days, you made a supply of rillettes to last for a whole winter.

Yield: about 2 pounds

For Rillettes de Porc

2 pounds pork shoulder (bones in, if any), fatty
½ pound pork belly (pork fat)
1½ teaspoons coarse salt (or regular salt)
¼ teaspoon pepper, fresh ground
¼ teaspoon Quatre Épices (page 528)

1 cup dry white wine
1 medium onion, peeled
2 cloves
1 bay leaf
1 garlic clove
2 tablespoons Armagnac or Cognac

For Rillettes de Lapin, Use the Following Amounts of Meat Instead

1 pound pork shoulder, fatty
1½ pounds rabbit (bones in)

½ pound pork belly (pork fat)

For Rillettes de Canard, Use the Following Amounts of Meat Instead

1 pound pork shoulder, fatty
1½ pounds duckling legs (bones in)

½ pound pork belly (pork fat)

1. Cut all the meats into 1½-inch cubes, bones in (if present). In a bowl, sprinkle the meats with the salt, pepper, and Quatre Épices. Toss the

Rillettes de Porc (ou Lapin, ou Canard) (continued)

meats and the seasonings thoroughly. Refrigerate, covered, for at least 6 hours, preferably overnight.

2. Remove the pieces of pork belly from the bowl. Put them in a heavy-bottomed pot, and let them melt over medium heat—about 10 minutes—stirring with a wooden spoon from time to time.

3. Add the remaining meat to the pot, and continue cooking slowly, browning the meats very lightly on all sides—another 10 minutes. The meat should color only a little.

4. Add the wine and 2 cups of water to the pot—the liquid should almost cover the meat. Pierce the onion with the 2 cloves, and add it. Add the bay leaf and garlic clove. Bring to the boil, lower the heat, cover, and cook very gently for 3 to 3½ hours, stirring from time to time.

5. Discard the onion, bay leaf, and garlic. Let the pot cool to room temperature. With a ladle, remove from the surface about ½ cup of the fat. Set this fat aside. Remove the meat from the pot, leaving the liquid and fat that remains in the pot.

6. With your fingers, remove the bones (if any) from the meat. With the tines of a fork, break the meat into fibers, teasing the pieces of meat into fine shreds. Return the meat to the pot.

7. Add the Armagnac (or Cognac) to the pot. Bring the pot to the boil, and cook over medium heat for 4 minutes. Let this pot cool, stirring constantly until you have a homogeneous mixture—10 to 15 minutes.

8. Put the meat in a 2-pound or 3-pound cast-iron terrine, or in an earthenware terrine, or in two 1-pound earthenware crocks. The meat must not fill the container. Smooth the top(s). Cover the top(s) with the reserved fat, using all the fat. Refrigerate for at least 24 hours. Remove from the refrigerator ½ hour before serving.

Note: Before using, scrape all the fat from the top. As long as the seal of fat on top has not been broken, the rillettes may be stored for several weeks. But once the seal is broken, the rillettes must be used promptly.

Saucisson Sec

HARD SAUSAGE (SALAMI)

Once in a while at Lutèce the staff and I make this for ourselves. We would never serve it to our customers, because this coarse, strong sausage is the furthest thing from what people expect to find at Lutèce. But we have fun making it together, and then, later, we all enjoy eating it. It is easy to make, but you need patience.

Yield: 3 salamis, each about 8″ long, 2″ to 2½″ thick

3 pounds pork shoulder or pork butt
¼ pound fatback
2 scant tablespoons salt
2 teaspoons pepper, fresh ground, coarse
1 scant tablespoon sugar

1 pinch curing salt
½ garlic clove, peeled, green germ removed, chopped fine
3 pork casings (or beef middle casing), 12 inches long (available from butchers)

1. Cut the leanest quarter of the pork (¾ pound) into ¼-inch cubes. Pass the remainder of the meat, together with the fatback, through the coarse blade of the meat grinder. Thoroughly mix together the cubed pork, the ground pork, and all the other ingredients.

2. With twine, tie one end of each casing, and pack the meat tightly into the casings. (At Lutèce we use a pastry bag for feeding the meat into the casings.) Then tie the casings at the other end.

3. Hang these sausages in a cool, well ventilated room—the room should be between 50° and 60°—for 10 to 15 weeks, until they have dried to the desired hardness.

Note: The sausage is ready to serve after it has hung for 10 to 15 weeks. You may find a mold on the outside of the casing, but do not worry about it—just wipe it off.

Terrine d'Anguille en Gelée
au Vin Rouge

TERRINE OF EEL WITH RED WINE JELLY

Where I grew up, in Alsace, we were far from the sea. So until recent times, in Alsace "fish" always meant river fish, like pike, trout, carp—and eel.

In America, people like eel, but not the way it looks, so in Lutèce I can always sell eel—as long as it does not look like eel, as in this delicious dish. It helps also if I do not call it eel, but call it instead "anguille."

Note: Step 1 can be performed for you by your fish dealer.

Serves 8 to 10

4 pounds eel
1 tablespoon peanut oil
1 medium onion, peeled and
   sliced
1 cup red wine
1 bay leaf
1 garlic clove, unpeeled, crushed
1 sprig thyme
1 tablespoon balsamic vinegar
   (or red wine vinegar)

½ teaspoon salt
pepper, fresh ground
4 hardboiled eggs (page 119),
   sliced
2 tablespoons parsley, chopped
   coarse
1 teaspoon chopped tarragon
1 tablespoon chopped chervil
1 scant tablespoon (or 1 envelope) powdered gelatin

1. Skin, eviscerate, and remove the heads of the eels. Fillet the eels and set aside the skin and bones to make a jelly. You will have about 2 pounds of eel fillets.

2. In a saucepan, heat the oil, add the skin, bones, and onion, and sauté for 3 to 4 minutes. Add 2 cups of water, the wine, bay leaf, garlic, thyme, vinegar, salt, and pepper, and bring to the boil. Reduce until 2 cups of liquid remain.

3. Put the eel fillets in a deep pot, and strain the 2 cups of liquid over them. Bring gently to the boil, and cook slowly, covered, for 15 minutes. With a skimmer, delicately remove the fillets of eel from the liquid. Set aside the liquid.

4. In a terrine of approximately 2 quarts, arrange successive layers of the eel, then the egg slices, then the herbs. (At Lutèce, the top layer is of herbs.)

5. Dissolve the gelatin in the reserved liquid, bring the liquid to the boil, simmer it for 1 minute, and strain it over the contents of the terrine. Refrigerate overnight.

6. The next day, about ½ hour before serving, remove the terrine from the refrigerator, and lower it into a pan of enough hot water so that the water reaches most of the way up the sides of the terrine. Leave it in the hot water for 1 minute. At this point it will be possible to remove the terrine from its container by inverting it over a serving plate.

Note: Serve sliced on a green salad, either with Mayonnaise (page 515) or with Mayonnaise au Gingembre et Curry (page 516).

❧❦❧

Terrine de Campagne

COUNTRY TERRINE

When it comes to Terrine de Campagne, the idea is not to do it in an original way, but to do it well. Nothing in this dish is invented by me; you cannot find a more basic French dish than this one.

The pâté must not be overcooked, it must not be done in too hot an oven, the ingredients must be fresh, and, for the best result, you should store it for three or four days before using it.

This terrine, and the other classic terrines in this book, are to many people passé. But this is the real French cooking, and it will never go out of style.

Serves 10

Terrine de Campagne (continued)

1½ pounds pork butt, boneless
¼ pound pork liver
1 medium onion, peeled and
  chopped
2 tablespoons chopped parsley
1 garlic clove, peeled, green
  germ removed, and chopped
  fine
½ tablespoon salt
pepper, fresh ground

1 ample tablespoon all-purpose
  flour
2 eggs
1 tablespoon Cognac
¼ cup heavy cream
1 pinch grated nutmeg
6 slices fatback, ⅛ inch thick
5 juniper berries
3 bay leaves

1. In a meat grinder, using the coarse blade, grind the pork and liver together. Put the ground meats in a mixing bowl and, with a wooden spatula, mix in the onion, parsley, garlic, salt, pepper, and flour. Mix in the eggs, one by one, then the Cognac, cream, and nutmeg. Keep mixing until the mixture is smooth.

2. Preheat the oven to 325°.

3. Line a terrine with the fatback, reserving some for the top. Put the mixture in the lined terrine, and smooth the top. Cover the top with the remaining sliced fatback. Put the juniper berries and bay leaves on top of the fatback. Cover the terrine with its lid or with aluminum foil. Set the terrine in a pan of hot water in the preheated oven, and cook for 1 hour. Refrigerate overnight. Remove from the refrigerator ½ hour before serving.

Note: This terrine may be served the next day, but it is best served after 3 or 4 days. It may also be preserved for future use. To preserve it, pour melted lard (or another fat) over the top as a seal. Sealed, it may be kept in the refrigerator for up to 3 weeks.

Terrine de Canard

TERRINE OF DUCK

Serves 10

1 duckling, about 5 pounds
1 pound pork butt, boneless
2 tablespoons Cognac
juice of 1 orange
½ cup red wine
1 bouquet garni (page 55)
2 teaspoons salt
½ teaspoon pepper, fresh ground
2 tablespoons (¼ stick) unsalted
  butter

4 shallots, peeled and chopped
  fine
1 garlic clove, peeled, green
  germ removed, and chopped
  fine
1 egg
¼ teaspoon Quatre Épices (page
  528)
2 slices fatback, ⅛ inch thick

1. Remove the skin from the duckling, without tearing it, and set it aside. Cut the duckling's liver in half, and set it aside.

2. Debone the duckling and trim the meat of its fat. Set the carcass, the bones, the meat of the legs, and the trimmings aside.

3. Cut the breast meat in ½-inch cubes. Cut ½ of the pork butt in ¼-inch cubes.

4. Marinate the cubed breast meat, the cubed pork butt, and the liver in the Cognac and orange juice for about 2 hours, at room temperature.

5. Put the carcass, bones, wine, bouquet garni, salt, and pepper in a pot. Cover with 6 cups of water, and bring to the boil. Skim the foam from the top. Cook, uncovered, until ½ cup of liquid remains. Pass the liquid through a fine sieve.

6. Preheat the oven to 325°.

7. In a sauté pan, melt the butter, and sauté the shallots for 1 minute. Add the garlic, and the liquid prepared in Step 5. Bring to the boil. *Immediately* turn off the heat, and let cool.

8. With the coarse blade of the meat grinder, grind together all the remaining duck meat, the trimmings, and the remaining ½ pound of pork butt. Put this ground meat in a bowl, stir in the cooled liquid, the egg,

Terrine de Canard (continued)

Quatre Épices, and salt and pepper to taste. Mix with a spatula until smooth. Add the cubed duck breast, cubed pork butt, and their marinade. Cut the 2 pieces of liver in half and add them. Mix again, but *do not over-mix.*

9. Line a terrine with the skin of the duckling. Fill the terrine with the mixture. Cover with the sliced fatback. Cover the terrine with its lid or with aluminum foil, set it in a pan of hot water in the preheated oven, and cook for 50 minutes.

10. Remove the terrine from the oven, and remove the lid or aluminum foil from the top. Put a lid (or a piece of wood or plastic) a little smaller than the terrine on top of the cooked mixture, and put a ½-pound weight on top.

Note: If the weight is too light, the terrine will not hold together; if it is too heavy, the liquid will be squeezed out, and it will be too dry.

11. Let the terrine stand this way at room temperature for 1 hour. Remove the weight and the lid, and refrigerate the terrine overnight. Remove from the refrigerator ½ hour before serving.

Note: The terrine may be served the next day. It may also be preserved for future use. To preserve it, pour melted lard (or another fat) over the top as a seal. Sealed, it may be kept in the refrigerator for up to 3 weeks.

Terrine de Foie Gras

TERRINE OF FOIE GRAS—TWO METHODS

Foie gras has a long history. Even in ancient Egypt there was foie gras, and in those days the geese were fed with figs. In Alsace, where it is still very popular, it has a long history too. There was even a time when foie gras was produced in Alsace, though today most of it comes from big commercial producers in other parts of Europe.

When I was young, most families kept two or three geese. In wintertime they stuffed them—force-fed them—and a week or two before Christmas, the geese were slaughtered for Christmas dinner. If the family was a poor one, and many of them were, they would keep the geese for themselves, but would sell the livers (the foie gras) to restaurants or hotels, and they would use this extra money for Christmas expenses—toys for the children, and so on.

I remember that when I was an apprentice, people came from all over the town to the hotel where I worked to sell us their goose livers. They knew that the hotel paid more than the other places. My boss, the chef, would inspect the livers that were brought to the door, and pay a price according to their quality.

My mother also kept geese, but we had enough money so that we did not have to sell the livers. (My father would not have appreciated it if my mother did not keep them for the family.) Instead, she would make them into terrine de foie gras.

I was a very young boy when a neighbor taught my mother how to force-feed the geese, and when I was a little older it was my job to do it. One at a time, I would hold each goose between my legs, and I would insert a funnel down its throat. Then I dropped whole kernels of corn into the funnel, and then I poured in a little water. I continued to do this until each goose was full. The geese did not seem to suffer.

Three times a day I fed the geese this way, for about the last month before the slaughter, which was when the geese were around a year old. Eventually I had to do the slaughtering also, because my father—though he was a big strong man, an athlete who had won dozens of medals, even a boxing championship— broke out in a sweat when it came to killing the geese.

In Alsace, foie gras is usually prepared in brioche pastry. In the southwest of France, the other major foie gras region, it is prepared more simply, which is how I make it at Lutèce.

These recipes call for kirsch or Cognac or Armagnac. In Alsace, kirsch is used, in the rest of France Cognac or Armagnac. At Lutèce I use sometimes one, sometimes another. Also, you will notice that even though many recipes for Terrine de Foie Gras call for truffles, I do not use them. They add nothing to the dish except cost.

For years, French chefs in America were stuck because there was no foie gras here—to us foie gras is one of the greatest of all culinary products. But today, many farms in this country do produce foie gras, but from ducklings, not geese. Duck livers are a little smaller than goose livers, but they are just as good.

The old way of preparing foie gras was for years my way, but recently I learned an easier way with just as good a result. Now I make it both ways at Lutèce, and I give here both ways.

Note: Though foie gras is now plentiful in America, you still do not find it in supermarkets or butcher shops. But many specialty shops carry it, and many butcher shops will order it for you.

Serves 10 to 12

Method I: The Classic Way

3 pounds duck foie gras (2 large livers or 3 small ones)

2 cups milk

3 tablespoons salt

½ teaspoon white pepper, fresh ground

1 teaspoon sugar

½ teaspoon Quatre Épices (page 528)

¼ cup kirsch (or Cognac, or Armagnac)

3 tablespoons goose fat or duckling fat (preferred), or lard

1. With both hands, break each foie gras into its 2 lobes (there is a natural separation into two parts, one part larger than the other). Each lobe has a smaller, somewhat pointed end—cut 1½ inches off each pointed end, and keep these pieces.

2. Put all the pieces (4 pieces from each liver—2 large pieces and the 2 pointed ends) in a bowl. Cover them with the milk, 2 quarts of water, and 2 tablespoons of the salt. Let this stand for at least 3 hours at room temperature. (If you wish, refrigerate it overnight.)

3. Remove the foie gras from the liquid, rinse the pieces quickly under cold water, and dry them with a paper towel. With a small knife cut away any green parts of the liver. Then peel away the liver's clear skinlike membrane.

4. Place the small pieces, cut side down, on a paper towel, to drain them. With a knife, cut an incision down the center of each large piece, along its length. Do not cut to a depth greater than 1 inch. Then, with 2 hands, using each incision as the beginning of a break, break each piece into 2 parts. (*Do not* cut all the way through with the knife, which would cut the blood vessels.)

5. When the large pieces are broken in two, a network of blood vessels is revealed, usually darker than the meat. Gently, gripping with your finger and the point of a knife, pull the blood vessels out, and discard them. *During this step, take special care to damage the liver as little as possible.*

6. Put all the pieces of liver on a plate. In a small bowl, mix together the remaining 1 tablespoon of salt, the pepper, sugar, and Quatre Épices. Sprinkle the foie gras on all sides with this mixture. Then sprinkle the kirsch (or Cognac, or Armagnac) on the foie gras. Refrigerate for at least 5 hours, preferably overnight. During this period turn the foie gras from time to time in the small amount of liquid it gives off.

7. Preheat the oven to 200°.

8. Heavily grease a 3-pound cast-iron or earthenware terrine with ½ of the goose fat or duck fat (or lard). Lay half of the larger pieces from the larger lobes of the foie gras in the terrine, the outer (smooth) sides down. Then put the cut-off tips and all the pieces of the smaller lobes in the terrine. Then put the remaining pieces of the larger lobes on top, the outer (smooth) sides up. When all the pieces are in the terrine, gently press the contents down, to form a smooth top and to eliminate air spaces in the terrine.

9. Cover the foie gras with the remaining fat. Cover the terrine with its lid or with aluminum foil.

10. Put the terrine in a pan of water that is hot, but not at the boiling point (the water should be about 180°), and transfer the terrine in its pan of water to the preheated oven for 50 minutes.

11. Remove the terrine from the oven, and remove it from the water bath. Let it cool for 2 hours at room temperature. Then refrigerate. (There

Terrine de Foie Gras (continued)

will be a layer of fat on the top, which will seal the terrine.) Remove from the refrigerator ½ hour before serving.

Note: Serve cold: The terrine may be served after 24 hours, but its flavor is better after 3 or 4 days. It may be kept for as long as 2 weeks, but once the seal of fat has been broken, the terrine must be used up promptly.

Foie gras is best served with Pain de Campagne (page 541), which is how we serve it at Lutèce.

Method II: The Modern Way

I was taught this way of making Terrine de Foie Gras by the son-in-law of my old partner, André Surmain.

This young man, Jean-Paul Battaglia, has a very successful restaurant in the south of France—Feu Follet, in the town of Mougins. When he first told me about this method, I was very skeptical. But when he showed it to me, I was amazed, because it worked—even though this way of making Terrine de Foie Gras ignores many of the rules of the classic recipe. Nowadays, I make it this way more often than the old way.

The ingredients are the same as for the Classic Way, except that, in place of the fat, you substitute:

¾ cup Gelée (page 514), or prepare a jelly
   with commercial aspic jelly powder

1 to 6. These steps are the same as in the Classic Way.

7. Melt the Gelée, put ½ of it in the terrine—this must be a cast-iron terrine, *not an earthenware terrine*—and let it stiffen in the refrigerator.

8. Lay half of the larger pieces from the larger lobes of the foie gras in the terrine, the outer (smooth) sides down. Then put the cut-off tips and all the pieces of the smaller lobes in the terrine. Then put the remaining pieces of the larger lobes on top, the outer (smooth) sides up. When all the pieces are in the terrine, gently press the contents down, to form a smooth top and to eliminate air spaces in the terrine.

9. Pour the remainder of the Gelée on top. Cover the foie gras with parchment paper. (*Do not* cover with aluminum foil or a lid.)

10. Preheat the oven to 450°.

11. Put the terrine in a pan of water that has been brought to the boil. The water should extend about ⅔ of the way up the sides of the terrine. Put the terrine, in its boiling-hot water bath, in the preheated oven *for exactly 7 minutes.*

12. Remove the terrine from the oven and from its water bath, and lower it immediately into ice water. Let it cool completely in the water—about 1½ hours. Then refrigerate.

Note: Serve cold. The terrine should be served after 1 or 2 days. Because the cooking is briefer than in the Classic Way, this terrine may be kept no longer than 1 week. And once the seal of jelly has been broken, it must be used up promptly.

As with the Terrine de Foie Gras prepared the Classic Way, we serve this terrine with Pain de Campagne (page 541).

Terrine de Roquefort

TERRINE OF ROQUEFORT CHEESE

The son-in-law of my old partner has a restaurant in the south of France, and it was there that I first saw this dish. He told me it was a big seller in his place. Now it is a big seller in my place.   *Serves 8*

1 pound Roquefort cheese	½ cup walnut halves, broken
½ pound (2 sticks) unsalted	into smaller pieces
butter	salt
¼ cup heavy cream, very cold	pepper, fresh ground
2 tablespoons Cognac	

1. In a bowl, with a wooden spatula, mash the cheese and butter into a paste.

2. Beat the cream until it is thick, but not stiff. Mix the cream into the

Terrine de Roquefort (continued)

Roquefort paste. Then mix in the Cognac, walnuts, salt, and pepper. (Be careful not to add too much salt, for the cheese is already salty.)

3. Put the paste into an earthenware terrine, cover it with plastic wrap or aluminum foil, and refrigerate overnight.

Note: To serve, remove the mixture in a block from the terrine, and serve it sliced, on a green salad, with Whole Wheat Bread (page 545).

Note: When preparing the green salad to be served with this terrine, it is a good idea to use a dressing made with walnut oil.

❧❧❧

Terrine de Lapin

TERRINE OF FARMED RABBIT

Note: Step 1 may be performed for you, in advance, by your butcher. The 2 fillets, combined, should weigh about ½ pound, the remaining meat about 2 pounds.

Serves 8 to 10

1 rabbit, about 5 pounds, including the liver
1 pound pork shoulder, fatty, cut in 1-inch cubes
1½ teaspoons salt
¼ teaspoon pepper, fresh ground
¼ teaspoon Quatre Épices (page 528)
½ cup dry white wine
3 shallots, peeled and chopped fine
1 garlic clove, peeled, green germ removed, and chopped fine

1 tablespoon lard
2 tablespoons Cognac
¼ cup Gelée (page 514) prepared with the rabbit bones (or prepare a jelly with commercial aspic jelly powder), liquefied but not heated
2 eggs
6 slices fatback, ⅛ inch thick

1. Cut the rabbit in 7 pieces. Bone the meat—*keeping the fillets whole*—and reserve the bones. Trim the meat—trimming the fillets very carefully—of all fat, skin, and fibers. Reserve the liver.

2. Put the rabbit meat (but not the fillets), the liver, and the pork shoulder in a bowl. Add the salt, pepper, Quatre Épices, wine, shallots, and garlic. Let this marinate, covered, in a cool place, or in the refrigerator, for at least 2 hours.

3. In a skillet, melt the lard, and sauté the 2 fillets quickly on all sides, browning them lightly—about 3 minutes. Add the Cognac, and set it aflame. When the flames subside, add the liquid and fat from the skillet to the marinating meat. Set the fillets aside.

4. When the marinating meat is ready, pass it through a meat grinder, using the medium blade. Put this meat in a bowl.

5. Preheat the oven to 300°.

6. With a wooden spatula, stir the Gelée and eggs into the ground meat. Taste for seasoning, and add salt and pepper if necessary.

7. Line a 3-pound terrine with the fatback, holding 1 slice of the fatback aside for the top. Lay ½ the ground meat in the bottom of the terrine. Put the 2 fillets on the ground meat, parallel to the length of the terrine. Put the remainder of the ground meat in the terrine. Cover the ground meat with the remaining slice of fatback. Cover the terrine with its cover or with aluminum foil.

8. Set the terrine in a pan of hot water in the preheated oven. The water in the pan should be almost at the boil. Bake for 1 hour.

9. Take the terrine from the oven, and remove the lid (or aluminum foil). Put a lid (or a piece of wood or plastic) slightly smaller than the terrine on top of the cooked mixture, and put a ½-pound weight on top.

Note: If the weight is too light, the terrine will not hold together; if it is too heavy, its liquid will be squeezed out, and it will be too dry.

10. Let the terrine stand this way at room temperature for 1 hour. Remove the weight and the lid. Refrigerate overnight.

Note: This terrine may be served the next day. It may also be preserved for future use. To preserve it: When it is cold pour melted lard (or another fat) over the top to form a seal. When sealed, it may be kept in the refrigerator for up to 3 weeks.

Terrine de Pintade
aux Champignons Sauvages

TERRINE OF GUINEA HEN WITH WILD MUSHROOMS

Note: Step 1 may be performed for you, in advance, by your butcher.

Serves 8 to 10

2 guinea hens, 2 to 2¼ pounds
    each
¼ pound pork fat (pork belly),
    cut in ¼-inch cubes
2 tablespoons Cognac
salt
pepper, fresh ground
1 pound pork shoulder, a little
    fatty
1 tablespoon peanut oil

½ pound wild mushrooms (or
    cultivated mushrooms),
    sliced
1 garlic clove, peeled, green
    germ removed, and chopped
    fine
1 small onion, cut in pieces
½ cup white wine
1 bouquet garni (page 55)
6 slices fatback, ⅛ inch thick

1. Bone the guinea hens. Cut the boned breasts in half, yielding 4
pieces of breast meat. Retain the liver, all bones, and all the additional
meat and trimmings of meat, but not the skin.

2. Put the breast meat, liver, and pork fat (pork belly) in a bowl. Add
the Cognac, a pinch of salt, and pepper. Refrigerate.

3. Cut the pork shoulder and all the remaining meat of the hens in
pieces. Add ½ teaspoon salt, pepper, and grind the meat in a meat grinder,
using the fine blade. Set aside.

4. In a skillet, heat the oil, and sauté the mushrooms. Add the garlic
and sauté for about ½ minute more. Put the mushrooms in a colander, and
let cool.

5. Cut the bones in pieces and put them in a saucepan. Add the onion,
wine, bouquet garni, a pinch of salt, pepper, and 6 ounces of water. Bring
to the boil, and cook over medium heat, skimming the foam from the top,

until there is ½ cup of liquid remaining. Strain this stock through a fine sieve. Let it cool. Add ½ of this stock to the ground meat prepared in Step 3. Then mix the mushrooms into the ground meat.

6. Preheat the oven to 325°.

7. Line a 3-quart terrine with the fatback, reserving 1 slice of the fatback for the top. Then layer the bottom of the terrine with half of the ground-meat-and-mushroom mixture. Arrange the breast meat and liver over that layer. Then layer the remainder of the ground-meat-and-mushroom mixture on top. Cover the top with the remaining slice of fatback. Pour the remaining stock over the fatback.

8. Cover the terrine with its lid or with aluminum foil, forming a tight seal. Set the terrine in a pan of hot water in the preheated oven, and bake for 1½ hours.

9. Remove the terrine from the oven. Remove the lid or aluminum foil from the terrine. Put a lid (or a piece of wood or plastic) a little smaller than the terrine on top of the cooked mixture, and put a ½-pound weight on top.

Note: If the weight is too light, the terrine will not hold together; if it is too heavy, the liquid will be squeezed out, and it will be too dry.

10. Let the terrine stand this way at room temperature for 1 hour. Remove the weight and the lid. Refrigerate for at least 24 hours.

Note: This terrine may be served the next day. It may also be preserved for future use. To preserve it, pour melted lard (or another fat) over the top as a seal. Sealed, it may be kept in the refrigerator for up to 3 weeks.

Terrine de Ris de Veau

TERRINE OF SWEETBREADS

Extremely popular in Lutèce, this terrine is available at the restaurant every day. It is moister and more tender than other terrines, and not exactly what people think of when they think of French terrines—even though how you make it is not so different from how you make the more familiar ones.

Serves 10 to 12

The Farce

1½ pounds pork shoulder (half lean, half fatty)
½ cup dry white wine
2 shallots, peeled and chopped
6 ounces fatback, cut in small cubes

¼ cup Cognac
2 teaspoons salt
1 teaspoon sugar
1 teaspoon pepper, fresh ground
½ teaspoon ground thyme
1 pinch saltpeter

The Sweetbreads and the Final Assembly

1 to 2 sweetbreads, approximately 2½ pounds
1 tablespoon unsalted butter
salt
pepper, fresh ground
3 tablespoons dry sherry

½ cup Fond Blanc de Volaille (page 512)
1 scant tablespoon (or 1 envelope) powdered gelatin
1 egg
6 slices fatback, ⅛ inch thick

The Farce

1. Grind the pork in a meat grinder, using the medium blade. Then pass it through the grinder again.

2. Put the wine and shallots in a small saucepan. Bring them to the boil, and cook for 1 minute. Let cool.

3. Put the ground pork, wine, shallots, and all the other ingredients listed under *The Farce* in a bowl, and mix them together. Cover the bowl with plastic wrap. Refrigerate for 1 day.

The Sweetbreads and the Final Assembly

4. Preheat the oven to 400°.

5. Blanch the sweetbreads in boiling water for 3 minutes. Chill them under cold running water. Peel them very carefully, and remove all the tough membranes.

6. Melt the butter in an ovenproof sauté pan. Add the sweetbreads, salt, and pepper. Sauté the sweetbreads gently until they are golden brown on all sides.

7. Add the sherry and the Fond Blanc de Volaille. Cover with parchment paper. Cook in the preheated oven for 20 minutes.

8. Remove the sauté pan from the oven, and lower the oven temperature to 325°.

9. Put the sweetbreads on a plate, and let them cool. Cook the liquid in the sauté pan down to ⅓ cup. Stir in the gelatin. Let cool. Strain this liquid over the farce. Mix in the egg.

10. Line a terrine with the fatback, reserving 1 slice for the top. Fill the terrine with alternate layers of the farce and the sweetbreads. The bottom and top layers should be of the farce. Cover with the last slice of fatback.

11. Cover the terrine with its lid, or with aluminum foil tightly sealed. Set the terrine in a pan of hot water in the oven. The water should extend about ⅔ of the way up the sides of the terrine. Bake for 1½ hours. Remove the terrine from the oven, remove its lid or aluminum foil, and let the terrine cool for ½ hour.

12. Put a lid (or a piece of wood or plastic) a little smaller than the terrine on top of the cooked mixture, and put a ½-pound weight on top.

Note: If the weight is too light, the terrine will not hold together; if it is too heavy, the liquid will be squeezed out, and it will be too dry.

13. Let the terrine stand this way at room temperature for 1 hour. Remove the weight and the lid. Refrigerate for at least 24 hours.

Note: The terrine may be served the next day. It may also be preserved for future use. To preserve it, pour melted lard (or another fat) over the top as a seal. Sealed, it may be kept in the refrigerator for up to 3 weeks.

Terrine de Tête de Porc Vinaigrette

TERRINE OF PORK HEAD, WITH VINAIGRETTE

I have an old friend from Normandy, Jacques de Chanteloup, who is an expert charcutier—pork butcher. He was head chef, at one time, at a well-known American restaurant, the Red Coach, in New York. When the Red Coach closed, he became the first instructor of charcuterie at the Culinary Institute of America.

He was a true charcutier, trained in the old way. And whenever I had a question about charcuterie, I asked Jacques de Chanteloup, and he always helped me out.

One morning, he visited Lutèce to show us how to make this terrine. Ever since we have been preparing it and serving it regularly.

Note: Your butcher probably does not have pork heads on hand, but he will probably be able to order one for you. Because it may be difficult to obtain less than a whole pork head, the recipe is given for 2 terrines. If your butcher will sell you half a head, cut in half the amounts of all the other ingredients.

Serves 8 to 10

The Terrine

1 pork head, cut in half by the butcher, brain removed (the brain may be used for another dish)

salt

1 medium onion, peeled, stuck with 2 cloves

2 bay leaves

3 sprigs thyme

2 celery stalks, peeled and washed

1 leek (including the greens), washed

2 carrots, trimmed, peeled, and washed

pepper, fresh ground

10 sprigs parsley

1 quart dry white wine

2 garlic cloves, peeled, green germs removed

1 tablespoon vinegar

powdered unflavored gelatin, as needed (see Step 5)

The Vinaigrette (Serves 6)

1 ample teaspoon Dijon mustard
¼ teaspoon salt
pepper, fresh ground
3 tablespoons tarragon vinegar
   (or another vinegar)
1 small pinch sugar
1 cup olive oil (or peanut oil)

1 hardboiled egg (page 119),
   chopped not too fine
3 shallots, peeled, chopped not
   too fine
5 cornichons (small French pickles), chopped not too fine
1 tablespoon chopped parsley

The Terrine

1. Put the pork head in a large pot. Cover it with cold water, add 1 tablespoon of salt, and let it soak for 3 hours. Discard the water and rinse the head.

2. Cover the head again with enough cold water barely to cover. Bring the water to the boil and skim the surface of the water of its foam. Add the onion, bay leaves, thyme, celery, leek, carrots, 1 teaspoon of salt, pepper, parsley, wine, and garlic. Cover the pot, but leave an opening for steam to escape. Cook gently until the meat is tender—about 1¼ to 2 hours.

3. Remove the vegetables (which may be sliced and served with vinaigrette). With a strainer, remove the 2 halves of the pork head from the pot. Continue to cook the liquid slowly, now uncovered, until it has been reduced by ½.

4. Let the head cool a little. Then separate the meat from the bones. Peel off and discard the skin of the tongue. Dice the meat and the tongue into ½-inch cubes. Put the diced meat and tongue in a terrine.

5. When the liquid has been reduced by ½, add the vinegar. Dissolve some gelatin in a little cold water, and add it to the liquid.

Note: If there is a pint of liquid, use 1 tablespoon of gelatin. If there is more or less liquid, increase or decrease the amount of gelatin accordingly.

6. Bring the liquid to the boil and let it cook for 2 minutes. Strain this liquid through a fine sieve over the meat. The meat should be barely covered by the liquid. Refrigerate overnight.

7. Serve sliced, with the vinaigrette.

Terrine de Tête de Porc Vinaigrette (continued)

The Vinaigrette

8. In a bowl, whisk together the mustard, salt, pepper, vinegar, sugar, and ½ tablespoon of water. Slowly whisk in the oil. Stir in the chopped egg, shallots, cornichons, and chopped parsley.

Note: The vinaigrette can be prepared a day in advance. If you prepare it in advance, do not add the shallots until just before it is used.

Note: The terrine may be served the next day. It may also be preserved for future use. To preserve it, pour melted lard (or another fat) over the top as a seal. Sealed, it will keep in the refrigerator for up to 3 weeks.

Terrine de Volaille au Foie Gras (ou Foie de Volaille)

TERRINE OF CHICKEN WITH FOIE GRAS (OR CHICKEN LIVER)

Serves 8 to 10

1 large capon, 5 to 6 pounds (or two 3-pound chickens)
¾ teaspoon salt, plus salt to taste
pepper, fresh ground
3 tablespoons peanut oil
1 medium onion, peeled and cut in small pieces
1 carrot, trimmed, peeled, washed, and cut in small pieces
1 celery stalk, peeled, washed, and cut in small pieces

1 quart Fond Blanc de Volaille (page 512), or water (see *Note* on page 58)
½ cup red wine
2 sprigs of thyme
1 bay leaf
4 juniper berries, crushed
½ pound foie gras (preferred), or chicken liver
¼ teaspoon Quatre Épices (page 528)
¼ cup port

2 tablespoons chopped shallots
½ pound pork butt, boneless
½ pound fatback
1 egg
2 slices fatback, ⅛ inch thick, for
    covering the terrine

1¼ cups Gelée (page 514), or
    prepare a jelly with commer-
    cial aspic jelly powder

1. Remove the skin from the capon (or chickens) without tearing it. Set aside.

2. Separate the meat from the bones, and trim the fat from the meat. Set the bones, trimmings, and dark meat aside.

3. Cut the white breast meat into long strips. Season it with ½ the salt, and with pepper to taste. Set aside.

4. Cut the carcass and all the bones into small pieces.

5. In a large skillet, in a few drops of the oil, sauté the carcass, bones, onion, carrot, and celery until lightly browned. Add the Fond Blanc de Volaille (or water), red wine, thyme, bay leaf, and juniper berries. Bring to the boil over high heat and cook until the liquid is reduced to ¼ of its original volume. There should be about 1 cup of liquid remaining. Pass the liquid through a fine sieve.

6. Cut the foie gras (or chicken liver) in strips. Season it with the remaining salt and with the Quatre Épices. Moisten it with the port wine. Refrigerate.

7. In a skillet, heat the remaining oil, and sauté the shallots for 1 minute. Add the reduced liquid, bring it to the boil, and pass it through a sieve over the chicken. Toss the chicken in a bowl with the liquid and set it aside to cool. Reserve the liquid that drains to the bottom.

8. Preheat the oven to 325°.

9. In a meat grinder, grind together the dark meat of the chicken, the trimmings, the pork butt, and the ½ pound of fatback, using the medium blade. *(Do not grind the 2 slices of fatback to be used for covering the terrine.)*

10. In a bowl, mix the egg into the ground mixture. Then mix in the liquid reserved in Step 7. Add salt and pepper to taste.

Terrine de Tête de Porc Vinaigrette (continued)

11. Line the terrine with the capon (or chicken) skins(s). Put ½ of the ground mixture into the terrine and smooth it down. Add alternate layers of the strips of white meat and the strips of foie gras (or chicken liver) to the terrine. Fill the terrine with the remainder of the ground mixture. Smooth the top and cover it with the 2 slices of fatback. Cover the terrine with its lid or with aluminum foil. Set the terrine in a pan of hot water in the preheated oven for 50 minutes.

Note: When the terrine is ready, the liquid that comes out of the hole will be clear when a needle is inserted into the center of the terrine.

12. Put a lid (or a piece of wood or plastic) a little smaller than the terrine on top of the cooked mixture, and put a ½-pound weight on top. Let the terrine stand this way at room temperature for 1 hour.

Note: If the weight is too light, the terrine will not hold together; if it is too heavy, the liquid will be squeezed out, and it will be too dry.

13. Remove the weight and the lid. Refrigerate overnight.
14. The next day, surface the terrine with the Gelée and refrigerate for another hour.

Note: The terrine may be kept for 1 or 2 days in the refrigerator.

Tourte de Vallée de Munster

COVERED MEAT PIE

My mother sometimes prepared this tourte, and in the hotel where I apprenticed it was served often. It is traditional Alsatian food.

At Lutèce we serve it once in a while at lunch—either hot with a Sauce Périgourdine, or cold with a green salad.

Note: This is the basic recipe, but sometimes at Lutèce we reduce by ⅓ the amount of pork and veal, and substitute venison or rabbit or duckling or squab. You may do the same thing at home, but when you substitute duckling or squab, be sure to remove all the skin and fat from the meat.

The dish may also be prepared entirely with rabbit or duck meat (in place of *all* the veal). Again, when you use duck meat for this dish remove all the skin and fat.

Serves 12

1 pound fillet of pork, lean	flour for flouring the work
1 pound fillet or leg of veal, lean	surface
2 shallots, peeled and chopped	1 recipe Feuilletage Rapide
2 tablespoons chopped parsley	(page 531)
2 teaspoons salt	1 egg beaten with a little cold
pepper, fresh ground	water
2 tablespoons dry white wine	2 eggs
2 tablespoons Cognac	1 cup heavy cream

1. Cut the pork and veal in thin strips. In a bowl, mix them with the shallots, 1 tablespoon of the parsley, the salt, pepper, wine, and Cognac. Let this mixture marinate for at least 1 hour.

2. On a floured work surface, roll out two 12-inch rounds of the Feuilletage Rapide. Put 1 of the rounds on a baking sheet. Add the remaining 1 tablespoon of parsley to the meats, and put the meats on this round of pastry, leaving a ¾-inch border. Brush the exposed border of the pastry with the beaten egg.

3. Preheat the oven to 350°.

4. Cover the meat with the other round of pastry. Firmly press the edge of the top pastry to the exposed border of the bottom pastry to seal. Cut a hole about ¾ of an inch in diameter in the middle of the top pastry. Insert a chimney formed of a strip of parchment paper or aluminum foil in this hole.

5. Brush the top pastry with the beaten egg. Cut a design in the top pastry with the tip of a sharp knife. Bake in the preheated oven for 55 minutes.

6. Beat together the 2 eggs, the cream, and a pinch of salt. Pour this into the tourte through the chimney. Bake 20 minutes more.

Note: The tourte may be served either hot or cold.

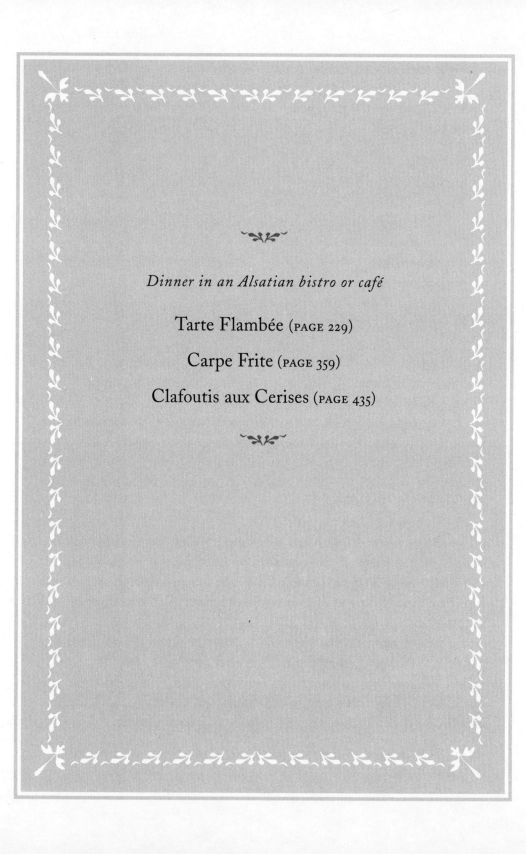

Dinner in an Alsatian bistro or café

Tarte Flambée <small>(PAGE 229)</small>

Carpe Frite <small>(PAGE 359)</small>

Clafoutis aux Cerises <small>(PAGE 435)</small>

HOT APPETIZERS

WHEN I GO BACK to France for my vacation, I always spend some time in Alsace to visit my family. And when I am there, I like to go to the bistros to have the good, simple traditional food in a traditional setting.

Here is a menu of this simple food. The three dishes are all things that we serve also at Lutèce, the first one a hot Alsatian appetizer—from the recipes that follow in this chapter of Hot Appetizers.

Beignets de Cervelles

BRAIN FRITTERS

I think this is a great dish, but it is not so easy to sell brains to Americans. Still, the ones I convince to try it, they love it.

In this recipe the fritters are served with a coulis of tomato, but at Lutèce we sometimes serve them with a green salad instead.

Serves 2

Beignets de Cervelles (continued)

1 veal brain
¼ cup vinegar
1 teaspoon salt, plus salt for sprinkling the beignets
1 sprig thyme
1 bay leaf
¼ teaspoon cracked pepper
3 cups oil for deep frying

½ cup Coulis de Tomates (page 506)
½ recipe Pâte à Frire (page 536)
½ cup parsley tops (stems removed), washed and thoroughly dried

1. Soak the brain in 1 cup of cold water and 2 tablespoons of the vinegar for at least 5 minutes.

2. Cut the brain into its 2 halves. Gently peel all the translucent surface membrane and blood vessels from the brain.

3. Put 1 cup of water in a small saucepan. Add the teaspoon of salt, the remaining 2 tablespoons of vinegar, the thyme, bay leaf, and cracked pepper. Bring to a rolling boil. Add the cleaned brain, and *immediately* remove from the heat. Let the brain cool for 15 minutes in the liquid.

4. In a deep fryer, heat the oil to 375°.

5. In a saucepan, warm the Coulis de Tomates.

6. With a slotted spoon, remove the 2 halves of the brain from the liquid, and drain them on a cloth napkin or paper towel. Cut each half of the brain into 4 pieces—8 pieces altogether.

7. One at a time, dip each piece into the Pâte à Frire, then plunge it into the deep fryer, until all 8 are in the hot oil. When the beignets come to the surface, turn them in the oil. When they are golden brown all over, remove them from the oil and drain them on paper towels. Sprinkle the beignets lightly with salt. Keep the oil hot.

8. Pour a pool of the warmed Coulis de Tomates on each of 2 plates. Put 4 of the beignets on each pool of coulis.

9. Plunge the parsley into the hot oil for 1 minute. Drain the parsley on paper towels, and arrange it over the beignets.

Note: This recipe may be prepared, in exactly the same way, substituting sweetbreads for the calf's brain.

Crêpes Soufflées aux Champignons

CRÊPES SOUFFLÉES WITH MUSHROOMS

This dish is very good when made with ordinary cultivated mushrooms, but it is even better when made with one or more wild mushrooms—morels, chanterelles, cèpes, black trumpets, whatever is in season. *Serves 4*

unsalted butter for buttering the gratin dish
8 small, fine crêpes, about 6″ across (page 345)
8 thin slices of ham
1 recipe Soufflé aux Champignons (page 221), uncooked, prepared with

either cultivated mushrooms or wild mushrooms
grated nutmeg
1 cup heavy cream
¾ cup grated Swiss cheese (Emmental or Gruyère)

1. Preheat the oven to 300°.
2. Butter a gratin dish that will hold the 8 crêpes when they are folded in half.
3. Arrange the crêpes on a work surface. Put a slice of ham over each crêpe. Then spread each slice of ham with ⅛ of the Soufflé aux Champignons mixture. Fold each crêpe in half.
4. Arrange the folded crêpes in the gratin dish. Grate a little nutmeg over each crêpe. Pour the cream over the crêpes, and then sprinkle them with the grated Swiss cheese.
5. Bake in the preheated oven for 15 minutes. Serve immediately.

Brioche de Kugelhopf aux Escargots

SNAILS IN KUGELHOPF (OR BRIOCHE) PASTRY

When we were children, in rainy weather we would go out to gather snails. We would bring them home, and my mother would put them in a container (with a cover, otherwise they would climb out) and let them fast for five or six days.

Then she would put vinegar, flour, and handfuls of coarse salt in with the snails to purge them. Five or six hours later she would wash them several times in cold water, and then she would blanch them. When they were cool, she drained them.

We took the snails out of their shells with a pin, we cut off their black ends, and then my mother cooked them—in white wine and water, with a bouquet garni, and salt and pepper—for three or four hours.

Today, when you buy snails in cans, that is the stage they are at. And today, in all restaurants canned snails are used. The best canned snails (the brand name is Helix) come from Burgundy, and they are the only ones we use at Lutèce.

This recipe is a special version of escargots, which I came up with at Lutèce. It can be made with Kugelhopf pastry or with brioche pastry.

Really, this dish is not entirely my original idea. A customer of mine was visiting Colmar, in Alsace, and when he was there he had a dish like this, except that it was made with Béchamel.

He described it to me, and I thought it would be better with snail butter, so I came up with this variation. *Serves 8*

48 canned snails
½ cup dry white wine, Alsatian
    wine preferred

½ cup Fond Blanc de Volaille
    (page 512), or water (see *Note*
    on page 58)

1 teaspoon powdered gelatin
1 bay leaf
1 sprig thyme
salt
pepper, fresh ground
unsalted butter, to butter the
    molds

1¼ pounds Kugelhopf pastry
    (page 446), or Pâte à Brioche
    (page 534)
1 recipe Beurre d'Escargot (page
    506)

1. Drain the snails free of the juice they are canned in, rinse them under cold water, and put them in a saucepan.

2. Combine the wine and Fond Blanc de Volaille (or water). Dissolve the gelatin in the combined liquids, and add this liquid to the snails. Add the bay leaf, thyme, salt to taste, and pepper. Bring to the boil, and cook slowly for 5 minutes. Let the snails cool in the liquid. Drain them.

3. Butter 8 molds—either small Kugelhopf molds or small brioche molds.

4. Preheat the oven to 300°.

5. Work the snails into the Kugelhopf pastry (or Pâte à Brioche). Divide the pastry into 8 portions. Put the portions in the buttered molds, and let them rise in a warm place until they double in size—about 20 minutes.

6. Bake for 12 minutes in the preheated oven. Remove the pastries from the molds and let them cool on a rack for about 30 minutes.

7. Lower the oven temperature to 275°.

8. Cut the pastries horizontally into 3 parts—to form a top layer, a center layer, and a bottom. Spread snail butter between the top and center layers, and between the center layers and the bottoms. Reassemble the pastries. Return them to their molds.

9. Put the pastries, in their molds, back in the oven until the butter is melted and hot—about 10 minutes. Before serving, make certain the snail butter is completely melted. Serve very hot.

Croissant de Truffe

WHOLE TRUFFLE IN PASTRY,
WITH FOIE GRAS AND MUSHROOMS

This has always been the most expensive dish we sell at Lutèce, and since the day the restaurant opened it has been on the menu. And yet, in more than thirty years, only one time did anyone send it back.

Many people order it, I think, out of curiosity, because it is so expensive. And some people, I am sure, do not like it—nothing can please everybody. But when they do not like it, I think they are afraid to admit it. They are afraid to admit they do not like something that is so expensive it *must* be good.

The recipe calls for either fresh black truffles (which are available from November to February in specialty shops) or canned truffles—the preparations are slightly different. The dish is excellent when you make it with canned truffles. But fresh truffles are the ultimate.

This is an expensive dish, but it is a great gastronomic experience.

Serves 4

4 whole, fresh black truffles (or canned truffles), approximately 1 ounce each

1 cup dry white wine (when using fresh truffles)

4 tablespoons (½ stick) unsalted butter

1 shallot, peeled and chopped fine

¼ pound mushrooms, washed and chopped coarse

salt

pepper, fresh ground

10 ounces Feuilletage Spécial (page 532), or Feuilletage Rapide (page 531)

¼ pound fresh foie gras in 1 piece, or Terrine de Foie Gras (page 182)

1 egg beaten with a little cold water

1. *When using fresh truffles.* Brush the truffles very carefully under cold running water, making sure that all soil is removed from the surfaces. Put the 4 truffles in a saucepan and add the wine. The saucepan must be small

enough that the wine will cover the truffles. Bring to the boil, and simmer gently, covered, for 25 minutes. Let the truffles cool in the liquid. Then separate the truffles from the cooking liquid. Set both aside.

When using canned truffles. Drain the truffles and keep their juice.

2. Peel the truffles. Chop coarse *the peel only.* Set aside.

3. In a skillet, over medium heat, melt 1 tablespoon of butter. Add the shallot and sauté for 1 minute. *Do not brown.* Add the mushrooms, and sauté until all the juice is evaporated—around 4 minutes. *Do not brown.* Turn off the flame. Add the chopped truffle peelings and salt and pepper to taste. Let cool.

4. Roll out the pastry to a rectangle about 14 by 6 inches. Then cut the rectangle in half so that you have 2 rectangles, each 7 by 6 inches. Then cut each of these rectangles in half diagonally, to make 4 triangles.

5. *When using fresh foie gras:* Cut the piece of foie gras in half, to form 2 thinner flat pieces, and sauté these pieces in a skillet, over medium heat, for 1½ minutes on each side. Then cut the pieces in strips about ¼ inch thick.

When using Terrine de Foie Gras: Cut the foie gras in strips about ¼ inch thick.

6. Put the triangles on a work surface, the longest sides toward you. Brush some of the beaten egg along the 3 edges of each triangle. Set aside the remainder of the beaten egg.

7. Preheat the oven to 350°.

8. Put 1 truffle on each triangle of pastry. Each truffle should be at the center point of the longest side of its triangle. Then put strips of foie gras on each side of the truffle—they should extend from the truffles like arms, parallel to the long side of the triangle. Then arrange the mushrooms along the strips of foie gras, the mushrooms partially overlapping the foie gras.

9. Roll up each triangle of pastry, starting from the long side, so that the truffle, foie gras, and mushrooms are enclosed in the cylinder of pastry. Then bend and seal the ends of each cylinder to form a crescent.

10. Arrange the pastries on a baking sheet. Brush them with the remainder of the beaten egg. Cook in the preheated oven until the pastries are golden brown—about 10 to 12 minutes.

11. In a small saucepan, reduce the truffles' cooking juice (or the juice

Croissant de Truffe (continued)

from the preserved truffles) to ⅓ of its original volume. Whisk in the remaining 3 tablespoons of butter, whisking vigorously over high heat. Add salt and pepper. Serve this sauce with the croissants.

~✣~

Escargots à l'Alsacienne

SNAILS, AS PREPARED IN ALSACE

One day, a long time ago, a man—a doctor who was sitting in the Garden of Lutèce with his wife—asked one of the captains a question. The man wanted to know, Did the chef ever work in the restaurant Chez Hansi, in Paris, in the 1950s?

The captain came to the kitchen to ask me this question, and I went out to the dining room to see the man, and to tell him that, yes, in those years I was the chef in Chez Hansi. He said to me, "I recognized your snails."

The man told me that years before, after the war, he had been a doctor in the American army, and that he was stationed at Fontainebleau, about fifty kilometers from Paris. Whenever he had a day off, he said, he would go to Paris. And whenever he went to Paris, he would go to Chez Hansi, because he liked very much the snails there. After that, wherever he went, this man would order snails, but he never found any snails like the ones he had at Chez Hansi—until this day at Lutèce. He recognized my snails ten years later.

For many years, he came back to Lutèce again and again, and always he ordered snails—these snails.

Note: Traditionally, snails are served in snail shells, but I prefer to serve them in small timbales, which are easier to clean. These snails can be served either way.

Serves 6

48 canned snails
½ cup dry white wine, Alsatian
    wine preferred

½ cup Fond Blanc de Volaille
    (page 512), or water (see *Note*
    on page 58)

1 teaspoon powdered gelatin
1 bay leaf
1 sprig thyme
salt

pepper, fresh ground
1 recipe Beurre d'Escargot (page 506)

1. Drain the snails of the juice they are canned in, rinse them under cold running water, and put them in a saucepan.

2. Combine the wine and Fond Blanc de Volaille (or water). Dissolve the gelatin in the combined liquids, and pour this liquid over the snails. Add the bay leaf, thyme, and salt and pepper to taste. Bring to the boil, and cook slowly for 5 minutes. Let the snails cool in the liquid.

Note: If the recipe is done in advance to this point, the snails may be cooled in the refrigerator.

3. Preheat the oven to 350°.

4. Put each snail in a small timbale (or in a snail shell) with ½ teaspoon of the slightly gelatinous juice they cooked in. Then fill each timbale (or shell) with Beurre d'Escargot, pushing it in with your thumb.

5. Arrange the timbales on an ovenproof plate (or put the snail shells on a snail plate), and put the snails in the preheated oven. The snails are ready when the snail butter bubbles—around 10 minutes.

Note: The snails must be served very hot—directly from the oven—otherwise the butter separates.

꧁꧂

Foie Gras aux Pommes

DUCK LIVER WITH CARAMELIZED APPLES

Foie gras is considered fancy food, but Alsatians have been eating it for hundreds of years as part of their everyday life, as if it was everyday food.

But in the Bordelais region in the old days it was less than that—not even part of everyday life. When migrant workers came for the harvest of the grapes every year, in the fall, the owners of the châteaux fed them goose—not the breast meat, which the château owners kept for themselves, and not the legs, which the farmers ate, but the livers, the foie gras. To the château owners it was food for the lower classes.

Today, foie gras is often prepared with fruit, all kinds of fruit. But for me it is best with Golden Delicious apples, which is how it is usually made in Alsace and in Lutèce. *Serves 6*

1 fresh foie gras, about 1½ pounds
4 medium apples, Golden Delicious, or another cooking apple
4 tablespoons (½ stick) unsalted butter
all-purpose flour for dredging
salt
pepper, fresh ground
2 tablespoons tarragon vinegar
½ cup Fond de Veau (page 510) or water (see *Note* on page 58)

1. Separate the foie gras into its 2 parts, and then cut it into 12 equal slices. Refrigerate.

2. Peel and core the apples. Cut each apple into 8 slices. In a large skillet heat 1 tablespoon of the butter. Add the apples, and brown them over medium heat, about 3 minutes on each side. The apples should be slightly caramelized. Remove the apples to a plate and keep them warm.

3. Dredge the slices of foie gras with the flour, and season them with salt and pepper. Melt 1 more tablespoon of butter in the skillet. Sauté the slices of foie gras, over medium heat, for 3 minutes on each side. The foie gras should be nicely browned on the outside, a little pink inside.

4. Arrange the apples and foie gras on 6 warm plates. Remove all fat from the skillet. Add the vinegar to the skillet and cook very briefly. Add the Fond de Veau (or water), and reduce it by ½ over high heat. Whisk in the remaining 2 tablespoons of butter and, still over high heat, cook for 2 minutes. Pour this sauce over the foie gras, and serve hot.

Fondue aux Oeufs à la Tomate

EGGS AND TOMATOES

We do serve this dish at Lutèce—but not to the customers. Sometimes it is the staff lunch. It is good home cooking, for lunch or a light dinner. *Serves 4*

2½ pounds tomatoes, ripe
3 tablespoons (⅜ stick) unsalted
    butter
2 large shallots (or 1 small
    onion), peeled and chopped
    fine
2 garlic cloves, peeled, green
    germs removed, and
    chopped

1 bouquet garni (page 55)
salt
pepper, fresh ground
4 large eggs
3 tablespoons heavy cream
1 tablespoon chopped chives (or
    chopped parsley)

1. Cut a conical plug from the stem end of each tomato and discard. Blanch the tomatoes in boiling water for 10 seconds, drain them under cold water, and peel off the skins. Cut the tomatoes in half, squeeze out and discard the juice and seeds, and chop the pulp in ¼-inch cubes.

2. In a skillet, melt 2 tablespoons of the butter. Sauté the chopped shallots (or onion) for 2 to 3 minutes. *Do not brown.* Add the tomatoes, garlic, bouquet garni, ½ teaspoon of salt, and pepper, and cook over medium heat, uncovered, for 20 minutes.

3. In a large saucepan, bring salted water to the boil. Put the whole eggs in a strainer, and lower the strainer into the boiling water. Bring the water back to the boil, and cook for 9 minutes.

4. Immediately transfer the eggs to a container of cold water, put them under cold running water, and leave them under the running water until they have cooled.

5. Preheat the oven to 375°.

6. Remove the shells from the eggs. Cut the eggs in half length-

Fondue aux Oeufs à la Tomate (continued)

wise. Without breaking the whites, remove the yolks, and put them in a bowl. Soften the remaining 1 tablespoon of butter and add it to the bowl. Then add 1 tablespoon of the cream, the chives (or parsley), and salt and pepper to taste. With a fork, mash the contents of the bowl into a paste.

7. Pack the paste into the halves of egg white, and arrange them, side by side, on an ovenproof earthenware or porcelain plate.

8. In a bowl, combine the chopped tomatoes and the remaining cream, and pour them over the eggs. Put the plate of eggs in the preheated oven for 10 minutes. Serve warm.

***

Oeufs Brouillés aux Pointes d'Asperges

SCRAMBLED EGGS WITH ASPARAGUS TIPS

This simple dish serves as an appetizer or, with a salad, as a light main course. *Serves 4*

16 thin green asparagus, washed
8 eggs
3 tablespoons (⅜ stick) unsalted butter
2 tablespoons heavy cream

salt
pepper, fresh ground
1 tablespoon chervil leaves (or chives, or Italian parsley), in small pieces

1. Cut a 3-inch spear from the tip of each asparagus. Cut each 3-inch spear in 1-inch lengths. Discard the remainder of the asparagus.

2. Cook the asparagus pieces in salted water for 8 minutes. Drain them. Set them aside and keep them warm.

3. Beat the eggs. In a small saucepan, melt ½ the butter. Add the beaten eggs. Put the saucepan in a pan of warm water, over heat. Stir constantly with a spoon until the eggs are smooth, homogeneous, and creamy—about 6 minutes.

4. Remove the saucepan from the heat. Stir the cream and the remaining butter into the eggs. Add salt and pepper to taste.

5. Put an equal portion of the eggs in each of 4 soup plates. Arrange the asparagus on top, and sprinkle with the chervil (or chives, or Italian parsley).

꧁꧂

Oeufs Brouillés aux Truffes

SCRAMBLED EGGS WITH TRUFFLES

During the first two weeks of January, I usually try to buy a year's supply of truffles. That is when you can usually get the best truffles, and, because they are also plentiful then, the price usually comes down. Of course, sometimes I outsmart myself, and the price goes up instead. Whatever they cost, truffles are wonderful with scrambled eggs.

This is a great and simple dish. But, because of the truffles, these are scrambled eggs for which at Lutèce we have to charge a lot. Mainly in December and January, when truffles are fresh and when they are at their best, we serve this as a first course at lunch. *Serves 2*

4 eggs	pepper, fresh ground
1 ounce truffles (fresh or canned), chopped coarse	3 tablespoons (⅜ stick) unsalted butter
½ teaspoon salt	1½ tablespoons heavy cream

1. With a fork, beat the eggs—*but not too thoroughly.* Add the truffles, salt, and pepper.
2. Put water in the bottom part of a double boiler, bring it to the boil, and set the upper part of the double boiler in place on top. Melt ½ the butter in the upper part of the double boiler. Add the eggs and truffles, and cook slowly, stirring continuously with a wooden spoon, until the eggs are smooth, homogeneous, and have the consistency of cream—about 6 minutes.
3. Remove the top of the double boiler from the heat, add the cream and the remaining butter to the eggs, stirring with a wooden spoon.

Note: Serve with Pain de Campagne (page 541), or with bread that has been toasted by frying it in butter.

Oeufs Cocotte à la Purée de Légumes

EGGS WITH PUREED VEGETABLES

Serves 6

salt

¼ pound string beans, washed
and trimmed

¼ pound shelled peas, washed

2 tablespoons (¼ stick) unsalted
butter

¼ pound spinach leaves, washed,
stems removed

pepper, fresh ground

5 tablespoons (almost ⅓ cup)
heavy cream

6 large eggs, very fresh

coarse salt

1. In a large saucepan, bring salted water to the boil. Add the string beans, and boil vigorously for 6 minutes. Add the peas, and continue boiling for 3 minutes more.

2. While the string beans and peas are cooking, melt 1 tablespoon of butter in a heavy-bottomed pot (not of aluminum) over low heat. Add the spinach. Cover, and cook for 5 minutes.

3. Drain the string beans and peas, and, when the spinach is ready, add them to the spinach. Add salt and pepper to taste. Cover, and cook over low heat for 20 minutes.

4. Put the vegetables in a food processor, and add 3 tablespoons of the cream. Process for a few seconds, until you have a puree. (If you do not have a food processor, use a food mill.)

5. Preheat the oven to 375°.

6. Butter 6 egg cocottes (or 6 porcelain ramekins that have lids) with the remaining butter. Fill each cocotte halfway with the puree of vegetables. Break an egg into each cocotte, and set the cocottes in a pan of warm water. The water in the pan should reach ⅔ of the way up the sides of the cocottes. Cover each cocotte with its lid.

7. On the top of the stove, bring the water in the pan to a gentle boil. Put the pan in the preheated oven for 8 minutes.

8. Remove the pan from the oven, and remove the cocottes from the

pan. Put equal amounts of the remaining 2 tablespoons of cream in the 6 cocottes. Sprinkle a few grains of coarse salt over each. Serve immediately.

⌁⤳⤷⌁

Oeufs Durs aux Poireaux à la Bretonne

HARDBOILED EGGS WITH LEEKS

Serves 4

3 leeks—the white part, plus a small amount of the green	1 cup heavy cream
	salt
1 tablespoon unsalted butter	1 pinch cayenne pepper
½ cup Sauce Béchamel, Method I or II (page 517 or page 518)	8 hardboiled eggs (page 119)

1. Trim the leeks, cut them in half lengthwise, and wash them thoroughly.

2. Again, cut the leeks in half lengthwise. Then cut them crosswise into ⅛-inch pieces.

3. Melt the butter in a skillet. Add the leeks, cover, and cook gently over low-to-medium heat, stirring from time to time, until the leeks are soft—about 10 minutes. *Do not brown.*

4. Add to the skillet the Sauce Béchamel, cream, salt to taste, and the cayenne. Bring to the boil, reduce the heat, and simmer gently for 5 minutes, stirring once or twice.

5. Peel the eggs. Add them, whole, to the skillet, and simmer for 2 to 3 minutes, until they are warm.

6. Put the eggs on 4 plates. Spoon the sauce around them. Serve with toast.

⌁⤳⤷⌁

Oeufs Pochés sur Lit d'Oseille au Vin Blanc

POACHED EGGS WITH SORREL

Serves 4

10 tablespoons (1¼ sticks) unsalted butter
4 slices white bread
¼ pound sorrel, washed, stems
removed, cut in ¼-inch
strands
salt

white pepper, fresh ground
3 shallots, peeled and chopped
fine
1½ cups white wine, Gewürz-
traminer preferred
3 tablespoons vinegar
8 eggs, very fresh

1. Melt 3 tablespoons of the butter in a skillet, and fry the bread in the butter until it is golden brown on each side.

2. Melt 2 tablespoons of the butter in a sauté pan. Add the sorrel, a little salt and pepper, and cook over medium heat for about 3 minutes. Set aside and keep warm.

3. Melt 1 tablespoon of butter in a frying pan. Add the shallots and cook slowly for 2 minutes. Add the wine, ½ teaspoon of salt, and pepper, and reduce by ½. Add the remaining 4 tablespoons of butter, a small piece at a time, and beat it vigorously into the liquid, over high heat, until all the butter is incorporated into the liquid. Continue cooking and beating until the sauce thickens. Set aside and keep warm.

4. In a wide, shallow sauté pan, bring 1 quart of water *barely* to the boil. Add the vinegar. *Do not add salt.* Crack the eggs into the water one by one, and cook, over very low heat, for 4 minutes.

Note: The cooking water should not actually boil. It should *almost* boil—that is, it should move a little, but not bubble.

5. Put each slice of bread on a plate. Arrange the sorrel on the slices of bread. With a skimmer or slotted spoon, remove the eggs from the water,

draining them well, and put them carefully on the sorrel, 2 to a plate. Spoon the sauce around the bread. Serve hot.

~❧~

Oeufs Pochés Vigneronne

POACHED EGGS IN RED WINE SAUCE

Serves 2

4 tablespoons (½ stick) unsalted butter

2 slices white bread, trimmed, each slice cut in 2 triangles

1 garlic clove, peeled, halved, green germ removed

8 cultivated mushrooms, or wild mushrooms, washed, cut in ½-inch matchsticks

2 slices ham, cut in ½-inch matchsticks

pepper, fresh ground

salt

3 tablespoons vinegar

4 eggs, very fresh

1 cup Sauce Vin Rouge (page 524)

1. Melt 3 tablespoons of the butter in a skillet. Fry the bread in the butter until it is golden brown on each side. Rub each slice of bread with the garlic clove.

2. Melt the remaining 1 tablespoon of butter in a skillet. Over high heat, sauté the mushrooms and ham—with pepper and a pinch of salt—for 3 minutes.

3. In a shallow sauté pan, bring 1 quart of water *barely* to the boil. Add the vinegar. *Do not add salt.* Crack the eggs into the water one by one, and cook, over very low heat, for 4 minutes.

Note: The cooking water should not actually boil. It should *almost* boil—that is, it should move a little, but not bubble.

4. Arrange 2 triangles of bread on each plate. Put a poached egg on each triangle of bread.

5. Add the Sauce Vin Rouge to the ham and mushrooms. Heat well, and pour this sauce over the eggs. Serve at once.

Ravioli de Ris de Veau

RAVIOLI OF SWEETBREADS

Serves 4

½ sweetbread
¼ pound spinach, stems
    removed, washed
salt
2 tablespoons (¼ stick) unsalted
    butter
3 shallots, peeled and chopped
    fine
1 cup sliced mushrooms
pepper, fresh ground

1 egg yolk
1 recipe Ravioli Dough (page
    540) (see *Note*)
1 egg beaten with a little cold
    water
2 bay leaves
⅓ cup Fond de Veau (page 510)
½ cup grated Swiss cheese
    (Emmental or Gruyère)

1. Soak the ½ sweetbread in cold water for 1 to 2 hours. Put it in a pan, cover it with cold water, bring the water to the boil, and cook for 5 minutes. Cool the sweetbread under cold running water, then remove it from the water.

2. Peel all the skin from the sweetbread, and trim off all the fat and cartilage. Cut the sweetbread in ½-inch cubes.

3. Cook the spinach in a pot (not of aluminum) of salted boiling water for 3 minutes. Cool the spinach under cold running water, drain it, and remove all the excess water by forming the spinach into balls between the palms of your hands, and squeezing it. Chop the spinach coarse.

4. Melt 1 tablespoon of the butter in a skillet, and sauté the shallots. *Do not brown.* Add the mushrooms, and sauté over high heat until all their liquid is cooked off—4 to 5 minutes.

5. Add the sweetbreads and spinach to the mushrooms. Add salt and pepper. Cook over high heat for 5 minutes. Stir in the egg yolk, and cook 1 minute more.

6. Put the contents of the skillet in a food processor, and process for 1 minute, to form a coarse-ground stuffing. Set this stuffing aside to cool.

7. Divide the Ravioli Dough in 2 equal pieces, and roll out each piece to a sheet as thin as possible. (The best way is to use a pasta rolling machine.)

8. Dot 1 sheet of the dough with small teaspoons of the stuffing. The dots of stuffing should be about 1 inch apart. Brush the exposed portions of this sheet of ravioli dough with the beaten egg. Put the second sheet of dough on top.

9. Press the 2 sheets of ravioli dough together, and with a pastry cutter or sharp knife, form the ravioli by cutting through the sheets of dough between the dots of stuffing.

10. Preheat the oven to 350°.

11. Bring a large pot of salted water, with the bay leaves, to the boil. Add the ravioli, and cook slowly for 4 minutes. With a slotted spoon, remove the ravioli to a colander to drain.

12. Using the remaining 1 tablespoon of butter, butter a gratin dish. Put the ravioli in the gratin dish. Pour the Fond de Veau over the ravioli, sprinkle them with the Swiss cheese, and put them in the preheated oven for 10 minutes. When ready, the cheese on top should be lightly browned. Serve hot.

Note: If you do not wish to prepare your own ravioli dough, wonton wrappers may be purchased in Chinese markets. Instead of following Steps 7 to 9, fill each wonton wrapper with a little of the stuffing, apply some of the beaten egg, and seal. Then proceed to Step 10.

Saucisson à l'Ail

GARLIC SAUSAGE

This is an ancient dish from the region around Lyon, where it is still common. In France, restaurants usually do not prepare their own sausages, because there are good sausage makers—charcutiers—all over.

Most French restaurants just buy sausages, wrap them in pastry, bake them, and serve them.

But when I first came to America I could not find a sausage that was good enough for Lutèce. (Today I probably could.) So I started making my own. It is not hard to do, and I still do it.

This is bistro food, and we serve it only at lunchtime.

Yield: 2 sausages

1 pound lean beef chuck
1 pound pork butt
½ pound fatback, cut in tiny dice
1 tablespoon salt
1 pinch curing salt (saltpeter)
white pepper, fresh ground

2 ounces (⅜ cup) cornstarch, or
    potato starch
½ teaspoon garlic chopped very
    fine
2 beef middle casings (available
    from butchers)

1. Grind the beef and pork in a meat grinder, using the medium blade.

2. Put the ground meat, 1 cup of very cold water, and all the other ingredients (except the beef middle casings) in the bowl of an electric mixer. Mix slowly—do not overmix—for 1 minute.

3. Pack the mixture into a pastry bag, and from the pastry bag force it into 2 beef middle casings. Prick the casings in several places with a needle. Tie the ends. Leave the sausages at room temperature overnight before cooking.

4. Simmer the sausages in water for 50 minutes. Refrigerate overnight, preferably longer.

Note: The sausage may be served cool with Salade de Pommes de Terre (page 243);

or, hot, with the casing removed, wrapped in a ⅛-inch layer of Feuilletage Rapide (page 531) and baked for 30 minutes in a 350° oven;

or, hot, with the casing removed, wrapped in a ⅓-inch layer of Pâte à Brioche (page 534)—which must be permitted to rise, after it has been wrapped around the sausage, at room temperature, for 15 minutes—and baked for 30 minutes in a 350° oven.

Soufflés Salés: au Fromage, aux Champignons, aux Asperges, et aux Poireaux

APPETIZER SOUFFLÉS, FOUR VERSIONS

Serves 5

The Appareil Soufflé (Basic Soufflé Mixture)

1 cup milk
2 tablespoons (¼ stick) unsalted
    butter, plus butter for butter-
    ing the soufflé dishes
2 tablespoons all-purpose flour,
    plus flour for flouring the
    soufflé dishes

¼ teaspoon salt
pepper, fresh ground
4 egg yolks
4 egg whites

The Appareil Soufflé (Basic Soufflé Mixture)

1. Heat the milk and keep it hot.

2. In a heavy-bottomed saucepan, melt the butter over medium heat, and mix in the flour. Cook for 2 minutes. *Do not brown.*

3. Remove the saucepan from the heat, and whisk in the hot milk, stirring until the mixture is smooth. Return the saucepan to the heat, and, stirring constantly, bring to the boil. Cook slowly for about 5 minutes, still stirring. Stir in the salt and pepper.

4. Still over heat, whisk in the egg yolks, and cook for 1 more minute, stirring constantly to prevent sticking.

Note: At this point, from this basic mixture various soufflés may be made by stirring in:

For a Cheese Soufflé

¾ cup grated Swiss cheese (Emmental or Gruyère)

Soufflés Salés (continued)

For a Mushroom Soufflé

¼ cup grated Swiss cheese (Emmental or Gruyère)
½ cup sliced mushrooms, sautéed in unsalted butter until dry

For an Asparagus Soufflé

¼ cup grated Swiss cheese (Emmental or Gruyère)
½ cup asparagus, cut in small sticks (approximately ½″ × ³⁄₁₆″ × ³⁄₁₆″)
   and cooked for 5 minutes in boiling water

For a Leek Soufflé

¼ cup grated Swiss cheese (Emmental or Gruyère)
2 leeks (mostly the white part, but with a little green)

Note: To prepare the leeks for the Leek Soufflé: Trim the leeks, cut them in half lengthwise, wash them thoroughly. Again, cut them in half lengthwise, then cut them crosswise in ⅛-inch pieces. Sauté the leeks in ½ tablespoon of unsalted butter for 8 minutes. Do not brown.

5. Preheat the oven to 300°.

6. After stirring in the Swiss cheese (or 1 of the three pairs of ingredients): Whip the egg whites in a bowl until stiff. Fold them gently into the mixture.

7. Butter the inside of 5 individual 8-ounce soufflé dishes (approximately 4 inches wide and 2 inches high). Then lightly flour the dishes.

8. Put equal amounts of the mixture in the 5 soufflé dishes. (The mixture will not—and must not—fill the dishes.) Bake for about 12 minutes in the preheated oven.

Note: The soufflé may also be prepared in a 3-cup soufflé dish. In the larger dish, the baking time is about 20 to 25 minutes.

Note: When done, the tops should be golden brown, and should have risen to about 1 inch above their molds.

Note: To prepare other variations on the basic soufflé, you may substitute other ingredients for the mushrooms, asparagus, or leeks.

Tarte à la Tomate

TOMATO TART

This is one of the dishes I came up with when more and more people started to ask me for vegetarian food. At Lutèce we serve it as a hot appetizer, and also as a garnish with vegetable platters.

Note: It is important that you prepare these tarts only when you have very ripe tomatoes.

Serves 4

3 medium tomatoes, very ripe
7 ounces Feuilletage Rapide
    (page 531)
oil for oiling the pastry sheet
½ teaspoon salt
pepper, fresh ground
6 tablespoons (¾ stick) unsalted
    butter
2 medium shallots, peeled and
    chopped

1 tablespoon white wine
1 large pinch coarse salt
1½ teaspoons chopped fresh
    basil (or chervil, or Italian
    parsley, or chives, depending
    on the season)

1. Cut a conical plug from the stem end of each tomato and discard. Blanch the tomatoes in boiling water for 10 seconds, drain them under cold water, and peel off the skins. Cut the tomatoes in half. Then cut each half into half-moon–shaped slices—about 9 slices per half, about 54 slices altogether.

2. Divide the Feuilletage Rapide into 4 equal parts, and roll the parts out into 4 rounds, each 7 inches in diameter. The rounds will be quite thin.

3. Oil a pastry sheet, using very little oil. Put the pastries on the baking sheet. Pinch up a very small edge all around each pastry. Refrigerate for 10 minutes.

4. Preheat the oven to 375°.

Tarte à la Tomate (continued)

5. Arrange the tomato slices in a circle on each round of pastry, placing them like overlapping petals of a flower, the petals extending to about ½ inch from the edge of the pastry. Put 2 or 3 additional slices at the center. (Use about 13 or 14 slices per tart.) Sprinkle the tomatoes with the salt and pepper.

6. Cut ½ of the butter into small pieces, and arrange the pieces over the tomatoes. Bake the tarts in the preheated oven for about 12 minutes—until the pastries are crisp and the tomatoes just beginning to brown.

7. While the tarts are in the oven, melt ½ of the remaining butter in a skillet. Cook the shallots in the hot butter for 30 seconds, stirring. Add the wine. Bring to a boil (this will take only a moment), and then stir in the remaining butter.

8. When the tarts come out of the oven, pour the hot shallot butter (prepared in Step 7) over them. Sprinkle the tarts with the coarse salt, then with the chopped basil (or one of the other herbs). Serve immediately, very hot.

❧

Tarte à l'Oignon

ONION TART

You could not find in the small village where I grew up all the things you could find in the bigger towns. So sometimes my mother would take me shopping with her to Mulhouse, the big town nearby, when she was looking for something special. We would go by bus.

In Mulhouse, in some of the bistros, I remember there was a sign in the window: TARTE À L'OIGNON PRÊTE À QUATRE HEURES. These places served no other food, just the onion tart, and at four o'clock everyone would go to these bistros, and they filled up.

When my mother was finished with her shopping, we would go too. We would each get a slice of onion tart, and my mother would have a glass of white wine—and I would take a sip.

Onion tarts are still popular in Alsace in the cafés. There are sophisticated ways to make them, but the best ones are more basic. The tart we make at Lutèce is based on my aunt's recipe—she is also my godmother.

At lunch, at Lutèce, the onion tart is on the menu. But at night I only make it every few weeks, usually when someone asks for it in advance. I make a very large one, and I send slices around to some of the tables. Of course I do not charge for that.

Other chefs may send a glass of champagne to a friend. But I think, why send a glass of champagne? If someone wants a glass of champagne, he can buy it. But an onion tart he cannot buy.   *Serves 5 or 6*

2 cups all-purpose flour, sifted
salt
8 tablespoons (1 stick) unsalted
    butter
2 tablespoons lard
1 pound onions, peeled and
    chopped

1 egg
½ cup heavy cream
pepper, fresh ground
grated nutmeg

1. Mix the flour and 1 scant teaspoon of salt in a bowl. Rub in the butter with the fingertips. *Do not work the dough too much.* Make a well in the center of the mixture, pour in ½ cup of cold water, and incorporate it into the mixture with the fingers until it is just moistened. Let the dough rest for at least 30 minutes.

2. Preheat the oven to 375°.

3. Heat the lard in a skillet, and sauté the onions until they are slightly browned and tender. Remove the skillet from the heat.

4. In a small bowl, beat the egg and cream together. Add this to the onions. Add a pinch of salt, pepper, and nutmeg.

5. Roll out the dough, and line a 10-inch pie tin or tart pan with it. Fill with the onion mixture.

6. Bake in the preheated oven for 25 minutes, and serve very hot.

Tarte à l'Oseille Gratinée

SORREL TART

Serves 6

The Tart

12 ounces Pâte Brisée
   (page 537)
2 tablespoons (¼ stick) unsalted
   butter
1 pound fresh sorrel, washed,
   stems removed, cut in
   ¼-inch strips

2 eggs
½ cup heavy cream
½ teaspoon salt
¼ teaspoon pepper, fresh ground

The Gratin

4 hardboiled eggs (page 119),
   yolks only
½ cup heavy cream

½ cup grated Swiss cheese
   (Emmental or Gruyère)

The Tart

1. Roll out the Pâte Brisée, and line a 10-inch pie tin with the rolled-out pastry. Refrigerate for at least 20 minutes.

2. Preheat the oven to 350°.

3. In a sauté pan heat the butter. Add the sorrel and sauté for about 3 minutes, moving the sorrel around in the pan. If the sorrel releases too much water, drain it.

4. In a bowl, beat together the 2 whole uncooked eggs and the cream. Add salt and pepper. Stir in the sorrel. Put this mixture in the pastry-lined pie tin, and bake in the preheated oven for 30 minutes.

The Gratin

5. While the tart is baking, push the hardboiled egg yolks through a sieve. Then mix them with the cream to form a soft paste. When the tart has baked for 30 minutes, remove it from the oven, and spread this mix-

ture over the tart. Then sprinkle the Swiss cheese on top. Return the tart to the oven for 10 more minutes.

Note: If the cheese is not nicely melted and browned after the final 10 minutes of baking, finish the tart by putting it under the broiler for 1 to 2 minutes.

Note: Onions (or the whites of leeks with a little bit of the green), may be substituted for the sorrel in this recipe. The onions (or leeks) should be peeled, chopped, and sautéed in butter until they are golden brown before proceeding with Step 4.

Celery may also be substituted. The celery should be peeled, washed, cut in small pieces, and sautéed in butter until soft before proceeding with Step 4.

Spinach may also be substituted. Proceed exactly as with sorrel.

~~≈≈~~

Tarte aux Pommes de Terre (in Alsatian, Tréflaï)

POTATO PIE

This is typical of my mother's Alsatian cooking, but it is not a dish that is popular in Alsace. It is a very hearty, heavy, solid thing—so much, that I am always afraid to do it in Lutèce. I would never put it on the regular menu. But once in a while, on a Friday, I make it a special for the day, and whoever eats it, they love it.

There are two brothers who eat at Lutèce together quite often, and they asked me what I ate at home. I described this potato pie, and they asked me to make it the next time they came.

I made a pie, a big one, big enough for eight people. They ate it.

Serves 6

Tarte aux Pommes de Terre (continued)

The First Day

1¾ cups all-purpose flour, sifted,
    plus flour for flouring the
    work surface
¾ teaspoon salt
4½ ounces (1 stick plus 1 table-
    spoon) unsalted butter

1 egg yolk, lightly beaten with
    enough ice water to make
    ¼ cup

The Second Day

5 ounces bacon (mild smoked),
    cut crosswise in ¼-inch
    strips
1¼ pounds smooth-skinned
    Long Island or Maine pota-
    toes, peeled, cut in ⅛-inch
    slices
¼ cup chopped parsley (chopped
    fine)

salt
pepper, fresh ground
5 small hardboiled eggs (page
    119), peeled and sliced thin
½ cup crème fraîche (or heavy
    cream)
1 egg beaten with a little cold
    water

The First Day

1. Mix the flour and salt in a bowl. Rub in the butter with the finger-tips until the mixture resembles coarse cornmeal. Make a well in the center, pour in the egg yolk beaten with water, and incorporate it into the mixture with the fingers until the mixture is just moistened.

2. With a cupped hand gather this dough into a ball. On a floured work surface, quickly roll it out into a rectangle. Fold it in thirds, enclose it in plastic wrap, and refrigerate it overnight.

The Second Day

3. In a skillet, gently sauté the bacon for a minute or two, stirring, until it is just wilted and browned on the edges. Drain the bacon.

4. Divide the dough into 2 equal parts. Roll ½ of it into a round about 12 inches across and fit it into a 9-inch pie pan. Leave the excess pastry in place, hanging over the rim. Chill for 10 minutes.

5. Preheat the oven to 400°.

6. Wash the sliced potatoes thoroughly in cold water. Drain them and pat them dry. Toss them with the parsley, and with salt and pepper to taste.

7. Arrange a layer of overlapping slices of potato in the pastry shell, using ½ the potatoes. Spread the bacon over the potatoes, and the egg slices over the bacon. Spread the crème fraîche (or cream) over the eggs. Then, using the remaining potatoes, arrange a layer of overlapping slices of potato on top. Fold the excess pastry around the sides over the top.

8. Roll the remaining pastry into a round large enough to cover the pie. Brush the exposed edges of the bottom crust with some of the egg-and-water mixture. Cover the pie, trim the pastry, and crimp the top and bottom layers together around the edges to seal them firmly. Prick the top once or twice with a larding needle or the point of a knife. Brush the top crust lightly with the egg-and-water mixture.

9. Bake on the middle shelf of the preheated oven for 20 minutes. Lower the oven temperature to 350°, and bake 1 hour longer. Lower the temperature to 300°, and bake 10 minutes longer. Let the pie rest at room temperature for 10 minutes before serving.

Note: At Lutèce, we serve this tart as a first course, but at home it is satisfying as a main course when served with a green salad.

꩜

Tarte Flambée
(in Alsatian, Flammeküeche)

ALSATIAN CHEESE TART

The name of the dish, either in French or in Alsatian, refers to a flame—even though there is no flame. But originally, these tarts were baked in a baker's oven, and during the baking the flames of the fire licked into the oven over the tarts.

This is a very traditional Alsatian dish, still popular today, in fact more popular now than it was thirty years ago. In the southern part of Alsace, where I come from, this dish was once rare—but now it is served all over

Alsace. Many Alsatians go to small restaurants for their light evening meal, and this is what they often have—with Alsatian wine.

Tarte Flambée is like pizza, but made with bacon, onion, cream, and fromage blanc. You usually cannot get fromage blanc in America, so I use cottage cheese, and it works very well. To those of my customers who do not mind having food that is not so fancy once in a while—as long as it tastes good—I occasionally serve this earthy and delicious dish. And when I go home to Alsace, we make a feast of eating Flammeküeche.

Serves 4

7 ounces Pâte à Pain Ordinaire (page 543)	pepper, fresh ground
2 tablespoons peanut oil	½ cup crème fraîche
½ cup fromage blanc, or cottage cheese	¼ pound smoked bacon, cut crosswise in ¼-inch strips
1 tablespoon all-purpose flour	1 small onion (about 4 ounces), sliced very thin
salt	

1. Divide the Pâte à Pain Ordinaire into 4 equal parts, and roll the parts out into 4 rounds, each 8 inches in diameter. The circles will be quite thin.

2. Oil a pastry sheet, using very little of the oil. Put the pastries on the baking sheet. Pinch up a very small edge of each pastry circle. Refrigerate.

3. Put the fromage blanc (or cottage cheese) in a food processor and process until smooth—about 30 seconds. Add the flour, salt and pepper to taste, 1 tablespoon of the oil, and the crème fraîche. Process again until smooth—about 30 seconds more.

4. Preheat the oven to 425°.

5. In a skillet, sauté the bacon and onion in the remaining oil, until the onion is barely tender.

6. Take the pastries from the refrigerator, and spread the cheese mixture over them, leaving a ¼-inch uncovered path between the mixture and the edges of the pastries. Sprinkle the bacon and onions on top.

7. Put the baking sheet, with the pastries, in the

preheated oven, and bake for 12 to 15 minutes—until the pastry is golden brown and the topping is also a little brown. Serve immediately.

Note: This recipe is for the traditional Alsatian way of preparing the Tarte Flambée. But at Lutèce, in place of the Pâte à Pain, we often use Feuilletage Rapide (page 531). Both methods are good, the Feuilletage Rapide a lighter pastry.

❧

Tartelettes de Champignons

MUSHROOM TARTS

This traditional Alsatian dish is excellent with a crisp green salad, even better when served also with a bottle of Alsatian white wine.

Serves 6

1 tablespoon unsalted butter, plus butter for buttering the tartelette molds
½ cup smoked bacon cut crosswise in ¼-inch strips
2 tablespoons chopped shallots
3 cups sliced mushrooms
½ cup dry white wine
salt

pepper, fresh ground
1 teaspoon chopped fresh tarragon
½ pound Feuilletage Rapide (page 531), or Pâte Brisée (page 537)
3 eggs, separated
1 cup heavy cream

1. In a pan, melt the 1 tablespoon of butter. Add the bacon, and sauté for 3 to 4 minutes. The bacon should brown a little. Add the shallots, and sauté for 1 minute more. Add the mushrooms and sauté 2 minutes more. Add the wine, a little salt, and pepper, and cook until the wine is reduced by ¾. Add the tarragon and set aside.

2. Preheat the oven to 325°.

3. Butter 6 tartelette molds about 3½ inches across and ¾ inch high. Roll out the dough to a sheet 1/16 inch thick.

Tartelettes de Champignons (continued)

4. Line the molds with the pastry, and prick the bottoms. Trim the edges so that the pastry fits the molds perfectly. Refrigerate the lined molds for at least 30 minutes.

5. Line the pastry in the molds, bottom and sides, with parchment paper. Fill each mold with dried beans (or lentils or split peas) to hold the pastry in place, and bake for 10 to 12 minutes in the preheated oven. Empty the tartelettes of the beans and remove the parchment paper. Leave the oven on.

6. Beat the egg yolks and cream together and stir them into the mushrooms.

7. In a bowl, whip the egg whites until stiff. Fold the whipped egg whites into the mushroom mixture.

Note: This step may be performed while the mushrooms are warm, but not while they are still hot.

8. Put equal amounts of the mushroom mixture in the prebaked pastries. Bake in the preheated oven for about 25 minutes—until golden brown.

❧

Tartelettes d'Oeuf aux Escargots

EGG TARTS WITH SNAILS

This is an old provincial recipe from Lorraine, a region that borders on Alsace. *Serves 4*

6 ounces Feuilletage Rapide
(page 531), or Pâte Brisée
(page 537)
2 tablespoons (¼ stick) unsalted
butter, plus butter for buttering the molds
2 shallots, peeled and chopped

½ tablespoon all-purpose flour
½ cup milk
1 dozen canned snails, rinsed
and cut in half
2 hardboiled eggs (page 119),
chopped coarse
¼ cup heavy cream

½ tablespoon chopped parsley
salt

cayenne pepper
½ tablespoon bread crumbs

1. Roll out the pastry to a very thin sheet. Butter four 3½-inch tartelette molds, and line the molds with the pastry. Trim the edges so that the pastry fits the molds perfectly.

2. With a fork, prick the bottoms of the pastries. Refrigerate the lined molds for at least 30 minutes.

3. Preheat the oven to 325°.

4. Line the pastry in the molds, bottom and sides, with parchment paper. Fill each mold with dried beans (or lentils or split peas) to hold the pastry in place. Bake in the preheated oven for 10 minutes.

5. Remove the tartelettes from the oven, remove the beans, and remove the parchment paper. Return the empty tartelettes to the oven, and continue baking until the pastry is slightly browned—about 3 to 5 minutes.

6. In a small pan, melt 1 tablespoon of butter. Add the shallots, and sauté for 2 minutes. *Do not brown.* Whisk in the flour and cook for 1 minute more.

7. Remove the pan from the heat. Add the milk and stir it in until the mixture is smooth, with no lumps. Return the pan to the heat, bring it to the boil, and cook gently for 5 minutes.

8. Stir in the snails, eggs, cream, and parsley. Add salt and cayenne pepper to taste. Pour this mixture into the tartelettes. Sprinkle the tops with the bread crumbs. Cut the remaining butter in little pieces and spread the pieces over the tops.

9. Put the tarts in the oven, and bake until the bread crumbs are golden brown—about 10 minutes. Serve hot.

A typical tasting menu dinner at Lutèce in the 1980s and 1990s (half portions—or even smaller portions)

Croissant de Truffe (PAGE 206)

Potage Cressonière aux Huîtres (PAGE 89)

Terrine de Homard (PAGE 132)

Saumon Glacé à la Mousse de Moutarde
(PAGE 157)

Sorbet au Kirsch (PAGE 458)

Pigeon Rôti aux Figues (PAGE 299)

Bibeleskaes (PAGE 236)

Beignets de Pommes (PAGE 428)

Tarte au Chocolat (PAGE 466)

SALADS AND OTHER COLD APPETIZERS

IN THE 1980s it was fashionable for people to go to the fashionable restaurants and order the "tasting menu." For these tasting menus, the chef would send out many different dishes, so that the customers could sample a large selection from his repertoire. Usually, the dishes were chosen by the chef. I never thought of Lutèce as so fashionable, but many people asked me to do these tasting menus, and I obliged.

Then the fashion passed. People do not want tasting menus so much anymore. But once in a while, someone will ask me to do it, and then I send out a series of dishes something like those on the menu that introduces this chapter. What exactly I include depends on the time of the year, and on what dishes I am in the mood to make, and also on what I think these people will enjoy.

In one way, for sure, this tasting menu is different from all other tasting menus. It includes a dish—Bibeleskaes, from this chapter of Salads and Other Cold Appetizers—that is as plain as food can be. Most chefs do not think that such food shows off their talent. But I think Bibeleskaes is delicious, and I think also that it fits very well with the more ambitious dishes.

Bibeleskaes
(in French, Fromage Blanc)

ALSATIAN GARLIC-FLAVORED COTTAGE CHEESE

In Lutèce we serve this as a cheese course—it is very good with walnut bread, though any good bread will do. But at home, in Alsace, this plain food is a main course, eaten with boiled potatoes.

Today the dish is made with cheese, but my mother remembers that when she was a child, when this was the food of poor people, it was made of milk that was allowed to separate—to turn.

She remembers also that in those days it was sold from wagons in the streets. The venders would call out their wares—"*Bibela . . . Bibela . . . Bibeleskaes!*"

Bibeleskaes is made also in Lyon. There it is called "cervelle de canus," which means "silk worker's brain." Maybe it means that the brains of the poor people who used to work silk in their houses were turned into cheese by their labor.   *Serves 6*

2 cups small-curd cottage cheese	germs removed, and
salt	chopped fine
pepper, fresh ground	1 tablespoon chopped parsley
2 garlic cloves, peeled, green	½ cup crème fraîche

1. Push the cheese through a sieve, or process it for about 2 minutes in a food processor, to make it into a smooth paste.

2. In a blender, or in the processor, add salt and pepper to taste and the remaining ingredients to the cheese. Blend or process until the mixture is thoroughly combined and smooth—about 1 minute. Refrigerate for several hours before serving. Serve on a lettuce leaf.

Céleri Rémoulade

KNOB CELERY (CELERIAC) IN SAUCE RÉMOULADE

Partly because I have customers who insist that I make it for them whenever they come, I still serve this dish often. It used to be served everywhere, all the time, but it is not so common anymore.

It is good as a first course, and it is perfect as a garnish for pâtés.

Serves 4

1 large knob celery, peeled, washed, and cut in ¹⁄₁₆-inch strips
juice of 1 lemon
2 teaspoons Dijon mustard

¾ cup Mayonnaise (page 515)
salt
white pepper, fresh ground

1. Toss the celery with the lemon juice, and refrigerate for at least 20 minutes.

2. Mix together the mustard and Mayonnaise. Add salt and pepper to taste. Toss this dressing gently with the celery. Serve cool.

Salade de Boeuf

BOILED BEEF SALAD

I have many customers who like French home cooking, and they ask me to make for them the kind of food you usually cannot find in restaurants. For them I sometimes make a dish like this.

When you make boiled beef, you want the soup to have good flavor, so you cannot make it with only a small amount of meat. That is why boiled beef is a common leftover.

Here is a dish that uses up the leftover boiled beef. It makes a good cold light supper at home.

Serves 4

Salade de Boeuf (continued)

1 pound boiled beef (leftovers)
1 teaspoon Dijon mustard
¼ cup vinegar
3 tablespoons peanut oil
¼ teaspoon salt
pepper, fresh ground
1 pinch cayenne pepper

1 small onion, peeled and
   chopped
4 cornichons (small French
   pickles or gherkins), sliced
2 hardboiled eggs (page 119)
1 tablespoon chopped parsley

1. Cut the boiled beef in cubes about ¾″ by ¾″ by ¼″. (You should have about 3 cups.)

2. In a bowl, mix together the mustard, vinegar, oil, salt, pepper, and cayenne pepper. Stir in the onion and the cornichons. Toss the beef with this dressing, and let it marinate in the dressing for 1 hour, either at room temperature or in the refrigerator.

3. Just before serving, arrange the marinated beef on a serving platter. Peel the eggs, slice them into circles, and arrange the slices over the beef salad. Sprinkle with the chopped parsley.

Salade de Champignons et Gruyère

MUSHROOM SALAD WITH SWISS CHEESE

Because it is light, refreshing, and stimulates the appetite, we serve this salad in Alsace just before choucroute. It is also an excellent garnish for charcuterie or pâtés. *Serves 6*

½ pound mushrooms, washed,
   dried, and sliced
juice of ½ lemon

3½ tablespoons peanut oil
2½ tablespoons vinegar
1 teaspoon Dijon mustard

½ teaspoon salt
pepper, fresh ground
1 pound Swiss cheese (Emmen-
    tal or Gruyère), cut in strips
    about 1¼″ × ⅛″ × ⅛″

1 medium onion
1 scant tablespoon chopped
    parsley

1. Toss the mushrooms with the lemon juice.

2. Prepare a vinaigrette by whisking together the oil, vinegar, mustard, salt, and pepper.

3. Combine the mushrooms and cheese, and toss them with the vinaigrette. Refrigerate for 30 minutes.

4. Just before serving the salad, peel the onion and cut it in fine rings. Arrange the onion rings over the salad. Sprinkle with the chopped parsley. Serve cool.

꧁꧂

Salade de Chou Blanc
aux Lardons

CABBAGE SALAD

Serves 6

1 medium green cabbage (as
    pale in color as possible)
1 cup vinegar
½ teaspoon caraway seeds
1 ample teaspoon coarse salt

½ teaspoon white pepper, fresh
    ground
½ pound smoked strip bacon,
    cut crosswise in ¼-inch
    strips

1. Remove and discard the outer leaves of the cabbage. Cut the cabbage in quarters, cut out and discard the core pieces. Wash the leaves, and then cut them in strips ⅛ inch wide.

2. In a large pot, bring the vinegar to the boil. Add the cabbage, caraway seeds, salt, and pepper. Cover, and cook slowly, over low heat, for 15 minutes. The cabbage should remain a little crunchy. Drain the cabbage.

Salade de Chou Blanc (continued)

3. In a skillet, sauté the bacon until it is browned. Pour the contents of the skillet—the bacon and the melted fat—over the cabbage. Add more salt to the salad if necessary. Refrigerate. Serve cold.

Salade d'Endives
aux Noix et Olives Noires

ENDIVE AND WALNUT SALAD WITH BLACK OLIVES

Serves 4

4 endives
2 tablespoons peanut oil
1 tablespoon vinegar
1 teaspoon Dijon mustard
¼ teaspoon salt
pepper, fresh ground

4 walnuts (8 halves), broken into
    smaller pieces
12 black olives, pitted and quar-
    tered
½ tablespoon chopped parsley

1. Cut a conical plug from the bottom of each head of endive and discard. Cut the endives into 1½-inch lengths. Separate the leaves. Wash and dry them.
2. Prepare a vinaigrette by whisking together the oil, vinegar, mustard, salt, and pepper.
3. Combine the endives, walnuts, and black olives, and toss them with the vinaigrette. Sprinkle with the chopped parsley, and serve.

Salade de Pissenlit

DANDELION SALAD

Here in America, dandelion greens grow wild in the fields near my country house. Early in the spring, my wife and I go out and pull the greens from the ground (with their roots, so they will not fall apart), take them home, and make with them salads like this one. (Just before we put the greens in a salad we cut away most of the root.)

There are only about two weeks of the year when you can pick dandelion, usually in late March. It is then that the plants are just appearing, pale green and tender, and are very good to eat.

In Alsace, a dandelion salad is considered health food. Many Alsatians believe that salads of this kind purify and restore the body. This salad is usually served as a garnish, but it is served also as a first course.

Serves 4

½ pound dandelion greens
2 ounces sliced bacon, cut in small pieces
3 tablespoons vinegar
2 slices of French bread, crusts removed
1 tablespoon unsalted butter
1 teaspoon Dijon mustard
½ teaspoon salt

pepper, fresh ground
2 tablespoons peanut oil
1 small onion, peeled and chopped fine
1 garlic clove, peeled, green germ removed, and chopped fine
1 hardboiled egg (page 119)

1. Wash the dandelion greens thoroughly, dry them, and put them in a salad bowl.

2. In a skillet, sauté the bacon in its own fat, and pour the bacon—and the fat it has given off—over the greens. Toss the salad a little.

3. Add 2 tablespoons of the vinegar to the skillet, heat it, and pour it over the greens. Toss the salad a little.

4. Cover the greens, and let them rest for 10 minutes.

5. Cut the bread in ½-inch squares. In the same skillet, melt the but-

Salade de Pissenlit (continued)

ter, and sauté the cubes of bread until they are golden brown and crisp. Set these croutons aside.

6. In a bowl, mix the mustard, the remaining 1 tablespoon of vinegar, salt, pepper, and oil, and whisk them together. Add this vinaigrette to the dandelion greens. Add the onion and garlic. Toss the salad.

7. Slice the egg into circles, and arrange the circles over the salad. Sprinkle the croutons on top.

˜ᴥᴥ˜

Salade de Poireaux, Betteraves, et Avocats

SALAD OF LEEKS, BEETS, AND AVOCADO

At Lutèce, I make this simple and healthful appetizer when people ask me for something very light. *Serves 4*

4 small red beets
4 medium leeks, the white part
    only
2 avocados, ripe
4 small shallots, peeled and
    chopped fine
1 teaspoon Dijon mustard

1½ tablespoons vinegar
    (tarragon vinegar preferred)
¼ teaspoon salt
pepper, fresh ground
2½ tablespoons olive oil
½ tablespoon chopped chervil
    (or Italian parsley)

1. Cook the beets, covered, in boiling salted water until they are tender—about 45 minutes. Peel the beets, cut them in ⅛-inch slices, and set them aside at room temperature. Do not chill them.

2. Split the leeks in half lengthwise, and wash them thoroughly. Tie them in a bundle, and cook them, uncovered, in boiling salted water until tender—about 15 to 20 minutes. Set the leeks aside at room temperature. Do not chill them.

3. Cut the avocados in half—to the seed—lengthwise. Twist the 2

halves in opposite directions to separate them. Remove and discard the seed. Peel off the skin, and cut the avocados in ⅛-inch slices. Arrange the slices decoratively on 4 plates with the beets and leeks.

4. In a bowl, mash the shallots. Add the mustard, vinegar, salt, and pepper. Whisk these ingredients together, and then, whisking constantly, slowly add the oil. Pour this vinaigrette over the vegetables. Sprinkle the salad with the chervil (or the parsley). Serve at room temperature.

Salade de Pommes de Terre

POTATO SALAD

Serves 6

2 pounds firm, waxy potatoes, White Creamer potatoes preferred
salt
½ cup dry white wine, or Fond Blanc de Volaille (page 512)
1 teaspoon Dijon mustard
5 tablespoons (almost ⅓ cup) peanut oil

2 tablespoons vinegar
pepper, fresh ground
1 small white onion, peeled and chopped fine
1 tablespoon chopped chives, or chopped parsley

1. Preheat the oven to 275°.

2. In an ovenproof pot, boil the potatoes, in their skins, in salted water, covered, until they are tender—about 25 minutes. Discard the water.

3. Put the pot of potatoes (its lid a little to the side, to let steam escape) in the preheated oven for 10 minutes. Remove the potatoes from

Salade de Pommes de Terre (continued)

the oven and let them cool partially, from hot to warm. While the potatoes are still warm, peel and slice them.

4. Warm the wine (or Fond Blanc de Volaille). In a bowl, whisk together the wine (or Fond Blanc de Volaille), mustard, oil, vinegar, ½ teaspoon of salt, and the pepper. Stir in the onion. Gently toss this dressing with the potatoes, taking care to break the potatoes as little as possible.

5. Sprinkle with the chives (or parsley). Serve lukewarm—do not refrigerate.

Note: This is a wonderful garnish for smoked pork or sausages.

Terrine de Confit de Légumes

VEGETABLE TERRINE

O f the recipes in this book, this is the latest, introduced at Lutèce in the spring of 1993, and immediately a big success.

Serves 6 to 8

3 tomatoes (must be ripe)
2 medium leeks (the white part plus a little of the green), trimmed and very carefully washed
salt
8 shallots or pearl onions, peeled
8 garlic cloves, peeled
5 ounces olive oil
½ teaspoon sugar
8 medium whole cultivated mushrooms, or wild mushrooms, washed

juice of ½ lemon
2 medium eggplants, washed
3 small zucchinis, washed
3 red and/or yellow peppers, washed
pepper, fresh ground
1 pinch cayenne pepper
½ cup Vinaigrette (page 525)
1 hardboiled egg (page 119), peeled and chopped
1 tablespoon chopped chives, or parsley

1. Cut a conical plug from the stem end of each tomato and discard. Blanch the tomatoes in boiling water for 3 minutes, drain them under cold water, and peel off the skins. Cut the tomatoes in half, squeeze out and discard the juice and seeds. Set aside.

2. Cook the leeks in boiling salted water until tender—about 8 minutes. Drain. Set aside.

3. Put the shallots (or pearl onions), the garlic, 2 tablespoons of the olive oil, the salt, sugar, and ¼ cup of water in a heavy-bottomed skillet. Bring to the boil, and cook, covered, until the vegetables are half cooked—about 5 minutes.

4. Uncover the skillet and continue cooking, frequently shaking the skillet, until the shallots (or pearl onions) and garlic cloves are tender and lightly glazed. (They should brown almost not at all.) Remove the shallots and garlic from the skillet, and set them aside.

5. Put the mushrooms in the same skillet. Add the lemon juice and salt, and cook over high heat until the mushrooms are tender—about 5 minutes. Remove the mushrooms from the skillet, and set them aside.

6. Preheat the oven to 375°.

7. Cut the eggplants lengthwise in ¾-inch-thick slices. Cut the zucchini lengthwise in ½-inch-thick slices.

8. With a fork, spear each pepper and hold it over the flame of a gas burner to singe the skin, turning it until it is charred on all sides. Peel the peppers and remove the stems. Cut the peppers in half. Remove and discard the seeds and white inner pulp.

9. Distribute the eggplant, zucchini, and red pepper over the bottom of a roasting pan. Sprinkle with salt, pepper, and the cayenne. Sprinkle the remaining olive oil over the vegetables, coating them on all sides.

10. Put the roasting pan in the preheated oven for 35 minutes. From time to time stir the vegetables around, being careful not to break the pieces.

11. Line a 2-quart terrine with parchment paper or plastic wrap in which you punch a few holes.

12. Four of the eggplant slices (the outer slices) will have large skin-covered surfaces. Put 2 of these on the bottom of the terrine, skin down,

Terrine de Confit de Légumes (continued)

cutting them to fit if necessary. (Set the remaining such slices aside for the top.) Layer ½ the remaining eggplant over those bottom slices.

13. Spread ½ the zucchini over the eggplant; ½ the peppers over the zucchini; ½ the tomatoes over the red peppers. Spread all the shallots and garlic over the tomatoes. Put the 2 leeks, parallel to the length of the terrine, over the shallots and garlic, and fill out this layer by arranging the mushrooms between and around the leeks.

14. Spread the remaining tomatoes over the leeks and mushrooms; the remaining peppers over the tomatoes; and the remaining zucchini over the tomatoes. Then arrange the remaining eggplant over the zucchini, the reserved outer slices (which have large skin-covered surfaces) on top, cutting them to fit if necessary, skin up.

15. Cover the terrine with parchment paper or plastic wrap. Set a second terrine on top. Put weights in this second terrine to compress the vegetables. Refrigerate overnight.

16. Mix the Vinaigrette with the chopped egg and chives (or parsley). Gently unmold the terrine, and with a sharp knife carefully cut it in ¾-inch slices. Serve on cold plates with the Vinaigrette.

Note: This is a wonderful spring or summer dish. At Lutèce, we sometimes serve it garnished with toasted goat cheese, or with smoked salmon.

Note: The terrine may also be served warm (not hot). To serve it warm, moisten individual plates with olive oil, put a slice of the terrine on each plate, and then brush each slice with olive oil. Put the plates in a preheated 300° oven for a few minutes, until they are warm.

When the terrine is served warm at Lutèce, it is sometimes garnished with a few grilled shrimp; and sometimes we serve it as a side dish with a main course.

Main Courses

A typical lunch at Lutèce today—summer

Gazpacho (PAGE 84)

Blanquette de Sole et St. Jacques (PAGE 251)

Glace Caramel (PAGE 445)

A typical dinner at Lutèce today—summer

Soupe Glacée à l'Oseille (PAGE 102)

Goujonettes de Bass Coulis de Tomates
(PAGE 267)

Soufflé Glacé au Citron (PAGE 462)

SEAFOOD

ONE SUMMER I spent part of my vacation in Italy, on the Italian Riviera. I was traveling with my wife and with my mother. Normally, I enjoy Italian food. But on this trip, everywhere we looked the food was disappointing. For me, that is enough almost to ruin a vacation.

Then one afternoon we were driving in very heavy traffic—it was so heavy that the people who were walking alongside of us were going faster than we were. I saw that one of these people was wearing a white kitchen uniform, and I saw that he was carrying an open box on his shoulder. In this box was a big fish, and the fish was steaming.

The traffic was not moving, we were standing still, so I got out of the car, I gave the wheel to my wife, and I told her that I would catch up with her. Then I ran and caught up with this man who was walking. I wanted to know where he was going with this fish—I thought that it was steaming because it was just poached.

But when I reached him I found out that it was not "steaming" because it was poached, but because it was frozen—in the warm moist air this ice-cold frozen fish only seemed to be steaming. I went back to my car.

In New York also the air is warm and moist in the summer, but the fish at Lutèce is never frozen. I introduce this chapter with two summer menus; one is a lunch and one is a dinner. The menus begin with cold summer soups and end with cold desserts, with main courses of fresh fish—from this chapter—in between.

Baby Bass Farci

STUFFED BABY BASS

E asy to eat (the bones are removed), and attractive (a whole fish, without the head, is served to each guest), here is a light, mild dish.

These little black bass used to be hard to get, and I could make this dish only when one of my suppliers called me up to say he had some baby bass for me. Now I get them all the time.   *Serves 2*

2 baby sea bass, about 1 pound
    each
3 tablespoons (⅜ stick) unsalted
    butter
1 small carrot, trimmed, peeled,
    washed, and cut in very fine
    strips
1 celery stalk, peeled, washed,
    and cut in very fine strips
1 small leek, the white part only,
    peeled, washed, and cut in
    very fine strips

½ small knob of fennel,
    trimmed, peeled, washed,
    and cut in very fine strips
⅓ cup fresh bread crumbs
salt
pepper, fresh ground
¾ cup Beurre Blanc (page 505)
½ tablespoon chopped Italian
    parsley

1. Eviscerate the 2 fish, and remove the heads and gills. With a sharp knife, fillet the fish, but leave the fillets attached to the tail. Remove the skins down to the tail.

2. In a small saucepan, melt 1 tablespoon of the butter. Add the vegetables, and cook them, covered, over low heat until they are soft, stirring once in a while. When the vegetables are ready, put them between the 2 filleted sides of each bass. Press each pair of fillets together.

3. Melt 1 tablespoon of the butter, and butter the outsides of the 2 fish. Spread the bread crumbs on a plate, and set each fish in the crumbs—first on one side, then on the other—to coat the surfaces. Firmly press the bread crumbs onto the surfaces of the fish. Salt and pepper the fish.

4. Preheat the oven to 325°.

5. In a skillet, heat 1 tablespoon of butter, and sauté the fish until

they are golden brown on both sides—about 3 minutes on each side.

6. Put the skillet of fish in the preheated oven for 5 minutes.

7. Transfer the fish to 2 warm plates. Pour the Beurre Blanc around them. Sprinkle the sauce with the chopped parsley.

Blanquette de Sole et St. Jacques

SOLE WITH SCALLOPS

Serves 4

1¼ cups Fumet de Poisson (page 513)

5½ tablespoons (⅝ stick plus ½ tablespoon) unsalted butter

2 tablespoons all-purpose flour

3 threads saffron

½ cup heavy cream

1 medium carrot, trimmed, peeled, washed, and cut in very fine 2-inch strips

1 leek (the white part, plus a little of the green), washed, and cut in very fine 2-inch strips

2 celery stalks, peeled, washed, and cut in very fine 2-inch strips

1 pound fillets of sole

½ pound scallops

1. Bring the Fumet de Poisson to the boil, and keep it simmering. In a saucepan, over medium heat, melt 1½ tablespoons of the butter. Whisk in the 2 tablespoons of flour, the boiling Fumet de Poisson, and the saffron. Simmer, uncovered, for 20 minutes, stirring occasionally.

2. Stirring constantly, and still over heat, add the cream. Then, piece by piece, add 3 tablespoons of the butter. Keep this sauce warm.

3. In a skillet, over medium heat, melt the remaining 1 tablespoon of butter. Sauté the vegetables in this butter for 5 minutes. Add the sole and the scallops. Strain the sauce over the sole, scallops, and vegetables, bring to the boil, and simmer for 4 minutes. Serve hot.

Bluefish Rôti au Persil à la Tomate

BAKED BLUEFISH WITH PARSLEY AND TOMATO

When I first came to America, I looked up the brother of a friend from my hometown. He was stranded in America when the war started, so he got married and stayed here.

He invited me to go fishing with him for bluefish. We went out on a boat from Sheepshead Bay, and we came home with three bluefish. At that time, I did not speak English, so I myself could not explain to his American wife that I wanted to cook the fish for the three of us. Finally she understood.

This is how I prepared the fish, and my friend was very happy. He thought it was the greatest thing in the world—because he had not had much French food after he left home.

Bluefish is a strong, oily fish. I do not serve it at Lutèce. But it was one of the first things I tasted in America that I had never had before. I thought it was delicious then, and I still do.   *Serves 6*

1 bluefish, whole, about 4 pounds, eviscerated, gills removed, scaled, cleaned, head and tail intact	1 large tomato, or 2 small ones, sliced
salt	3 tablespoons (⅜ stick) unsalted butter
pepper, fresh ground	½ cup dry white wine
1 tablespoon chopped parsley	lemon slices

1. Preheat the oven to 400°.
2. Rinse the fish under cold running water. Pat it dry with paper towels. Sprinkle it inside and out with salt and pepper.
3. Put the fish in a roasting pan. Sprinkle the parsley around it. Surround it with the slices of tomato, and dot it with the butter.
4. Bake the fish in the preheated oven, basting it every 3 minutes. When the fish flakes easily when tested with a fork—after about 30 minutes—remove it from the oven, and put it on a hot serving platter.

5. On top of the stove, over heat, add the wine to the roasting pan. Reduce the liquid for 3 minutes over high heat, and pour it over the fish. Arrange the lemon slices around the fish.

Note: Boiled potatoes are the perfect garnish for this bluefish.

Bouillabaisse de Morue

BOUILLABAISSE OF CODFISH

Americans think of bouillabaisse as made with all different kinds of fish and shellfish. But in the south of France, this simple version, made only with salted codfish, is common. *Serves 4*

The First Step
2 pounds salted codfish

The Remaining Steps, 2 Days Later

2 whitings, about ½ pound each
¼ cup olive oil
1 medium onion, peeled and
    sliced
1 small knob of fennel, washed
    and cut in ¼-inch pieces
2 celery stalks, peeled, washed,
    and cut in ¼-inch pieces
1 carrot, trimmed, peeled,
    washed, and cut in ¼-inch
    pieces
2 garlic cloves, peeled, green
    germs removed, and
    chopped

2 tomatoes, quartered
1 tablespoon tomato puree
2 cups dry white wine
1 bay leaf
2 sprigs thyme
5 threads saffron
1 pinch cayenne pepper
salt
2 medium potatoes
1 tablespoon chopped parsley

Bouillabaisse de Morue (continued)

The First Step

1. Soak the codfish in cold water for 2 days. Change the water several times during this period.

The Remaining Steps, 2 Days Later

2. Eviscerate the whitings, remove the gills, wash them under cold water, and cut them in 2-inch lengths.

3. Heat the olive oil in a large, heavy-bottomed pot, over high heat. Add the whitings, onion, fennel, celery, and carrot, and sauté, constantly stirring, over high heat for 5 minutes. The contents of the pot must be kept moving throughout this step.

4. Add the garlic, tomatoes, and tomato puree. Cook for 15 minutes more, still over high heat, stirring frequently, until the contents of the pot are almost a puree.

5. Add 6 cups of water, the wine, bay leaf, thyme, saffron, cayenne, and a little salt. Bring to the boil, cover, and boil very vigorously, over high heat, for 1 hour, stirring occasionally.

6. Push everything through a fine sieve, pressing firmly so that all the solids except the bones are forced through. Return everything that passes through the sieve to the pot.

7. Peel and wash the potatoes, cut them in ¼-inch slices, and add them to the pot. Bring to the boil, and cook for 10 minutes.

8. Cut the codfish in 8 pieces, and add it to the pot. Bring to the boil, and simmer gently, over low heat, for 10 minutes. Do not boil. Serve hot, in soup plates, sprinkled with parsley.

Cervelas de Homard

LOBSTER SAUSAGE—MAY BE PREPARED
WITH MIXED SEAFOOD

I first saw a dish like this in Paris in the 1970s. It was in the restaurant Taillevent. Their sausage was a large one, of *fruits de mer*, from which they sliced portions. But I changed the dish and make it my own way. My sausage is made with lobster. It is a small sausage—like a meat sausage—and I serve these sausages whole.

For a few years, seafood sausages were served in dozens of New York restaurants—it was a fad. Now the fad is over, but Cervelas de Homard is still popular at Lutèce.   *Serves 8*

The Julienne

2 tablespoons (¼ stick) unsalted butter

1 medium carrot, trimmed, peeled, washed, and cut in very fine 2-inch strips

1 leek (the white part, plus a little of the green), washed and cut in very fine 2-inch strips

2 celery stalks, peeled, washed, and cut in very fine 2-inch strips

½ fennel bulb, washed and cut in very fine 2-inch strips

salt

pepper, fresh ground

The Finished Sausages

2 quarts Court Bouillon (preferred) (page 507), or salted water with a little vinegar

2 lobsters, 1½ pounds each

1 pound Mousseline de Poisson (page 527), prepared with pike (or whiting)

pork casing, enough for 8 sausages, each 4 inches long

1 tablespoon peanut oil

1 recipe Sauce Homard à la Crème (page 522)

The Julienne

1. In a saucepan, melt the butter. Add the carrot, leek, celery, fennel, salt, and pepper, and stew, covered, over low heat, stirring occasionally, until the vegetables are soft—about 12 minutes. *The vegetables must not brown.* Set aside and keep warm.

The Finished Sausages

2. In a large pot, bring the Court Bouillon (or vinegared water) to the boil. Add the lobsters, return to the boil, and cook for 5 minutes. Remove the lobsters from the pot, remove the meat from the shells, and cut it into ¼-inch cubes.

Cervelas de Homard (continued)

3. Thoroughly mix together the lobster meat, the Mousseline of pike (or whiting), and the julienne of vegetables, and pack this mixture into the pork casing. Tie the packed casing in 8 equal lengths and at both ends with string, and pierce each sausage in several places with a needle.

Note: The mixture may be put in a pastry bag and then forced from the bag into the sausage casings.

4. In a saucepan, cover the sausages with water. Bring the water *almost* to the boil, and cook gently for 20 minutes. *The water must not boil.*

Note: The dish may be prepared a day in advance to this point. If prepared in advance, the sausages should be warmed in hot water (not boiling water) before you go on to Step 5.

5. In a frying pan, sauté the sausages *very gently* in the oil, about 4 minutes on each side, until they are lightly browned. Serve with the Sauce Homard à la Crème.

⤙⤛⤜

Civet de Thon

TUNA STEW

I n this dish, I prepare the tuna as if it were meat. When it is cooked, it looks like a veal stew.

Serves 4

The Stew

1½ pounds tuna, skinned

2 cups red wine

1 onion, peeled, and cut in ¼-inch cubes

1 carrot, trimmed, peeled, washed, and cut in ¼-inch cubes

2 garlic cloves, broken

1 bouquet garni (page 55)

1 tablespoon vinegar

¼ teaspoon cracked pepper

¼ cup peanut oil

2 tablespoons flour

1 tablespoon tomato paste (or tomato puree)

1 tablespoon Cognac

salt

pepper, fresh ground

The Garnish

16 pearl onions, peeled
5 ounces bacon, smoked or
    salted, cut crosswise in ¼-
    inch strips
1 tablespoon unsalted butter

salt
1 pinch sugar
1 cup small cultivated mush-
    rooms, peeled

The Final Assembly

2 tablespoons (¼ stick) unsalted butter

The Stew

1. Cut the tuna in 1-inch cubes, put it in a bowl, and add the wine, onion, carrot, garlic, bouquet garni, vinegar, and cracked pepper. Refrigerate overnight. The next day, drain the contents of the bowl thoroughly. Set aside in separate containers the tuna, the vegetables, and the liquid.

2. Preheat the oven to 350°.

3. In a skillet, heat the oil and sauté the tuna until it is golden brown—about 3 minutes. Sprinkle the tuna with the flour, and sauté 2 minutes more. Remove the tuna from the skillet, and put it in an oven-proof pot.

4. Add the vegetables to the skillet, and sauté them until they are golden brown. Add them to the tuna, and put the pot in the preheated oven for 5 minutes.

5. Put the pot over heat on top of the stove. Stir in the tomato paste (or tomato puree), the liquid reserved in Step 1, and the Cognac. Add salt and pepper. Bring to the boil, and cook slowly, covered, for 25 minutes.

The Garnish

6. Meanwhile, blanch the pearl onions for 30 seconds in boiling water, and drain. Cook the bacon in boiling water for 8 minutes, and drain.

7. In a skillet, melt the 1 tablespoon of butter. Add the pearl onions, salt, and sugar, and cook over medium heat until the onions are tender and glazed—about 8 minutes. Remove the pearl onions and set them aside.

8. In the same skillet, sauté the bacon for 1 minute. It should brown just a little. Add the mushrooms to the bacon, and sauté until the juice from the mushrooms is evaporated—about 5 minutes. Return the pearl onions to the skillet. Keep warm.

Civet de Thon (continued)

The Final Assembly

9. When the tuna is ready, remove the pieces of fish from the pot with a slotted spoon, and arrange them in a deep serving plate. Rectify the sauce in the pot with salt and pepper to taste. Over heat, stir in the 2 tablespoons of butter. Pass the sauce through a fine sieve over the tuna. Arrange the mushrooms, bacon, and pearl onions on top.

Note: At Lutèce I usually serve this stew with boiled potatoes or buttered spaghetti.

❧

Couscous de Poissons

COUSCOUS PREPARED WITH FISH

The first time I had couscous was when I was in the French army in Tunisia. I was in a mixed regiment; some of the other soldiers in my regiment were Arabs, and the couscous they made was a traditional one, with mutton.

But then, one time when I went into Tunis, the capital of Tunisia, on a weekend pass, in a very small and very humble restaurant I had a couscous made with fish, and I liked it. Now I make it for myself at home.

There are many steps in this recipe, but each of them is easy to do.

Note: To make this dish the standard way calls for a couscousier, a special steamer just for this purpose. If you have no couscousier, it is possible to work with any pot as the bottom pot, and a colander (for which you will need a well-fitting lid) lined with a cloth as a top pot.

Note: The fish you use depends on your own taste and what is available. But you should use a firm fish, such as snapper, or bass, or halibut, or a mixture of them.

Note: The recipe calls for durum semolina wheat cereal (couscous). There are two kinds of this couscous: unprepared semolina cereal (called for in this recipe) and pre-prepared semolina couscous. You may use either kind. You will have a better result using the unprepared semolina cereal, but you will have a good dish either way. If you use pre-prepared semolina couscous, of which there are many kinds, follow the cooking instructions on the package.

Note: Harissa is a hot sauce that is sold packaged in Middle Eastern food stores.

Serves 4

2 pounds fillet of fish (see second *Note*)
salt
pepper, fresh ground
juice of 1 lemon
¼ cup olive oil
1 pound mussels
1 pound couscous (durum semolina wheat cereal—see third *Note*)
1½ cups water, lukewarm and lightly salted
1 small onion, peeled and sliced
1 celery stalk, peeled, washed, and cut in cubes
¾ pound carrots, trimmed, peeled, washed, and cut in pieces 1½″ × ¼″ × ¼″

1 ample tablespoon tomato puree
2 small garlic cloves, peeled, halved, green germs removed
½ teaspoon paprika
1 pound small potatoes, washed, peeled, and cut in ¼-inch slices
1 pound small firm zucchini, washed but not peeled, and cut in pieces 1½″ × ¼ × ¼″
One 10-ounce can chickpeas
2 tablespoons (¼ stick) unsalted butter
1 tablespoon harissa (see fourth *Note*)

1. Wash the fillets of fish and cut them in 8 pieces (12 pieces if you are using 3 kinds of fish). Put them on a plate, sprinkle them with a little salt, then with pepper, lemon juice, and 1 tablespoon of the olive oil. Set aside.
2. Squeeze each mussel in your hand, pushing the top and bottom of the shell in opposite directions. Discard any mussels you can open this way. Scrub the mussels to remove the beards, and wash them in 2 or 3 changes of cold water. Set aside.
3. Put the couscous on a large, deep plate. Using 1 cup of the lukewarm, lightly salted water, sprinkle the couscous with a little of the water.

Couscous de Poissons (continued)

Then roll handfuls of it between your hands. Repeat the sprinkling of the water and the rolling of the couscous until all the water has been absorbed, and the individual grains are well separated. (The process will take at least 5 minutes.) Set aside.

4. Heat the remaining 3 tablespoons of olive oil in the bottom part of the couscousier. Sauté the onion, celery, and carrots for 5 minutes. Add the tomato puree, garlic, paprika, and 1½ quarts of water. Add salt and pepper, and bring to the boil.

5. Put the reserved couscous in the upper portion of the couscousier, and then cover it with a clean cloth or napkin. Put the lid on the top portion of the couscousier, and set the top portion over the bottom portion. Cook for 30 minutes.

6. Remove the lid, and put the couscous in a large, deep plate. With a fork, separate the grains, while sprinkling them with the remaining ½ cup of lukewarm, lightly salted water. Move the fork through the grains until they are well separated.

7. Return the couscous to the top portion of the couscousier, cover it with the cloth, replace the lid, and cook 15 minutes more.

8. Remove the upper portion of the couscousier, and add the potatoes and zucchini to the vegetables in the bottom portion. If necessary, add a little water to the vegetables. Set the top portion back on the bottom and cook 10 minutes more.

9. Remove the upper portion of the couscousier. Take ½ cup of the liquid (bouillon) from the bottom portion, put it in a separate saucepan, and set it aside. Add the chickpeas and the reserved fish to the bottom portion.

10. Remove the top lid. Remove the cloth. Add the butter to the couscous and thoroughly stir it in. Again cover the couscous with the cloth, and replace the lid. Put the top portion of the couscousier back on the bottom, and cook for 10 minutes more.

11. Add the reserved mussels to the ½ cup of bouillon in the saucepan. Cover the saucepan, bring it to the boil, and cook until the mussels open—about 3 minutes. Separate the 2 halves of each mussel shell, keeping the halves that hold the mussels.

12. In a small bowl, with a little of the bouillon from the bottom of the couscousier, dilute the harissa.

13. With a fork, work the couscous again, until the grains are well separated. Put equal amounts of the couscous on 4 plates. Arrange the fish, and the mussels in their half-shells, on top. Surround the couscous and seafood with the vegetables and bouillon. Serve the diluted harissa separately—each guest uses the hot sauce according to his taste.

⌇⌇

Darne de Saumon au Lard

SALMON WITH BACON

When I was an apprentice, poachers would come to the kitchen of the hotel where I worked and sell to my boss salmon they had taken from the Rhine. It was the season when the fish were spawning. He would always buy one or two, because these salmon were fantastic.

Today, most of the salmon that you can buy is farmed salmon. It is all right—but it does not have the real salmon flavor.

So whenever a supplier offers me wild salmon I take it—except when the price is out of the question. Very often this wild salmon that I get is from Scotland, and it is great.

For me, all wild salmon, as long as it is fresh, is better than all farmed salmon. It is certainly better in this dish, where the salmon stays tender and moist and is very tasty.

Note: The word "darne" refers to a slice of fish, like a steak, cut from a fillet.

Serves 4

The Batter

3 ounces smoked strip bacon, cut crosswise in ¼-inch strips
½ cup milk
1 sprig thyme
1 egg
½ cup fresh bread crumbs
½ tablespoon chopped parsley
½ teaspoon salt
pepper, fresh ground

Darne de Saumon au Lard (continued)

The Vegetables and Salmon

½ medium green cabbage (Savoy cabbage preferred), washed, core removed, and cut in ¼-inch strips

1 carrot, trimmed, peeled, washed, and shredded with a vegetable peeler into ¼-inch-wide strips

1½ pounds fillets of salmon, skin removed

2 tablespoons peanut oil

1 tablespoon unsalted butter

salt

pepper, fresh ground

The Sauce

6 tablespoons (¾ stick) unsalted butter

2 tablespoons vinegar

2 tablespoons heavy cream

salt

pepper, fresh ground

The Batter

1. In a small skillet, sauté the bacon for about 2 minutes. Add the milk and the thyme. Bring the milk to the boil, cover, and cook for 10 minutes. Discard the thyme.

2. Put the milk and bacon in a food processor, and process to a puree—about 1 minute.

3. Put the puree in a bowl, and, with a spatula, mix in the egg, bread crumbs, parsley, salt, and pepper. (This is the "batter"—not a real batter, but used as one.)

The Vegetables and Salmon

4. In a large saucepan, bring salted water to the boil. Add the cabbage and carrot to the water, and boil vigorously, over high heat, for 6 minutes. The vegetables should still be a little crunchy. Put the vegetables in a colander, and cool them under cold running water. Drain.

5. Remove any remaining small bones from the salmon with needlenose pliers, or by gripping them between a finger and the tip of a small knife. Cut the salmon into 4 equal scallops. If necessary, flatten the scallops with the side of a cleaver between sheets of waxed paper, to make them of equal thickness.

6. In a frying pan, heat the 2 tablespoons of oil. Dip the pieces of salmon in the batter so that both sides are coated. Fry the salmon in the oil until golden brown—about 4 minutes on each side.

7. In a skillet, heat the 1 tablespoon of butter, and quickly sauté the cabbage and carrots until they are hot—about 2 minutes. Add salt and pepper to taste. Arrange the vegetables on 4 plates, and arrange the salmon on the vegetables. Keep warm.

The Sauce

8. Discard the oil from the frying pan, add the 6 tablespoons of butter, and melt the butter to a beurre noisette—slightly browned. Remove the frying pan from the heat, and add the vinegar. Briefly whisk the vinegar and butter together over heat, until they are hot. Then, still over heat, whisk in the cream. Season with salt and pepper to taste. Pour this sauce on the plates around the vegetables. Serve hot.

❧

Gambas au Beurre d'Escargot

FRESHWATER PRAWNS WITH SNAIL BUTTER

Serves 6

24 freshwater prawns
(preferred), or large shrimp,
rinsed in cold water

1 recipe Beurre d'Escargot (page
506)

1. Preheat the oven to 450°.
2. With a sharp knife, split (butterfly) the prawns, but leave the shells on. Discard the stomach (the small sac behind the eyes) and the intestinal vein.
3. Put the prawns in a gratin dish. Cover them with the Beurre d'Escargots. Put the dish in the preheated oven for 8 minutes. Serve hot.

❧

Gambas à la Nage

FRESHWATER PRAWNS IN BROTH

I make this dish with the beautiful fresh prawns that I get from Hawaii. These prawns are meaty, and they have wonderful flavor.

I order prawns every week, and every week I make them a special of the day at least once. I make them either this way, or as Gambas au Beurre d'Escargots (page 263), or in other variations.

Serves 4

1 carrot, trimmed, peeled, washed, and chopped
1 onion, peeled and chopped
3 shallots, peeled and chopped

1 leek (the white part only), washed and chopped
1 garlic clove, peeled, green germ removed, and chopped

1½ cups Riesling, or another dry white wine
½ cup white vinegar
bouquet garni (page 55), but with a sprig of tarragon instead of the bay leaf, wrapped in cheesecloth

salt
pepper, fresh ground
20 freshwater prawns (preferred), or large shrimp, rinsed in cold water

1. Put all the ingredients, except the prawns, in a saucepan. Add 3 cups of water. Cook slowly for 30 minutes.

2. Wash the prawns, leaving the shells on. Add them to the saucepan and simmer for 8 minutes.

3. Remove and discard the bouquet garni. Remove the prawns and put them in 4 soup bowls. Spoon some of the liquid over them, with some of the vegetables. Serve warm.

Flétan au Curry

SAUTÉED HALIBUT, CURRIED SAUCE

Halibut is not common in France, so I never really worked with this beautiful fish until I came to America. *Serves 6*

2 tomatoes
¼ cup olive oil
1 small onion, peeled and chopped fine
1 garlic clove, peeled, green germ removed, and chopped fine
1 scant tablespoon curry powder
salt

pepper, fresh ground
1 pinch cayenne pepper
½ cup dry white wine
1 cup heavy cream
1 ample tablespoon flour
2 pounds fillets of halibut, in 12 pieces
1 tablespoon fresh basil cut in threads (or chopped parsley)

1. Cut a conical plug from the stem end of each tomato and discard. Blanch the tomatoes in boiling water for 10 seconds, drain them under cold water, and peel off the skins. Cut the tomatoes in half, squeeze out and discard the juice and seeds, and chop the pulp in ¼-inch cubes.

2. In a saucepan, heat 1 tablespoon of the olive oil. Add the chopped onion, and sauté for 2 minutes. *Do not brown.* Add the garlic, tomatoes, ⅓ of the curry powder, salt, pepper, cayenne pepper, and white wine. Bring to the boil, stir in the cream, return to the boil, and cook slowly for about 10 minutes. Set aside and keep warm.

3. Combine the flour and the remaining curry powder. Dust the fish with this mixture on both sides. Then salt the fish on both sides.

4. In a large skillet, heat the remaining 3 tablespoons of olive oil. Sauté the fish until it is golden brown—about 4 minutes on each side.

5. Spoon the reserved sauce onto 6 hot plates. Arrange 2 pieces of fish on each of the plates. Sprinkle with the cut basil (or chopped parsley). Serve very hot.

Note: Rice is a perfect garnish for this dish.

Gigot de Lotte Rôti

ROASTED MONKFISH

I n France lotte has always been very much in demand, but when I first came to America, I learned that in this country lotte was thrown away. Americans would not eat it because it is ugly to look at when it is whole.

It is still ugly, but nobody throws it away anymore. Lotte, known in America as monkfish or anglefish, is now recognized as an excellent eating fish—so firm that you can make with lotte any dish you usually make with lobster. But this recipe is strictly for lotte.   *Serves 4*

4 monkfish, about 1 to 1¼ pounds each, eviscerated, gills, heads, and skins removed, tails left on
8 sprigs of thyme
8 garlic cloves, peeled, quartered lengthwise, green germs removed

4 slices white bread, crusts removed
1 tablespoon flour
¼ cup olive oil
salt
pepper, fresh ground
1 cup Sauce Gribiche (page 519)

1. With a sharp knife cut away the dark second skins left behind when the outer skins of the monkfish were removed by the fish dealer. Then cut away the yellow fat just under the second skin. Finally cut 2 parallel incisions in each fish: the first incision just to the left of the central bone, the second just to the right. These incisions should extend only to within an inch of each end of the fish, and they should be cut halfway down the sides of the fish, revealing the bones.

2. Lay 1 sprig of thyme in each of the 8 incisions (2 in each fish).

3. Within each of the 8 incisions, pierce the meat of the fish with 4 of the slivers of garlic, leaving each sliver in its puncture hole.

4. Put the bread and the flour in a food processor, and process until you have fine bread crumbs. In a small bowl, mix the bread crumbs with 1 tablespoon of the olive oil.

5. Preheat the oven to 375°.

6. Heat the remaining 3 tablespoons of olive oil in an ovenproof skillet. Salt and pepper the fish, and brown the fish in the oil, tops and bottoms, until they are golden brown—first the tops (where the incisions were made), then the bottoms. The browning should take 3 to 4 minutes on each side. Spread the bread crumbs over the tops of the fish.

7. Put the skillet in the preheated oven for 20 minutes. Baste the fish with the juice in the skillet twice during the 20 minutes. The bread crumbs should turn golden brown.

8. Serve hot, with the Sauce Gribiche served separately.

Note: This dish takes very well to a garnish of boiled potatoes.

Goujonnettes de Bass Coulis de Tomates

SAUTÉED GOUJONETTES OF BASS,
COULIS OF TOMATOES

Goujon is a fish—in English, "gudgeon." So "goujonnette" is a little gudgeon.

But in French cooking, the word always means small pieces from a large fish, with the pieces more or less in the shape of a small fish—a goujonnette.

Serves 4

½ cup fresh bread crumbs
1 tablespoon flour
4 tablespoons (½ stick) unsalted
   butter
1½ pounds fillet of bass
2 tablespoons peanut oil
1 teaspoon salt

¼ teaspoon white pepper, fresh
   ground
½ recipe Coulis de Tomates
   (page 506), hot
1 tablespoon chopped parsley

1. In a bowl, stir together the bread crumbs and flour.
2. In a pan, melt 3 tablespoons of the butter. Cut the bass into pieces

Goujonnettes de Bass (continued)

around 2½ inches long and ½ inch wide, or a little less. Moisten the pieces of bass in the melted butter, and roll them in the mixture of bread crumbs and flour, to coat them lightly. Roll each piece between your hands to press the bread crumbs and flour into the surface.

3. Put the oil and the remaining 1 tablespoon of butter in a large skillet over high heat. When the oil and butter are hot, add the fish in one layer and sauté over high heat until the fish is browned—about 2½ minutes on each side. Add salt and pepper.

4. Put equal portions of the fish on 4 plates, pour the Coulis de Tomates around each serving, and sprinkle with the chopped parsley. Serve hot.

❧

Goujonnettes de Sole, Julienne de Carotte et Nouilles Chinoises

SAUTÉED GOUJONNETTES OF SOLE, JULIENNE OF CARROT AND ANGEL HAIR NOODLES

Serves 4

The Carrot and Angel Hair Noodles

1 carrot, trimmed, peeled, washed, and cut in strips 2″ × ⅟16″ × ⅟16″	2 ounces angel hair noodles

The Beurre Blanc

⅓ cup white vinegar	¼ teaspoon white pepper, fresh ground
½ cup dry white wine	
2 tablespoons chopped shallots	¼ pound (1 stick) unsalted butter, cut in small pieces
½ teaspoon salt	

The Sole

½ cup fresh bread crumbs	4 tablespoons (½ stick) unsalted butter
1 tablespoon all-purpose flour	

1½ pounds fillet of sole
2 tablespoons peanut oil
1 teaspoon salt

¼ teaspoon white pepper, fresh
   ground

The Final Assembly

1 tablespoon chopped parsley

The Carrot and Angel Hair Noodles

1. Blanch the carrot in boiling water for 1 minute. Immediately cool it in ice water. Drain. Set aside.

2. Soak the noodles in cold water for 10 minutes. Cook them in boiling salted water for 4 to 5 minutes. Cool them under cold running water. Drain. Set aside.

The Beurre Blanc

3. In a saucepan, combine the vinegar, wine, shallots, salt, and pepper. Cook over medium heat until the mixture is syrupy.

4. Reduce the heat to low. Whisk in the butter, piece by piece, strain the sauce through a fine sieve, and keep it warm.

The Sole

5. In a bowl, stir together the bread crumbs and flour.

6. In a pan, melt 3 tablespoons of the butter. Cut the sole into pieces around 2½ inches long and ½ inch wide or a little less. Moisten the pieces of sole in the melted butter, and roll them in the mixture of bread crumbs and flour to coat them lightly. Roll each piece between your hands to press the bread crumbs and flour into the surface.

7. Bring a saucepan of salted water to the boil and keep it simmering.

8. Put the oil and the remaining 1 tablespoon of butter in a large skillet over high heat. When the oil and butter are hot, add the fish in one layer and sauté over high heat until the fish is browned—about 2½ minutes on each side. Add salt and pepper. Keep warm.

Goujonnettes de Sole (continued)

The Final Assembly

9. Toss the carrot and noodles together, heat them quickly in the boiling water. Drain.

10. Put equal amounts of the carrot and noodles onto 4 hot plates. Arrange the fish over the carrot and noodles. Add the chopped parsley to the beurre blanc and pour it around each serving. Serve hot.

❦

Homard au Beurre d'Escargot

LOBSTER WITH SNAIL BUTTER

Serves 2

1 live lobster, about 1¼ pounds
3 tablespoons (⅜ stick) unsalted
   butter, softened
1 scant tablespoon chopped
   parsley (chopped fine)
2 shallots, peeled and chopped
   fine

1 garlic clove, peeled, green
   germ removed, and chopped
   fine ·
¼ teaspoon salt
pepper, fresh ground
1 tablespoon Pernod (preferred),
   or Ricard

1. Preheat the oven to 450°.

2. With a sharp knife, split the lobster in half. Remove and discard the stomach (the small bag behind the eyes) and the intestinal vein. Put the lobster halves in a gratin dish, the exposed meat up.

3. In a bowl, thoroughly mix the other ingredients. Spread this mixture over the lobster and bake in the preheated oven for 10 minutes. Serve hot.

Gratin de Morue au Fromage

FRESH CODFISH, CHEESE GRATIN

The main difference between Lutèce and the other more formal French restaurants in New York—and in the rest of the country, and even in France—is that most of those restaurants would never serve a dish like this. Maybe they think it would destroy their image, or maybe they think that such dishes cannot be sold at their prices.

The result is that most people who choose to eat only in the most expensive restaurants never get the real home cooking, which is too bad.

But whoever comes to Lutèce and wants me to cook for them such dishes—dishes you do not usually get in four-star restaurants—they always come back for more. This is one of those dishes.

In France this Gratin de Morue is served on Good Friday. I do not know why. Whatever the reason, at Lutèce, on Good Friday, we serve it to the staff.

Serves 4

1 cup milk
1 bouquet garni (page 55)
salt
pepper, fresh ground
1½ pounds fillets of fresh cod-
    fish
1 tablespoon unsalted butter,
    plus butter for buttering the
    gratin dish
1 medium onion, peeled and
    chopped fine
2 medium leeks (the white parts
    only), washed and chopped
    fine

1 garlic clove, peeled, green
    germ removed, and chopped
    fine
2 tablespoons tarragon vinegar
2 cups heavy cream
1¼ cups grated Swiss cheese
    (Emmental or Gruyère)
2 slices of white bread, crusts
    removed, toasted, processed
    in a food processor to make
    bread crumbs

1. In a pot, combine the milk with 2 cups of water, the bouquet garni, a little salt, and pepper, and bring to the boil. Add the codfish, return the

Gratin de Morue au Fromage (continued)

pot to the boil, and simmer slowly for 8 minutes. Drain the fish and keep it warm. (Discard the liquid and the bouquet garni.)

2. In a saucepan, melt the 1 tablespoon of butter. Add the onion and leeks, and cook slowly until the vegetables are soft—about 8 minutes. *Do not brown.* Add the garlic, vinegar, cream, salt, and pepper, and cook slowly until the sauce is slightly thick—about 10 minutes.

3. Preheat the oven to 300°.

4. Flake the codfish, removing any remaining bones as you do so.

5. Butter a gratin dish. Put ½ the onion, leeks, and their liquid in the gratin dish. Spread ½ the cheese on top. Spread the codfish over the grated cheese, and spread the remainder of the onion, leeks, and their liquid over the fish.

6. In a small bowl, mix the bread crumbs with the remainder of the grated cheese. Add this mixture to the gratin dish, spreading it evenly over the top.

7. Put the gratin dish in the preheated oven for 30 minutes. If at this point the top is not golden brown, brown it by putting the dish under the broiler until the top browns. Serve hot.

Note: This Gratin de Morue may also be prepared with salted codfish. To make it that way, start by desalting the fish, soaking it in cold water for 24 hours, and changing the water 3 times during the 24-hour period.

✥

Navarin de Homard

LOBSTER IN PERNOD CREAM SAUCE

Originally, a "navarin" was a lamb stew. Then people started calling all kinds of stews "navarins." French cooking dictionaries still say that this is wrong, even though people have been calling all kinds of stews "navarins" for fifty years.

I do this dish at home, and I do it at Lutèce also. It is old-fashioned cooking, and delicious, though the way we present it in the restaurant—with a julienne of vegetables—is modern. *Serves 6*

3 live lobsters, 1¼ pounds each
1 tomato
6 tablespoons (¾ stick) unsalted
    butter
1 cup carrots, trimmed, peeled,
    washed, and cut in strips 2"
    × ¹⁄₁₆" × ¹⁄₁₆"
1 cup celery, peeled, washed, and
    cut in strips 2" × ¹⁄₁₆" × ¹⁄₁₆"
1 cup leeks, white part only,
    washed, and cut in strips 2"
    × ¹⁄₁₆" × ¹⁄₁₆"

¼ cup peanut oil
½ cup Pernod or Ricard
1½ cups heavy cream
1 teaspoon coarse salt, plus salt
    to taste
pepper, fresh ground
½ pound fresh sea scallops
1 tablespoon parsley, chopped
    fine
1 tablespoon chives, chopped
    fine

1. Put one of the lobsters on a cutting board. Cut the tail from the body at the joint. Then cut the tail into 4 sections. Twist and pull off the 2 large claws. Break each claw into 2 pieces at the joint. Cut the body in half lengthwise. Remove and discard the stomach (the small bag behind the eyes) and the intestinal vein.

2. Repeat Step 1 with each of the other lobsters.

3. Cut a conical plug from the stem end of the tomato and discard. Blanch the tomato in boiling water for 10 seconds, drain it under cold water, and peel off the skin. Cut the tomato in half, squeeze out and discard the juice and seeds, and chop the pulp in ¼-inch cubes.

4. Heat 1 tablespoon of the butter in a sauté pan over medium-low heat. When the foam subsides, add the carrots, celery, and leeks, and sauté for 5 minutes. Set aside in a warm place.

5. Heat the oil in a large skillet until it is sizzling. Add all the lobster pieces, and sauté, turning once or twice, until the shells just begin to turn red—2 to 3 minutes. Add 1 tablespoon of the butter and continue to sauté until the shells are all red—1 to 2 minutes.

6. Add the Pernod (or Ricard) and ignite it. When the flame subsides, add the cream, the tomato, the 1 teaspoon of coarse salt, and pepper. Cook for 6 minutes.

7. Add the scallops, and cook for 2 minutes. With a slotted spoon, remove the lobster and scallops to a warm serving platter and keep warm.

8. Add the parsley and chives to the skillet. Then, 1 tablespoon at a time, stir in the remaining butter, adding another piece only when the pre-

vious piece has been incorporated into the sauce. Check for seasoning, and, if needed, add salt and pepper.

9. Strain the sauce over the lobster. Scatter the vegetables on top. Serve immediately.

❧

Matelote d'Anguille au Vin Rouge

EELS IN RED WINE

To most French people, when they see the word "matelote" they think of red wine. But when Alsatians see the word "matelote," they think of white wine—because almost all Alsatian wine is white. In making this dish with red wine I am going back to my days in Paris.

If you want to make a typical Alsatian matelote, there is a recipe for one on page 368, Matelote de Poissons au Riesling. *Serves 4*

2 pounds eel, eviscerated, skinned, and washed
2 cups red wine
1 medium onion, peeled and cut in ¼-inch dice
1 carrot, trimmed, peeled, washed, and cut in ¼-inch dice
1 garlic clove, cracked
¼ cup Cognac
1 bouquet garni (page 55)
20 pearl onions, peeled
2 ounces smoked bacon, cut crosswise in ¼-inch pieces
¼ pound (1 stick) unsalted butter

salt
pepper, fresh ground
1 cup Fumet de Poisson (page 513), or water (see *Note* on page 58)
1 pinch sugar
½ pound small mushrooms, washed and drained
2 slices white bread, trimmed, each slice cut in 4 triangles
3 ample tablespoons all-purpose flour
1 tablespoon chopped parsley

1. Cut the eel in 2½-inch lengths. Put the eel in a bowl, and add the wine, onion, carrot, garlic, Cognac, and bouquet garni. Refrigerate overnight (preferably), or for at least 4 hours.

2. The next day (or at least 4 hours later), drain the contents of the bowl. Set aside the vegetables (with the bouquet garni), the eel, and the liquid in 3 separate containers.

3. Blanch the pearl onions for 30 seconds in boiling water. Drain. Set aside.

4. Cook the bacon in boiling water for 8 minutes. Drain. Set aside.

5. In a sauté pan, melt 2 tablespoons of the butter. Add the eel, the reserved vegetables, salt, and pepper. Sauté over low heat for 5 minutes, but *do not brown.*

6. Add the reserved liquid and Fumet de Poisson (or water) to the sauté pan, and bring to the boil. Cover, and cook slowly for 12 to 15 minutes.

7. In a skillet, melt 1 tablespoon of the butter. Add the pearl onions, salt, and sugar, and cook over medium heat until the onions are tender and glazed—about 8 minutes. Remove the pearl onions and set them aside.

8. In the same skillet, sauté the bacon for 1 minute. It should brown just a little. Add the mushrooms, and sauté until the juice from the mushrooms is cooked off—about 5 minutes. Return the pearl onions to this skillet. Set aside and keep warm.

9. In a frying pan, melt 2 tablespoons of the butter, and fry the triangles of bread until they are golden brown.

10. In a saucepan, melt 1 tablespoon of the butter. Mix in the flour, and cook slowly for about 5 minutes. *Do not brown.* Let cool to room temperature.

11. With a slotted spoon, put the eel in a deep serving dish, and keep it warm. Pour the liquid the eel cooked in into the butter and flour. Then, whisking vigorously and constantly, bring this mixture to the boil. Lower the heat and cook gently for 10 minutes, stirring occasionally. Still over heat, whisk the remaining 2 tablespoons of butter into this sauce. Strain through a fine sieve over the eel.

12. Arrange the bacon, mushrooms, and pearl onions over the eel. Distribute the triangles of toasted bread around the eel. Sprinkle with the parsley. Serve hot.

Osso Buco de Lotte

MONKFISH IN THE SHAPE OF OSSO BUCO

This dish gets its odd name from the fact that when the fish is cut into portions, with the center bone running through, each portion looks like a small veal shank—osso buco.   *Serves 4*

1 monkfish, about 4½ pounds, eviscerated, head, gills, tail, and skin removed, net weight about 2½ pounds
salt
pepper, fresh ground
flour for dredging
2 tomatoes
3 tablespoons peanut oil
½ cup chopped onions in ¼-inch dice
½ cup chopped carrots in ¼-inch dice
½ cup chopped celery in ¼-inch dice

4 garlic cloves, peeled, green germs removed, and chopped fine
1½ cups dry white wine
1 cup Fond de Veau (page 510), or water (see *Note* on page 58)
1 bay leaf
2 sprigs thyme
½ teaspoon grated orange rind
½ teaspoon grated lemon rind
1 tablespoon chopped parsley

1. With a sharp knife, cut away the dark second skin of the monkfish left behind when the outer skin was removed. Then cut away the yellow fat just under the second skin. Finally, cut the fish into 4 portions—these will be, approximately, 2½-inch lengths of fish. Season the sections of fish with salt and pepper, and dredge them with flour.

2. Cut a conical plug from the stem end of each tomato and discard. Blanch the tomatoes in boiling water for 10 seconds, drain them under cold water, and peel off the skins. Cut the tomatoes in half, squeeze out and discard the juice and seeds, and chop the pulp in ¼-inch cubes.

3. In a heavy-bottomed skillet, heat 2 tablespoons of the oil. Add the

fish and brown over medium heat, about 4 minutes on each side. Remove the fish from the skillet, set it aside, and keep it warm.

4. Add the remaining 1 tablespoon of oil to the skillet, then the onions, carrots, and celery. Sauté, stirring from time to time, until very lightly browned—about 5 minutes. Add the garlic, and sauté 1 minute more.

5. Add the tomatoes, wine, Fond de Veau (or water), bay leaf, thyme, and salt and pepper to taste. Add the fish. Bring to the boil, cover, and simmer for 15 minutes.

6. Add the orange rind and lemon rind, and continue to simmer, covered, for 5 minutes more.

7. Arrange the fish on a serving plate, and pour over it the sauce from the skillet. Sprinkle with chopped parsley, and serve.

Note: At Lutèce we usually garnish the Osso Buco de Lotte with buttered spaghetti.

Pompano Braisé à la Julienne de Légumes

BRAISED POMPANO WITH
JULIENNE OF VEGETABLES

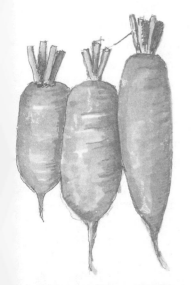

When I first tasted this American fish in restaurants, I thought it was terrible, a disaster. That was long ago, when all the pompano in New York was frozen. Today I can get fresh pompano whenever I want it, and now I know that it is a wonderful fish.

But with this fish especially, you must be very careful not to overcook—it is very easy for a pompano to become dry and to lose its flavor. *Serves 4*

Pompano Braisé (continued)

1½ tablespoons unsalted butter, plus butter for buttering the roasting pan

¾ cup julienned carrots, trimmed, peeled, washed, and cut in strips 2″ × ¹⁄₁₆″ × ¹⁄₁₆″

¾ cup julienned celery, peeled, washed, and cut in strips 2″ × ¹⁄₁₆″ × ¹⁄₁₆″

½ cup julienned leeks (the white part only), washed and cut in strips 2″ × ¹⁄₁₆″ × ¹⁄₁₆″

2 ample tablespoons shallots chopped fine

salt

pepper, fresh ground

2 pompanos, 1¾ to 2 pounds each, filleted

1 cup dry white wine

½ cup Fond Blanc de Volaille (page 512), or water (see *Note* on page 58)

1 cup heavy cream

juice of ½ lemon

1 tablespoon chopped parsley

1. In a saucepan, melt the 1½ tablespoons of butter. Add the vegetables, stir, cover, and cook over low heat for about 10 minutes—until they are softened, but not overcooked. Drain the vegetables, retaining the small amount of liquid. Set aside, separately, the vegetables and the liquid.

2. Preheat the oven to 300°.

3. Butter the bottom of a roasting pan that is big enough to hold all the pompano fillets in one layer. Spread the chopped shallots over the bottom of the roasting pan. Salt and pepper the fillets on both sides and arrange them over the shallots. Add the wine and Fond Blanc de Volaille (or water), and bring *almost* to the boil on top of the stove.

4. Cover the fish with a sheet of parchment paper that has been cut to just fit inside the roasting pan. Put the pan in the preheated oven for 12 to 15 minutes. Remove the pan from the oven. Put the juice from the roasting pan into a saucepan, but leave the fish in the roasting pan, and keep it warm.

5. Add the reserved liquid from Step 1 to the saucepan. Add the cream, and bring to the boil. Cook until this sauce thickens slightly. Add the lemon juice, salt and pepper to taste, and strain over the reserved vegetables.

6. Bring the sauce and vegetables to the boil, and simmer for 2 to 3 minutes.

7. Put the pompano on 4 plates. Surround the fish with the sauce and vegetables. Sprinkle with the parsley. Serve hot.

~~∗~~

Red Snapper à la Vapeur d'Algues

RED SNAPPER STEAMED WITH SEAWEED

Serves 4

1 pound seaweed (for
   presentation)
salt
1 red snapper, about 3 pounds,

eviscerated, gills removed,
   and scaled
pepper, fresh ground

1. Blanch the seaweed in salted boiling water for 1 minute. Cool it in ice water, to obtain a nice green color.

Note: This seaweed is prepared only for the presentation of the dish, and is not meant to be eaten.

2. Put ⅓ of the seaweed in a fish kettle, preferably one with a steaming platform. (If there is a steaming platform, the seaweed should be under it.) Add 1 cup of water and salt.

3. Wash the fish, salt and pepper it inside and out, and put it on the steaming platform. (If there is no steaming platform, put the fish directly on the seaweed in the water.) Cover the snapper with another ⅓ of the seaweed. Cover the pot with its lid or, tightly, with aluminum foil. Bring to the boil, and let it boil gently for 20 minutes.

4. When the snapper is ready, carefully separate it from the seaweed, put it on a long fish plate, and surround it with the remaining ⅓ of the seaweed for the presentation.

5. After presenting the fish, peel away the skin, separate the meat from the bones, and serve. The snapper *must* be served at once, otherwise it will dry out.

Note: Serve with Sauce Choron (page 521) or with Sauce Hollandaise (page 519). At Lutèce the snapper is often garnished with boiled potatoes.

Sole à la Catalane

TOMATOES STUFFED WITH PAUPIETTES OF SOLE

This is one hundred percent a classic French dish, which means it is in Escoffier, which is to French chefs the Bible.

In 1968 I was given the award Meilleur Ouvrier de France, the first time anyone got this award who was working outside of France.

To win, you have to take a test. In this test you have to make three dishes from Escoffier. This was one of them. I must have done it right, because I won the award. Sole à la Catalane is a tasty dish, and I still make it. *Serves 2 (serves 4 as an appetizer)*

4 medium tomatoes, ripe
salt
pepper, fresh ground
7 tablespoons (⅞ stick) unsalted
  butter, plus butter for buttering the baking dish and
  parchment paper
4 small white onions, peeled,
  sliced thin

2 fillets of sole (about 6 ounces
  each), split lengthwise to
  make 4 pieces
2 tablespoons shallots chopped
  fine
½ cup dry white wine
1 tablespoon chopped parsley
1 tablespoon chopped chives

1. Cut and discard a conical plug from the stem end of each tomato, making as small a hole as possible. Blanch the tomatoes in boiling water for 10 seconds, drain them under cold water, and peel off the skins. Cut a lid from the smooth bottom of each tomato (opposite the stem end). With a melon scoop or a small spoon, carefully remove the pulp and seeds from the tomatoes, leaving a neat shell.

2. Put the tomatoes, stem end down, their lids in place, in a small buttered baking dish, and sprinkle them with salt and pepper.

3. In a small skillet, heat 1 tablespoon of the butter. Add the onions, and sauté over medium heat until they are soft but not browned—around 5 to 7 minutes. Spoon ¼ of the onions into each of the tomatoes.

4. Preheat the oven to 300°.

5. On a work surface, flatten the fillets by lightly tapping them with the side of a wide knife blade or cleaver. Carefully roll up each fillet, beginning with the small (tail) end, and with the shiny-skinned surface inside.

6. Lightly butter a shallow, flameproof baking dish into which the rolled fillets will fit snugly. Scatter the chopped shallots in the baking dish, and then arrange the rolled fillets over the shallots. Add a little salt and pepper. Pour the wine over the fillets, then cover them with a sheet of buttered parchment paper, buttered side down.

7. Put the baking dish over medium heat and bring the liquid almost to the boil. Then put both the baking dish of fish and the baking dish of tomatoes in the preheated oven. Bake until the fillets are just cooked through—6 to 8 minutes. *Do not overcook.*

8. Remove the fish and tomatoes from the oven. Remove the lids from the tomatoes and set them aside. With a slotted spoon, lift the fillets one at a time, draining all liquid back into the baking dish, and put each fillet, upright, into one of the hollowed tomatoes.

9. Set the pan of fish-cooking liquid over high heat and boil it until the liquid is reduced to a few syrupy tablespoons. Reduce the heat to very low. Whisk in the remaining 6 tablespoons of butter, 1 or 2 tablespoons at a time, adding more butter only when the previous addition has been absorbed and the sauce is creamy and smooth. Strain this sauce into a small bowl. Stir in the parsley and chives and season to taste with salt and pepper.

10. Put 2 stuffed tomatoes on each of two warm plates. Spoon sauce over and around the stuffed tomatoes. Replace the lids. Serve at once.

Truite Grillée à la Crème

GRILLED TROUT, CREAM SAUCE

I used to have a neighbor in the Catskill Mountains who was a chef and also a trout fisherman. In the trout season, he would catch the fish, and he and I would cook them—this way.

In the Catskills, we could cook these trout over a barbecue, but in Lutèce we have to cook them under the broiler. The barbecue is better, because the cream sauce takes on some of the special taste of the barbecue grilling. But the trout we make in Lutèce are very good too.

Serves 4

The Julienne

2 tablespoons (¼ stick) unsalted butter
2 medium carrots, trimmed, peeled, washed, and cut in very fine strips
1 leek (the white part only), washed, and cut in very fine strips

3 celery stalks (or 1 small knob celery), peeled, washed, and cut in very fine strips
salt
pepper, fresh ground

The Trout

4 trout, eviscerated, gills removed
1 tablespoon peanut oil
1 tablespoon butter

salt
pepper, fresh ground
1 cup heavy cream
½ cup dry white wine

The Julienne

1. In a saucepan, melt the butter. Add the carrots, leek, celery, salt, and pepper, and stew over low heat, covered, stirring occasionally, until the vegetables are soft—about 12 minutes. *The vegetables must not brown.* Set aside and keep warm.

The Trout

2. Thoroughly wash the trout under cold running water, and dry them with paper towels. Brush them with oil, and grill them on both sides on a barbecue (or under the broiler) until they just begin to blacken.

3. Preheat the oven to 325°.

4. Butter an ovenproof dish in which the 4 trout will fit nicely, and put the trout in the dish side by side. Add the salt, pepper, cream, and wine. Bake in the preheated oven for about 12 minutes, until the trout are done (the exact time will depend on the size of the trout—they are ready when they are tender).

The Final Assembly

5. Remove the trout from the oven, and gently transfer them to a plate. (Retain the cooking liquid.) Spread the reserved vegetables over the trout. Set aside and keep warm.

6. Reduce the cooking liquid on top of the stove until it thickens. Add salt and pepper to taste. Strain this sauce through a fine sieve over the trout. Serve hot.

Note: Boiled potatoes are the perfect garnish for this trout.

Lunch at Lutèce when the restaurant was new—in the 1960s

Chausson aux Crabes Sauce Béarnaise
(PAGE 144)

Fricassée de Volaille aux Échalotes (PAGE 297)

Bombe au Pralin (PAGE 431)

A typical dinner at Lutèce today—spring

Grenouilles Sautées Provençale (PAGE 148)

Canard aux Framboises (PAGE 287)

Cerises Jubilées (PAGE 433)

A typical dinner at Lutèce today—fall

Sole à la Catalane (PAGE 280)
(served as an appetizer)

Côtelettes de Chevreuil au Poivre Vert
(PAGE 295)

Mille Feuilles à la Mousse de Pistache
Sauce Chocolat Amer (PAGE 448)

℘OULTRY AND ℊAME

WHEN LUTÈCE WAS NEW, the words "Sauce Béarnaise" and "Fricassée" and "Bombe" were familiar on New York menus. You do not see them so much anymore, but if you want an idea of how people ate at Lutèce in those days, I suggest you prepare together the three dishes that make up the first of the menus that introduce this chapter. These are old Lutèce dishes, but I still like them, my customers still like them, and I still serve them. The spring and fall menus are more typical of what I serve at Lutèce today.

The main courses on all three of these menus are in this chapter on Poultry and Game.

Cailles Vigneronne

QUAILS WITH GRAPES

Wild quails are common in the wine regions of France, so in the old days the wine makers' wives—the "vigneronne" is the wine maker's wife—devised dishes of quails and grapes, including this very old one.

Note: This recipe calls for Creamer potatoes, if available—they have great flavor, and the cubes of Creamer potato hold their shape very well.

Serves 2

Cailles Vigneronne (continued)

4 tablespoons (½ stick) unsalted
butter, divided in 3 pieces
6 small Creamer potatoes (or 2
medium potatoes cut in
cubes), peeled, washed, and
drained

salt
pepper, fresh ground
4 quails
20 grapes, seedless
2 tablespoons Cognac
⅓ cup Fond de Veau (page 510)

1. In a heavy-bottomed skillet, melt 1 piece of the butter. Add the potatoes, and sprinkle them with salt. Cover, and cook slowly on top of the stove until the potatoes are golden brown and soft—about 12 to 15 minutes. Shake the skillet from time to time, to turn the potatoes and to prevent them from sticking.

2. Preheat the oven to 425°.

3. While the potatoes are cooking, salt and pepper the quails inside and out. Then truss them.

4. Melt the second piece of butter in another skillet, and brown the quails on all sides. Put the quails, in their skillet, in the preheated oven for 8 minutes. Remove the skillet from the oven, add the grapes, and return the skillet to the oven for 2 more minutes.

5. Remove the skillet from the oven, add the Cognac, and set it aflame. When the flame has subsided, add the Fond de Veau. Cover the skillet, bring it to the boil, and cook for 2 minutes on top of the stove.

6. Remove the trussing twine from the quails. Arrange the birds on 2 plates. Over high heat, stir the remaining butter into the sauce in the skillet, and cook over high heat for 2 minutes. Pour this sauce, and the grapes that are in it, around the quails. Garnish with the potatoes.

Canard aux Framboises

DUCK WITH RASPBERRIES

By now I have served thousands of ducks this way. But there was a time in French cooking when the only fruit you could cook a duck with was the orange. So this is really a modern way.

This is another one of the dishes of new combinations that came along when the so-called nouvelle cuisine was popular. And it is one of those that I preserve even though nouvelle cuisine is almost gone now.

Note: The recipe calls for 8 serving pieces, that is, each leg cut in 2 parts, and each half of the breast cut in 2 parts. It also calls for Fond Blanc de Canard, which may be prepared in advance using the carcass, wings, and neck.

Serves 4

3 tablespoons (⅜ stick) unsalted
   butter
1 duck, about 5 pounds, cut in 8
   serving pieces
2 sugar cubes
2 garlic cloves, unpeeled
½ cup raspberry vinegar

1 tablespoon tomato puree
2 fresh tomatoes, squashed
1 bouquet garni (page 55)
1½ cups Fond Blanc de Canard
   (page 509)
1 cup fresh raspberries

1. Melt 1 tablespoon of the butter in a heavy pot, and brown the serving pieces of duck on both sides over medium heat. Add the sugar cubes and garlic cloves. Cover the pot and cook for 20 minutes.

2. Remove all the fat from the pot. Add the vinegar, tomato puree, tomatoes, and bouquet garni. Cook 10 minutes longer, covered.

3. Remove the pieces of duck from this pot and put them in a second pot, or in a flameproof casserole that can be brought to the table. Set aside.

4. Preheat the oven to 400°.

5. Add the Fond Blanc de Canard to the first pot and boil it until it is reduced by ½. Stir in the remaining 2 tablespoons of butter. Strain this sauce, pushing it firmly through a fine sieve, over the duck.

Canard aux Framboises (continued)

6. Sprinkle the raspberries over the duck, and put the duck in the preheated oven, uncovered, for 2 minutes before serving. Serve hot.

Confit de Canard

PRESERVED DUCK

Note: For this dish, we use only duck legs, which you can buy separately. The duck fat called for in this recipe you can also buy from certain butchers. Of course, if you buy whole ducks, you can use the breasts for other purposes, and the fat rendered from the ducks for this confit. Lard can also be used, instead of the duck fat—but duck fat is better.

Serves 4

salt
pepper, fresh ground
4 large duck legs (the legs of 2
    large ducks), cut in half at
    the joint, yielding 8 pieces
2 bay leaves, each broken into a
    few pieces

3 sprigs thyme
4 garlic cloves, peeled, cut in
    half, green germs removed
4 cups duck fat (preferably), or
    lard

When the Confit Is Served Hot

2 large potatoes, peeled, and cut
    in ½-inch cubes

1. Generously salt and pepper the 8 pieces of duck on all sides. Put the pieces of duck on an earthenware plate. Add the bay leaves, thyme, and cloves of garlic. Cover with plastic wrap, and refrigerate for 24 hours.

2. With a wet cloth, carefully wipe away all salt from the surfaces of the duck.

3. In a pot, melt the fat, and put the pieces of duck in the fat, with the garlic, thyme, and pieces of bay leaf.

Note: The pot should be large enough so that the pieces of duck are not crowded together. The fat should barely cover the duck.

4. Slowly bring the pot up to heat. The fat should become quite hot, but must not boil. Cook for 2 hours, uncovered, until the meat is tender.

Note: The fat should barely simmer, but not boil. If the fat boils, the meat will be dry.

5. When the duck is ready, remove the pieces from the pot with a slotted spoon, and put them in an earthenware terrine. Immediately strain the fat over the duck, and let the duck cool in the fat—first at room temperature; then, when the duck is at room temperature, in the refrigerator.

Note: In this state—with the duck covered by the fat—the duck may be kept for weeks or months. But once any of the duck has been removed from the terrine, the rest must be consumed promptly—within a day or two.
To serve cold, take the duck directly from the fat, and serve.

When the Confit Is Served Hot

6. Slowly warm the terrine of fat and duck until the fat is melted and the duck is warm. Then remove the pieces of duck from the fat with a slotted spoon, put them on a plate, and put them under the broiler until the skin is crisp and golden brown—about 3 minutes.

7. While the duck is being warmed and crisped, sauté the potatoes in 2 tablespoons of the duck fat, until they are browned and crisped—about 12 to 15 minutes. Serve them with the duck.

Note: The duck should be garnished also with a green salad.

Chevreuil en Ragoût

VENISON STEW

There was a time when if I wanted to serve venison, I had to buy the whole deer. What I wanted to serve at Lutèce was the loin, but I prepared this dish to use up the other cuts.

Today, venison is almost like any other meat, and I can buy loins alone. Still, from time to time, I make this ragoût—especially when people who remember it from the old days call me up in advance and ask for it.

Serves 4

The First Day

3 pounds boneless venison (shoulder, neck, breast, or a mixture) cut in 1½-inch cubes

1 carrot, trimmed, peeled, washed, and cut in ¼-inch cubes

1 medium onion, peeled and cut in ¼-inch cubes

2 garlic cloves, unpeeled

2 sprigs thyme

½ bay leaf

1½ cups red wine

½ teaspoon cracked pepper

The Second Day

2 tablespoons peanut oil

1 ample tablespoon flour

1 cup Fond de Veau (page 510)

1 scant teaspoon salt

½ cup smoked bacon cut crosswise in ¼-inch strips

¾ cup button mushrooms (or quartered larger mushrooms), washed

The First Day

1. Put the meat in an earthenware or glass bowl. Add the carrot, onion, garlic, thyme, bay leaf, wine, and pepper. Refrigerate for at least 24 hours.

The Second Day

2. Drain the meat well. Set aside the liquid and vegetables separately.

3. In a cocotte or heavy-bottomed pot, over very high heat, heat 1½ tablespoons of the oil. When the oil is smoking, add the venison. Brown the meat, in batches if necessary, frequently turning the pieces so they color on all sides—5 to 8 minutes.

4. Add the reserved vegetables, and brown for 2 more minutes. Sprinkle the venison and vegetables with the flour. Mix well, and, still over high heat, cook 2 minutes more.

5. Add the reserved liquid and the Fond de Veau. With a wooden spoon, mix thoroughly. Add the salt. Bring to the boil, cover, and simmer gently. The venison will be ready—tender—in 1 to 1½ hours, depending on the age of the meat.

6. While the pot is simmering, blanch the bacon for 2 minutes in boiling water. Drain.

7. In a skillet, heat the remaining ½ tablespoon of oil. Sauté the bacon for 1½ minutes. Add the mushrooms, and sauté for 3 minutes more.

8. When the venison is ready, put the meat on a serving plate. Strain the remaining contents of the pot through a fine sieve over the meat, pressing firmly, so that almost everything passes through.

9. Arrange the mushrooms and bacon over the venison. Serve hot.

Note: Nouilles à l'Alsacienne (page 411) or Spätzele (page 418) are excellent garnishes with this stew.

Confit de Lapin aux Lentilles

PRESERVED RABBIT WITH LENTILS

When I first came to America, I had to go to Italian markets on Ninth Avenue to find a rabbit to cook at home.

In those days, to try to sell rabbit at Lutèce made no sense. First of all, suppliers could not sell me rabbit, because they did not carry it, because there was no demand. And customers would not eat it.

Today I sell ten to fifteen orders of rabbit every evening in Lutèce. Sometimes I make it the plat du jour at lunchtime—confit of rabbit, rabbit sauté, whatever—and sell it out. And when I want to make a rabbit at home I no longer have to go to Ninth Avenue.   *Serves 4*

salt
pepper, fresh ground
1 rabbit, about 3 pounds (a
    fryer), cut in 12 pieces (see
    Note on page 188)
2 bay leaves, each broken into a
    few pieces
3 sprigs thyme
4 garlic cloves, peeled, cut in
    half, green germs removed
4 cups duck fat (preferably), or
    lard

¾ cup lentils
1 carrot, trimmed, peeled, and
    washed
1 medium onion, peeled, and
    stuck with 2 cloves
1 bouquet garni (page 55)
½ cup smoked bacon cut cross-
    wise in ¼-inch strips
½ cup Fond de Veau (page 510)

1. Generously salt and pepper the pieces of rabbit on all sides. Put them on an earthenware plate. Add the bay leaves, thyme, and garlic. Cover with plastic wrap, and refrigerate for 24 hours.

2. With a wet cloth, carefully wipe all salt from the surfaces of the rabbit pieces.

3. In a pot, melt the fat, and put the pieces of rabbit in the fat, with the garlic, thyme, and bay leaf.

Note: The pot should be large enough that the pieces of rabbit are not crowded together. The fat should barely cover the rabbit.

4. Slowly bring the pot up to heat. The fat should become hot, but not boil. Cook for 1½ hours, uncovered, until the meat is tender.

Note: The fat must barely simmer, but not boil. If the fat boils, the meat will be dry.

5. When the rabbit is ready, remove the pieces from the pot with a slotted spoon, and put them in an earthenware terrine. Immediately strain

the fat over the rabbit, and let the rabbit cool in the fat—first at room temperature; then, when the rabbit is at room temperature, in the refrigerator.

Note: In this state—covered by fat—the rabbit may be kept for weeks or months. But once any of it has been removed from the terrine the rest must be consumed promptly—within a day or two.

6. Soak the lentils in cold water for 4 hours. Drain them and put them in a saucepan. Add 2 cups of water. Bring to the boil, and skim off all foam. Add the carrot, onion, bouquet garni, salt, and pepper. Simmer, covered, until tender—about 30 minutes. *Do not overcook.*

7. In a skillet, over high heat, sauté the bacon until about ½ its fat is melted off—about 4 minutes. Add the bacon, *but not the melted fat,* to the lentils. Put the lentils and bacon in a nonmetallic dish.

8. Preheat the oven to 350°.

9. Slowly warm the terrine of fat and rabbit until the fat is melted and the rabbit is warm.

10. Heat the Fond de Veau.

11. When the rabbit is hot, remove the pieces from the fat with a slotted spoon. Put them on the lentils. Pour the Fond de Veau over the rabbit, and put the dish in the preheated oven for 5 minutes. Serve hot.

❧

Dinde Farcie aux Marrons

TURKEY STUFFED WITH CHESTNUTS

In France, we say, Sad is the house that does not have, on Christmas Eve, a turkey to put in the oven. Turkey is not really eaten very much in France, but almost everyone has it for Christmas Eve dinner.

When I came to America, of course I started eating turkey on Thanksgiving—every year, at the home of an Alsatian chef in New York who more or less adopted me when I was a young man in this country.

At Lutèce, I occasionally prepare turkey at holiday times, especially when a large group of customers asks for it in advance. *Serves 8*

Dinde Farcie aux Marrons (continued)

The Stuffing

1 pound chestnuts
2 cups Fond Blanc de Volaille
    (page 512)
1 tablespoon unsalted butter
the turkey liver, cut in 4 parts
the turkey heart, cut in half
2 tablespoons chopped parsley

salt
pepper, fresh ground
1 medium onion, peeled and
    chopped
1 cup milk
3 slices of bread,
    trimmed

The Turkey and the Sauce

1 turkey, around 8 pounds
salt
pepper, fresh ground
1 tablespoon peanut oil
1 tablespoon unsalted butter,
    softened

1 medium onion, peeled, and cut
    in ½-inch pieces
2 medium carrots, trimmed,
    peeled, washed, and cut in
    ½-inch cubes
¾ cup dry white wine

The Stuffing

1. With a sharp knife, score each chestnut once, on the flat side, through the shell. In a saucepan, cover the chestnuts with water, bring the water to the boil, and cook over medium heat for 10 minutes. Remove the chestnuts from the water, 5 or 6 at a time, and quickly remove the shells and the inner skins.

2. Put the chestnuts in a saucepan, add the Fond Blanc de Volaille, and cook for 30 minutes. Remove the chestnuts from the liquid, and break them into coarse pieces—4 to 6 pieces per chestnut.

3. In a skillet, heat the 1 tablespoon of butter, and sauté the turkey liver and the turkey heart for 3 minutes. Mix in the parsley, and season with salt and pepper to taste. Put the contents of the skillet on a cutting board and chop them coarse. Put the onion in the skillet and sauté for about 4 minutes, browning it lightly.

4. In a saucepan, heat the milk. Remove the saucepan from the heat, add the bread, and leave it in the milk until the milk is completely absorbed. Mash the bread with a fork. Mix the chopped liver, heart, and onion with the bread. Then gently mix in the chestnuts.

The Turkey and the Sauce

5. Preheat the oven to 325°.

6. Thoroughly rinse the inside of the turkey with cold water, and dry it with a paper towel. Season the inside of the turkey with salt and pepper. Pack the stuffing into the turkey. Then truss the turkey with string. Season the outside of the turkey with salt and pepper. Put the turkey in a roasting pan. Brush on the oil, then the butter.

7. Roast the turkey in the preheated oven for 2½ hours, as follows: 1 hour on its side; then 1 hour on the other side; then add the onion and carrots to the roasting pan, and roast it for the last ½ hour on its back (breast up).

Note: Throughout the 2½ hours of roasting, the turkey should be basted with its roasting juices every 15 minutes.

8. Remove the turkey from the pan, and keep it warm. Remove all fat from the roasting pan. Add the white wine, ½ cup of water, and simmer on top of the stove for 5 minutes. Slice the turkey, and serve it with the stuffing and with this sauce.

Note: Chou Rouge Braisé aux Marrons (page 401) and Purée de Pommes de Terre (page 419) are excellent garnishes with turkey.

❦

Côtelettes de Chevreuil au Poivre Vert

VENISON CUTLETS WITH GREEN PEPPER

The hunting laws in Alsace are different from the hunting laws everywhere else in France. Large pieces of land are rented out for a number of years, and only the people who rent them can hunt on them.

Because of this limited hunting, game is plentiful, and Alsace is famous for its game cooking. People come to Alsace just to eat game dishes like this one.   *Serves 2*

Cotelettes de Chevreuil (continued)

4 venison cutlets, cut from the loin
⅓ teaspoon cracked pepper
1½ tablespoons peanut oil
1 sprig thyme
½ bay leaf
3 ounces rosé wine (preferred), or white wine
salt

1 tablespoon unsalted butter
½ cup mushrooms, washed and sliced
1 tablespoon Cognac
2 tablespoons heavy cream
½ cup Fond de Veau (page 510)
16 green peppercorns

1. Arrange the cutlets on a plate. Sprinkle them with the cracked pepper, ½ tablespoon of the oil, the thyme, bay leaf, and 1 ounce of the wine. Refrigerate for 4 to 5 hours, and turn the meat every hour while it is marinating.

2. Remove the venison from the plate, and retain the marinade. Dry the meat with paper towels, and sprinkle it with salt.

3. In a skillet, over high heat, heat the remaining 1 tablespoon of oil, and sauté the cutlets for 2 minutes on each side. The meat should be pink inside. Discard the oil from the skillet. Set the meat aside and keep it warm.

4. Melt the butter in the skillet. Add the mushrooms, and sauté them over high heat for 2 minutes. Add the Cognac, and set it aflame. Then add the cream, Fond de Veau, peppercorns, and the remaining wine. Reduce until the sauce starts to thicken. Pour this sauce over the venison, and serve hot.

Note: Good garnishes for this venison include a puree of knob celery, or a chestnut puree, or Spätzele (page 418).

Fricassée de Volaille aux Échalotes

CHICKEN FRICASSEE WITH SHALLOTS

Note: This recipe may also be prepared with a guinea hen, which in French is "pintade."

Serves 2 or 3

12 shallots, unpeeled
salt
1 bunch scallions, the white part only, trimmed (see also the last ingredient listed)
1 chicken, about 2½ pounds, cut in 8 serving pieces, the breast bone and the back bones of the legs removed and reserved
pepper, fresh ground

4 tablespoons (½ stick) unsalted butter
2 shallots, peeled and sliced fine
1 cup dry white wine
1 cup heavy cream
juice of ½ lemon
1 scant teaspoon sugar
¾ recipe Nouilles à l'Alsacienne (page 411)
4 scallion greens, chopped

1. Cook the 12 unpeeled shallots in salted water for 3 minutes. Remove them from the water, peel them, and set them aside.

2. Cook the whites of the scallions in salted water for 3 minutes. Remove them from the water, and set them aside.

3. Season the chicken with salt and pepper. In a heavy skillet, melt 2 tablespoons of the butter, and sauté the pieces of chicken, the skin sides first, over medium heat until browned—about 6 minutes. Remove the chicken from the skillet. Set aside.

4. In the same skillet, sauté the bones until lightly browned—about 6 minutes. Add the 2 sliced shallots and sauté 1 minute more. Add 1 cup of water and the wine, and cook for 15 minutes.

5. Add the cream, lemon juice, and chicken. Cover, and cook over medium heat for 10 minutes.

6. In another heavy skillet, melt the remaining 2 tablespoons of butter. Add the 12 whole, peeled shallots, and sprinkle them with salt,

Fricassée de Volaille (continued)

pepper, and the sugar. Add 2 tablespoons of water. Cook over high heat, *shaking the skillet constantly, so the shallots keep moving,* until they are caramel colored all over—about 8 minutes. Add the whites of the scallions and cook 2 minutes more.

7. Remove the chicken from its skillet, then cook the sauce down over high heat until it is reduced by ⅓.

8. Put the Nouilles à l'Alsacienne on a serving platter, and surround them with the pieces of chicken. Strain the sauce over the chicken. Arrange the whites of the scallions and the caramelized shallots on top. Sprinkle with the chopped scallion greens.

❧

Noisettes de Chevreuil aux Marrons

VENISON CUTLETS WITH CHESTNUTS

Serves 6

½ pound chestnuts
12 small venison cutlets, very
    well trimmed
salt
pepper, fresh ground
4 tablespoons (½ stick) unsalted
    butter
¼ cup Cognac

½ cup dry white wine
1 cup venison stock, or Fond de
    Veau (page 510)
juice of ½ lemon
½ pound button mushrooms,
    washed and sliced
1 tablespoon chopped parsley

1. With a sharp knife, score each chestnut once, on the flat side, through the shell. In a saucepan, cover the chestnuts with water, bring the water to the boil, and cook over medium heat for 10 minutes. Remove the chestnuts from the water, 5 or 6 at a time, and quickly remove the shells and the inner skins. Set the peeled chestnuts aside.

2. Season the venison with salt and pepper. Melt 1 tablespoon of the butter in a skillet and sauté the venison cutlets, about 3 minutes on each

side. The meat must be pink inside. Arrange the cutlets on a hot serving platter, and keep them warm.

3. Discard the butter from the skillet. Add the Cognac and flame it. Then add the wine and venison stock (or Fond de Veau), and cook until the liquid has been reduced by ½.

4. With the liquid still boiling, stir in 2 tablespoons of the butter, then the lemon juice. Strain this sauce through a fine sieve over the venison.

5. In the same skillet, melt the remaining 1 tablespoon of butter, and sauté the mushrooms until almost all the liquid they produce has been cooked away. Add the chestnuts and cook briefly—only long enough to heat them. Distribute the mushrooms and chestnuts over the venison, and sprinkle with the chopped parsley.

Note: Ideally, this dish is garnished with both red cabbage (a recipe for Chou Rouge Braisé aux Marrons appears on page 401); and Spätzele (page 418).

Pigeon Rôti aux Figues

ROAST PIGEON WITH FIGS

When I was in the French army in Tunisia, in 1954, we were not very well supplied with good French food. And sometimes when supplies were delayed our rations were short. So in our spare time, on Sundays, my friends and I went with our rifles to shoot wild pigeons. In the army, I was not a cook, but when we shot these pigeons I did the cooking.

Sometimes we went into town and bought cans of French peas, and I cooked the pigeons with peas. Sometimes I made them with figs—not with the figs you buy today in American or French markets, but with *figues de barbarie,* wild figs, which grew in Tunisia on desert plants that are like cactus.

So in Tunisia the pigeons were wild and the figs were wild. But the pigeons at Lutèce are raised on farms, and the figs are grown in orchards. So this dish of Roast Pigeon with Figs is really a second cousin of what I cooked in Tunisia. *Serves 2*

Pigeon Rôti aux Figues (continued)

6 fresh figs
2 pigeons (squabs)
salt
pepper, fresh ground
1 tablespoon peanut oil
1 small carrot, trimmed, peeled,
    washed, and chopped fine
1 medium onion, peeled and
    chopped fine
1 stalk celery, peeled, washed,
    and chopped fine
2 garlic cloves, peeled, halved,
    green germs removed

1 sprig thyme
1 bay leaf
2 tablespoons (¼ stick) unsalted
    butter
½ cup dry white wine
½ cup Fond de Veau (page 510),
    or water (see *Note* on page
    58)
1 teaspoon tarragon vinegar (or
    another vinegar)

1. Set the figs on a cutting board with the stem down. Cut through the figs as if to quarter them, but cut only halfway down. They should remain whole, but cut open. Put the figs on an ovenproof plate, the cut sides up. Set aside.

2. Preheat the oven to 375°.

3. Season the pigeons with salt and pepper. In a roasting pan, heat the oil on top of the stove, and, over medium heat, brown the pigeons on all sides—around 2 minutes on each surface.

4. When the pigeons are browned, add the carrot, onion, celery, garlic, thyme, and bay leaf to the roasting pan. Put the pan in the preheated oven for 12 minutes. Interrupt the roasting a few times to baste the birds with the pan juices, and to stir the vegetables so that they do not stick to the pan.

5. Melt the butter and pour it over the figs. When the pigeons are half done—that is, after 6 minutes of their roasting—put the figs in the oven (but *not* in with the pigeons) for the final 6 minutes.

6. When the 12 minutes are up, remove the pigeons and the figs from the oven. Remove the pigeons from the roasting pan. Set the figs aside, set the pigeons aside, and keep them both warm.

7. Add the white wine and Fond de Veau (or water) to the roasting pan. Return the roasting pan to the oven and let the liquid simmer for 6

minutes. Then add the juice from the figs (there will be around a spoon-ful) to the roasting pan, and the vinegar.

8. Carve the pigeons by detaching the legs and cutting the breast meat, whole, from the carcass. Spoon the vegetables from the roasting pan, together with the pan juices, onto 2 plates. Arrange the legs and breasts over the vegetables. Surround each pigeon with 3 figs. Serve hot.

Pigeonneaux aux Nouilles Fraîches, Sauce Vin Rouge

SQUAB WITH FRESH NOODLES, RED WINE SAUCE

Note: This dish may be prepared with the breast of 1 Muscovy duckling in place of the breasts of 2 squabs. When prepared with Muscovy duckling, the breasts require longer browning (in Step 2): 10 minutes on the skin side, 2 minutes on the other side, 12 minutes altogether.

Note: At Lutèce, this dish is always garnished with Nouilles à l'Alsa-cienne (page 411).

Serves 2

2 squabs
salt
pepper, fresh ground
½ tablespoon peanut oil
3 tablespoons (⅜ stick) unsalted
butter
2 large shallots, peeled and
chopped

1 tablespoon Cognac
½ cup red wine
½ cup squab stock—use the ~~chicken stock~~
recipe for Fond Blanc de
Volaille (page 512), substituting the carcass and
trimmings of the squabs for
the chicken

1. Remove the breast meat, whole, with the skin attached, from the squabs. Detach the legs. Season the breasts and legs with salt and pepper.

2. In a skillet, heat the oil and ½ tablespoon of the butter until very

Pigeonneaux aux Nouilles Fraîches (continued)

hot. Brown the breasts and legs on both sides, over high heat, for about 8 minutes altogether. Put them on a cutting board and let them rest for 5 minutes.

3. Add another ½ tablespoon of butter to the skillet and sauté the shallots, without browning them. Add the Cognac and red wine and cook for 2 to 3 minutes. Add the stock, bring to the boil, and reduce the liquid by ½.

4. With the liquid rapidly boiling, stir in the remaining 2 tablespoons of butter. Add salt and pepper to taste. Strain through a fine sieve.

5. With a sharp knife, carve the breasts in thin slices. Pour the sauce onto 2 serving plates, and arrange the slices of breast in a fan shape, the legs beside them, on the sauce.

~❧~

Poussin Basquaise

BASQUE CHICKEN

Serves 2

2 large artichokes, bottoms trimmed
salt
1 large tomato, ripe
2 baby chickens, 1 to 1¼ pounds
pepper, fresh ground
2 to 3 tablespoons unsalted butter
3 ounces fresh cèpes (or chanterelles), sliced

1 small garlic clove, peeled, green germ removed, and chopped fine
2 tablespoons dry white wine
2 tablespoons Fond Blanc de Volaille (page 512), or water (see *Note* on page 58)
chopped chives
chopped parsley

1. Poach the artichokes in salted water until they are tender—about 8 to 10 minutes. (The artichokes are tender when you can easily remove an outer leaf.) Cut out and slice the bottoms, and set them aside. Discard the leaves.

2. Cut a conical plug from the stem end of the tomato and discard. Blanch the tomato in boiling water for 10 seconds, drain it under cold water, and peel off the skin. Cut the tomato in half, squeeze out and discard the juice and seeds, and chop the pulp coarse.

3. Preheat the oven to 350°.

4. Season the inside of the chickens lightly with salt and pepper. Truss the chickens with string, so that the legs are up close to the breasts and the wings are firmly in place. (It is not necessary to close the openings.) Season the outside of the chickens with salt and pepper.

5. Melt 2 tablespoons of butter in a heavy pot that is large enough to hold both chickens. Brown the chickens on all sides, until well browned, turning them by the trussing strings. *Do not pierce the chickens with a fork.* Add the third tablespoon of butter if necessary. The browning should take about 5 minutes. Cover the pot and put it in the preheated oven for 12 minutes.

6. Remove the pot from the oven, spoon the sliced artichoke bottoms, sliced cèpes (or chanterelles), and the chopped tomato around the chickens. Return the pot to the oven for 10 minutes. Remove the pot from the oven again, and remove the chickens from the pot. Set them aside, and keep them warm.

7. Put the pot, uncovered, on a burner. Add the garlic, wine, and Fond Blanc de Volaille (or water). Bring to the boil and cook over high heat until the liquid is slightly reduced and the juices and liquids are blended.

8. Serve the chickens whole or cut in half, with the pan juices and vegetables spooned around them, and sprinkled with chopped chives and parsley.

꧁꧂

Poussin Poché aux Petits Légumes, Sauce Suprême

BABY CHICKEN POACHED WITH SPRING VEGETABLES

I usually prepare this dish with young chickens, but it is just as good made with squabs, or with one two-pound chicken instead of the two baby birds.

Serves 2

The Baby Chickens

2 white turnips, small to medium size, peeled and washed, and cut in sticks 1¼" × ¼" × ¼"

2 carrots, small to medium size, trimmed, peeled, washed, and cut in sticks 1¼" × ¼" × ¼"

3 celery stalks (or ½ knob celery, or 1 small knob celery), peeled, washed, and cut in sticks 1¼" × ¼" × ¼"

6 pearl onions, peeled

2 baby chickens, about 1 pound each (or a single 2-pound chicken)

4 cups Fond Blanc de Volaille (page 512)

2 leeks, the white part plus a little of the green, washed, the 2 leeks tied together

½ small cabbage, washed, bound with twine to hold it together

2 cloves

1 bouquet garni (page 55)

salt

10 peppercorns, roughly broken

The Sauce Suprême

1 tablespoon unsalted butter

scant ½ tablespoon all-purpose flour

1 cup bouillon (the liquid from the pot the chickens are cooked in)

juice of ½ lemon

¼ cup heavy cream

1 egg yolk

salt

pepper, fresh ground

The Baby Chickens

1. Wrap the turnips, carrots, celery, and pearl onions in cheesecloth and tie with a string.

2. Wash the chickens inside and out under cold running water. Truss the chickens with string, and put them in a pot. Add the vegetables (in the cheesecloth), all the other ingredients listed under *The Baby Chickens,* and bring the pot to the boil over medium heat. When the bouillon has come to the boil, skim off the foam, and simmer slowly for about 30 minutes.

The Sauce Suprême

3. In a small saucepan, melt the butter. Mix in the flour, and cook for about 3 minutes. Do not brown. Remove the pan from the heat.

4. Remove 1 cup of the cooking liquid from the pot the chickens were cooked in, strain it, and whisk it into the saucepan.

5. Bring the saucepan to the boil, and cook slowly for 10 minutes, whisking constantly. Add the lemon juice.

6. In a small bowl, combine the cream and egg yolk, and, with the saucepan still over heat, whisk this mixture in. Bring back *almost* to the boil. Remove from the heat, and strain through a fine sieve. Add salt and pepper to taste.

Note: If the sauce is too thick, dilute it with bouillon strained from the pot.

The Final Assembly

7. Remove the chickens from the pot. Cut off the legs and breasts, and put them on 2 plates. Remove the vegetables from the cheesecloth, untie the leeks, and untie the cabbage and cut it in half. Divide the vegetables and arrange them around the chickens.

Note: Serve hot. Serve the Sauce Suprême separately.

Poitrine de Canard Sautée aux Pommes en l'Air

BREAST OF DUCK WITH APPLES

Serves 4

2 whole breasts of duckling
  (the breasts of 2 ducklings),
  skin on
salt
pepper, fresh ground
1 tablespoon peanut oil, plus a
  few additional drops
¾ cup Fond de Canard (page

509), or Fond de Veau
  (page 510)
¾ cup natural apple juice
2 apples, Golden Delicious
  preferred
3 tablespoons (⅜ stick) unsalted
  butter

1. Split the 2 whole breasts, making 4 pieces in all. Score the skin of the breasts in a diamond pattern, 3 cuts in each direction. The cuts should go through the skin, and through the fat that is under the skin, *but not into the meat itself.* Season the breasts with salt and pepper.

2. Heat the oil in a skillet. Put the duck breasts in the skillet, skin down, and cook slowly, uncovered, for about 12 minutes. The skin should become golden brown and crisp, and the fat under the skin should be completely—or almost completely—melted away.

3. Pour off some of the duck fat, leaving enough to cook the breasts on the other side. Turn the duck breasts over, and cook them on the other side for 5 minutes. Remove the breasts from the skillet, and keep them warm.

4. Pour off all the fat from the skillet. Add the Fond de Canard (or Fond de Veau) and apple juice to the skillet. Reduce this liquid by ½.

5. While the liquid is being reduced, peel and core the apples, and cut each apple into 8 sections.

6. In a second skillet, heat 1 tablespoon of butter with the few drops of oil. Add the apples to this skillet and sauté them until they are lightly caramelized and just tender—about 4 minutes on each side.

7. Over heat, whisk the remaining 2 tablespoons of butter into the reduced liquid. Strain this sauce through a fine sieve.

8. With a sharp knife, slice the duck breasts. Arrange the slices in a fan shape on 4 plates. Garnish the duck with the apples, and spoon the sauce around the apples and duck. Serve hot.

Note: Either Spätzele (page 418) or rice makes an excellent garnish with this duck.

Poussin Rôti

ROAST BABY CHICKEN

Of all my dishes, the recipe for this simple and very popular chicken dish is asked for the most often by food writers and others. And of all my recipes it has been published the most often. We have served it at Lutèce every day since we opened.   *Serves 2*

2 baby chickens, about 1 pound each	2 small onions, peeled
1 teaspoon salt	2 teaspoons peanut oil
½ teaspoon black pepper, fresh ground	¼ cup white wine
4 sprigs thyme	¼ cup Fond Blanc de Volaille (page 512)
5 sprigs tarragon	2 tablespoons Italian parsley, minced
4 sprigs parsley	1 tablespoon unsalted butter

1. Wash the chickens inside and out with cold running water, and pat them dry with paper towels. Sprinkle the chickens with the salt and pepper, inside and out.

2. Put 2 sprigs of thyme, 2 sprigs of tarragon, 2 sprigs of parsley, and 1 onion in the cavity of each chicken. Truss the chickens with string. Remove the leaves from the remaining sprig of tarragon, and set them aside.

Poussin Rôti (continued)

3. Preheat the oven to 450°.

4. On top of the stove, over high heat, heat the oil in a roasting pan, and brown the chickens on all sides.

5. Put the pan, with the chickens, in the oven, and roast, basting about every 5 minutes, until the chickens are crisp and golden brown—about 20 to 25 minutes.

Note: It is a good idea to throw 1 or 2 tablespoons of hot water into the oven—to create steam—after each basting. This will keep the chickens moist.

Remove the chickens from the oven, put them on a serving platter, and keep them warm.

6. Pour off the fat from the pan, and put the pan over medium heat on top of the stove. Add the wine, and scrape the pan thoroughly with a wooden spoon. Add the Fond Blanc de Volaille, the reserved tarragon leaves, and the Italian parsley. Simmer for 2 minutes.

7. Remove the pan from the heat, and stir in the butter. Pour this sauce around the chickens. Serve immediately.

～✫～

Râble de Lapin à l'Ail

SADDLE OF RABBIT WITH GARLIC

For twenty years I could not sell rabbit in Lutèce. I tried, but no one ordered it. If I suggested rabbit to my customers, they told me that they used to have rabbits as pets, or that they used to play with rabbits in the children's zoo, or something like that, and that they could not imagine eating rabbit.

Then everything changed, starting around 1980. I do not know why. Maybe it was because people wanted low-fat food—rabbit has almost no fat at all.

Anyway, we now offer rabbit every day, and it is very popular. In Alsace, of course, we have always eaten rabbit.   *Serves 2*

20 garlic cloves, unpeeled
2 saddles of rabbit (also called
    the loin)
salt
pepper, fresh ground
1 tablespoon peanut oil
1 sprig thyme

½ cup dry white wine
½ cup Fond de Veau (page 510),
    or water (see *Note* on page
    58)
1 tablespoon unsalted butter
1 pinch sugar

1. In a small saucepan, cover the unpeeled garlic with cold water. Bring to the boil, and boil for 4 minutes. Peel 10 of the garlic cloves and set them aside.

2. Preheat the oven to 325°.

3. Season the rabbit with salt and pepper. In an ovenproof skillet, heat the oil. Add the saddles of rabbit to the skillet, and brown them over medium heat on all sides—about 5 minutes. Add the 10 *unpeeled* cloves of garlic to the skillet.

4. Put the skillet in the preheated oven for 10 minutes. Remove the skillet from the oven. Remove the rabbit from the skillet and set it aside. Leave the garlic in the skillet.

5. Add to the skillet the thyme, wine, and Fond de Veau (or water). Over high heat, reduce the liquid by ½. Then push the contents of the skillet through a fine sieve, using a lot of pressure. Everything should pass through the sieve except the garlic peels.

6. In a small sauté pan, melt the butter. Add the 10 peeled garlic cloves, salt, pepper, and the sugar, and sauté over medium heat until the garlic cloves are nicely caramelized—about 4 to 5 minutes.

7. Detach the 2 fillets from the bones of each saddle. With a sharp knife, slice the fillets diagonally, in ¼-inch slices, and then return the sliced fillets to their original positions on the bone.

8. Put the saddles on 2 plates, spoon the sauce around them, and garnish each with 5 caramelized cloves of garlic. Serve hot.

Note: This dish goes very well with a garnish of Nouilles à l'Alsacienne (page 411), or with any vegetable puree.

Volaille Pochée Grand-Mère

POACHED CHICKEN GRAND-MÈRE

Even though this is a very solid and satisfying dish, it is not rich. No butter, no cream.

When a customer asks me for something along those lines, this is one of the dishes I like to make. Naturally when I make it just for one person, I use a smaller bird, and the cooking time of the chicken is cut in half.

Serves 4

1 truffle, in large slices
   (optional)
1 chicken, 3 to 4 pounds
2 large carrots, trimmed, peeled,
   washed, and cut in 4 lengths
2 leeks (the white part only),
   washed

1 bouquet garni (page 55)
1 veal shank (with its meat)
1½ quarts Fond Blanc de
   Volaille (page 512), or water
   (see *Note* on page 58)
salt
pepper, fresh ground

1. Slip the slices of truffle (if used) under the skin of the chicken. Tie the entire bird in a sheet of cheesecloth.

2. In a pot, cover the carrots, leeks, bouquet garni, and veal shank with the Fond Blanc de Volaille (or water). Add salt and pepper to taste, and cook for 1 hour. Remove the vegetables, but not the veal shin.

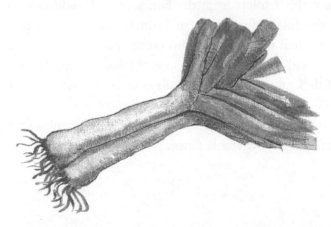

3. In this liquid, simmer the chicken together with the veal shank, covered, for 45 minutes. Strain the liquid through a fine sieve.

Note: The liquid the chicken was cooked in may be served first as a soup. Then serve the chicken, hot, with assorted condiments—coarse salt, gherkins, mustard, horseradish, vinegared cherries, etc., and with the carrots and leeks that the cooking broth was prepared with.

Note: The veal shank may be served cold the next day, with Mayonnaise (page 515).

Dinner at the Hôtel du Parc when I was an apprentice there in the 1940s

Consommé Madrilène (PAGE 76)

Terrine d'Anguille en Gelée au Vin Rouge (PAGE 178)

Selle de Veau Farcie aux Ris de Veau (PAGE 323)

Soufflé au Kirsch (PAGE 458)

VEAL

THIS CHAPTER is introduced with a menu not of how I ate when I was an apprentice at the Hôtel du Parc, but of dishes that I helped to prepare—for the people who ate so very well in the hotel dining room.

To me it is a menu with a kind of historic interest, but it is also more than that, because I keep all these dishes alive today by serving them from time to time at Lutèce.

You will find the recipe for the main course, Selle de Veau Farcie aux Ris de Veau, in this chapter of main courses prepared with veal.

Côte de Veau Pojarski

PATTIES OF VEAL (OR RABBIT, OR CHICKEN)

A lmost nobody makes this famous old dish anymore. And even though it is good, I rarely serve it. At most, maybe once a year I offer it to customers. But from time to time I make Côte de Veau Pojarski for the five-o'clock staff dinner. That way I preserve the dish at Lutèce.

Serves 4

Côte de Veau Pojarski (continued)

4 ounces white bread, crusts removed	salt
¾ cup milk	pepper, fresh ground
1 pound veal—any cut of veal that is very lean	2 tablespoons Madeira
	½ cup Fond de Veau (page 510)
11 tablespoons (1⅜ sticks) un-salted butter	1 tablespoon chopped truffles (optional)

1. Soak the bread in the milk for 5 minutes. Squeeze the milk out of the bread.

2. Cut the veal into small pieces and put it in a food processor. Add the bread, 8 tablespoons of the butter, and salt and pepper to taste. Process for 2 to 3 minutes, to make a fine puree.

3. Divide the meat in 4 parts, and form each part into the shape of a cutlet.

4. In a heavy-bottomed skillet, melt 1 tablespoon of the butter. Sauté the cutlets over medium heat until they are golden brown—about 5 minutes on each side. Put the cutlets on a plate and keep them warm.

Note: When done, the "cutlets" should be cooked through, but pale and juicy inside.

5. Add the Madeira and the Fond de Veau to the skillet, and reduce the liquid by ½. Add the truffles (if used), and simmer them for 2 minutes. Over medium heat, stir in the remaining 2 tablespoons of butter, and cook for 1 minute more. Add salt and pepper to taste. Spoon this sauce around the cutlets.

Note: The dish may be prepared in the same way with chicken or rabbit. But whatever meat is used, it must be very lean.

Any vegetable is an appropriate garnish.

Foie de Veau aux Olives Vertes

CALF'S LIVER WITH GREEN OLIVES

Serves 2

3 ounces smoked bacon, cut in
   ¼-inch cubes (or sliced
   bacon cut in small pieces)
18 green olives, pitted
2½ tablespoons unsalted butter
1 small onion, peeled, cut in ¼-
   inch cubes
1 small carrot, trimmed, peeled,
   washed, and cut in ¼-inch
   cubes
1 stalk celery, peeled, washed,
   and cut in ¼-inch cubes
1½ tablespoons all-purpose flour

1 tablespoon tomato puree
1 garlic clove, peeled, green
   germ removed, and chopped
   fine
½ cup dry white wine
½ cup Fond de Veau (page 510)
1 bouquet garni (page 55)
salt
pepper, fresh ground
4 slices calf's liver, about 2½
   ounces each
½ tablespoon chopped parsley

1. Blanch the bacon in boiling water for 2 minutes. Cool it under cold running water. Drain.

2. Blanch the olives in boiling water for 3 minutes. Drain.

3. In a saucepan, melt 1 tablespoon of the butter. Add the bacon, and sauté it for 1 minute. Add the onion, carrot, and celery, and sauté until very lightly browned. With a wooden spoon, stir in ½ the flour. Add the tomato puree and garlic. Stir over heat for 1 more minute.

4. Add the wine, Fond de Veau, and bouquet garni. Stir, bring to the boil, and simmer gently for 7 minutes. Add the olives, and continue simmering until the vegetables are cooked through and soft—about 5 minutes more.

5. Salt and pepper the liver, then dust it with the remaining flour. Pat the liver, so that the flour sticks to it.

6. In a sauté pan heat the remaining 1½ tablespoons of butter, and sauté the liver until it is golden brown—about 3 minutes on each side. The center of the liver should be slightly pink.

7. Put the liver on plates. Pour the vegetables, bacon, and olives over the liver, sprinkle with the parsley, and serve at once.

Note: Purée de Pommes de Terre (page 419) or rice is a fine garnish for this liver.

※

Médaillons de Veau aux Champignons

MEDALLIONS OF VEAL WITH MUSHROOMS

On the Lutèce menu, this dish is listed "aux Morilles," which means "with morels." Because morels are often hard to get, I give it here with regular (cultivated) mushrooms, and it is fine this way. You can also make it with any other kind of wild mushroom, such as chanterelles or cèpes.   *Serves 4*

8 slices boned loin of veal, ½
  inch thick, carefully
  trimmed
salt
pepper, fresh ground
flour for dusting the veal
2 tablespoons (¼ stick) unsalted
  butter

½ pound fresh mushrooms (or
  wild mushrooms), washed
  and sliced
1 ounce Madeira
¾ cup heavy cream
1 scant tablespoon chopped
  parsley

1. Season the veal lightly with salt and pepper, and dust it with flour.
2. In a large skillet, melt the butter. Over medium heat, brown the veal—about 2 minutes on each side. Lower the heat, add the mushrooms, cover, and let simmer for about 4 minutes. Remove the veal from the skillet (but not the mushrooms), and set it aside on a warm platter.
3. Cook the mushrooms in the skillet until all the liquid is evaporated. Add the Madeira to the mushrooms, bring to the boil, and cook briefly. Whisk in the cream, and simmer until the sauce thickens and becomes velvety—about 6 to 8 minutes.

4. Correct the sauce for seasoning and pour it over the medallions. Sprinkle with the chopped parsley. Serve hot.

Note: Garnish with Nouilles à l'Alsacienne (page 411).

❦

Médaillons de Veau en Croûte

MEDALLIONS OF VEAL IN PASTRY

Serves 6

The Veal and the Sauce

1½ pounds boneless loin of veal, well trimmed
salt
white pepper, fresh ground
flour for dusting the veal

2 tablespoons (¼ stick) unsalted butter
3 tablespoons chopped shallots
½ cup dry white wine
2 cups Fond de Veau (page 510)

The Optional Brains

1 small pair of calf's brains, 10 to 12 ounces (optional)
4 tablespoons white wine vinegar

salt
1 bay leaf

The Mushroom Stuffing

2 tablespoons (¼ stick) unsalted butter
2 tablespoons chopped shallots
10 ounces mushrooms, washed, bottoms trimmed, chopped coarse

2 tablespoons chopped parsley
salt
pepper, fresh ground

The Assembly, Baking, and Serving

1 recipe Feuilletage Rapide (page 531)
1 egg beaten with a little cold water

sprigs of watercress for the garnish

Médaillons de Veau en Croûte (continued)

The Veal and the Sauce

1. Cut the loin of veal into 6 equal medallions. Pat the slices dry, and sprinkle them with salt and pepper. Dust them with flour, and pat the flour into the surface of the meat.

2. In a wide skillet, over high heat, heat the 2 tablespoons of butter. Add the meat (if necessary, do 3 slices at a time), and sauté until they are golden brown—about 2 minutes on each side. Reduce the heat to low, cover, and cook for 2 minutes. Set the veal aside.

3. Pour off all but 1 tablespoon of butter from the skillet. Add the shallots, and sauté for 2 minutes. Add the white wine, scraping up the browned bits from the pan, and boil until the liquid is reduced by ½.

4. Add the Fond de Veau. Add any juices from the plate in which the veal was set aside. Boil again, until reduced by ½. Strain this sauce through a fine sieve, and set it aside. Refrigerate the meat, covered.

The Optional Brains

5. If you are using the optional calf's brains, soak the brains in cold water with 2 tablespoons of the vinegar for 30 minutes. Drain, and carefully remove all membranes and veins. Set aside.

6. In a small saucepan, combine 3 cups of cold water, the remaining 2 tablespoons of vinegar, salt, and the bay leaf. Bring to the boil, and simmer for 10 minutes. Carefully lower the brains into the water, and immediately turn off the heat. Let the brains sit in the water, covered, for 8 minutes. Remove the brains from the water and set aside.

The Mushroom Stuffing

7. In a large skillet, heat the 2 tablespoons of butter over medium-high heat. Add the shallots and sauté for a few seconds, then add the mushrooms and sauté, stirring, until they are nearly dry—about 8 minutes. Add the calf's brains (if using them), and stir, breaking up the brains as you do so, until they are in very small pieces.

8. Add ¼ cup of the reserved sauce, and simmer briefly, until thick. Turn off the heat. Stir in the parsley. Add salt and pepper. Allow this mixture to cool, then refrigerate it, covered.

The Assembly, Baking, and Serving

9. On a lightly floured work surface, roll out ⅓ of the pastry into a rectangle about 1⁄16 inch thick. Cut 6 pastry ovals from this sheet, each oval roughly the size and shape of the slices of veal, plus a generous border.

10. Roll out the remaining ⅔ of the pastry into a rectangle about ⅛ inch thick. Cut 6 pastry ovals from this sheet, each oval roughly the size and shape of the slices of veal, plus a generous border. These ovals should be slightly larger than those prepared in Step 9.

11. Put the smaller, thinner pastry ovals on a large ungreased baking sheet. Put a veal medallion on each oval, and spread a layer of the mushroom stuffing on each medallion. Mound the stuffing slightly, and put equal amounts of it on the 6 medallions. Brush the exposed edges of the pastry with the beaten egg.

12. Top each medallion with one of the larger, thicker pastry ovals. Smooth the top pastries gently without stretching them. Firmly press the overhanging edges of the top pastries to the exposed edges of the bottom pastries. Brush the top pastries with the beaten egg. Refrigerate for at least ½ hour on the pastry sheet.

13. Preheat the oven to 425°.

14. Brush the top pastries again with the egg-and-water mixture. Trim the edges of the pastries, if necessary, leaving a ½-inch border. Trace a leaf pattern in the top pastries with the sharp tip of a knife.

Note: At this point it is a good idea to refrigerate the meat for 10 to 15 minutes on the pastry sheet, but you may, to save time, proceed immediately with the baking.

15. Put the pastry-wrapped medallions, on the baking sheet, on the center rack of the preheated oven, and bake for 5 minutes. Lower the oven temperature to 400°, and continue baking until the pastries are golden brown—about 15 minutes more.

16. While the veal is baking, heat the sauce, reducing it further, if necessary, until it is slightly thick. Serve the veal surrounded by some of the

sauce, and garnished with sprigs of watercress. Serve the rest of the sauce separately.

Note: At Lutèce we often serve this dish with Épinards en Branches (page 402) or a combination of carrots and snap peas.

❧

Ris de Veau Panés aux Câpres

SWEETBREADS WITH CAPERS

This dish has been on the Lutèce menu for years and years. Every once in a while, I decide that it has been on the menu too long, and I take it off. As soon as I do, people start complaining, and I have to put it back on. Certainly it is not my most popular dish, but the people who like it *love* it.

Serves 2

1 pair sweetbreads (the
    2 attached lobes)
salt
pepper, fresh ground
1 tablespoon all-purpose flour
1 egg
½ tablespoon peanut oil

¼ cup fresh bread crumbs
3 tablespoons (⅜ stick) unsalted
    butter
1 tablespoon vinegar
⅓ cup Fond de Veau (page 510)
1 ample tablespoon capers

1. Soak the sweetbreads in cold water for at least 3 hours. Put them in a saucepan, cover them with cold water, and bring to the boil. Cook gently for 5 minutes. Remove the sweetbreads from the heat, drain them, and cool them under cold running water.

2. When the sweetbreads are thoroughly cooled, pull apart the 2 lobes. Remove and discard all filament, fat, and cartilage. Cut the sweetbreads into slices about ⅓ inch thick. Sprinkle the slices with salt and pepper, then dust them with flour.

3. Beat together the egg, oil, and ½ tablespoon of water. Dip each

slice of sweetbread into the beaten egg mixture, and then in the bread crumbs. Pat the slices so that the bread crumbs stick to the meat.

4. In a large skillet, heat ½ of the butter. Add the slices of sweetbread to the skillet, and cook gently until golden brown—about 3 minutes on each side. Put the slices on a warm plate, and keep them warm.

5. To the same skillet, add the vinegar and the Fond de Veau. Reduce for a few minutes. Add the remaining butter to the skillet, and cook by shaking the skillet until the butter is melted and the sauce is bound. Add the capers. Bring to the boil, and immediately pour the sauce around the sweetbreads.

Note: The sweetbreads must be crisp. When you add the sauce, pour it *around* the sweetbreads, not on them, so they keep their crispness.

Rognons de Veau Aigrelets

VEAL KIDNEYS IN A TART SAUCE

Note: This recipe may also be prepared with pork kidneys (3 pork kidneys per serving), or with calf's liver (5 ounces per serving).

Serves 2

1 veal kidney
2 tablespoons (¼ stick) unsalted
    butter
salt
pepper, fresh ground
5 mushrooms, washed and sliced
3 shallots (or 1 onion), peeled
    and chopped

½ tablespoon all-purpose flour
½ cup Fond de Veau (page 510),
    or water (see *Note* on page
    58)
2 tablespoons vinegar
1 tablespoon chopped parsley

1. Cut the kidney in half. Cut out and discard all the fat from the inside of the kidney. Cut the kidney in ½-inch cubes.

2. In a skillet, over high heat, melt 1 tablespoon of the butter. Add the

Rognons de Veau Aigrelets (continued)

kidney to the skillet, with salt and pepper, and sauté over very high heat until browned—about 2 minutes. Add the mushrooms and shallots (or onion), and continue to sauté over very high heat for 2 minutes more.

3. Sprinkle the flour into the skillet, and stir it in thoroughly with a wooden spatula. Continue cooking over high heat for 1 minute more.

4. Add the Fond de Veau (or water), stir, and bring the skillet to the boil—but do not let it continue to boil.

5. Add the vinegar and the remaining butter, and stir until the butter is incorporated.

Note: This step is performed over heat, but the liquid must not boil for more than a few seconds once the vinegar and butter have been added.

6. Sprinkle with parsley. Serve hot.

Note: Pommes Sautées (page 414), Purée de Pommes de Terre (page 419), and Nouilles à l'Alsacienne (page 411) all go very well with kidneys.

❧

Rognons de Veau à la Moutarde

VEAL KIDNEYS, MUSTARD SAUCE

Serves 4

1 cup white button mushrooms (or larger mushrooms, quartered), washed
juice of ½ lemon
3 tablespoons (⅜ stick) unsalted butter
salt
2 veal kidneys
pepper, fresh ground

2 tablespoons peanut oil
3 tablespoons Cognac or Armagnac
1 tablespoon chopped shallot
⅓ cup dry white wine
1 ample tablespoon Dijon mustard
½ cup heavy cream

1. Toss the mushrooms with the lemon juice.
2. In a sauté pan, heat 1 tablespoon of the butter. Lightly salt the

mushrooms, add them to the pan, and sauté over high heat for 5 minutes—or until dry. Set the mushrooms aside, and keep them warm.

3. Cut the kidneys in half. Cut out and discard all the fat from the inside of the kidneys. Cut the kidneys in ½-inch cubes. Add salt and pepper.

4. In a skillet, over high heat, heat the oil, and sauté the kidneys for 4 minutes. Drain them of all oil, and remove all oil and fat from the skillet. Return the kidneys to the skillet. Add the Cognac (or Armagnac), and flame. Add the kidneys to the mushrooms and keep them warm.

5. In the same skillet, melt the remaining 2 tablespoons of butter. Add the shallot, and sauté for 1 minute. Add the wine. Bring to the boil, and reduce by ½. Whisk in the mustard and cream. Return to the boil, and cook for 2 minutes. Strain this sauce through a fine sieve over the kidneys and mushrooms.

6. Return the kidneys and mushrooms to the skillet, and bring to the boil. Immediately remove from the heat. Serve hot.

Note: Serve with Pommes Sautées (page 414).

Selle de Veau Farcie aux Ris de Veau

BONED SADDLE OF VEAL STUFFED
WITH SWEETBREADS

Note: The boned saddle called for in this recipe consists of 2 joined parts: a flat part called the flank, and a ridgelike column of meat called the fillet.

Note: The recipe calls for caul fat, a sheet of fatty membrane that surrounds the abdominal cavity. You can get it from your butcher.

Serves 8

Selle de Veau Farcie (continued)

The Stuffing

¼ pound spinach, washed, stems removed

1 pound lean veal, cut in 1-inch cubes

½ teaspoon salt

pepper, fresh ground

3 egg whites

3 ounces heavy cream, cold

The Package

½ saddle of veal, boned

1 pair sweetbreads, blanched, peeled, and cut in 4 lengths

3 or 4 pieces caul fat—enough to wrap the roast

The Cooking and Serving

¼ cup peanut oil

2 medium carrots, trimmed, peeled, washed, and cut in ½-inch pieces

1 medium-large onion, peeled and cut in ½-inch pieces

2 stalks celery, peeled, washed, and cut in ½-inch pieces

1 cup dry white wine

salt

pepper, fresh ground

The Stuffing

1. Bring a pot (not of aluminum) of water to the boil, put the spinach in the boiling water, and cook for 1 minute. Cool the spinach in cold water, drain it in a colander, pressing out all excess water, and chop it coarse. Set aside.

2. Grind the cubed veal in a meat grinder, using the fine blade. Put the ground veal in a bowl. Add salt, pepper, and the egg whites to the veal, and mix until smooth. Add the cream quickly, and mix until the cream has been absorbed. *Do not overmix.* Mix in the chopped spinach. Set aside.

The Package

3. Spread the boned saddle flat on a work surface, and trim it of all fat. Arrange the ground veal mixture on the flank of the saddle, alongside the fillet. The filling should *not* extend all the way to the edges of the meat. Arrange the lengths of sweetbread over the mixture. Fold the flank over the filling and sweetbreads, to form the package.

4. Spread the caul on a work surface, the overlapping pieces forming a sheet large enough to wrap the roast. Put the saddle on the middle of the caul, and fold the caul over it. Tuck the ends under the saddle. Firmly tie the package with string.

The Cooking and Serving

5. In a skillet, over medium heat, heat the oil. Reduce the heat to low, put the saddle in the skillet, flank up, and cook for 45 minutes. Turn the saddle over and cook for 5 minutes more.

6. Preheat the oven to 350°.

7. Put the saddle in a pot. Add the carrots, onion, and celery. Cover, and cook in the preheated oven for 45 minutes. Remove the pot from the oven, put the meat on a warm platter, and let it rest for 20 minutes. Leave the vegetables in the pot.

8. While the roast is resting, pour all fat from the pot, and add the wine and ½ cup of water to the vegetables. Add salt and pepper. Bring to the boil, and cook on top of the stove for 5 minutes.

9. Pour the sauce around or over the roast. Serve the vegetables with the roast.

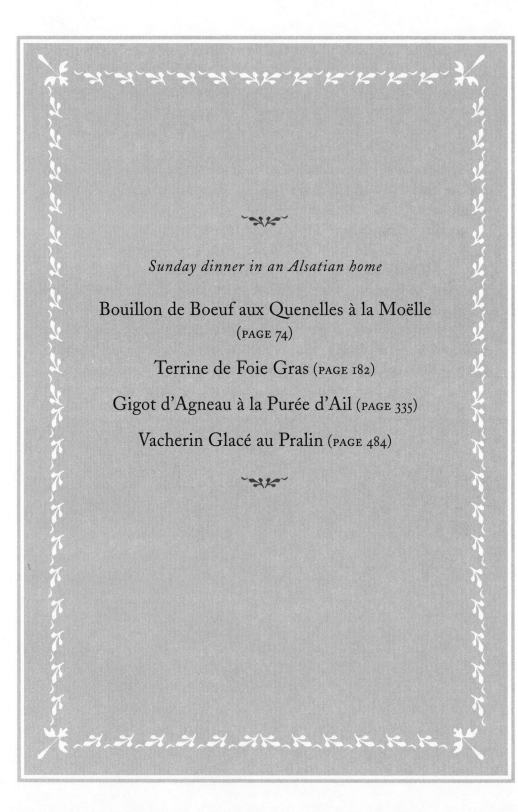

Sunday dinner in an Alsatian home

Bouillon de Boeuf aux Quenelles à la Moëlle
(PAGE 74)

Terrine de Foie Gras (PAGE 182)

Gigot d'Agneau à la Purée d'Ail (PAGE 335)

Vacherin Glacé au Pralin (PAGE 484)

LAMB

I INTRODUCE THIS CHAPTER with a menu that I think will frighten some people. Printed on the page, one right after the other, these dishes together may seem like too much. But an Alsatian family on a Sunday afternoon would enjoy a dinner of exactly these dishes. None of them are really heavy if they are made right. And of course the servings of each dish should be not too large.

So I do recommend to the people who use this book that they try this entire dinner—when there is the time to prepare it, and when there is the time to eat it. I recommend also that with it you drink an Alsatian wine.

The recipe for the main course, Gigot d'Agneau à la Purée d'Ail, appears in this chapter of main courses made with lamb.

Carré d'Agneau Caramelisé

CARAMELIZED RACK OF LAMB

For a long, long time everybody made Carré d'Agneau the very well known Provençale way, with garlic and parsley—Carré d'Agneau Persillé. It is good that way, but I got tired of it. I started looking for other ways to make lamb, and this is one of the ways I came up with. (I also began to make lamb chops in a potato crust. The recipe for the lamb chops is on page 330.)

In the end I stopped making rack of lamb the Provençale way

altogether, though of course I am happy to do it whenever anyone asks for it. You can try both ways yourself, and see which one you like better—the recipe for Carré d'Agneau Persillé is on the opposite page.

Note: Have your butcher prepare the rack by removing most of the fat and the chine (backbone), and by cutting the rib bones so that they extend from the meat by ¾ of an inch. And be sure that with your rack the butcher gives you the chine and the ends of the ribs.

Serves 2

1 tablespoon honey
1 scant tablespoon Dijon
   mustard
1 teaspoon crumbled thyme
juice of ½ lemon
salt
pepper, fresh ground
1 rack of lamb—1 side of the
   double rack, 8 chops, including the trimmed bones (see
   Note above)

1 tablespoon peanut oil
1 small onion, peeled and cut in
   ⅓-inch pieces
1 medium carrot, trimmed,
   peeled, washed, and cut in
   ⅓-inch pieces
1 garlic clove, unpeeled
¾ cup dry white wine, or water
   (see *Note* on page 58)

1. Preheat the oven to 375°.

2. In a bowl, mix together the honey, Dijon mustard, thyme, lemon juice, salt, and pepper. Set the bowl aside.

3. Salt and pepper the rack of lamb, and brush it with oil. Put it in a roasting pan, and surround it with the bones. Put the roasting pan in the preheated oven for 12 minutes. Turn and baste the meat twice during this time.

4. Add the onion, carrot, and garlic to the roasting pan, and roast for 10 more minutes. Once during the 10 minutes, turn and baste the meat and stir the vegetables and bones.

5. Remove the roasting pan from the oven, put the lamb on a plate, and let it rest in a warm place for 5 or 6 minutes. Leave the bones and vegetables in the pan.

6. While the lamb is resting, remove all fat from the roasting pan. Add the wine (or water) to the bones and vegetables. Boil the liquid for a

few minutes, and move the bones and vegetables about with a wooden spoon. When the liquid has been reduced by ½, strain it through a sieve into a sauceboat. Press the vegetables through the sieve as well, but do not attempt to push all the solids through the sieve.

7. Preheat the broiler at maximum heat.

8. With the meat side of the rack up, brush the top of the rack with the reserved honey mixture. Put the meat under the broiler for about 3 minutes—until the top of the rack is nicely caramelized.

9. Cut the rack into 8 chops, and arrange them on 2 plates, with the liquid from the roasting pan.

Note: Serve with string beans or potatoes, garnished with sprigs of watercress.

❧

Carré d'Agneau Persillé

RACK OF LAMB WITH PARSLEY

Serves 2 or 3

1 rack of lamb, about 1¼ pounds
1 tablespoon peanut oil
salt
pepper, fresh ground
1 tablespoon Dijon mustard
½ cup fresh bread crumbs
2 tablespoons chopped parsley

1 small garlic clove, peeled, green germ removed, and chopped fine
⅛ teaspoon thyme
2 teaspoons unsalted butter, melted

1. Preheat the oven to 400°.

2. Brush the rack with the oil, and sprinkle it with salt and pepper. Put the rack in a roasting pan, and roast it in the preheated oven for 12 minutes.

3. Remove the meat from the oven, and coat it with the mustard.

4. Lower the oven temperature to 350°.

5. Combine the bread crumbs, parsley, garlic, thyme, and melted but-

Carré d'Agneau Persillé (continued)

ter. Spread this mixture over the top of the rack. Put the rack in the 350° oven, and roast for another 15 minutes.

6. Remove the rack from the oven, and let it rest for 10 minutes before carving it into chops. The lamb will be medium rare.

Côtes d'Agneau à la Croûte de Pommes de Terre

LAMB CHOPS IN A POTATO CRUST

Serves 2

1 pound medium potatoes, unpeeled, washed
salt
4 rib lamb chops
pepper, fresh ground
1 tablespoon peanut oil

1 ample tablespoon all-purpose flour
1 egg
3 tablespoons (⅜ stick) unsalted butter

1. In a saucepan bring the potatoes to the boil in salted water. Cover, and simmer until the potatoes are soft—about 20 minutes. Discard the water. Cook the potatoes over low heat, uncovered, for about 5 minutes more, to dry them.

2. Set the potatoes aside, uncovered, to cool.

3. Trim most of the fat from the lamb chops. Salt and pepper them.

4. In a skillet, heat the oil. Brown the lamb chops quickly—about 1½ minutes on each side. Put the chops on a plate, and let them cool.

5. Peel the potatoes, and then grate them into a bowl, using the coarsest side of a four-sided grater (or the grater attachment of a food processor). Add salt and pepper, the flour, and the egg. Mix gently with a wooden spatula. Press this mixture onto the surfaces and sides of the lamb chops. The potato mixture should form a shell around ¼ inch thick.

6. In a skillet, melt the butter. Sauté the chops over medium heat for about 5 minutes on each side. The potato crust should be nicely browned and crisp, and the meat inside should be pink but warmed through.

Note: Serve with a green salad.

Filet d'Agneau Pané au Poivre Blanc

LOIN OF SPRING LAMB WITH WHITE PEPPER

Serves 5

1 saddle of spring lamb, boned and carefully trimmed (2 loins—excludes the 2 filets mignons)
salt
2 tablespoons cracked white pepper

5 tablespoons (⅝ stick) unsalted butter
½ cup Cognac
1 cup Demi-Glace (page 508), or 3 cups Fond de Veau (page 510) reduced by ⅔

1. Cut the loins of lamb into 15 ½-inch-thick medallions (3 per person). Season each slice lightly with salt, then with the pepper. Press the pepper into the meat.

2. In a sauté pan, over high heat, melt 2 tablespoons of the butter. Still over high heat, brown the medallions in the butter, about 1½ minutes on each side. Transfer the meat to a warm platter, and keep it warm.

3. Add the Cognac to the pan, and set it aflame. Add the Demi-Glace (or the reduced Fond de Veau), bring to the boil, and cook over medium heat for 4 to 5 minutes. Stir in the remaining butter. Taste for seasoning. Add salt and pepper if needed. Strain through a fine sieve over the lamb.

Filet d'Agneau en Feuilleté

LOIN OF LAMB IN PASTRY

Serves 6

The Lamb and the Sauce

1 saddle of spring lamb, boned
   and carefully trimmed (2
   loins—excludes the 2 filets
   mignons), approximately 1¼
   pounds net weight
salt
pepper, fresh ground

2 tablespoons (¼ stick) unsalted
   butter
3 tablespoons chopped shallots
½ cup dry white wine
2 cups Fond de Veau or Fond
   d'Agneau (page 510)

The Optional Brains

1 small pair calf's brains, 10 to
   12 ounces (optional)
¼ cup vinegar

salt
1 bay leaf

The Stuffing

2 tablespoons (¼ stick) unsalted
   butter
2½ cups sliced mushrooms
   (about 10 ounces), or 3 cups
   if the optional brains are
   omitted

2 tablespoons chopped shallots
2 tablespoons chopped parsley
salt
pepper, fresh ground

The Stuffed Lamb in the Pastry

flour for flouring the work
   surface
1½ pounds Feuilletage Rapide
   (page 531)

1 egg beaten with a little cold
   water

The Lamb and the Sauce

1. Preheat the oven to 400°.

2. Sprinkle the 2 loins of lamb with salt and pepper. In a large oven-proof skillet, melt the butter over high heat. Brown the meat in the skillet on all sides—about 3 minutes. Put the skillet in the preheated oven for 4 minutes.

3. Remove the skillet from the oven, put the meat on a platter, and pour off all but 1 tablespoon of the butter from the skillet. Refrigerate the meat.

4. Over heat, add the shallots to the skillet and sauté for 1 to 2 minutes. Add the white wine. With a wooden spoon, scrape free any browned bits clinging to the pan. Boil the wine until it is reduced by ½. Add the Fond de Veau or Fond d'Agneau, and boil until the liquid is reduced by almost ⅓. Strain this sauce through a fine sieve. Set aside.

The Optional Brains

5. In a bowl, cover the brains with cold water. Add 2 tablespoons of the vinegar, and soak for 15 minutes. Drain. Carefully remove all membrane and veins from the brains. Set aside.

6. Put 3 cups of water, the remaining 2 tablespoons of vinegar, a little salt, and the bay leaf in a small saucepan. Bring to the boil. Gently lower the brains into this water. *Immediately* remove the saucepan from the heat. Let the brains sit in the water, covered, for 8 minutes. With a slotted spoon, remove the brains from the water to a small bowl. Set aside.

The Stuffing

7. In a large skillet, melt the 2 tablespoons of butter over medium-high heat. Add the mushrooms, and sauté, stirring, until they are almost dry—about 8 minutes. Add the shallots, and cook 2 minutes more.

8. Add the brains (if used), and stir, breaking them up until the mixture is almost a puree. Add ¼ cup of the reserved sauce, and simmer briefly until the mixture is thick. Remove from the heat. Stir in the chopped parsley, salt, and pepper. Cool to room temperature. Then refrigerate.

The Stuffed Lamb in the Pastry

9. On a lightly floured work surface, roll out 10 ounces of the Feuilletage Rapide into a 10-inch square. It should be about ¹⁄₁₆ inch thick. Cut the square in half, so that you have 2 rectangles, each 5″ by 10″.

10. Roll out the remaining pastry to about a 10-inch square. Cut it in half, so that you have 2 somewhat thicker rectangles, each 5″ by 10″.

Filet d'Agneau en Feuilleté (continued)

11. Put the thinner pastry rectangles on an ungreased baking sheet. Put a piece of loin of lamb on each, and spread ½ the stuffing over each piece of lamb, mounding the stuffing slightly near the center. Brush the exposed edges of the pastries with some of the beaten egg.

12. Put a thicker pastry rectangle over each of the pieces of lamb. Smooth the pastries down gently, without stretching them. Firmly press the edges of the top pastries to the bottom pastries to seal them. Brush the top pastries with the beaten egg. With a sharp knife, trim off the edges of the pastries so that a ½-inch border of pastry encircles each package. With the tip of a knife cut a pattern in the top pastries. Refrigerate, on the baking sheet, for at least ½ hour.

Note: The recipe may be prepared to this point 2 to 3 hours in advance.

The Baking and the Final Assembly

13. Preheat the oven to 425°.

14. Put the lamb, on its baking sheet, in the preheated oven for 5 minutes.

15. Lower the oven temperature to 375°.

16. Continue baking until the pastries are golden brown—about 15 minutes more.

17. While the lamb is baking, heat the remaining reserved sauce, reducing it if necessary until it coats a spoon lightly.

18. Cut each piece of lamb in 6 slices. Serve 2 slices per person, surrounded with some of the sauce.

Note: Serve with string beans or wax beans, and garnish with sprigs of watercress.

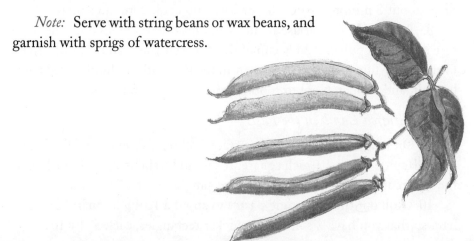

Gigot d'Agneau à la Purée d'Ail

LEG OF LAMB WITH GARLIC PUREE

There is a lot of garlic in this dish, but made this way, the garlic is really a mild, gentle flavor.   *Serves 8*

1 leg of lamb, approximately 5 pounds, pelvic bone removed	5 heads of garlic, cloves peeled, halved, green germs removed
unsalted butter for coating the lamb	1 cup milk
salt	1 cup heavy cream
pepper, fresh ground	¼ cup dry white wine

1. Preheat the oven to 375°.

2. Coat the leg of lamb with the butter, and season it with salt and pepper. Put the leg in a roasting pan, and roast it in the preheated oven for 50 minutes. Baste the meat and turn it over about every 8 minutes.

3. While the lamb is in the oven, in a saucepan blanch the garlic in boiling water for 3 minutes. Pour off the water.

4. Add the milk, cream, salt, pepper, and ½ cup of water. Bring to the boil, and cook gently over medium heat for 15 minutes. Put the garlic and the liquid in a food processor and process for 1 minute, to obtain a light puree. Set aside and keep warm.

5. When the lamb is ready, turn off the oven, open the oven door and leave it ajar. Let the lamb rest in the turned-off oven, its door ajar, for about 10 minutes. Remove the lamb from the roasting pan and keep it warm.

6. Discard all fat from the roasting pan, add the wine and ½ cup of water. Bring to the boil on top of the stove, and cook for a few minutes.

7. Stir 3 tablespoons of the liquid from the roasting pan into the garlic puree. Serve this puree as a garnish with the roast lamb.

Note: In addition to the garlic puree, we usually serve this dish at Lutèce with flageolets or lima beans.

Épaule d'Agneau Braisée aux Petits Légumes

LAMB SHOULDER WITH SPRING VEGETABLES

Most lamb is expensive, but here is an excellent dish you can make with an inexpensive cut. You do not have to spend top dollar all the time to make good food.

Serves 5 or 6

1 lamb shoulder, boned, rolled, and tied with twine
salt
pepper, fresh ground
1 tablespoon peanut oil
1 cup dry white wine
1½ cups Fond d'Agneau or Fond de Veau (page 510), or water (see *Note* on page 58)
1 bouquet garni (page 55)
2 tablespoons (¼ stick) unsalted butter
15 pearl onions, peeled
¾ pound carrots, trimmed, peeled, washed, and cut into olive-shaped pieces (or sticks 1¼″ × ¼″ × ¼″)
¾ pound white turnips, washed, peeled, and cut into olive-shaped pieces (or sticks 1¼″ × ¼″ × ¼″)
½ pound celery, peeled, washed, and cut into olive-shaped pieces (or sticks 1¼″ × ¼″ × ¼″)
6 garlic cloves, peeled, halved, green germs removed
1 teaspoon sugar

1. Sprinkle the lamb with salt and pepper. In a cocotte, or heavy-bottomed ovenproof pot, heat the oil. Put the lamb in the cocotte, and brown it on all sides on top of the stove.

2. Preheat the oven to 300°.

3. Add the wine to the lamb. Cover, and cook on top of the stove until the wine is reduced by ⅓—about 20 minutes.

4. Add the Fond de Veau or Fond d'Agneau (or water) and bouquet garni. Cover, and put the cocotte in the preheated oven for 1¼ hours.

5. While the meat is in the oven, melt the butter in a sauté pan. Add the onions, carrots, turnips, celery, garlic, and sugar. Cook until the vegetables are slightly browned.

6. When the lamb has been in the oven for 1¼ hours, remove the pot from the oven, and add the vegetables. If there is only very little liquid in the pot, add some water. Return the pot to the oven for another 20 minutes. During this 20-minute period, inspect the lamb from time to time, and if there is only very little liquid left, again add some water. (At the end of the cooking, there should be just enough liquid remaining to serve with the lamb.)

7. Remove the lamb from the oven. Discard the bouquet garni. Slice the meat, and pour the vegetables and juices over it.

Médaillons de Filet d'Agneau au Gratin

MEDALLIONS OF LAMB AU GRATIN

Serves 5

2 tomatoes, ripe
½ cup olive oil
1 large onion, peeled
    and sliced
2 pounds eggplant, unpeeled,
    cut in ¼-inch cubes
2 pounds zucchini, unpeeled,
    cut in ¼-inch cubes
4 garlic cloves, peeled, halved,
    green germs removed
1 bouquet garni (page 55)

salt
pepper, fresh ground
1 saddle of spring lamb,
    boned and carefully
    trimmed (2 loins—excludes
    the 2 filets mignons)
1 tablespoon unsalted butter,
    plus butter for buttering the
    gratin dish
3 ounces Swiss cheese (Emmen-
    tal or Gruyère), grated

1. Cut a conical plug from the stem end of each tomato and discard. Blanch the tomatoes in boiling water for 10 seconds, drain them under cold water, and peel off the skins. Cut the tomatoes in half, squeeze out and discard the juice and seeds, and chop the pulp in ¼-inch cubes.

2. In a saucepan, heat the oil. Add the onion, and cook over low heat

Médaillons de Filet d'Agneau (continued)

for 5 minutes. Add the eggplant, zucchini, tomatoes, garlic, bouquet garni, salt, and pepper. Cover. Cook over low heat for 30 minutes. Stir from time to time to avoid burning.

3. Remove the bouquet garni. Put the contents of the saucepan in a food processor, and process until pureed—about 30 seconds.

4. Preheat the oven to 300°.

5. Cut the loins of lamb into 15 ½-inch-thick medallions (3 per person). Season lightly with salt and pepper. In a sauté pan, melt the butter, and brown the medallions in the butter for 2 minutes on each side.

6. Butter a gratin dish. Cover the bottom of the dish with ½ of the vegetable puree. Arrange the medallions of lamb on the puree. Cover the lamb with the remainder of the puree. Sprinkle the Swiss cheese on top.

7. Bake in the preheated oven for 20 minutes.

Sauté d'Agneau Printanière

LAMB STEW WITH YOUNG VEGETABLES

I make this dish mostly in the springtime, when there are young vegetables. You can do it in the winter too, but you will have to use older vegetables. The dish will still be good, but not as good as when the carrots and turnips and string beans and peas are young, small, and tender.

Serves 4

2 tablespoons (¼ stick) unsalted butter

1½ pounds lamb (breast, shoulder, or both), thoroughly trimmed of fat, cut in pieces of approximately 1½ ounces

1 medium carrot, trimmed, peeled, washed, and cut in ½-inch pieces

1 medium onion, peeled and cut in ½-inch pieces

1 garlic clove, peeled, halved, green germ removed

salt

pepper, fresh ground

1 teaspoon plus 1 scant teaspoon sugar

1 tablespoon all-purpose flour

1 tablespoon tomato puree
1 bouquet garni (page 55)
4 potatoes, trimmed to the size
   and shape of small eggs
½ cup young carrots, peeled,
   washed, and trimmed to the
   size and shape of large olives
8 pearl onions, peeled

½ cup young white turnips,
   peeled, washed, and
   trimmed to the size and
   shape of large olives
½ cup string beans, trimmed
½ cup green peas

1. In a heavy-bottomed pot, heat 1 tablespoon of butter and add the lamb. Over high heat, brown the meat well on all sides.

2. Add the 1 medium carrot, the 1 medium onion, the garlic, salt, and pepper. Continue to sauté, still over high heat, for 5 more minutes. Sprinkle on the teaspoon of sugar, and sauté, stirring, until the sugar is caramelized—about 2 to 3 minutes.

3. Remove all the fat. Add the flour, mix well, and sauté, still over high heat, for 2 more minutes. Add the tomato puree and the bouquet garni. Add water barely to cover. Bring to the boil, lower the heat, cover, and simmer gently for 1 hour.

4. With a fork, transfer the pieces of lamb to another pot. Add the potatoes to the lamb. Strain the contents of the first pot over the meat, firmly pushing the contents through the strainer. This sauce should just cover the meat and potatoes. If it does not, add water to cover. Taste for seasoning, and add salt and/or pepper if needed.

5. Bring the stew to a light boil. Cover, and simmer gently for 45 minutes.

6. While the meat is cooking, put the young carrots, pearl onions, and turnips in a wide, deep sauté pan. Add the remaining 1 tablespoon of butter, the remaining scant teaspoon of sugar, and ½ cup of water. Bring to the boil, and cook, uncovered, until the water is completely cooked off, and the vegetables are tender and glazed. Set aside.

7. Cook the string beans and peas, separately from each other, in boiling salted water, until tender. Drain. Set aside.

8. When the meat is ready, remove all fat from the surface of the liquid. Put the stew in a deep serving plate. Arrange the vegetables over and around it. Serve very hot.

Lunch at Lutèce today—winter

Soupe de Lentilles à l'Alsacienne (PAGE 98)

Queue de Boeuf Bourguignonne (PAGE 354)

Charlotte Chaude aux Pommes (PAGE 434)

Dinner at Lutèce today—winter

Brioche de Kugelhopf aux Escargots (PAGE 204)

Filet Mignon au Foie Gras (PAGE 350)

Beignets de Pommes (PAGE 428)

BEEF

FOR ME, beef is great winter food, so here are two winter menus of Lutèce today, one for lunch and one for dinner. On both menus the main course is from this beef chapter.

If you are in New York on a cold winter day, I suggest you come to Lutèce for a lunch or dinner like these. If you prefer, you can stay at home and prepare the same dishes yourself.

Boeuf Braisé à la Mode

BRAISED BEEF

Boeuf à la Mode is such an old-fashioned dish, I almost did not put it in this book. It is a great, great dish, but hardly anybody makes dishes like this anymore. Still, at Lutèce, I continue to make it, maybe two or three times a year. And when I make it my customers like it very much, so I decided to include it here.

This is a dish I encourage you to make at home. Hot, it is wonderful home cooking, a winter dish. Cold, it is an excellent summer dish that you can make in advance.

Boeuf Braisé is simple—but it takes time and attention. None of the steps are hard to do, but you have to give each one time and care. If you do not have the time, it is better if you do not do this dish until you do.

Almost any cut of beef can be used to make Boeuf Braisé, but I recommend highly that you use the cut called by American butchers "chicken steak." It is perfect for this dish, the only cut I ever use. Chicken steak is part of the shoulder, and it has a tender, gelatinous layer in the center, so when you cut the meat in slices there is a band of this enriching layer in each slice.

Note: Calf's feet are an optional part of this recipe. If you use them, ask your butcher to bone them, and to keep the bones for you.

Serves 6

Preparing the Beef, Parts I and II

1 whole "chicken steak" of beef, 3 to 3½ pounds

1 carrot, trimmed, peeled, washed, and cut in ½-inch pieces

1 medium onion, peeled and cut in ½-inch pieces

2 stalks celery, peeled, washed, and cut in ½-inch pieces

1 bouquet garni (page 55)

4 garlic cloves, slightly crushed

1 scant teaspoon cracked pepper

2 cups dry white wine

2 ounces Cognac

2 calf's feet (optional)

2 to 3 ounces pork rind (if available)

salt

2 tablespoons lard or peanut oil

4 cups Fond de Veau (page 510), or water (see *Note* on page 58)

The Garnish

1½ cups carrots, trimmed, peeled, washed, and cut in olive-shaped pieces

20 pearl onions, peeled

2 tablespoons (¼ stick) unsalted butter

1 teaspoon sugar

salt

1 cup mushrooms, washed and cut in ⅓-inch dice

To Serve Cold

1 scant tablespoon (or 1 envelope) powdered gelatin

10 cornichons (small French pickles or gherkins), cut in ¼-inch pieces

Preparing the Beef, Part I

1. Put the meat, carrot, onion, and celery in a nonmetallic bowl or pot. Add the bouquet garni, garlic, pepper, wine, and Cognac. Let the meat marinate for 24 hours.

Note: You may marinate the meat as long as several days. If you do, the dish will have an even better flavor.

2. Put the calf's feet (if used), their bones, and the pork rind (if used) in a pot. Cover with cold water, bring the water to the boil, and cook for 10 to 15 minutes. Run cold water into the pot until the contents are thoroughly chilled. Pour off all the water. Set aside.

3. Drain the meat and vegetables of their marinade. Keep the marinade. Dry the meat with paper towels, then salt it.

4. Preheat the oven to 225°.

5. In a heavy-bottomed ovenproof pot, heat the lard (or oil). Over high heat, sear the meat on all sides. Add the vegetables, and lightly brown them—about 2 minutes. Add the calf's feet (if used) and their bones, and the pork rind (if used). Cover with the marinade and the Fond de Veau (or water).

6. Bring the pot slowly to the boil. Put the pot, covered, in the preheated oven, and cook for 3 to 3½ hours.

The Garnish

7. While the meat is in the oven, put the 1½ cups of carrots and the pearl onions in a wide sauté pan in which they will not be crowded. Add 1 tablespoon of the butter, the sugar, salt, and ½ cup of water.

8. Bring to the boil, and cook, uncovered, stirring the vegetables around from time to time, until the water is completely cooked off, and the vegetables are tender and glazed. Set aside in a warm place.

9. In a sauté pan, over high heat, melt the remaining 1 tablespoon of butter. Add the mushrooms and a little salt. Sauté the mushrooms until dry, about 5 to 6 minutes, and set them aside.

Preparing the Beef, Part II

10. When the meat is ready, transfer it to another pot that barely holds it. Set aside the liquid that the meat cooked in, and let the fat rise to the surface.

Boeuf Braisé à la Mode (continued)

11. If used, cut the calf's feet and the pork rind into ¼-inch cubes, and add them to the meat.

Note: If the dish is to be served cold (see Steps 15 to 17 below), do not cut up the calf's feet or pork rind in this step.

12. With a spoon, remove and discard all the fat from the surface of the liquid that the meat cooked in. Pour the remaining liquid through a fine sieve over the meat. Put the cooking vegetables in the sieve as well, and press them against the sieve so that their juices pass through the sieve onto the meat—but do not push the vegetables themselves through the sieve.

13. Add *The Garnish*—the carrots, pearl onions, and mushrooms—to the meat. Bring the pot to a slow boil, and cook slowly, covered, until the meat is very tender—about ½ hour to 1 hour. Test the tenderness with a needle or a cooking fork. Remove all fat, if any, from the surface of the liquid.

To Serve Hot

14. Delicately cut the meat into ½-inch slices. Surround it with the vegetables and calf's feet, and cover lightly with the sauce.

Note: When served hot, the Boeuf Braisé à la Mode goes well with a garnish of Purée de Pommes de Terre (page 419).

To Serve Cold

15. Eliminate Step 14. Dissolve the gelatin in a little cold water, and stir it into the pot of meat. Cook for 2 minutes.

16. Discard the pork rind. Put the meat, calf's feet, vegetables, and cornichons in a terrine in which they fit snugly. Pour the sauce over the meat. Refrigerate overnight.

17. The next day, briefly lower the terrine into hot water. Then invert the terrine onto a cutting board. The meat will be encased in the jellied sauce and the vegetables.

Note: Serve the cold Boeuf Braisé à la Mode sliced, with a green salad.

Entrecôte en Chemise au Coulis de Poivrons

SIRLOIN IN A CRÊPE, COULIS OF RED PEPPERS
(May Be Prepared with Endives)

Serves 4

The Crêpes

1 cup all-purpose flour, sifted
2 eggs
1 scant teaspoon salt
pepper, fresh ground
½ cup milk

3 tablespoons (⅜ stick) unsalted
  butter, melted
1 tablespoon parsley chopped
  fine

The Steaks in the Crêpes

1 tablespoon peanut oil
4 sirloin steaks, about 6 ounces
  each
½ recipe Coulis of Red Peppers
  (page 506)

3 tablespoons heavy cream
salt
pepper, fresh ground

The Crêpes

1. Put the flour in a bowl. Add the eggs, salt, and pepper. Whisk in the milk and ⅓ cup of water. Work this batter with the whisk until it is smooth.

2. Add 2 tablespoons of the melted butter and the parsley. If the batter is too thick to flow out into a thin crêpe, add a little more milk. Let the batter rest for 10 minutes before using it.

3. Brush a little of the melted butter on a 7- to 8-inch nonsticking skillet, and heat. Prepare a crêpe by pouring in enough batter to cover the bottom of the

Entrecôte en Chemise (continued)

skillet. Brown it lightly on 1 side. Then turn it over and brown it lightly on the other side.

4. Perform the last step 3 more times.

The Steaks in the Crêpes

5. In a large skillet, over high heat, heat the 1 tablespoon of oil. Still over high heat, sauté the sirloins 2 minutes on each side. At this point the steaks will be rare.

6. Put the 4 crêpes on 4 ovenproof plates. Put a steak on each crêpe. Spread 3 tablespoons of the Coulis of Red Peppers on each steak. Then wrap each steak in its crêpe.

7. Preheat the oven to 400°.

8. Bring the remaining Coulis to the boil, and whisk in the heavy cream. Add salt and pepper, and pour this sauce around the wrapped steaks. Put the plates in the preheated oven for 1 minute. Serve hot.

Note: The Entrecôte en Chemise requires no garnish.

Filet de Boeuf en Brioche

BEEF TENDERLOIN IN BRIOCHE PASTRY

Although this is similar to Beef Wellington—it is made with brioche pastry instead of puff pastry—it is really an old Alsatian dish that is sometimes called Filet de Boeuf Strasbourgeoise. Strasbourg, of course, is the capital of Alsace.

Serves 6

oil for the roasting pan
½ large tenderloin of beef, carefully trimmed and tied
2 tablespoons (¼ stick) unsalted butter
3 shallots, peeled and chopped

1 pound mushrooms, chopped
¼ pound foie gras, cut in ¼-inch cubes
salt
pepper, fresh ground
½ tablespoon chopped parsley

1½ pounds Pâte à Brioche (page 534)

1 egg beaten with a little cold water

1. Preheat the oven to 450°.

2. Oil a roasting pan. Roast the beef in the pan in the preheated oven for 12 minutes. Baste and turn the beef from time to time, so that it browns evenly on all sides. Remove it from the oven and let it cool at least to room temperature.

3. In a sauté pan, over medium heat, melt the butter. Sauté the shallots for 1 minute. Add the mushrooms, and continue sautéing until the mushrooms are dry. Turn off the heat. Stir in the foie gras, salt and pepper to taste, and the parsley. Let cool.

4. Roll out the Pâte de Brioche to a rectangle ¼ inch thick, and large enough to enclose the beef.

5. Put the beef on the center of the pastry, and coat it with the mixture of mushrooms, shallots, and foie gras. Wrap the beef in the pastry, and brush the pastry with the beaten egg. Let the pastry rise for 45 minutes at room temperature.

6. Preheat the oven to 325°.

7. Bake in the preheated oven for 30 minutes. The pastry should be nicely browned.

Note: Serve with Sauce Périgourdine (page 523).

Bavette de Boeuf Farcie

STUFFED FLANK STEAK

This is a recipe I came up with for a cooking demonstration I give every year at Macy's. I have also given many demonstrations on television, and when a young schoolgirl in New York saw me one day on TV, she wrote about it. She did this for a school assignment on famous people and important places—and she won a prize. Here is what she wrote about me:

"Chef André Soltner is famous because he is a good cook. He cooks at a restaurant in New York City. He makes yummy food. He is important to my community because food is important to our life. I like him because he cooks and I like to eat. I watched him on TV with Julia Child. He looks like he knows what he is doing."

Serves 6

The Stuffing

½ tablespoon goose fat, or lard, or chicken fat

1 medium onion, peeled and cut in ¼-inch cubes

2 shallots (optional), peeled and cut in ¼-inch cubes

1 medium to large carrot, trimmed, peeled, washed, and cut in ¼-inch cubes

1 leek (the white part and a few inches of the green), washed and cut in ⅛-inch pieces

2 medium potatoes, peeled, cut in ¼-inch cubes, washed, and set aside in cold water

salt

pepper, fresh ground

½ cup milk

3 slices white bread, trimmed

1 pound pork butt (or veal)

2 eggs

1 ample tablespoon chopped parsley

The Stuffed Flank Steak

1 flank steak (not peeled), about 2½ pounds, with a pocket cut into one edge; the pocket must not reach to the other edge of the steak (may be prepared ahead by your butcher)

salt

pepper, fresh ground

½ tablespoon goose fat, or lard, or chicken fat

1 teaspoon sugar

2 cups dry white wine

2 cups chicken stock, or water (see *Note* on page 58)

10 ounces sliced smoked bacon (optional), lightly sautéed and drained of its fat

3 pounds white turnips, peeled, washed, and cut in ⅛-inch slices

The Stuffing

1. In a skillet, melt the goose fat (or lard, or chicken fat). Add the onion, shallots (if used), carrot, and leek, and sauté gently until the vegetables are a little bit softened—about 3 to 4 minutes.

2. Add the potatoes, and continue to sauté gently for another 4 minutes, moving the vegetables about from time to time. Add a little salt and pepper.

3. In a saucepan, warm the milk, and then soak the bread in the warm milk. The bread should just about soak up all the milk.

4. In a meat grinder, grind together the pork butt (or veal) and the bread. (You may do this step in a food processor, but do not overprocess.)

5. Put the meat-and-bread mixture in a bowl and, with a wooden spoon, stir in the eggs and chopped parsley. Add ½ teaspoon of salt and a little pepper. Stir in the sautéed vegetables.

The Stuffed Flank Steak

6. Preheat the oven to 350°.

7. Fill the pocket of the flank steak with the stuffing. Sew the pocket closed with a needle and string. Season the outside of the steak with salt and pepper on all sides.

8. In an ovenproof pot, melt the fat over medium heat. Brown the stuffed steak on all sides for about 10 minutes. Sprinkle the sugar over the meat, and bake, uncovered, in the preheated oven for about 5 minutes—until the sugar is lightly caramelized.

9. Lower the oven temperature to 300°.

10. Add the wine and the chicken stock (or water). Cover tightly, and cook in the oven for 30 minutes. Add the bacon (if used) and the turnips. Again cover tightly, and cook for 1¼ hours more.

11. Slice the stuffed steak, and arrange the slices, surrounded by the turnips and the juice, on a serving platter.

Filet Mignon au Foie Gras

SAUTÉED FILET MIGNON WITH FOIE GRAS

This is a wonderful dish, wonderfully rich, and still popular with Lutèce customers, as it has been for more than thirty years.

Serves 2

salt
pepper, fresh ground
2 filets mignons, about 5 ounces
  each
2 tablespoons (¼ stick) unsalted
  butter
1 scant tablespoon peanut oil
2 slices fresh foie gras, about 2

ounces each, or 2 slices of
Terrine de Foie Gras (page
182), about 1 ounce each
6 mushrooms, washed and sliced
1 tablespoon Madeira
2 tablespoons heavy cream
3 tablespoons Fond de Veau
  (page 510)

1. Salt and pepper the filets mignons. In a skillet, melt ⅓ of the butter with the oil, and sauté the filets mignons over high heat for 4 minutes on each side. (The filets will be rare. To do them medium rare, sauté them for 1 more minute on each side.) Remove the meat from the skillet. Set aside, and keep warm.

2. In the same skillet, sauté the slices of foie gras (or Terrine de Foie Gras), 1½ minutes on each side, and put each slice on 1 of the filets mignons.

3. Discard most of the fat from the skillet, and sauté the mushrooms in the remaining fat over high heat for 3 minutes. Still over high heat, add the Madeira. Then add the cream, and cook for 2 minutes more.

4. Add the Fond de Veau. Bring to the boil, and stir in the remaining butter while cooking for 1 minute more. At this stage the sauce should be silky.

5. Pour the mushroom sauce over the meat. Serve hot.

Note: Any vegetable is a good garnish for this beef.

Filet Mignon en Croûte Lutèce

FILET MIGNON IN PUFF PASTRY

Beef Wellington was once very fashionable. In this version I make it in servings for one person. *Serves 4*

salt

pepper, fresh ground

4 filets mignons, about 5 ounces each

1 tablespoon peanut oil

4 slices of fresh foie gras, about 1 ounce each, or 4 slices of Terrine de Foie Gras (page 182)

1 tablespoon unsalted butter

2 shallots, peeled and chopped

6 ounces mushrooms, washed and chopped coarse

flour for flouring the work surface

1 pound Feuilletage Rapide (page 531)

1 egg beaten with a little cold water

1. Salt and pepper the filets mignons. In a skillet, heat the oil over high heat, and sear the filets mignons for 1 to 1½ minutes on each side, depending on the thickness of the meat. Remove the meat from the skillet. Set aside and let cool.

2. In the same skillet, over high heat, sauté the slices of foie gras (or Terrine de Foie Gras) for ½ minute on each side. Salt and pepper the foie gras while it is in the skillet. Remove it from the skillet. Set aside and let cool.

3. In a sauté pan, over medium heat, melt the butter. Add the shallots, and sauté for 1 minute. Add the mushrooms, salt, and pepper, and continue sautéing until all the liquid has cooked off and the mushrooms are dry. Set aside and let cool.

4. On a lightly floured work surface, roll out the Feuilletage Rapide in a sheet ¹⁄₁₆ of an inch thick. Cut out 4 rounds, each the size of a filet mignon, plus a generous border. Cut out 4 more rounds, each a little larger than the first 4.

5. Put the first 4 pastry rounds on an ungreased pastry sheet. Put 1

Filet Mignon en Croûte Lutèce (continued)

filet mignon at the center of each round. Put a slice of foie gras on each of the filets mignons. Spread ¼ of the reserved mushrooms on each slice of foie gras. Brush the exposed edges of the pastry with a little of the beaten egg.

6. Put 1 of the remaining pastry rounds on each of the filets mignons. Firmly press the overhanging edges of the top pastries to the exposed edges of the bottom pastries, to seal them. Brush the top pastries with the beaten egg. Refrigerate for at least 15 minutes on the pastry sheet.

7. Preheat the oven to 425°.

8. Trim off the excess pastry, leaving a ¼-inch border of sealed pastry around each filet mignon. Put the filets mignons, on the pastry sheet, on the center rack of the preheated oven. Bake for 12 minutes—until the pastries are golden brown.

Note: Serve with Sauce Périgourdine (page 523), and garnish with any vegetable.

❧

Pommes de Terre Farcies

STUFFED POTATOES

There are dishes you cannot make in small amounts, but when meat is left over, it can be turned into a satisfying dish, if not a great one.

This dish was one of my mother's ways of using leftovers—boiled beef, veal, even chicken, though beef is best. She served this to us many times when I was young. With a salad it is a good simple dinner.

Serves 4

The Stuffing

½ pound leftover meat (boiled beef, veal stew, etc.)
2 slices white bread, trimmed
¼ cup milk

1 tablespoon unsalted butter
1 medium onion, peeled and chopped

¼ pound smoked bacon, cut
   crosswise in ¼-inch
   pieces
1 garlic clove, peeled, green
   germ removed, and chopped
   fine

1 tablespoon chopped parsley
salt
pepper, fresh ground

Stuffing and Baking the Potatoes

4 large baking potatoes, peeled
   and washed
8 strips smoked bacon
1 garlic clove, peeled
1 medium onion, peeled and
   sliced
2 tablespoons lard, melted

¾ cup Fond Blanc de Volaille
   (page 512), or water (see *Note*
   on page 58)
salt
pepper, fresh ground
1 bouquet garni (page 55)

The Stuffing

1. Grind the meat through the fine blade of a meat grinder, or process it in a food processor. Soak the bread in the milk.

2. In a saucepan, heat the butter. Add the onion, and sauté for 1 minute. Add the ¼-inch strips of bacon, and sauté for 1 more minute. Add the ground meat and garlic.

3. Squeeze the excess milk from the bread, and add the bread to the saucepan. Add the parsley.

4. Over low heat, stir the contents of the saucepan until they are well mixed. Continue cooking and stirring for 5 minutes. Add salt and pepper to taste. Set aside.

Stuffing and Baking the Potatoes

5. Cut a thin slice from the bottom of the potatoes, so that they will be stable on a flat surface. Cut a ½-inch-thick slice from the top of the potatoes, for the lid. Hollow out the body of the potatoes with a melon scooper or spoon, leaving a shell ½ inch thick.

6. Fill the potatoes with the filling. Cover them with the lids. Wrap each potato with 2 strips of bacon.

7. With the garlic clove, rub the bottom of a pot that will just hold the

Pommes de Terre Farcies (continued)

4 potatoes. Put the sliced onion in the pot. Add 1 tablespoon of the melted lard. Put the potatoes in the pot side by side. Add the Fond Blanc de Volaille (or water). Pour the remaining melted lard over the potatoes. Sprinkle with a little salt and pepper. Add the bouquet garni.

8. Preheat the oven to 400°.

9. Cover the pot with its lid. Bring it to the boil on top of the stove, and then put it in the preheated oven for 50 minutes. Baste the potatoes once or twice during the baking. At the end of the 50 minutes, the liquid should be almost all gone, and the potatoes should be tender and nicely browned.

Queue de Boeuf Bourguignonne

OXTAIL STEW

A certain Central American ambassador always writes me a letter a month ahead of time when he is going to be in New York. He wants to make sure I will make for him this Oxtail Stew when he comes to Lutèce.

Serves 3 to 4

1 oxtail, 3 to 4 pounds
½ pound pork skin (optional)
3 cups red wine
1 teaspoon sugar
1 tablespoon lard (or oil)
½ pound carrots, trimmed, peeled, washed, and cut in ⅓-inch discs
4 shallots, peeled

2 garlic cloves, peeled, halved, green germs removed
1 small onion (about 1½ inches in diameter), peeled and cut in ¼-inch disks
1 tablespoon all-purpose flour
1 bouquet garni (page 55)
pepper, fresh ground
salt

1. Trim the oxtail of all fat. Cut the tail in pieces by slicing between the bones at each joint.

2. Blanch the pork skin (if used) briefly in boiling unsalted water.

3. In a pan, bring the wine and sugar to the boil. Set aside.

4. In a heavy-bottomed ovenproof pot, over medium heat, melt the lard (or heat the oil). Add the pieces of oxtail and brown them on all sides. It takes about 8 minutes.

5. With a slotted spoon, remove the oxtail from the pot. Discard all the fat from the pot. Return the oxtail to the pot, and add the carrots, shallots, garlic, and onion. Sauté, constantly stirring, for 3 minutes. Sprinkle the flour over the oxtail and vegetables, and sauté for another 2 minutes.

6. Preheat the oven to 225°.

7. If using the pork skin, remove the oxtail and vegetables from the pot, and layer the pork skin on the bottom of the pot, fat side down. Return the meat and vegetables to the pot. Add the reserved wine, bouquet garni, pepper, and a moderate amount of salt. Bring to the boil, cover with a well-fitting lid, and then transfer the pot to the preheated oven for 3½ hours—until the meat is tender. (The cooking may take as long as 4 hours.)

8. Remove the pot from the oven, and let it stand at room temperature for 10 to 15 minutes. Then, with a ladle or a large spoon, skim all fat from the surface of the liquid.

9. With a slotted spoon, remove the pieces of oxtail from the pot. Strain everything else in the pot through a fine sieve, pushing the vegetables through. Return this sauce to the pot. Add the oxtail. Bring to the boil, and serve.

Note: Purée de Pommes de Terre (page 419) or a puree of knob celery is very good with this stew.

*An Alsatian dinner at Chez Hansi, in Paris, where I
was the chef in the late 1950s and early 1960s*

Foie Gras aux Pommes (page 209)

Choucroute Garni à l'Alsacienne (page 388)

Crêpes à l'Alsacienne (page 438)

SPECIAL ALSATIAN DISHES

ACCORDING TO an old definition, a "brasserie" is a restaurant that sells beer. So it is not so surprising that in France brasseries are also places that sell choucroute, because with choucroute beer is a very good drink.

But even when I was a young man brasseries could be much more than just restaurants with beer. When I worked in Paris at Chez Hansi, for example, the restaurant was a brasserie, but it offered a big selection of classic French dishes and bistro food as well.

Still, it was a brasserie, and also an Alsatian one—so we served huge amounts of choucroute and other Alsatian dishes.

Because all the dishes in this section of the book are Alsatian, I introduce it with an Alsatian dinner—dishes that we served all the time at Chez Hansi when I was the chef there.

Carpe à la Juive

COLD CARP IN WHITE WINE

At one time, the largest Jewish community in France, outside of Paris, was in Alsace. That is why this traditional old Jewish dish was a part of regular Alsatian cooking, and still is.

Note: Carp is a difficult fish to clean and bone. Ask your fish dealer to

clean and bone the fish, to cut it in fillets with the skin on, and to retain the
bones and head (split in half).   *Serves 6*

1 carp, around 3 pounds
2 tablespoons olive oil
2 medium onions, peeled and
   sliced
½ tablespoon all-purpose flour
2 garlic cloves, peeled, green
   germs removed, and sliced

2 cups dry white wine
1 bouquet garni (page 55)
salt
cracked pepper
1 tablespoon chopped parsley

1. Wash the head and bones of the carp under cold water, and drain
them. Rinse the fillets under cold water, and cut each fillet into 6 pieces—
12 pieces altogether.

2. Preheat the oven to 300°.

3. In a saucepan, heat the oil. Add the onions, and sauté, without
browning, for 2 to 3 minutes. Add the head and bones, and sauté for a few
minutes more, again without browning. Add the flour, stir it in well, and
sauté until the flour browns slightly.

4. Add the garlic, wine, bouquet garni, a little salt, pepper, and 2 cups
of water. Bring to the boil, and cook for 20 minutes over medium heat.

5. Arrange the fillets in a roasting pan. Pass the
cooking liquid through a fine sieve over the fish. Put
the pan over heat, and bring it to the boil. Cover the
fish with a sheet of parchment paper, and put the
roasting pan in the preheated oven for 20 minutes.

6. Leaving the liquid in the roasting pan,
put the fillets in a deep porcelain dish. Over high
heat, reduce the liquid in the baking pan by ½. Correct
the seasoning of the liquid, and pass it through
a fine sieve over the fish. Sprinkle with
chopped parsley.

7. Let the fish cool, then refrigerate it for at least 2 hours. The
juice will become slightly gelatinous. Serve cold.

Note: This carp may be prepared with red wine instead of white. When it is, the dish is served hot. To make this hot red-wine version, follow the recipe through Step 6, using red wine instead of white. Serve hot, garnished with Nouilles à l'Alsacienne (page 411), or with boiled potatoes.

✺

Carpe Frite

DEEP-FRIED CARP

A lsatians go out for Carpe Frite on Saturday and Sunday nights. They go to cafés that offer all the Carpe Frite you can eat for a fixed, very moderate price. Of course, with the Carpe Frite you drink Alsatian white wine, and for that you pay according to how much you order.

Big platters of the fried fish are delivered to the table, one after the other, until you say stop. It is very easy to eat too much, and on my visits home to Alsace I sometimes do, to my regret.

There are several ways to make Carpe Frite. Some cafés roll the carp in semolina before frying it. Some fry it with nothing on the outside at all. Others fry it in batter—which is the way I myself prefer, and which is how I prepare it when I make it at Lutèce once in a while.

Each way has its fanatical fans. Here are two methods—with a batter (Pâte à Frire), and rolled in semolina.

Note: Carp is a difficult fish to clean and bone. Ask your fish dealer to clean and bone the fish, remove the skin, and cut it in fillets.

Serves 4

Method I

1 carp, 3 to 3½ pounds, cleaned, skinned, and filleted (yield: about 1½ pounds of carp fillets)
juice of ½ lemon

salt
pepper, fresh ground
1 tablespoon chopped parsley
1 recipe Pâte à Frire (page 536)
1 quart oil for deep frying

Carpe Frite (continued)

1. Cut the fillets of carp into 12 equal pieces, and put them in a deep plate. Add the lemon juice, sprinkle lightly with salt, pepper, and chopped parsley, and let the carp marinate for 1 hour. Turn it occasionally during this period.

Note: The Pâte à Frire may be prepared while the carp is marinating.

2. Heat the oil in the deep fryer to 375°.
3. Dip each piece of fish in the Pâte à Frire, and plunge it into the hot oil. (This step should be carried out in 2 batches of 6 pieces each.) Fry the fish until it is golden brown. The fillets should be turned in the fat once or twice during the frying, so that they brown all over. It takes about 8 minutes to fry each batch.
4. When the fish is ready, remove it from the oil, drain it on paper towels, and sprinkle it with a little salt. Serve hot.

Note: Serve with Sauce Gribiche (page 519), or with Mayonnaise (page 515).

Method II

1 carp, 3 to 3½ pounds, cleaned, skinned, and filleted (yield: about 1½ pounds of carp fillets)	1 tablespoon chopped parsley
	1 quart oil for deep frying, plus 1 tablespoon oil
	2 eggs
juice of ½ lemon	⅓ cup semolina
salt	⅓ cup all-purpose flour
pepper, fresh ground	

1. Cut the fillets of carp into 12 equal pieces, and put them in a deep plate. Add the lemon juice, sprinkle lightly with salt, pepper, and chopped parsley, and let marinate for 1 hour. Turn the fish occasionally during this period.
2. Heat the quart of oil in the deep fryer to 375°.
3. In a bowl, beat the eggs with the 1 tablespoon of oil and a pinch of salt.
4. Mix the semolina and flour.

5. Dip the carp in the egg mixture, and then in the mixture of semolina and flour. With your hands, pat the fillets to press the semolina and flour into the surface of the fish.

6. Plunge the fillets into the hot oil. (This step should be carried out in 2 batches of 6 pieces each.) Fry the fish until it is golden brown. The fish should be turned at least once in the oil. It takes about 6 minutes to fry each batch.

7. When the fish is ready, remove it from the oil, drain it on paper towels, and sprinkle it with a little salt. Serve hot.

Note: Serve with Sauce Gribiche (page 519), or with Mayonnaise (page 515).

Cervelas de Brochet de Choucroute au Genièvre

PIKE SAUSAGES WITH SAUERKRAUT AND JUNIPER BERRIES

We did not start making this dish at Lutèce until the restaurant was almost thirty years old.

It happens that one time I was invited to Colmar to demonstrate some of my cooking. It was a big event, and all the best chefs of Alsace came to show what they do. There is nothing like this in America. It goes on for days. Thousands of people come. The demonstrations go on nonstop. When a chef is showing how he makes a dish, the demonstration is shown on huge screens all around the convention hall.

This dish was done by my friend Emile Jung. He has a very popular three-star restaurant in Strasbourg, called Le Crocodile. By now I no longer make it exactly the way he makes it—after a while, when you make a dish, your own feelings take over. But it is basically Emile Jung's idea.

Serves 4

1 pound sauerkraut
1 tablespoon lard
¼ pound smoked pork shoulder,
   cut in small pieces
1 medium onion, peeled and
   sliced
1½ cups dry Sylvaner, or
   another dry white wine
salt
pepper, fresh ground
24 juniper berries
1 bay leaf
1 clove

1 garlic clove, peeled, halved,
   green germ removed
½ teaspoon cumin seeds
2 tablespoons chopped shallots
½ cup Fond Blanc de Volaille
   (page 512)
7 tablespoons (⅞ stick) unsalted
   butter
1 fillet of pike (or bass), about 1
   pound

1. Set aside 2 tablespoons of the sauerkraut juice, then wash the sauerkraut several times in cold water. Drain well.

2. Preheat the oven to 350°.

3. In a pot, melt the lard over medium heat. Add the pork shoulder and the onion, and sauté until the onion is wilted. Add 1 cup of the wine, the sauerkraut, ½ cup of water, a little salt, and pepper.

4. In a piece of cheesecloth, tie 4 of the juniper berries, the bay leaf, clove, garlic, and cumin seeds, and add to the pot. Bring to the boil, and cook in the preheated oven for 1¼ hours.

5. While the pot is in the oven, put the shallots and ½ cup of the wine in a small saucepan, and cook over medium heat until the liquid is reduced by ⅔. Add the Fond Blanc de Volaille and the reserved sauerkraut juice. Whisk in the butter a few pieces at a time. Add salt and pepper to taste. Strain this sauce into a bowl, and add the 20 remaining juniper berries. Keep warm.

6. Cut the pike (or bass) into 4 equal parts. With the side of a wide knife or cleaver, flatten them between 2 pieces of parchment paper or waxed paper.

7. When the sauerkraut is done, remove it from the oven and stir in 4 tablespoons of the sauce.

8. Put equal parts of the sauerkraut along the center of each of the pieces of pike (or bass). Roll each piece into a sausage, wrap it securely in plastic wrap, and tie each sausage at both ends with string. Cook these sausages in hot water for 6 minutes. *The water must not boil.*

9. Remove the sausages from their wrappers, put each at the center of a heated plate, and spoon the remainder of the sauce around the sausages. Serve immediately.

꧁

Filets de Brochet au Vinaigre

PIKE IN VINEGAR SAUCE

Serves 4

The Nage

2 tablespoons (¼ stick) unsalted
   butter
1 leek, washed and cut in ¼-
   inch dice
1 carrot, trimmed, peeled,
   washed, and cut in ¼-inch
   dice
1 onion, peeled and cut in ¼-
   inch dice
1 stalk celery, peeled, washed,
   and cut in ¼-inch dice

1 small fennel head, washed,
   and cut in ¼-inch dice
1 garlic clove, cracked
1 bay leaf
1 sprig thyme
1 clove
1 cup dry white wine
¼ teaspoon cracked pepper
½ teaspoon salt

The Sauce

¼ pound (1 stick) unsalted
   butter
2 tablespoons chopped shallots
½ cup tarragon vinegar

½ cup nage (prepared in Step 1)
¼ cup heavy cream
salt
pepper, fresh ground

Filets de Brochet au Vinaigre (continued)

The Pike and the Final Assembly

1½ pounds fillets of pike
1½ tablespoons peanut oil
salt

pepper, fresh ground
½ tablespoon chopped chives

The Nage

1. Melt the 2 tablespoons of butter in a sauté pan, and sauté the leek, carrot, onion, celery, and fennel for about 10 minutes. Do not brown. Add the garlic, bay leaf, thyme, clove, white wine, cracked pepper, salt, and 1 cup of water. Bring to the boil and cook for 20 minutes. Drain through a fine sieve, and set aside this liquid (the "nage"). (You will have more of the nage than you need. Keep the balance for another use.)

The Sauce

2. In a skillet, melt 2 tablespoons of the butter. Add the shallots and sauté for a few minutes. Do not brown. Add the vinegar and reduce the liquid to ⅓ of its volume. Add the ½ cup of the nage, and again reduce the liquid to ⅓ of its volume. Add the cream, and cook until the sauce thickens a little—about 3 minutes. Whisk in the remaining butter, and salt and pepper to taste. Set aside and keep warm.

The Pike and the Final Assembly

3. Remove the skin from the pike, and cut it into 4 portions.
4. In a skillet, heat the oil. Salt and pepper the fillets of pike on both sides, and sauté them for about 4 minutes on each side, until they are golden brown. Arrange the fillets on 4 plates. Pour the sauce over them. Sprinkle with the chives.

Note: At Lutèce this dish is served with simple haricots verts, zucchini, and carrots, all arranged on the plate with the fish.

Filets de Sole aux Nouilles

SOLE WITH NOODLES

In the small Alsatian town of Ammerschwihr there is a restaurant called Aux Armes de France. In that restaurant the chef Pierre Gaertner made this dish popular. Pierre Gaertner is gone now, but his family carries on Aux Armes de France, and they probably still serve this dish.

Serves 4

1 tomato
1 tablespoon unsalted butter, softened
1½ pounds fillets of sole
1 tablespoon chopped shallot
salt
pepper, fresh ground
1 cup dry white wine
1⅓ cups Fumet de Poisson (page 513), or water (see *Note* on page 58)
1 cup heavy cream

12 ounces egg noodles or fettuccine, fresh if possible
1 recipe Sauce Hollandaise (page 519)
cayenne pepper

1. Cut a conical plug from the stem end of the tomato and discard. Blanch the tomato in boiling water for 10 seconds, drain it under cold water, and peel off the skin. Cut the tomato in half, squeeze out and discard the juice and seeds, and chop the pulp in ¼-inch cubes.

2. Preheat the oven to 375°.

3. Spread ½ of the softened butter in a large ovenproof sauté pan. Put the fillets in the pan in one layer, folding them slightly to fit if necessary. Sprinkle the fish with the shallot, salt, pepper, and the chopped tomato. Pour the wine and Fumet de Poisson (or water) over the fish, and cover it with a sheet of parchment paper buttered with the remaining butter.

4. On top of the stove, over medium heat, bring the pan to the boil.

Filets de Sole aux Nouilles (continued)

Transfer the pan to the preheated oven, and bake until the fillets are just firm—about 6 minutes. *Do not overcook.*

5. Remove the sauté pan from the oven, and pour the cooking liquid from the pan into a heavy saucepan. Keep the fish in the sauté pan, covered. Over high heat, reduce the liquid in the saucepan by ¾. (You should end up with about ½ cup.) Add ½ of the cream, and boil until the sauce is slightly thickened—about 3 minutes. Set aside.

6. Meanwhile, bring a large pot of salted water to the boil. Add the noodles. Return to the boil, and cook until the noodles are tender but still firm. Rinse the noodles under cold water, and drain.

7. Preheat the broiler.

8. Put the noodles and the remaining cream in a gratin dish that is large enough to hold the fish in one layer.

9. Drain any exuded juices from the reserved fish into the reserved sauce. Arrange the fish over the noodles.

10. Whisk the Sauce Hollandaise into the sauce. Add salt, pepper, and cayenne to taste. Spread this sauce evenly over the fish. Put the fish under the broiler until the sauce is golden and bubbly—about 1 minute. Serve at once.

Suprêmes de Bass sur Choucroute

FILLETS OF BASS ON SAUERKRAUT

In the old, old days, fish with sauerkraut was not a rare combination. Then it was forgotten.

But in the 1970s, in Paris, an Alsatian cook by the name of Guy-Pierre Baumann—his restaurant was called Baumann—started making fish-and-sauerkraut dishes, and they caught on. Today Baumann has a restaurant in Strasbourg—Maison Kammerzell—where of course he continues to serve these marvelous dishes.

Everybody thinks of heavy food—meat and sausages—when they think of sauerkraut, but here is a wonderful light way to enjoy it.

Serves 4

The Sauerkraut

1 pound sauerkraut
1 ounce lard
¼ pound smoked pork, cut in
    ¼-inch pieces
1 medium onion, peeled and
    sliced thin
1 cup Sylvaner, or another dry
    white wine

salt
pepper, fresh ground
4 juniper berries
1 bay leaf
1 clove
1 garlic clove, peeled and
    crushed
½ teaspoon cumin seeds

The Sauce

2 tablespoons shallots chopped
    fine
½ cup Sylvaner, or another dry
    white wine
½ cup Fond Blanc de Volaille
    (page 512)

2 tablespoons juice from the
    prepared sauerkraut
6 tablespoons (¾ stick) unsalted
    butter
salt
pepper, fresh ground

The Bass

2 pounds fillet of sea bass, in 8
    pieces, each ½ inch thick
salt

pepper, fresh ground
2 tablespoons (¼ stick)
    unsalted butter

The Sauerkraut

1. Set aside 2 tablespoons of the sauerkraut juice for use in making *The Sauce*.

2. Wash the sauerkraut several times in cold water. Drain well.

3. Preheat the oven to 350°.

4. In a pot, melt the lard over medium heat. Add the pork and the onion and sauté until wilted, about 5 minutes.

5. Add the wine, ½ cup of water, the sauerkraut, and salt and pepper to taste. In a piece of cheesecloth, tie the juniper berries, bay leaf, clove, garlic, and cumin seeds. Add this bag to the pot. Bring to the boil and cook

Suprêmes de Bass (continued)

in the preheated oven for 1¼ hours. Adjust the seasoning, set aside, and keep warm.

The Sauce

6. In a small saucepan cook the shallots and wine until the liquid has been reduced by ⅔. Add the Fond Blanc de Volaille and the sauerkraut juice and return to the boil. Whisk in the butter a small amount at a time. Add salt and pepper to taste. Set aside and keep warm.

The Bass

7. Season the fillets with salt and pepper.

8. In a large skillet, melt the butter, add the fillets, and sauté them for about 3 minutes on each side.

The Final Assembly

9. With a slotted spoon, remove the sauerkraut from its pot and mound it on the center of 4 heated plates. (The sauerkraut should be moist, but all excess liquid should be drained off before it is placed on the plates.) Spoon the warm sauce around the sauerkraut. Lean 2 fillets on opposite sides of each mound of sauerkraut. Serve immediately.

Matelote de Poissons au Riesling

FISH STEW IN ALSATIAN WHITE WINE

Walk into any really good Alsatian restaurant, ask for this dish, and it will be made for you—it does not matter if it is on the printed menu or not.

An everyday dish in restaurants, at home this is usually a holiday dish, because several different kinds of fish are needed to make it the right way.

Note: If you have your fish filleted for you by your fish dealer, be sure that he gives you the heads, bones, and trimmings of the filleted fish, so that you can make the stock.

Serves 6

The Stock

the heads, bones, and trimmings
  of the filleted fish (the eel,
  pike, trout, and perch listed
  below)
1 leek, washed and cut in large
  pieces
1 medium onion, peeled,
  washed, and cut in large
  pieces
1 carrot, trimmed, peeled,
  washed, and cut in large
  pieces
2 garlic cloves, peeled, halved,
  green germ removed
1 bay leaf
1 sprig tarragon
1 sprig thyme
1 teaspoon salt
½ teaspoon cracked pepper

The Stew

¼ pound (1 stick) unsalted
  butter
¼ cup all-purpose flour
1½ cups sliced mushrooms
1½ pounds eel, eviscerated,
  washed, and filleted
1½ pounds pike, eviscerated,
  gills removed, washed, and
  filleted
1 pound trout (or bass), eviscerated, gills removed, washed,
  and filleted
1 pound perch (or bass), eviscerated, gills removed, washed,
  and filleted
2 tablespoons chopped shallots
1 bottle Riesling
salt
pepper, fresh ground
3 egg yolks
1 cup heavy cream
juice of ½ lemon
1 pinch grated nutmeg
1 tablespoon chopped parsley

The Stock

1. Put the heads, bones, and trimmings of the fish in a pot. Add the leek, onion, carrot, garlic, bay leaf, tarragon, thyme, salt, and pepper. Cover with 1½ quarts of water. Bring to the boil and simmer for 30 minutes. Strain through a fine sieve and set aside.

The Stew

2. In a saucepan, melt 4 tablespoons of the butter. Stir in the flour over a low flame. Cook slowly for 5 minutes. The butter should barely brown. Set aside and let cool.

3. In a skillet, melt 2 tablespoons of the butter. Sauté the sliced mush-

Matelote de Poissons (continued)

rooms in the butter until the liquid from the mushrooms is completely cooked off—about 5 minutes. Set aside.

4. Cut the fish fillets crosswise into 2-inch pieces.

5. In a pot, melt the remaining 2 tablespoons of butter. Add the chopped shallots and sauté gently for 2 to 3 minutes. Add the Riesling, 1 quart of the stock (prepared in Step 1), salt, and pepper. Bring to the boil.

6. Add the eel, and cook for 5 minutes. Add the pike and cook 4 minutes more. Add the perch (or bass) and trout (or bass) and cook another 4 minutes. Set aside, covered.

7. Whisk into the reserved flour-and-butter mixture all the liquid that the fish cooked in. Bring to the boil, and, whisking constantly, simmer for 10 minutes. Turn off the heat.

8. In a small bowl, combine the egg yolks and cream, then whisk them into the liquid. Bring up to heat, but do not boil. Add the lemon juice and nutmeg. Strain this sauce through a fine sieve. Add the mushrooms to the sauce.

9. Put equal amounts of the fish on 6 plates. Pour the sauce over the fish. Sprinkle with the chopped parsley.

Note: This dish goes very nicely with a garnish of Nouilles à l'Alsacienne (page 411).

Coq Sauté à la Bière d'Alsace

SAUTÉED CHICKEN IN BEER

Half the beer drunk in France comes from Alsace, where beer drinking is a thousand years old, and where beer is the second drink after Alsatian white wine.

In Alsace, beer is even drunk as an aperitif. Particularly on Sunday, people go to the bistros after mass and drink "amer seidel," which is beer to which an ounce of the bitters called Amer Picon, and a few drops of lemon syrup, have been added.

There used to be dozens of breweries in Alsace—almost every village had its own. Most of the old breweries are gone now, bought up by the big beer companies, but the tradition of cooking with beer is still strong.

At Lutèce, customers are surprised to learn that I sometimes cook with beer, but as an Alsatian it is natural to me. There are no beer dishes on the Lutèce printed menu, but I often serve one as the lunchtime special of the day.

Now, lately, all over France chefs are coming up with new dishes made with beer. To cook with beer has become fashionable.   *Serves 4*

salt
pepper, fresh ground
1 chicken, about 4 pounds, cut
    in 8 serving pieces
3 tablespoons (⅜ stick) unsalted
    butter
1 onion, peeled and chopped
1 garlic clove, peeled, green
    germ removed, chopped

1 bay leaf
2 cloves
3 cups beer (light colored)
1 tablespoon flour
1 pinch grated nutmeg
3 egg yolks, beaten
1 cup heavy cream

1. Salt and pepper the chicken. In a large skillet, melt 2 tablespoons of the butter over medium heat. Sauté the chicken until the pieces are golden brown on all sides.

2. Add the onion, garlic, bay leaf, cloves, and beer. Bring to the boil,

Coq Sauté à la Bière (continued)

and simmer until the drumsticks are tender to the fork—about 40 minutes. Remove the chicken from the skillet, set it aside, and keep it warm.

3. Over medium heat, cook the liquid in the skillet until it is reduced by ⅓. Strain this bouillon through a sieve, and set it aside.

4. In a saucepan, melt the remaining tablespoon of butter. Stir in the flour, and cook for 2 minutes. Then gradually stir in the bouillon and the nutmeg. Cook gently for 10 more minutes.

5. Put the egg yolks and cream in a bowl. Whisking constantly, *slowly* add 1 cup of the bouillon. Then, still whisking, pour in the rest of the bouillon. Return this sauce to the saucepan, and, whisking constantly, slowly reheat it. *Do not boil.*

6. Pour the sauce over the chicken, and serve hot.

Note: Nouilles à l'Alsacienne (page 411) are the right accompaniment to this dish.

Coq Sauté au Riesling

Note: Coq Sauté à la Bière d'Alsace may also be prepared as Coq Sauté au Riesling. Substitute 2 cups of Riesling (or another dry white Alsatian wine) and 1 cup of water for the 3 cups of beer.

Poitrine de Veau Farcie

STUFFED BREAST OF VEAL

Where I come from, the small town of Thann, in Alsace, every year there is a Poitrine de Veau Festival. The festival is held on a weekend in late spring, when the weather is warm. The whole town comes, and people from the region all around.

There is a giant tent. There is music and dancing, which goes on long into the night. The town orders huge amounts of poitrine de veau, and they sell it by the slice. All the money goes to the town—for the fire department, or for something like that.

Of course, with all that poitrine de veau the people drink a large amount of cold beer, and also a large amount of Alsatian white wine. Everyone has a good time.

Some people say that this dish was brought to Alsace by the Romans. It could be. But the festival is a local invention. *Serves 6*

The Stuffing

1 tablespoon unsalted butter
1 small onion, peeled and sliced
1 cup milk
½ pound white bread, sliced
½ pound veal (neck or shoulder)
½ pound pork butt

2 eggs
1 tablespoon chopped parsley
1 ounce Cognac
salt
pepper, fresh ground

The Stuffed Breast of Veal

1 breast of veal, about 3 pounds, with a pocket cut into edges of the breast (may be prepared ahead by your butcher)
salt
pepper, fresh ground
1 tablespoon unsalted butter
1 tablespoon peanut oil

1 carrot, trimmed, peeled, washed, and cut in ¾-inch pieces
1 medium onion, peeled, cut in ¾-inch pieces
2 celery stalks, peeled, washed, and cut in ¾-inch pieces
1 cup dry white wine

The Stuffing

1. In a skillet, melt the butter, and sauté the onion for 5 minutes.
2. Warm the milk. Trim the crusts from the bread, and cut the bread in 1-inch squares. Soak the bread in the warmed milk. When the bread has soaked in the milk for a few minutes, squeeze it to remove some but not all of the milk.
3. Cut the veal and the pork in cubes. Grind the meat, onion, and bread in a meat grinder, using the medium blade. Put the ground ingredients in a bowl and, with a wooden spoon, stir in the eggs, parsley, Cognac, salt, and pepper. Mix until you have a uniform blend.

Poitrine de Veau Farcie (continued)

Note: This step may be performed with a food processor, but care must be taken not to overprocess. The mixture must have texture. *It must not become a mousse.*

The Stuffed Breast of Veal

4. Preheat the oven to 325°.

5. Fill the pocket of the breast of veal with the stuffing. Sew the pocket closed with a needle and string. Season the outside of the breast with salt and pepper on all sides.

6. In a roasting pan, melt the butter with the oil. Over medium heat, brown the stuffed breast on all sides—about 12 minutes altogether. Add the carrot, onion, celery, salt, and pepper.

7. Put the roasting pan in the preheated oven for 20 minutes. Turn the breast over. Roast for another 20 minutes. During this 40 minutes of roasting, the breast should be basted with the pan juices from time to time. At this point, the breast should be golden brown.

8. Lower the oven temperature to 300°.

9. Add the wine and ½ cup of water to the roasting pan. Cover the breast with a sheet of parchment paper. Roast for another 1 hour and 15 minutes. Baste 2 or 3 times during this period.

10. Remove the roasting pan from the oven, put the veal on a cutting board, and let it rest for 10 to 15 minutes. Remove the string.

11. Skim the grease from the juice in the roasting pan and discard. Taste the remaining juice and adjust the seasoning if necessary. Cut the stuffed breast in ½-inch slices. Spoon the sauce from the roasting pan around the slices of veal.

Note: When served hot at Lutèce we garnish this veal either with Spätzele (page 418), or with Nouilles à l'Alsacienne (page 411), or with Purée de Pommes de Terre (page 419).

Note: This dish is excellent cold, served with Sauce Raifort (page 523) and Salade de Pommes de Terre (page 243).

Délice de Veau Vosgienne à la Mama

VEAL CORDON BLEU, BRAISED

Here is my mother's version of what is usually called Veal Cordon Bleu. It is country cooking, far away from classic French food. Chefs of haute cuisine will have nothing to do with it.

But in my childhood, my mother made it for us often. Sometimes, she would put it in a very slow oven, and then go to church. When she got home, it would be just ready.

This was one of my favorites of the many dishes my mother made, and I have it as a regular item on the lunch menu at Lutèce. *Serves 4*

1 pound veal (loin or top round), boned and trimmed, cut into 8 scallops

6 ounces Swiss cheese (Emmental or Gruyère), cut in 16 2-inch squares

3 ounces smoked ham (2 slices, each slice cut in 4 parts, each part approximately a 2-inch square)

salt

pepper, fresh ground

flour for dusting the veal

2 eggs beaten with a little cold water

¾ cup dry bread crumbs

2 tablespoons peanut oil

2 tablespoons (¼ stick) unsalted butter

½ cup Fond de Veau (page 510), or water (see *Note* on page 58)

juice of ½ lemon

1. Put the scallops of veal between sheets of oiled parchment paper, and flatten them with the side of a cleaver to a thickness of about ¼ inch. Each scallop should be about 4″ by 5″.

2. Put a slice of cheese over one end of each scallop, then put a slice of ham on each slice of cheese, then a slice of cheese on each slice of ham. Fold the exposed end of each scallop over the top slice of cheese. Season the veal with salt and pepper. Then sprinkle the veal with the flour, top and bottom.

3. Brush the veal with the beaten egg, top and bottom. Then sprinkle

Délice de Veau Vosgienne (continued)

the veal with the bread crumbs. Press the bread crumbs into the surface of the meat.

4. Preheat the oven to 275°.

5. In an ovenproof skillet large enough to hold the 8 scallops, heat the oil and butter. Over medium heat, sauté the scallops on both sides until they are golden brown—about 3 minutes on each side.

6. Add the Fond de Veau (or water) and lemon juice to the skillet. Cover the skillet with aluminum foil, or with a tight-fitting lid, and put it in the preheated oven for 30 minutes. Put the scallops on serving plates. Strain the cooking juices through a fine sieve.

Note: Serve immediately, with the cooking juices. The veal may be served with Purée de Pommes de Terre (page 419) or with any vegetable puree. At Lutèce we garnish the veal also with mushrooms.

჻

Quenelles de Foie de Veau à l'Alsacienne

ALSATIAN CALF'S LIVER DUMPLINGS

At home in Alsace, this is a traditional main course, but at Lutèce I usually serve it either as an appetizer—especially on Fridays, when I often make fish the special main course—or as a garnish with choucroute.

This recipe makes sixteen to twenty quenelles (depending on how big you make them), a main course for four or five people. But of course you can serve it as an appetizer for eight or ten people.

Serves 4 or 5 (8 or 10 as a first course)

3 ounces soft bread
½ cup milk
1 medium onion (approximately
    ¼ pound), peeled and sliced
    very thin
1 tablespoon peanut oil

5 ounces smoked strip bacon
1 garlic clove, peeled, green
    germ removed, and chopped
½ pound calf's liver
2 ounces semolina
3 eggs, well beaten

2 ample tablespoons chopped
   parsley and chopped chervil,
   mixed
1 pinch grated nutmeg
salt
pepper, fresh ground

1 tablespoon unsalted butter
1 medium onion, peeled and
   chopped
½ cup Fond de Veau (page 510)
   (optional), reduced by ⅓, hot

1. Soak the bread in the milk.

2. Over medium heat, sauté the sliced onion in the oil until golden brown.

3. Over medium heat, sauté the bacon in its own fat for 2 minutes.

4. Squeeze the excess milk from the bread. Grind the bread, sautéed onion, bacon, garlic, and the calf's liver in a meat grinder, using the fine blade. (A food processor may be used, but do not overprocess.)

5. Put the mixture in a bowl. Add the semolina, eggs, ⅔ of the parsley and chervil mixture, the nutmeg, and salt and pepper to taste. Stir with a wooden spoon.

6. Bring a large pot of salted water to the boil, and keep the pot boiling at a simmer. With a spoon, form the liver mixture into egg-shaped dumplings (quenelles). Add the quenelles to the pot of boiling water one at a time. They are ready when they float to the surface—about 12 minutes.

Note: The quenelles can be of almost any size, depending on whether you form them with a teaspoon, tablespoon, or even a serving spoon.

7. With a slotted spoon, remove the quenelles from the boiling water as they become ready, and put them on a cloth towel to drain.

8. In a small skillet, melt the butter, and sauté the chopped onion in the butter for 2 minutes.

9. Arrange the quenelles on a platter, sprinkle them with the remainder of the parsley and chervil mixture and the sautéed chopped onions. Pour the Fond de Veau (if used) over them. Serve very hot.

Note: When served as a main course, the quenelles may be garnished with Choucroute (page 384) or Spätzele (page 418).

Bacheofe

AN ALSATIAN MEAT STEW

The name "Bacheofe" means "baker's oven," and this is a very classic Alsatian dish. It is popular all over Alsace, but it is not known too much outside.

Long ago—not when my mother was a child, but when my grandmother was a child—Bacheofe always was eaten on Monday. On that day the women were too busy to cook, because it was laundry day.

The day before, on Sunday, they would put meat and Alsatian wine and other things in an earthenware pot to marinate. And on Monday morning, when the children went to school, they took the pot with them to the bakery. At that time in the morning all the bread for the day was already baked, but the ovens were still warm, and the pots would be left in the baker's warm ovens.

When the children passed the bakery on their way home from school at noon, they would pick up the pots, which were just ready. The men home from work, and the children home from school, would take the lid off the pot and scoop out the food. That was their lunch.

This is basic, hearty food, and to me it is a very great dish. It is the kind of food people ate in the old days, and in Alsace they still do.

Serves 6

The First Day

1 pig's foot
½ pound lamb shoulder
½ pound pork shoulder
½ pound breast of beef, boned
1 bouquet garni (page 55)
2 cups dry Alsatian white wine,
    or another dry white wine

1 small onion, peeled and sliced
    thin
1 garlic clove, peeled, halved,
    green germ removed
salt
pepper, fresh ground

The Second Day

1 pound potatoes, peeled and
    sliced thin
¼ pound onions, peeled and
    sliced thin
dry Alsatian white wine, or an-
    other dry white wine, as
    needed to cover

salt
pepper, fresh ground
½ cup all-purpose flour

The First Day

1. Cut the pig's foot, lamb, pork, and beef in 1-inch pieces. Tie the bouquet garni in a piece of cheesecloth. Put the meats, bouquet garni, wine, onion, and garlic in a pot. Add salt and pepper. Refrigerate for 24 hours.

The Second Day

2. Preheat the oven to 300°.
3. Line the bottom of a cocotte with ½ the potatoes. Discard the bouquet garni. Put the meat, with its marinade, on the potatoes. Add the sliced onions, then the rest of the potatoes on top. Add wine to cover. Season with salt and pepper.
4. Put the flour in a bowl and work in enough water to make a soft dough. Roll the dough into a rope long enough to go around the cocotte. Cover the cocotte with its lid, then seal the lid all around with the dough. Cook in the preheated oven for 2½ hours. Serve hot, right from the oven.

Note: Serve with a green salad.

Civet de Lapin aux Nouilles

RABBIT STEW WITH NOODLES

Before I went away to the army, I came home from my job in Switzerland to be with my family in Thann.

While I was home, a big wedding was held about twenty kilometers outside of Thann. It was arranged that a friend of mine would do the cooking, and he got me to do it with him. The family that had this wedding were farmers, and they also ran a bistro. The men took care of the farm, and the women took care of the bistro.

What went on at this wedding was something I never saw before— even though I grew up in the same region where this wedding took place.

There were 180 people, and the celebrating carried on for three days. The eating and drinking and dancing went on morning, noon, and night. Calves and pigs and chickens were slaughtered. The people drank wine by the barrel.

We cooked until two in the morning, and then everybody was ready to start eating again at seven in the morning. At the end of the three days, I was almost dead.

I do not remember if we prepared rabbit this way for the wedding, but all the French love rabbit, so we probably did. If we did, we must have made about a hundred pounds of it. But it is just as good in small quantities.

Note: The recipe calls for carving the rabbit in 12 pieces, bones on. This may be done ahead for you by your butcher. The 12 pieces are: the 2 shoulders, including the forelegs; the 2 hind legs, cut in half; the neck; the left side and the right side of the rib section; and the loin, cut in 3 lengths.

Serves 4

The Marinating

1 rabbit (fryer), about 3 pounds, in 12 pieces, bones on

1 bottle red wine

1 medium onion, peeled and chopped

2 shallots, peeled and halved

3 garlic cloves, peeled, green
    germs removed
1 carrot, trimmed, peeled,
    washed, and chopped
1 bay leaf

1 sprig thyme
salt
cracked pepper

The Sautéing, Stewing, and Serving

¼ pound smoked bacon (a solid
    piece, not strip bacon), cut
    in pieces about ¾″ × ¼″ ×
    ¼″
3 tablespoons (⅜ stick) unsalted
    butter
16 pearl onions, peeled
¼ pound mushrooms, washed
    and sliced

1 tablespoon lard
salt
pepper, fresh ground
1 ample tablespoon flour
1 pound fresh noodles (or
    ½ pound dry commercial
    noodles)

The Marinating

1. Put the pieces of rabbit in a terrine or a bowl. Cover with the remaining ingredients listed under *The Marinating*. Put the bowl in a cool place (or, if a cool place is not available, in the refrigerator) for 12 to 24 hours. Mix from time to time.

The Sautéing, Stewing, and Serving

2. Put the bacon in a saucepan and cover it with cold water. Bring to the boil, and cook for 4 minutes. Drain.

3. In a heavy-bottomed pot, melt ½ tablespoon of the butter. Add the bacon. Over medium-high heat, sauté the bacon for about 3 minutes—it should brown a little. Add the pearl onions, and cook until they are golden brown—about 8 minutes. Add the mushrooms, and sauté quickly over high heat.

4. With a slotted spoon, remove the bacon, pearl onions, and mushrooms from the pot, and set them aside. Leave all the fat in the pot. Add the lard.

5. Remove the pieces of rabbit from the marinade and drain them. Save the marinade, including the vegetables and herbs.

6. Wipe the pieces of rabbit dry. Add them to the fat in the pot. Over

Civet de Lapin (continued)

medium heat, sauté the meat until it is nicely browned—about 10 minutes. Season with salt and pepper. Sprinkle the rabbit with the flour and stir the pieces of rabbit around. Sauté for another 1 to 2 minutes, until the flour is slightly browned.

7. Add the marinade, with its vegetables and herbs, to the pot, and bring to the boil. Cover with a lid, and cook slowly, over low heat, until tender—about 35 minutes. Look at the meat from time to time and add water, about ½ cup at a time, as necessary.

8. With a slotted spoon, remove the pieces of rabbit, and put them on a shallow plate. Spoon the onions, mushrooms, and bacon over the meat. Taste the sauce in the pot, and add salt and pepper to taste. Strain this sauce through a fine sieve over the rabbit.

9. Meanwhile, cook the noodles in salted water. Then sauté them in the remaining butter for 2 minutes. Serve with the rabbit.

CHOUCROUTE: GENERAL INFORMATION

Many people think that in Alsace we eat choucroute (sauerkraut) all the time. But it is not so. At home, when I was growing up, my mother served choucroute maybe three times a year, and only in the winter. That was normal in Alsatian families. Still, Choucroute Garni is the Alsatian national dish par excellence, and no other dish in all gastronomy is as well known worldwide.

When I was an apprentice at the Hôtel du Parc, there too we served Choucroute Garni only a few times a year. Of course we prepared our own choucroute. In September, or early October, when the cabbages were ready, we cut them, salted them, added juniper berries, and put the cabbage in barrels in a cold cellar. We would cover the cabbage with cloths and wood, and weight it down with big stones. Every few days we uncovered the barrels and skimmed the choucroute. After three weeks, we had the "new choucroute." After six weeks, the choucroute was ready—and because it was cured with a lot of salt, it could be stored and used throughout the winter. It was beautiful choucroute.

We apprentices were not so happy on the days when the chef decided to serve choucroute, because we had to go to the ice-cold cellar to get it, and there was the heavy work of washing it—in hot water once, and then in cold water twice—which was necessary with such strong choucroute.

Years later, when I worked in an Alsatian restaurant in Paris, we had choucroute on the menu all the time, because that is what Parisians expected in Alsatian restaurants. We made a fancy version—with champagne—but that is a dish for tourists, not the real Alsatian article.

At Lutèce I have never put Choucroute Garni on the printed menu— it is not what people think of as Lutèce food. But, really, Choucroute Garni is a wonderful dish, and for customer friends who ask for it in advance, I make it. In fact, there are large groups who come every year for my Choucroute Garni—and everyone in the group eats it. For me, the version I serve in Lutèce is equal to the best you can get in Alsace.

To make Choucroute Garni at home, you will probably buy sauerkraut already prepared. When you buy it, look for sauerkraut that is lightest in color. And avoid canned choucroute—the vacuum-packed choucroute sold in plastic bags is better. (When I use pre-prepared sauerkraut, I buy it in New York at Schaller & Weber, and it is very good. There may be other suppliers who are just as good.) If you follow the recipes for preparing the choucroute step by step, the Choucroute Garni you make at home can be excellent. Of course if you wish to make your own sauerkraut it is not so hard. The recipes follow.

Choucroute has a reputation for being very heavy, but it is really very digestible. The reputation has to do with the meats and sausages that are usually served with it.

Actually, there are two kinds of choucroute. The most popular, of course, is made of white cabbage. But in Alsace, a version made with white turnips is also common. It is called Suara Riva or, in French, Navelines Confites.

Commercially, this Navelines Confites is available only in Alsace, nowhere in America. But every fall, late in September or early in October, when New York State turnips are at their best, I make a few pounds of Navelines Confites at Lutèce—for myself and for customer friends.

You cannot really prepare only a small quantity of either kind of choucroute. These recipes—for Choucroute and for Navelines Confites—are for the minimum amount that it is practical to make.

~᪣~

Choucroute

SAUERKRAUT

Yield: approximately 5 pounds drained weight

2 large white cabbages, about 5 pounds each	1 cup rock salt ¼ cup juniper berries

1. Remove all damaged and green leaves from the cabbages, and cut out the cores. Wash the heads of cabbage and drain them. Then, cutting perpendicular to the cores of the cabbages, slice them fine, so that the leaves of cabbage are cut into thin strands.

2. In a stoneware or enamel pot—*not a metal pot*—arrange the cabbage in layers, spreading some of the rock salt and juniper berries on each layer. Cover the cabbage with a cloth napkin. On the cloth place a lid that is a little smaller than the diameter of the pot. Then weight the lid down with a weight of about 3 pounds. Usually a clean stone is used. Any weight may be used, *but neither the lid nor the weight should be of metal.*

3. Let the cabbage marinate. After 24 hours, the cabbage will be covered with some rendered liquid. Do not remove the liquid. Let the cabbage continue to marinate for 3 or 4 days more. At this point, remove the weight, the lid, and the cloth. With a ladle or a large spoon, remove the foam that has formed on top. Then add enough cold water just barely to cover the cabbage.

4. Replace the cloth, the lid, and the weight. Keep in a cool place or in the refrigerator. The sauerkraut will be ready 3 weeks after the marinating begins.

~᪣~

Navelines Confites
(in Alsatian, Suara Riva)

TURNIPS PREPARED AS SAUERKRAUT

Yield: approximately 5 pounds drained weight

10 pounds large white turnips   ¼ cup juniper berries
1 cup rock salt

1. Peel the turnips, wash them, and cut them in long strips. The strips should be about ⅛″ by ⅛″ in thickness, and as long as the turnip they are cut from. (If you have a blade with large enough holes, this step can be performed with the grater attachment of a food processor.)

Steps 2, 3, and 4 are the same as for Choucroute, the strips of turnip in place of the cabbage.

Note: Though Choucroute (sauerkraut of cabbage) may be kept for months, Navelines Confites should not be kept longer than 30 days.

Choucroute à la Juive

SAUERKRAUT WITH KOSHER MEATS

There was a very large Jewish community in Alsace, and the members of that community did not want to do without the festive meal that was Choucroute Garni. So the Jews of Alsace created a choucroute with no pork.

Today this recipe is still in use, not only by people who eat only kosher food, but also by people who think that beef is more healthful than pork.

Serves 6

Choucroute à la Juive (continued)

4 pounds homemade
   Choucroute (page 384), or
   commercial sauerkraut
¼ cup goose fat or duck fat
1 medium onion, peeled and
   sliced thin
2 cups dry white wine, Alsatian
   wine preferred
1 bay leaf
2 pounds corned beef (cured,
   but uncooked)

salt
pepper, fresh ground
3 shallots, peeled and chopped
   fine
6 medium potatoes, peeled,
   washed, and quartered
2 garlic cloves, peeled, green
   germs removed, and
   chopped fine
6 frankfurters, all beef

1. Wash the Choucroute in cold water. Drain. Wash it a second time, in hot water. Drain again. Squeeze the water out of the sauerkraut by forming it into balls and pressing it between your hands.

2. In a heavy-bottomed ovenproof pot, melt 2½ tablespoons of the goose fat (or duck fat). Sauté the onion for a few minutes. *Do not brown.* Add the wine, 1 cup of water, and the bay leaf.

3. Wash the corned beef, and add it to the pot. Cover, and cook slowly for 45 minutes.

4. Preheat the oven to 325°.

5. Add the sauerkraut, salt, and pepper. Cover. Transfer to the preheated oven, and cook for 1½ hours.

6. While the sauerkraut is in the oven, melt the remaining 1½ tablespoons of fat in a saucepan. Add the shallots, and sauté for 30 seconds. Add the potatoes and garlic. Then add water to ½ the depth of the potatoes. (The water must *not* cover the potatoes.) Bring to the boil, and cook, covered, over low heat until the potatoes are soft—about 30 minutes. Pass the potatoes with their cooking liquid through a food mill, and keep them hot.

7. Ten minutes before the cooking is done, add the frankfurters to the sauerkraut. *Once the frankfurters have been added to the pot, the pot must not boil.*

8. Put the Choucroute in the center of a serving plate. Slice the corned beef, and

arrange it on top. Surround the Choucroute with the frankfurters. Serve the potatoes as a garnish.

Note: This recipe calls for corned beef that is cured but not cooked. If your corned beef is precooked, skip Step 3. Put the corned beef on the sauerkraut 15 minutes before the end of Step 6. (The corned beef will be in the oven 25 minutes altogether—the last 15 minutes of Step 6 plus the 10 minutes of Step 7.)

~✖~

Choucroute de Navelines de Colmar

SAUERKRAUT OF TURNIPS
WITH MEATS AND SAUSAGE

Serves 6

2 salted pig knuckles (ham
    hocks)
4 pounds Navelines Confites
    (page 385)
2 tablespoons lard
2 medium onions, peeled and
    sliced thin
1 cup dry white wine, Alsatian
    wine preferred
1 cup Fond Blanc de Volaille
    (page 512), or water (see *Note*
    on page 58)

2 garlic cloves, peeled, green
    germs removed, chopped
    fine
1 bay leaf
1½ pounds smoked pork
    shoulder
6 medium potatoes
salt
3 tablespoons kirsch

1. Wash the pig knuckles and cook them in *unsalted* boiling water until they are soft—about 1¼ hours.
2. Meanwhile, preheat the oven to 325°.
3. Wash the Navelines Confites in 3 changes of cold water, and drain. Squeeze the water out of the Navelines Confites by forming it into balls and pressing it between your hands.
4. In a heavy-bottomed ovenproof saucepan, melt the lard, and sauté

Choucroute de Navelines de Colmar (continued)

the onions for a few minutes. *Do not brown.* Add the wine, Fond Blanc de Volaille (or water), garlic, and the bay leaf. Bring to the boil, and add the Navelines. Add the pork shoulder, cover, transfer to the preheated oven, and cook for 1 hour.

5. Cook the potatoes in salted water until tender, and peel them.

6. When the Navelines are ready, add the kirsch, and gently stir it in with a fork.

7. Arrange the Navelines on a hot plate. Cut each knuckle in 3 pieces. Slice the pork shoulder in 6 slices. Arrange the knuckles and pork shoulder on top of the Navelines. Surround the Navelines with the potatoes.

Note: Other meats and sausages served with Choucroute Garni à l'Alsacienne may also be served with this dish.

✎

Choucroute Garni à l'Alsacienne

SAUERKRAUT WITH MEATS AND SAUSAGES

Traditionally, Choucroute Garni is a lunchtime Sunday dinner. In the old days, a housewife prepared the choucroute Sunday morning, put it in the oven, and went to mass, which took about two hours. When she came home, the dinner was *à point*—just right.

On this subject, Hansi, the most famous Alsatian poet and artist, and a great French patriot, told the story of a distracted farmer's wife who put her prayer book in the sauerkraut and went to church with a slab of bacon in her hand.

Choucroute Garni is a very hearty dish. It is the kind of dish that, when people eat it, they eat a lot. So I say that this recipe "Serves 6," though it could also serve more than that.

If you have food left over, save it and reheat it—you may think it is better that way. In France, to people who care very much about this dish, there is controversy about whether choucroute should be served fresh at all—or if it should be served only reheated. There are even people who insist that choucroute is not at its best until it has been reheated seven times!

Serves 6 (or more)

2 salted pig knuckles (ham hocks)

4 pounds homemade Choucroute (page 384), or commercial sauerkraut

3½ tablespoons lard, or goose fat, or duck fat

1 large onion, peeled and sliced fine

2 cups dry white wine, Alsatian wine preferred

1 pound smoked bacon (in a single piece)

pepper, fresh ground

salt

2 garlic cloves, unpeeled, cracked

8 juniper berries

1 teaspoon caraway seeds

1 bay leaf

1 pound precooked, smoked pork loin

12 small potatoes, peeled

2 smoked bratwursts

6 frankfurters

2 blood sausages (blutwurst)

6 Quenelles de Foie de Veau à l'Alsacienne (optional) (follow the recipe on page 376, but do not brown the Quenelles until Step 9 of this recipe)

2 tablespoons kirsch

1. Wash the pig knuckles and cook them in *unsalted* boiling water until they are soft—about 1¼ hours.

2. Wash the Choucroute in cold water. Drain. Wash it a second time, in hot water. Drain again. Squeeze the water out of the Choucroute by forming it into balls and pressing it between your hands.

3. In a heavy-bottomed ovenproof pot, melt 3 tablespoons of the lard (or goose fat, or duck fat). Sauté the onion in the lard until it is wilted. *Do not brown.* Add the wine and 1 cup of water. Add the smoked bacon. Cover, and cook for 20 minutes.

4. Preheat the oven to 325°.

Choucroute Garni à l'Alsacienne (continued)

5. Season the sauerkraut with pepper, and very lightly with salt. Add the sauerkraut to the pot, covering the bacon.

6. Tie in a piece of cheesecloth the garlic, juniper berries, caraway seeds, and bay leaf. Bury this in the sauerkraut. Put a circular piece of parchment paper over the sauerkraut. Cover the pot with a lid, bring it to the boil, and put it in the preheated oven for 1 hour.

7. Add the pork loin to the pot, and return the pot to the oven for another 30 minutes.

8. Boil the potatoes in salted water and keep them hot.

9. Add the smoked bratwursts to the pig knuckles for 10 minutes to heat them. Then add the frankfurters to this pot for another 10 minutes. *Once the frankfurters have been added to the pot, the pot must not boil.*

10. In a sauté pan, melt the remaining ½ tablespoon of lard, and sauté the blood sausages (blutwursts) and the Quenelles de Foie de Veau (if used) until they are browned.

11. Just before serving, add the kirsch to the sauerkraut. Taste the sauerkraut for seasoning, and add salt if necessary.

12. Slice the bacon and pork loin. Cut the bratwursts and blood sausages in thirds (cutting on a diagonal). Cut each pig's knuckle in 3 pieces. Put the sauerkraut in the center of a large platter and surround it and top it with the sausages, sliced meats, and boiled potatoes. (Usually, the pigs' knuckles and frankfurters are put on top, the potatoes and the other meats around the sides.)

VEGETABLES AND NOODLES

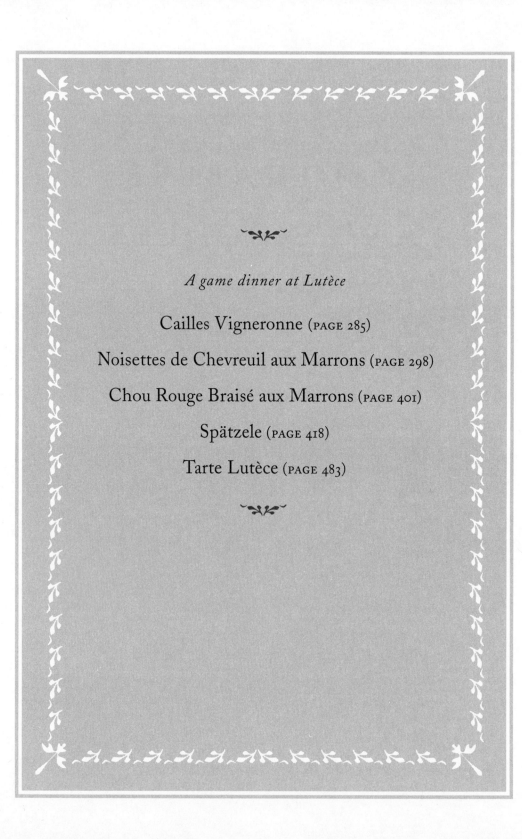

A game dinner at Lutèce

Cailles Vigneronne (PAGE 285)

Noisettes de Chevreuil aux Marrons (PAGE 298)

Chou Rouge Braisé aux Marrons (PAGE 401)

Spätzele (PAGE 418)

Tarte Lutèce (PAGE 483)

FOR MANY OF THE main courses in this book I suggest what I think are good garnishes. The recipes for almost all of these garnishes are in this chapter of vegetable and noodle dishes. Of course the garnish that you will decide to use depends on many things—what you like to eat, what is in season, what is available, and so on—so finally it is up to you.

But for one dish in this book, Noisettes de Chevreuil aux Marrons, I give what I think are two perfect garnishes. These garnishes make the dish complete. So for this menu of a game dinner at Lutèce I include these perfect garnishes—Chou Rouge Braisé aux Marrons, and Spätzele—as part of the menu.

Artichauts, Choux-Fleurs, et Champignons Barigoule

ARTICHOKES, CAULIFLOWER FLORETS, AND MUSHROOMS IN VEGETABLE BROTH

In Lutèce, as now in many restaurants, we have guests who ask not just for vegetable dishes, but for whole vegetarian meals. Of course we oblige them, sometimes with dishes like this one. *Serves 6*

Artichauts, Choux-Fleurs, et Champignons Barigoule (continued)

The Vegetable Broth

3 ounces olive oil
3 medium white onions, sliced
3 young carrots, trimmed,
    peeled, washed, and sliced
6 small garlic cloves, peeled,
    green germs removed

2 bay leaves
¼ teaspoon dried thyme
1½ cups dry white wine
½ teaspoon whole coriander
juice of 2 lemons

The Vegetables

¾ pound cauliflower florets
18 small artichokes, coarse
    outer leaves removed,
    smaller leaves trimmed

¾ pound button mushrooms

The Vegetable Broth

1. In a sauté pan, heat the olive oil. Add the onions and carrots, and sauté, but do not brown. Add 1 cup of water, the garlic, bay leaves, thyme, wine, coriander, and lemon juice. Bring to the boil and cook for 2 minutes.

The Vegetables

2. Blanch the cauliflower in unsalted boiling water for 1 minute. Cool the cauliflower under cold running water.

3. Put the cauliflower, artichokes, and mushrooms in 3 separate small saucepans. Add ⅓ of the broth to each pan.

4. Over medium heat, cook each vegetable until tender (until it is easily pierced with a knife). Set the vegetables aside to cool to room temperature in the broth. Serve in 3 separate serving dishes.

Aubergines à la Tomate au Four

ROASTED EGGPLANT WITH TOMATOES

This is a beautiful dish, completely foreign to the cooking I grew up with, but a dish that, as soon as I learned it, I cooked with pleasure. I serve it in the restaurant mostly as a garnish with a main course, but at home it is a nice first course.

Note: This dish will work best if you make it only with ripe tomatoes, so it is a good idea to do it only during the tomato season.   *Serves 6*

½ cup olive oil
3 medium onions, peeled and
   sliced
2 pounds tomatoes—the tomatoes must be ripe
1 bouquet garni (page 55)
3 garlic cloves, peeled, green
   germs removed, and
   chopped fine

salt
pepper, fresh ground
2 pounds small eggplants, unpeeled
3 garlic cloves, peeled, green
   germs removed, and cut in
   thin slivers

1. In a skillet, heat half the oil. Gently sauté the onions until they are soft. *Do not brown.*

2. Cut a conical plug from the stem end of each tomato and discard. Blanch the tomatoes in boiling water for 10 seconds, drain them under cold water, and peel off the skins. Cut the tomatoes in half, squeeze out and discard the juice and seeds, and chop the pulp fine.

3. Add the tomatoes to the onions. Add the bouquet garni, the chopped garlic (*but not the garlic that is cut in thin slivers*), salt, and pepper. Bring the skillet to the boil, and cook gently for 15 minutes.

4. Slice the eggplant, from end to end, in ¾-inch-thick slices. Stick the thin slivers of garlic into the surfaces of the slices of eggplant.

5. Preheat the oven to 300°.

6. Oil an ovenproof gratin dish with some of the olive oil. Salt the

Aubergines à la Tomate (continued)

gratin dish. Arrange the slices of eggplant in the dish and cover them with the tomato-and-onion mixture. Sprinkle the remaining olive oil over the top.

7. Put the gratin dish in the preheated oven, uncovered, for 45 minutes. Serve hot.

Aubergines Farcies

STUFFED EGGPLANT

Serves 4

4 small eggplants, unpeeled
5 tablespoons olive oil, plus oil for oiling the ovenproof dish
2 tomatoes—the tomatoes must be ripe
3 shallots, peeled and chopped fine
1 garlic clove, peeled, green germ removed, and crushed

2 sprigs thyme
16 black olives, pitted and sliced thin
salt
pepper, fresh ground
2 tablespoons dry bread crumbs
2 tablespoons grated Swiss cheese (Emmental or Gruyère)

1. Preheat the oven to 350°.
2. Cut the eggplants in half, from top to bottom. In an ovenproof skillet, heat 2 tablespoons of the olive oil. Put the eggplants in the skillet, cut sides down, and put the skillet in the preheated oven for 8 minutes.
3. Cut a conical plug from the stem end of each tomato and discard. Blanch the tomatoes in boiling water for 10 seconds, drain them under cold water, and peel off the skins. Cut the tomatoes in half, squeeze out and discard the juice and seeds, and chop the pulp in ¼-inch cubes.
4. With a spoon, empty the eggplant shells, leaving a ⅛-inch thickness of the meat of the eggplants adhering to the skins. Chop the spooned-out eggplant meat coarse.
5. In a saucepan, heat 1 tablespoon of the olive oil. Sauté the shallots

for 1 minute. Add the tomatoes, chopped eggplant meat, garlic, and thyme. Cook gently for 10 minutes. Add the olives, salt, and pepper.

6. Fill the eggplant shells with the mixture from the saucepan.

7. Increase the oven temperature to 475°.

8. Oil an ovenproof dish, and sprinkle it lightly with salt. Put the filled eggplants shells side by side in the dish. Combine the bread crumbs and Swiss cheese, and sprinkle the tops of the eggplants with this mixture. Pour the remaining 2 tablespoons of olive oil over the eggplants. Put the dish in the oven for 8 minutes.

Note: This vegetable goes beautifully with lamb.

⤳⤲

Betteraves Sautées à la Crème

SAUTÉED BEETS IN CREAM

You can tell by the cream that this is an old Normandy dish—old, but still not very common.

I prepare this dish only rarely at Lutèce, not because it is not delicious, but because it does not suggest itself to me. Maybe I do not feel it fits so well with my food. But it is a wonderful way to cook beets.

Serves 6

2 pounds red beets	3 garlic cloves, peeled, green
salt	germs removed, and
1 tablespoon vinegar	chopped fine
4 tablespoons (½ stick) unsalted	2 tablespoons chopped chives, or
butter	chopped parsley
pepper, fresh ground	¾ cup heavy cream

1. Wash the beets. Put them in a pot and cover them with water. (The pot should not be full. There should be at least 1 inch between the surface of the water and the top of the pot.) Add ½ tablespoon of salt and the vinegar. Bring to the boil, cover, and cook at a slow boil until tender—

Betteraves Sautées à la Crème (continued)

about 1 to 1½ hours. The beets are ready when a knife goes into them easily.

2. Set the pot aside and let the beets cool in the water. It is best not to refrigerate them.

3. Remove the skins, and pull off the roots and stems of the beets with your fingers. Cut the beets in ⅛-inch slices.

4. In a skillet, heat the butter. Add the beets. Add salt and pepper to taste. Sauté for 8 minutes. Add the garlic and sauté for 2 minutes more.

5. Add 1 tablespoon of the chives (or parsley) and the cream. Bring to the boil, and simmer for a few minutes. Put the beets on a plate, and sprinkle them with the remaining chives (or parsley). Serve hot.

Carottes Glacées aux Raisins

GLAZED CARROTS WITH RAISINS

Note: This dish is best when prepared with baby carrots.

Serves 6

3 ounces white raisins

4 tablespoons (½ stick) unsalted butter

2 pounds carrots, trimmed, peeled, washed, and cut in pieces about 1½″ × ¼″ × ¼″

1 cup Fond Blanc de Volaille (page 512), or water (see *Note* on page 58)

1 pinch sugar

salt

pepper, fresh ground

¾ cup heavy cream

1 tablespoon chervil (or parsley), chopped coarse

1. Soak the raisins in lukewarm water for 5 minutes.

2. In a skillet, heat the butter. Add the carrots, and sauté for 8 minutes over low heat, stirring from time to time. *Do not brown.*

3. Add the Fond Blanc de Volaille (or water), sugar, salt, and pepper.

Drain the raisins and add them to the skillet. Bring to the boil, cover, and cook gently, stirring from time to time, until the carrots are tender—about 35 minutes.

Note: At this point the liquid should be almost completely cooked off, with only a little yellow liquid remaining. If too much liquid remains, remove the cover and continue cooking until it is almost all cooked off.

4. Add the cream, and cook over medium heat, uncovered, stirring occasionally, until the cream starts to thicken—about 5 minutes. Put the carrots on a plate, sprinkle them with the chervil (or parsley), and serve hot.

Note: These carrots are an excellent garnish for veal.

Beignets de Courgettes

ZUCCHINI FRITTERS

Deep-fried dishes are made all over France, and even all over the world. But in Alsace they are especially well liked. This simple dish is no more Alsatian than French fried potatoes, but to me it is a dish that is part of my tradition.   *Serves 4 to 6*

1 pound small to medium zucchini, washed
1 teaspoon salt
3 eggs
½ teaspoon pepper, fresh ground
1 scant tablespoon shallots chopped fine

2 tablespoons chopped chives or chopped parsley—or 1 tablespoon of each, mixed
3 tablespoons all-purpose flour
¾ cup peanut oil

1. Grate the zucchini on the coarsest side of a grater (or use the grater attachment of a food processor). Toss the grated zucchini with the salt. Put

Beignets de Courgettes (continued)

the zucchini in a strainer, and let it drain for at least 1 hour. At the end of the draining, press the zucchini to release all excess moisture.

2. In a bowl, beat the 3 eggs. Add the pepper, shallots, and the chives—or the parsley, or the mixture of the two. Stir in the flour, then the grated zucchini.

3. In a large skillet, heat the oil.

Note: There should be a ¼-inch depth of oil in the skillet. If there is not, add more oil.

4. Spoon the batter-and-zucchini mixture onto a plate to form a circle of the mixture about 2 inches across. Slip this mixture into the hot oil. Continue forming these circles and slipping them into the oil. Turn the fritters so that they brown on both sides. As they do, remove them one at a time from the oil. When done right, they are crisp on the outside, creamy and moist inside.

Note: These fritters are an excellent garnish, but they may also be served as a simple appetizer.

Céleri Rave au Jus

KNOB CELERY (CELERIAC)

In France, when we say "celery," we mean this kind of celery—knob celery, or celeriac—which is more popular there than the branch celery common in America. (In France, branch celery is often called "English celery.") This recipe can be prepared only with knob celery.   *Serves 6*

2 pounds knob celery, peeled, all
    black spots removed,
    washed, and cut in sticks
    1½" × ¼" × ¼"
juice of 1 lemon
salt

1 cup Fond de Veau (page 510)
pepper, fresh ground
2 tablespoons (¼ stick) unsalted
    butter
1 tablespoon chopped parsley

1. In a bowl, toss the sticks of knob celery with the lemon juice.

2. Bring 3 quarts of salted water to the boil, and cook the celery in the boiling water for about 5 minutes. Drain in a colander.

3. Put the celery and Fond de Veau in a saucepan. Add pepper. Bring to the boil. Cook slowly for about 8 minutes. At the end of this cooking, there should be almost no liquid left.

4. Add the butter. Cook for 3 more minutes, moving the saucepan constantly, so that the celery does not stick to the almost dry pan.

5. Toss with the chopped parsley and serve hot.

Chou Rouge Braisé aux Marrons

BRAISED RED CABBAGE WITH CHESTNUTS

For the best result, you should cook this dish with goose fat. If you cannot get goose fat, you can use duck fat instead, or lard—or even a combination of oil and butter. But goose fat is the best. *Serves 6*

1 head red cabbage	1 cup dry red wine
2 tablespoons vinegar	1 bay leaf
1 pound chestnuts	salt
2 tablespoons goose fat (or duck fat, or lard)	pepper, fresh ground
	2 apples, Golden Delicious
1 medium onion, peeled, sliced fine	preferred

1. Remove and discard the outer damaged leaves of the cabbage. Wash the cabbage and cut it in quarters. Cut away the portions of the central core attached to each quarter, and discard them. Slice the cabbage into ¼-inch strands.

2. In a bowl, toss the cabbage with the vinegar.

3. With a sharp knife, score each chestnut once, on the flat side, through the shell. In a saucepan, cover the chestnuts with water, bring the water to the boil, and cook over medium heat for 6 minutes. Remove the

Chou Rouge Braisé (continued)

chestnuts from the water, 5 or 6 at a time, and quickly remove the shells and the inner skins.

4. In a heavy-bottomed pot, heat the fat. Sauté the onion until it is slightly browned. Add the wine and ¾ cup of water. Bring to the boil, and add the cabbage, chestnuts, bay leaf, salt, and pepper. Cover, and cook slowly for 45 minutes.

5. Peel and core the apples. Cut each apple into 8 slices. Stir the apples into the cabbage, cover, and cook slowly for 15 minutes more. Once or twice during the cooking, move the pot about. Serve hot.

Note: At Lutèce we serve this red cabbage with venison and pheasant, but it also garnishes nicely other game birds and rabbit.

꿎

Épinards en Branches

LEAF SPINACH

I do not know why the memory sticks in my mind, but when Lutèce was a new restaurant, a retired general of the American army came to me after his dinner to tell me how much he enjoyed it. Then he worked up his courage and asked me how I made the spinach he liked so much.

It must have been better than army spinach. But to me it was remarkable that such an important man, of all the things he could ask me, asked me about what is maybe the simplest dish I make.   *Serves 6*

salt
2 pounds spinach, washed,
   stems removed

3 tablespoons (⅜ stick) unsalted
   butter
3 shallots, peeled and chopped

1. Bring to the boil 3 quarts of salted water (not in an aluminum pot). Add the spinach, and cook vigorously, over high heat, for 4 minutes.

2. Plunge the spinach into ice water to cool it. Drain. Press the excess

water out of the spinach by forming it into a ball in your hands and squeezing it.

3. In a saucepan, melt the butter. Sauté the shallots for 1 minute. Add the spinach, and heat it quickly.

⊱❧⊰

Flan de Broccoli

BROCCOLI CUSTARD

For years, I just discarded broccoli stems. I think most of the French chefs in America did. I do not remember how I discovered that when you peel away the outer layer of the thick stems you find a delicious marrow inside.

All this may be because I never saw broccoli in France, and did not cook it until I came to this country. I wasted a lot of good broccoli before I learned all about this excellent vegetable.   *Serves 6*

1½ bunches broccoli, about 2¼
    pounds
salt
2 cups heavy cream
2 eggs
1 egg yolk
pepper, fresh ground
3 tablespoons (⅜ stick) unsalted
    butter

2 shallots,
    peeled
    and
    chopped fine
¼ cup Fond de Veau
    (page 510)

1. Separate the small florets from the large stems of the broccoli. With a vegetable peeler or a sharp knife, remove the fibrous outer layer of the large stems, leaving just the soft marrow.

2. In a saucepan, bring salted water to the boil. Put the florets in the boiling water and cook, uncovered, until tender—about 6 minutes. Re-

Flan de Broccoli (continued)

move the florets from the water (retain the liquid), and immediately submerge them in ice water to cool them. Drain thoroughly. Set aside.

3. To the same boiling water, add the peeled stems, and cook them, uncovered, until tender—about 10 minutes. Immediately submerge them in ice water to cool them. Drain thoroughly. Set aside.

4. Preheat the oven to 275°.

5. In a food processor, process the stems and ⅔ of the florets until they are pureed. In a bowl, beat together 1 cup of the cream, the eggs, and the egg yolk. Add this mixture to the processor. Add salt and pepper. Process for a few seconds more to combine thoroughly.

6. Melt 1 tablespoon of the butter, and butter 6 4-ounce ramekins. Put equal amounts of the broccoli mixture in the 6 ramekins. Set the ramekins in a baking pan of hot water. Put a sheet of parchment paper over the ramekins. Bake in the preheated oven for 30 minutes.

7. While the ramekins are in the oven, melt 1½ tablespoons of the butter. Add the shallots, and cook gently for 2 minutes. Add the Fond de Veau, the remaining 1 cup of cream, salt, and pepper. Bring to the boil, and simmer for a few minutes. Set this sauce aside, and keep it warm.

8. In a sauté pan, melt the remaining ½ tablespoon of butter, and sauté the remaining florets of broccoli until they are warm.

9. Unmold each ramekin onto a hot plate. (The flans should slip out easily. If not, use a knife to separate them from the ramekins.) Spoon the hot sauce around each custard. Sprinkle the florets on the sauce.

Flan d'Épinards à l'Ail

SPINACH CUSTARD WITH GARLIC

Serves 4

salt   4 garlic cloves, unpeeled
½ pound spinach, washed, stems   1 scant teaspoon arrowroot
   removed   2 eggs

3 tablespoons heavy cream
pepper, fresh ground
1 pinch grated nutmeg
1 tablespoon unsalted butter, at
room temperature, plus butter for buttering the egg
cocottes

1. Bring to the boil 1 quart of salted water (not in an aluminum pot). Add the spinach, and cook vigorously over high heat for 4 minutes.

2. Plunge the spinach into ice water to cool it. Drain. Press the excess water out of the spinach by forming it into a ball in your hands and squeezing it.

3. In a saucepan, cook the unpeeled garlic cloves for 6 minutes in boiling water. Drain and peel the cloves.

4. Preheat the oven to 375°.

5. Put the spinach and garlic in a food processor. Process until they are barely pureed—1 to 2 minutes.

6. Add the arrowroot, eggs, cream, salt, pepper, nutmeg, and the 1 tablespoon of butter. Process until pureed—about 1 to 2 minutes.

7. Butter 4 earthenware egg cocottes, and fill them with the spinach puree. Cover and seal each cocotte with aluminum foil. Set the cocottes in a pan of hot water in the preheated oven. Cook for 12 minutes.

8. Invert the flans onto plates.

Note: This is a garnish principally for meat or fowl.

Friture de Courgettes sur Coulis de Tomate

FRIED ZUCCHINI WITH TOMATO COULIS

At Lutèce, these crisp-fried zucchini sticks are served as a garnish, but at home they make a good first course.   *Serves 4*

Friture de Courgettes (continued)

The Batter

¾ cup beer
2 eggs, separated
1 tablespoon peanut oil

1 pinch sugar
salt
1 cup all-purpose flour

The Frying and Serving

1 quart oil for deep frying
1 cup Coulis de Tomates (page 506)

1 pound zucchini, small to medium size, unpeeled, cut in pieces approximately 2½″ × ⅓″ × ⅓″

The Batter

1. In a bowl, mix the beer, the egg yolks, the 1 tablespoon of oil, the sugar, and ½ teaspoon of salt. Stir in the flour, and whisk until you have a smooth batter. Cover with plastic wrap and let rest for 15 minutes at room temperature.

2. After the 15 minutes, beat the egg whites until stiff, and gently fold them into the batter.

The Frying and Serving

3. Heat the quart of oil in a deep fryer to 375°.

4. Heat the Coulis de Tomates and keep it hot.

5. One at a time, dip the pieces of zucchini in the batter, and then drop them into the deep fryer. They are done when they are golden brown—about 4 minutes. As they brown, remove them from the deep fryer with a skimmer or slotted spoon, and put them on paper towels to drain. Salt them lightly.

6. Spread the hot Coulis on 4 plates. Mound the fried zucchini on the Coulis at the center of each plate. Serve hot.

Galettes de Maïs

CORN FRITTERS

In France we do not have the kind of corn you find in America, so the French have never learned to enjoy it. But I love it.

In the fall, when I can get fresh ears of corn from the farms near my house in the Catskill Mountains I bring them to Lutèce to prepare this simple garnish.   *Serves 4*

4 ears of corn (off season, use ½ pound, net drained weight, of pre-prepared corn)
5 tablespoons (⅝ stick) unsalted butter
¼ cup all-purpose flour

2 eggs
salt
pepper, fresh ground
½ envelope active dry yeast
¾ cup milk
½ cup peanut oil

1. With a sharp knife, cut the kernels from the ears of corn. (You should end up with approximately ½ pound.)

2. In a skillet, heat 1 tablespoon of the butter. Sauté the corn for 2 minutes. Set aside.

3. Put the flour in a bowl, and form a well in the flour.

4. In another bowl, beat together the eggs, salt, and pepper. Stir in the yeast and the milk. Pour this mixture into the well, and with a whisk or with a wooden spoon, mix it into the flour until you have a smooth batter. Stir in the corn.

5. Melt the remaining 4 tablespoons of butter, and mix this butter into the batter. Cover the bowl with plastic wrap, and let the batter rest at room temperature for 15 minutes.

6. In a large, heavy-bottomed skillet, heat some

Galettes de Maïs (continued)

of the oil over medium heat. Put large tablespoons of the batter, one by one, side by side, in the oil. These form circular fritters about 2 inches in diameter.

7. Cook the fritters 1½ minutes on the first side. Turn them with a spatula, and cook them for 1 minute on the second side. The fritters should be golden brown. As the fritters become ready, set them aside and keep them warm until they are all done. Add oil to the skillet as needed.

Note: Do not overcook, or the fritters will be rubbery.

Galettes de Pommes de Terre

POTATO CRÊPES

My old partner André Surmain got this recipe from a member of the Blanc family, a famous old family in the world of French food. They have had restaurants, published cookbooks, and so on.

This was the recipe of a grandmother Blanc. Or maybe it was a great-grandmother Blanc. At Lutèce we do it often as a garnish.   *Serves 6*

1 pound potatoes, peeled, washed, and quartered	3 eggs
salt	4 egg whites
¼ cup milk	¼ cup heavy cream
3 tablespoons all-purpose flour	4 tablespoons (½ stick) unsalted butter

1. Cook the potatoes in salted water until tender. Drain. Put the potatoes through a food mill or strainer.

2. Bring the milk to the boil, and stir it into the potato puree. Let cool.

3. With a wooden spatula, stir the flour into the puree. Then stir in the whole eggs, one by one. Then stir in the egg whites, and then the cream. Add salt to taste. Mix, but *do not overwork*.

4. In a skillet, melt some of the butter. Fry small crêpes of the potato mixture (about ¾ of a tablespoon per crêpe) in the butter, about 2 minutes on each side—until they are nicely browned. (The crêpes will be about 2½ inches across.) Work in batches, and add more butter as needed. Serve hot.

❦

Légumes Mélangés au Spätzele

MIXED VEGETABLES WITH NOODLE DUMPLINGS

Serves 4

1½ cups baby carrots, trimmed, peeled, washed, and cut in strips 1″ × ⅛″ × ⅛″

1½ cups zucchini, unpeeled, washed, cut in strips 1″ × ⅛″ × ⅛″

salt

2 tablespoons (¼ stick) unsalted butter

½ recipe Spätzele (page 418)

1. Cook the carrots and zucchini in separate pots, in boiling salted water, until they are tender but still crunchy—about 4 minutes for the carrots, 1 to 2 minutes for the zucchini.

2. In a skillet, melt 1 tablespoon of the butter until browned. Sauté the Spätzele in the browned butter.

3. In another skillet, melt the remaining 1 tablespoon of butter, and sauté the vegetables, together, until hot—about 3 or 4 minutes.

4. Mix the vegetables and Spätzele, salt them, and serve hot.

❦

Haricots Beurre Braisés

BRAISED WAX BEANS

By "haricots beurre" we mean beans that are long, like string beans, except that these are white or pale yellow.

Serves 6

2 pounds wax beans, stems and
    strings removed
4 tomatoes
¼ cup olive oil
3 ounces sliced bacon (optional),
    cut in small slivers
2 onions, 1½" to 2" in diameter,
    peeled, and chopped coarse

2 garlic cloves, peeled, green
    germs removed, and
    chopped fine
1 bouquet garni (page 55)
salt
pepper, fresh ground

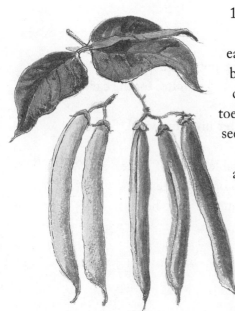

1. Soak the beans in cold water for 10 minutes.

2. Cut a conical plug from the stem end of each tomato and discard. Blanch the tomatoes in boiling water for 10 seconds, drain them under cold water, and peel off the skins. Cut the tomatoes in half, squeeze out and discard the juice and seeds, and chop the pulp in ¼-inch cubes.

3. In a heavy-bottomed pot, heat the oil, and add the bacon (if used) and onions. Sauté for 2 minutes, stirring with a spatula.

4. Add the tomatoes, beans, garlic, bouquet garni, salt, pepper, and ¼ cup of water. Bring to the boil, cover, and cook over low heat for 40 minutes. Stir gently a few times during the cooking, taking care not to break the beans.

Note: Be certain there is always enough liquid in the pot to prevent burning. When necessary, add a little water. At the end of the cooking, almost all the liquid should be cooked off, and the beans should be very tender.

5. Discard the bouquet garni. Serve hot.

Note: This is a nice garnish for lamb or beef.

Nouilles à l'Alsacienne

HOMEMADE ALSATIAN NOODLES

Today we make noodles with a noodle machine. But when I was a boy, when I helped my mother to make noodles, I rolled out the dough by hand, which was hard work.

When I first started to help my mother with the noodles, she would always say to me, The dough is not rolled out thin enough. It is not ready until you can read the newspaper through it.

Then, to please her, I would try to roll it out as thin as possible.

Serves 4

1 pound all-purpose flour, sifted	1 teaspoon vinegar
1 pinch salt	2 teaspoons peanut oil
3 eggs	5 tablespoons (⅝ stick) unsalted
6 egg yolks	butter

1. In a mixing bowl, combine the flour, salt, eggs, egg yolks, and vinegar. Mix these ingredients until the dough is smooth and elastic. Let the dough rest for 1 hour. (This step may be performed with an electric mixer.)

2. Divide the dough into pieces the size of a small egg. On a floured surface, roll out each piece to a paper-thin sheet. Cut the dough into strips less than ¼ inch wide and about 2 inches long. (Or make strips of the dough with a pasta machine, and then cut them by hand into 2-inch lengths.)

3. Set aside a handful of these noodles.

Nouilles à l'Alsacienne (continued)

4. Put 2 quarts of water in a pot and add the oil. Bring the water to the boil. Add the noodles (except those that have been set aside) to the boiling water, and cook until tender but not soft—about 5 minutes.

Note: The noodles should be checked often during the cooking, and removed from the heat as soon as they are ready.

5. In a colander, cool the noodles under cold water. Drain.
6. In a skillet, melt 1 tablespoon of the butter. Sauté the reserved noodles until they are lightly browned.
7. In another skillet, melt 4 tablespoons of the butter and let it brown. Sauté the cooked noodles in the melted butter until lightly browned. Serve hot, sprinkled with the sautéed noodles prepared in Step 6.

Oignons Farcis

STUFFED ONIONS

I was first served these Oignons Farcis in the south of France by the mother of a friend. They were delicious. Whenever I think about that time, I can taste this dish again.

It is not really part of what I do at Lutèce. I usually make it only when somebody asks for it.   *Serves 4*

4 large white onions, about ½ pound each, unpeeled
1 egg yolk
¼ cup heavy cream
¼ cup grated Swiss cheese (Emmental or Gruyère)
salt
pepper, fresh ground

1 pinch cayenne
2 tablespoons fresh bread crumbs
2 tablespoons (¼ stick) unsalted butter
1 cup Fond Blanc de Volaille (page 512)

1. Preheat the oven to 275°.

2. Put the onions in a baking pan, and bake in the preheated oven for 1 hour. With a pin, test to see if the onions are done—they are ready when they are soft. If the onions are not yet soft, leave them in the oven until they are.

3. When the onions are ready, let them cool. Peel them. With a melon scooper, or with a demitasse spoon, scoop out the centers (reserve the part that you scoop out), leaving a shell 2 layers thick.

4. Raise the temperature of the oven to 350°.

5. Chop the scooped-out part of the onions, and put them in a bowl. Stir in the egg yolk, cream, cheese, salt, pepper, and cayenne.

6. Fill the onions with the mixture, and sprinkle the tops with the bread crumbs.

7. Butter a gratin dish that will just hold the onions. Arrange the onions in the dish side by side, and put equal amounts of the remaining butter on the tops of the onions. Add the Fond Blanc de Volaille, and put the dish in the oven, uncovered, for about 30 minutes. The liquid should be almost entirely cooked off, and what little remains should be syrupy. Put the onions on plates and pour the remaining liquid over them. Serve hot.

Note: These onions may be served with any meat or fowl. They also make a good first course.

~≈~

Poireaux Ménagère

LEEKS AND POTATOES

When I was an apprentice, each of the three apprentices had to take a turn, for three months, cooking lunch and dinner for the whole staff of eighty people. The chef decided every day what the staff would eat the next day, and because leeks were cheap and potatoes were cheap, this simple dish of leeks and potatoes came up quite often.

Those three-month periods were the nightmares of my apprenticeship. You could never please the staff. No matter what you did they were not happy. But it was good experience in simple cooking.

Serves 4

4 leeks (the white part, plus a little of the green)

3 tablespoons (⅜ stick) unsalted butter

1 medium white onion, peeled and sliced thin

2 pounds potatoes, peeled, cut in ¼-inch slices, washed very thoroughly, and drained

salt

pepper, fresh ground

1. Cut the leeks in half lengthwise, and wash them very thoroughly. Cut the leeks in ½-inch lengths.

2. In a cocotte or heavy-bottomed pot, melt 1 tablespoon of the butter. Add the onion and leeks, and cook gently until very lightly browned. Add the potatoes. Add water, but not enough to cover. (The surface of the water should be about ½ inch below the top of the vegetables.) Add salt and pepper.

3. Bring to the boil, cover, and cook slowly for 25 minutes. Some liquid will remain in the pot. *Do not discard it.*

4. With a whisk, smash the vegetables, in the liquid, breaking them up. Add the remaining butter, and stir everything together with a wooden spoon.

Pommes Sautées

SAUTÉED POTATOES

Serves 3

1 pound potatoes, Yellow Creamer preferred, unpeeled, washed

salt

2 tablespoons (¼ stick) unsalted butter

1 tablespoon peanut oil

pepper, fresh ground

1 teaspoon chopped parsley

1. In a saucepan, cover the potatoes with water. Add salt, and bring to the boil. Cover, and simmer until tender—about 25 minutes.

2. Pour off the water, and dry the potatoes in the saucepan over a low flame—or in a 200° oven—for 5 to 10 minutes. The saucepan should be covered, but with the lid a little ajar to let steam escape. Let the potatoes cool to room temperature.

3. Peel the potatoes, and cut them in ⅛-inch slices.

4. In a skillet—preferably a nonsticking skillet—heat the butter and the oil. Add the potatoes to the skillet, pepper them, and sauté over medium heat until they are golden brown and slightly crisp—about 8 minutes.

5. Sprinkle with the chopped parsley just before serving.

Pommes Lyonnaise

Note: To make Pommes Lyonnaise, sauté ¼ pound of sliced onions in unsalted butter until they are tender and lightly browned. Add the onions to the potatoes halfway through Step 4.

Panaché de Petits Pois et Carottes

PEAS AND CARROTS

Serves 4

1 small Boston lettuce

4 tablespoons (½ stick) unsalted butter

1 medium onion, peeled and sliced thin

3 small carrots, trimmed, peeled, washed, and cut in ⅛-inch disks

2 pounds (unshelled weight) petits pois (small young green peas), shelled

1 teaspoon sugar

salt

pepper, fresh ground

¾ cup Fond Blanc de Volaille (page 512), or water (see *Note* on page 58)

¼ cup heavy cream

1 tablespoon chervil (or parsley), chopped coarse

Panaché de Petits Pois et Carottes (continued)

1. Wash the lettuce leaves in cold water. Drain. Cut them in ¼-inch strands.

2. In a heavy-bottomed pot, heat the butter. Add the onion and sauté for 3 minutes. Do not brown.

3. Add the carrots, petits pois, lettuce, sugar, salt, and pepper. Cover, and cook for 10 minutes over low heat. Stir a few times during the cooking.

4. Add the Fond Blanc de Volaille (or water), bring to the boil, cover, and cook slowly for 10 minutes more. Stir once or twice.

5. Add the cream and cook, uncovered, until the liquid begins to thicken—about 5 minutes. Stir once or twice. Put the vegetables on a serving plate, sprinkle them with the chervil (or parsley), and serve hot.

Note: This is an excellent vegetable garnish for squab or chicken.

Petits Artichauts à la Nage de Légumes

BABY ARTICHOKES IN VEGETABLE BROTH

Serves 2

10 baby artichokes
1 tomato
3 tablespoons olive oil
2 small white onions, peeled and sliced
1 medium carrot, trimmed, peeled, washed, and sliced
2 celery stalks, peeled, washed, and sliced

2 garlic cloves, peeled, green germs removed, each clove cut in 8 lengthwise slivers
1 sprig thyme
1 small bay leaf, or ½ bay leaf
1 scant ½ teaspoon salt
½ teaspoon cracked pepper
5 threads saffron
½ cup dry white wine

1. Remove one or two layers of outer leaves from the artichokes. With a sharp knife, cut a thin slice from the bottom of each artichoke, and cut ½ inch from the tops. Halve each artichoke, cutting from top to bottom. If there is a choke (dry, stringy material) in any of the artichokes, remove and discard it. Set aside in cold water.

2. Cut a conical plug from the stem end of the tomato and discard. Blanch the tomato in boiling water for 10 seconds, drain it under cold water, and peel off the skin. Cut the tomato in half, squeeze out and discard the juice and seeds, and chop the pulp in ¼-inch cubes.

3. In a saucepan, heat the olive oil. Add the onions, carrot, and celery, and sauté for 2 minutes. Do not brown.

4. Add the artichokes, tomato, and all the other ingredients. Add ¾ cup of water. Bring to the boil, cover, and cook over medium heat for 12 minutes. Check to see that the artichokes are tender. Serve lukewarm in the broth.

Note: At home, this is a nice appetizer by itself. But at Lutèce, we usually add shrimps; or we poach fillets of fish in the broth, and add them to the vegetables—mostly we use bass, but any fish will do.

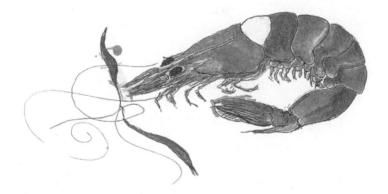

Purée de Légumes

VEGETABLE PUREE

Note: You can make this dish with carrots, knob celery (celeriac), broccoli, or almost any other vegetable. Whatever vegetable you use, prepare it with three parts of the vegetable to one part potato.   *Serves 4*

Purée de Légumes (continued)

½ pound potatoes, peeled, cut in
　　large chunks, and
　　thoroughly washed
1½ pounds vegetables, washed
　　and cut in large chunks

salt
6 tablespoons (¾ stick) unsalted
　　butter, cut in small pieces
white pepper, fresh ground
¾ cup heavy cream

1. Cook the potatoes and vegetables—in separate pots—in boiling salted water until they are tender. If one reaches tenderness before the other, speed up the cooking of the other.

Note: Once the vegetables and potatoes are removed from the hot water, the succeeding steps should be performed quickly, otherwise the puree will be rubbery.

2. Drain the vegetables and the potatoes, and put them in a food processor.
3. Add the butter and pepper, and process for 1 minute. Add the cream, and process for 1 minute more. Add salt to taste.

Spätzele

SMALL NOODLE DUMPLINGS

Serves 6

2 cups all-purpose flour, sifted
3 eggs
salt
1 pinch grated nutmeg

1 tablespoon chopped parsley
1 tablespoon peanut oil
6 tablespoons (¾ stick) unsalted
　　butter

1. Put the flour in a bowl.
2. Beat the eggs to break them up. Add 1 scant teaspoon of salt, the nutmeg, and 5 ounces of cold water. With a wooden spatula, vigorously stir this mixture into the flour. Continue stirring until small bubbles form

and the mixture no longer sticks to the spoon. The paste should be soft. Stir in the parsley.

3. In a large pot, bring salted water to the boil. (The pot should be tall enough so that when a colander is placed over it, there is clearance of a few inches between the bottom of the colander and the surface of the water.) Add the oil to the boiling water. Choose a colander with large holes, and put it over the pot of boiling water.

4. Put the paste in the colander, and press down on the paste with a spatula to force it through the holes into the boiling water. Cook for about 2 minutes—until the spätzeles rise to the surface. Drain.

5. Put the spätzeles in ice water or hold them under cold running water until they are thoroughly chilled. In a colander, drain the spätzeles carefully, tossing them so that all the water drains off.

6. In a skillet, over medium heat, melt the butter until it browns a little. Sauté the spätzeles in this butter to heat them. Add salt to taste. Serve very hot.

❧

Purée de Pommes de Terre

MASHED POTATOES

Just as in America, this is a very important dish in France. It went out of fashion in both countries for about twenty years, the 1970s and the 1980s. But now you find it again in restaurants of all kinds.

This is great home cooking. It seems like simple food, but for good results you have to do it carefully.   *Serves 4*

1½ pounds baking potatoes, peeled, quartered, and washed thoroughly
salt
7 tablespoons (⅞ stick) unsalted butter, cold, in pieces

1 cup milk, very hot
1 pinch grated nutmeg (optional)

Purée de Pommes de Terre (continued)

1. Put the potatoes in a saucepan, cover with cold water, and add 1½ teaspoons of salt. Bring to the boil, and cook until you can slip the tip of the knife into a potato easily—about 15 to 18 minutes. *Do not overcook.*

2. Drain the potatoes, and rapidly push them through a food mill. *They must stay hot.* Return the potatoes to a saucepan and put them over a very low flame. Cook for about 5 minutes, to dry them, moving them frequently with a spatula.

3. Still over a low flame, vigorously beat in the pieces of butter with a wooden spoon, to incorporate the butter thoroughly and to make the puree light.

4. Still over heat, add the hot milk a little at a time, working it in with a wooden spoon until it is totally absorbed and the puree is smooth. *Do not boil.* Add the nutmeg (if used). Add salt if necessary.

Note: Serve as soon as possible. Once prepared, mashed potatoes cannot be reheated.

⚜

Salsifis en Beignets

SALSIFY FRITTERS

As a child, I was crazy about salsify, and at Lutèce I often serve it with the plat du jour at lunchtime.

Though it is an excellent vegetable, salsify is not well known in America. Years ago a food writer wrote that the asparagus he had at Lutèce was not good—and also that the tips were missing! What he thought was asparagus was really salsify.

Serves 6

salt
2 tablespoons all-purpose flour
1½ pounds fresh salsify, peeled, washed, and cut in 3-inch lengths

1½ quarts oil for deep frying
½ recipe Pâte à Frire (page 536)

1. Bring to the boil 2 quarts of salted water. In a small bowl, make a paste of the flour and some water. Stir it into the boiling water.

2. Add the salsify to the water, and cook over high heat, for 12 to 15 minutes, until the salsify is tender but still firm. Drain. Dry the salsify on paper towels.

3. Heat the oil in a deep fryer to 375°.

4. Dip each piece of salsify in the Pâte à Frire, and plunge it into the hot oil. Move these beignets around until they are golden brown on all sides.

5. Remove the beignets from the oil, and drain them on paper towels. Sprinkle them with a little salt. Serve hot.

Note: These beignets are an excellent garnish for veal in any form.

Note: Salsify is still not easy to find in this country, even though you find it everywhere in Europe. But sometimes it is sold in farmers' markets and in fancy greengrocers', often under the name "oyster plant."

Terrine de Carottes et Endives

CARROT AND ENDIVE TERRINE

Serves 4

½ pound carrots, trimmed, peeled, washed, and cut in ½-inch pieces
4 tablespoons (½ stick) unsalted butter, plus butter for buttering the terrine
salt

4 eggs, beaten
¼ cup heavy cream
pepper, fresh ground
1 pinch grated nutmeg
½ pound endive, washed and trimmed, cut in ½-inch slices

1. Put the carrots in a saucepan. Add 2 tablespoons of the butter and 1 cup of water. Add salt. Bring to the boil, cover, and cook until the carrots are tender and the water is evaporated. The carrots must still be moist.

Terrine de Carottes et Endives (continued)

2. Puree the carrots in a food processor. Put the carrots in a bowl, mix in 2 of the beaten eggs and 2 tablespoons of the heavy cream. Add salt, pepper, and the nutmeg. Mix well.

3. Preheat the oven to 200°.

4. Put the carrots in a small buttered terrine. Set the terrine in a pan of hot water, and put it in the preheated oven for 20 minutes.

5. Prepare the endive exactly as the carrots were prepared in Steps 1 and 2.

6. Put the puree of endives in the terrine, over the puree of carrots. Cook in the oven for another 30 minutes.

7. Let the terrine rest for 10 to 15 minutes before inverting it onto a plate.

Note: Serve sliced, hot or cold. The terrine is delicate, so it must be sliced carefully. Serve with Vinaigrette (page 525). (When the terrine is served hot, the Vinaigrette must be at room temperature.)

❧

Tomates Farcies aux Épinards

TOMATOES STUFFED WITH SPINACH

With the tomatoes you sometimes get—tomatoes as white as turnips—this dish is a disaster. You must have ripe tomatoes to make these Tomates Farcies, so you should make them only in the tomato season.

Serves 4

salt

2 pounds spinach, washed, stems removed

2 tablespoons (¼ stick) unsalted butter, plus butter for buttering the gratin dish

½ cup heavy cream

pepper, fresh ground

1 pinch grated nutmeg (optional)

4 medium tomatoes, ripe

½ cup grated Swiss cheese (Emmental or Gruyère)

1. In a large saucepan (not of aluminum), bring salted water to the boil. Add the spinach and cook vigorously over high heat for 4 minutes.

2. Plunge the spinach into ice water to cool it. Drain. Press the excess water out of the spinach by forming it into a ball in your hands and squeezing it. Chop the spinach coarse.

3. In a sauté pan, heat the 2 tablespoons of butter until it is golden brown. Add the spinach, cream, salt, pepper, and nutmeg (if used). Mix well, and cook for 3 minutes.

4. Preheat the oven to 250°.

5. Cut a conical plug from the stem end of each tomato, making as small a hole as possible, and discard. Cut each tomato in half, so that this small hole is at the center of one half. With a spoon remove the seeds and juice from each half. Fill the tomato halves with the spinach.

6. Butter a gratin dish, and salt it lightly. Set the stuffed tomatoes in the gratin dish, and sprinkle them with the cheese. Bake in the preheated oven for 30 minutes.

Tomates Provençales Grand-Mère

STUFFED TOMATOES PROVENÇALE

A great friend of mine, Gérard Galian, used to have an excellent French restaurant in New York called Le Cygne, which was not far from Lutèce. Once, when he and his wife, Huguette, were visiting her mother in France, in Grasse, I visited them there. This is one of the wonderful dishes Huguette's mother made on that visit. *Serves 4*

Tomates Provençales Grand-Mère (continued)

5 tomatoes, ripe

2 medium potatoes, washed and peeled

1 slice white bread, soaked in water

3 garlic cloves, peeled, green germs removed, and chopped fine

1 tablespoon chopped parsley

1 garlic clove, peeled

olive oil for oiling the gratin dish

1¼ cups Fond Blanc de Volaille (page 512), or water (see *Note* on page 58)

salt

pepper, fresh ground

½ cup grated Swiss cheese (Emmental or Gruyère)

1. Cut a plug from the stem end of 1 of the tomatoes and discard. Blanch the tomato in boiling water for 10 seconds, drain it under cold water, and peel off the skin. Cut the tomato in half, squeeze out and discard the juice and seeds, and chop the pulp in ¼-inch cubes.

2. Cut the potatoes in ¼-inch-thick slices, wash them, and drain them.

3. Squeeze the excess water out of the bread.

4. Preheat the oven to 350°.

5. In a bowl, mix the chopped tomato, the bread, the chopped garlic (but not the whole clove of garlic), and the parsley into a paste.

6. Rub a gratin dish with the whole clove of garlic. Brush the dish with the olive oil. Put the potatoes on the gratin dish, cover them with the Fond Blanc de Volaille (or water), and add salt and pepper. Cook in the preheated oven for 12 minutes. Remove the gratin dish from the oven, but leave the oven on.

7. Lower the oven temperature to 300°.

8. Cut a plug from the stem end of each of the remaining 4 tomatoes and discard. Cut each tomato in half, so that the hole you cut is at the center of one half. Arrange the tomato halves with the cut surfaces up, sprinkle them with salt, and mound some of the chopped-tomato mixture on each of the tomato halves.

9. Put the tomatoes on the potatoes. Sprinkle them with the cheese, and return the dish to the oven for 30 minutes. Serve hot.

DESSERTS

A dinner of American foodstuffs at Lutèce

Soupe de Clams (PAGE 96)

Pompano Braisé à la Julienne de Légumes
(PAGE 277)

Tarte aux Pommes Rapées (PAGE 476)

❧

*Dinner at Lutèce when the restaurant was new in
the 1960s*

Bisque de Crevettes (PAGE 82)

Filet Mignon en Croûte Lutèce (PAGE 351)

Soufflé Glacé aux Framboises (PAGE 460)

❧

DESSERTS AND DESSERT SAUCES

WHEN I CAME TO AMERICA I was more or less adopted by one of New York's old French restaurateurs and his wife. From the time that I met them, I went every year to their house for Thanksgiving. He is dead now, but his wife is still alive, and I continue every year to have Thanksgiving with her.

Her name is Jeanne Luthringshauser, and each year, at her house, as part of Thanksgiving dinner she makes two desserts. She makes a mince pie and, always, a Tarte aux Pommes Rapées—because when she first made it for me, I liked it so much.

This menu of Lutèce dishes made with American foodstuffs begins with a recipe her husband taught me—for Clam Chowder—and it ends with Jeanne Luthringshauser's wonderful tart.

The second menu that I use to introduce this chapter on desserts also goes back to my early days in America. It ends with the Soufflé Glacé aux Framboises, which has always been the most popular dessert at Lutèce.

Beignets de Pommes

APPLE FRITTERS

Serves 4 to 5

4 apples
2 tablespoons Calvados
3 tablespoons sugar

1 quart oil for the deep fryer
1 recipe Pâte à Frire (page 536)
½ teaspoon powdered cinnamon

1. Peel and core the apples. Cut the apples in ¼-inch slices, so that each slice has a hole at the center. Arrange the slices over a large plate on which they more or less fit in 1 layer.

2. Sprinkle the apples with the Calvados and with 1 tablespoon of the sugar. Let the apples marinate for 30 minutes. Turn them from time to time so that all the slices are moistened with the Calvados.

3. Heat the oil in the deep fryer to 350°.

4. Working in batches of 5 or 6 slices, dip the apple rings in the Pâte à Frire one by one, and then put them in the hot oil. When the fritters rise to the surface, turn them with a fork and continue frying until they are golden brown on all sides—about 5 minutes.

5. Remove the fried apples from the oil and drain them on paper towels. Mix together the remaining 2 tablespoons of sugar and the powdered cinnamon, and sprinkle on the beignets. Serve warm.

Note: At Lutèce we serve these fritters in a pool of Crème Anglaise (page 488) that has been flavored with Calvados.

Beignets Soufflé Crème Anglaise

FRITTERS WITH VANILLA SAUCE

On the very first day of my apprenticeship, when I was a fifteen-year-old boy, the chefs in the kitchen kept feeding me these beignets—which I had never tasted. It was their way of playing a joke. They kept saying, Here, have another one. I was very excited, and they really stuffed me.

Another time, they stuffed me with éclairs au chocolat. I thought they were fantastic. They packed me with them until I was sick. For about forty years after that I never ate an éclair au chocolat. Today I can eat one, though not enthusiastically. But for the beignets I never lost my taste.

Later I figured out that it was more or less the chef's policy to stuff you with everything when you were just starting out. Eventually you had enough, and after that you were a professional—you could work with this food and not be tempted to eat it all the time.   *Serves 8*

1 cup sugar   1 recipe Pâte à Choux (page 535)
½ teaspoon powdered cinnamon
1 quart oil for deep frying

1. Prepare cinnamon sugar by mixing together the sugar and cinnamon. Set aside.

2. Heat the oil in a deep fryer to 325°.

3. With a tablespoon, scoop up about ½ tablespoon at a time of the Pâte à Choux. With your thumb push the Pâte à Choux that is in the spoon into a lump and, at the same time, out of the spoon and into the hot oil. Work in batches of 10 or 12 beignets.

4. During the frying of each batch, gradually increase the temperature of the frying oil to 375°, and keep the beignets moving so that they fry on all sides. Drain the beignets on paper towels in a warm place.

5. Lower the deep fryer setting to 325°. Pause a few minutes to let the oil cool, and repeat Step 3 with another batch of 10 or 12 beignets. Continue in this way until you have used all the Pâte à Choux.

6. Roll the beignets in the cinnamon sugar.

Note: Serve hot, with hot Crème Anglaise (page 488).

Bierewecke

ALSATIAN FRUIT CAKE

In Alsace, people exchange these traditional cakes every year at Christmas time. You make a lot of cakes, and you give one to each of your friends, and they give them to you. Of course each person's cake is a little different from the others.

It takes time to make this cake. Some people start months in advance, drying their own fruit as early as May or June. My sister does that, and to this day she makes a Bierewecke for me every Christmas and sends it to me in New York from France.

In Alsace, even some restaurants give these cakes as gifts—they make dozens of them, and give whole cakes to their regular customers. I cannot do that at Lutèce—I would have to make hundreds of them. But one year the Lutèce Christmas card, which I change every year, had a picture of a Bierewecke on the front, and this recipe on the back.

Serves 6 to 8

The Night Before

¼ pound dried pears
¼ pound dried prunes, seedless
¼ pound dried figs
2 ounces white raisins
2 ounces black raisins
1 ounce shelled filberts (hazelnuts), chopped coarse
1 ounce shelled almonds, chopped coarse

1 ounce shelled walnuts, chopped coarse
grated rind of ½ lemon
1 pinch grated nutmeg
1 pinch powdered cinnamon
1 cup kirsch
¼ cup sugar

The Next Day

½ pound Pâte à Pain Ordinaire
   (page 543)
1 egg, beaten with a little water

unsalted butter for buttering
   the pastry sheet

The Night Before

1. Cook the pears and prunes in water for a few minutes, to soften them. Cut the pears, prunes, and figs in ¼-inch-wide strips. Wash the raisins.

2. In a bowl, combine the pears, prunes, figs, raisins, filberts, almonds, walnuts, lemon rind, nutmeg, and cinnamon. Add the kirsch and sugar, and mix thoroughly. Refrigerate overnight—or for at least 12 hours.

The Next Day

3. Preheat the oven to 350°.

4. Mix the fruits, nuts, and marinade into the Pâte à Pain. Form the dough into a long loaf. Brush the top of the loaf with the beaten egg.

5. Butter a pastry sheet, put the loaf on it, and bake in the preheated oven for 1 hour. Serve at room temperature.

Note: Store the Bierewecke in plastic wrap at room temperature. It will keep for weeks, or longer.

Bombe au Pralin

FROZEN PRALINE CREAM IN ALMOND PASTRY

Serves 6

The Almond Pastry

4 egg whites
1 cup sugar
6 ounces (1⅓ cups) blanched
   almonds, ground

1 tablespoon all-purpose flour
oil for oiling the parchment
   paper

Bombe au Pralin (continued)

The Praline Cream

6 egg yolks	2 teaspoons rum
1 egg	2 teaspoons brewed coffee, very
1 scant cup sugar	strong
1 tablespoon light corn syrup	1 quart heavy cream
5 ounces praline (page 484)	

The Almond Pastry

1. Preheat the oven to 200°.

2. Whip the egg whites until stiff. Mix in the sugar, ground almonds, and flour.

3. Put a sheet of parchment paper on a pastry sheet. Lightly oil the paper. Spread the mixture on the paper in a layer ½ inch thick. Bake in the preheated oven until dry—about 1½ hours. Let cool on a rack.

Note: The almond pastry may be prepared in advance and stored. It must be kept at room temperature in an airtight container.

The Praline Cream

4. In an electric mixer, whip the egg yolks and egg together until they are frothy.

5. In a saucepan, cook the sugar and corn syrup, with 3 tablespoons of water, to 275° on a candy thermometer.

6. With the electric mixer running, pour the hot liquid into the eggs. Continue mixing until the eggs and sugar are at room temperature—about 10 minutes. Mix in the praline, rum, and coffee.

7. Whip the cream. Remove the bowl from the mixer, and fold in the whipped cream by hand, with a spatula.

The Final Assembly and the Freezing

8. Cut a piece of the almond pastry to fit the bottom of a 2-quart metal cake pan. Add the praline cream to the cake pan as the second layer. Cut another piece of the almond pastry to fit into the cake pan as the top layer. Freeze for at least 3 hours.

Cerises Jubilées

CHERRIES FLAMED IN KIRSCH

I never saw this dish in France. But when I came to the United States, I found that almost all the French restaurants in New York served it.

I was shown this recipe by an Alsatian chef, Ernest Luthringshauser. He was a great man, and he was also a great chef of bourgeois cooking.

Today Cerises Jubilées is considered old-fashioned, but to me it is still a wonderful recipe.

Serves 4

½ tablespoon arrowroot
2 cups red wine (California wine preferred, or another heavy red wine)
½ cup sugar

1 pound black cherries, washed, stemmed, and pitted
3 tablespoons kirsch
⅓ recipe (1 pint) Vanilla Ice Cream (page 442)

1. In a small bowl, dissolve the arrowroot in 2 tablespoons of the wine.

2. In a saucepan, bring the sugar and the remaining wine to the boil, stirring a few times to dissolve the sugar. Add the cherries, bring to the boil, and cook for 2 minutes. With a slotted spoon, remove the cherries from the wine and keep them warm.

3. Add the wine-and-arrowroot mixture to the saucepan and, whisking, bring to the boil and simmer for 2 minutes. Strain this sauce through a fine sieve.

4. In a sauté pan, heat the cherries. Add the kirsch, and set it aflame.

5. Put equal amounts of the ice cream in 4 serving bowls. Spoon ¼ of the cherries onto each portion of ice cream. Spoon the sauce over the cherries, and serve immediately.

Charlotte Chaude aux Pommes

APPLE CHARLOTTE

Serves 6

1 ounce (about ⅓ cup) seedless raisins

1 tablespoon rum

2 pounds apples, Golden Delicious preferred

¼ cup sugar

3 tablespoons (⅜ stick) unsalted butter, plus butter for buttering the mold

grated rind of 1 orange

¼ cup apricot jam, pureed

2 tablespoons honey

1 loaf Pâte à Brioche (page 534), its height at least equal to the height of the charlotte mold

1. In a small bowl, combine the raisins and rum. Set aside.

2. Core, peel, and quarter the apples. Toss them with the sugar.

3. In a skillet, melt 1 tablespoon of the butter, and sauté the apples until they are soft and golden brown—about 2 minutes. Stir in the grated orange rind, apricot jam, honey, raisins, and rum. Set aside.

4. Cut the brioche loaf into ¼-inch-thick slices. In a skillet, melt 2 tablespoons of the butter, and sauté the slices of brioche on both sides until they are lightly browned.

5. Preheat the oven to 375°.

6. Butter a 1½-quart charlotte mold, and line it with parchment paper. Then line it with slices of the brioche, trimming the slices as necessary to fit. The sides and bottom of the mold should be completely covered with the brioche.

7. Fill the mold with the apple mixture. Cover with another slice of the sautéed brioche—2 slices, if necessary. Cover with aluminum foil.

8. Put the charlotte mold, in a pan of hot water, in the preheated oven

for 40 minutes. Remove the charlotte from the oven, and let it stand for 15 minutes before inverting it onto a plate to serve it.

Note: Serve with warm Crème Anglaise (page 488).

Clafoutis aux Cerises

CHERRIES BAKED IN BATTER

In France this is a farmer's dish. We were not farmers, but my mother cooked it all the time. Really it is popular all over France. Sometimes it is made with other fruits, including pears, but for me the best version is this one, with black cherries. *Serves 6*

4 tablespoons (½ stick) unsalted butter, plus butter for buttering the gratin dish	¾ cup sugar
	1¾ cups milk
	4 eggs
2 pounds black cherries, pits removed	1 cup all-purpose flour, sifted
	1 pinch salt

1. Butter an oval, straight-sided gratin dish that is large enough to hold the cherries. Toss the cherries with ¼ of the sugar, then put them in the gratin dish.

2. In a pan, warm the milk, but do not make it hot. In another pan, melt the 4 tablespoons of butter.

3. Preheat the oven to 300°.

4. In a bowl, whisk together the eggs, flour, salt, and the remaining sugar. Stir in the warm milk. Then stir in the melted butter. Let this mixture rest for 10 minutes.

5. Strain the mixture through a fine sieve over the cherries. Put the Clafoutis in the preheated oven for 35 minutes. Turn off the heat, but leave the Clafoutis in the oven for 10 minutes more. Remove it from the oven and let it rest at room temperature for another 10 minutes.

Note: Serve lukewarm or cold. Cold, the Clafoutis is served with Sauce Sabayon (page 488), made with kirsch instead of Grand Marnier.

Crème Bavarois au Grand Marnier

BAVARIAN CREAM WITH GRAND MARNIER

Serves 8

8 egg yolks
1 cup sugar
2 scant tablespoons (or 2 envelopes) powdered gelatin

2 cups milk, boiled
3 tablespoons Grand Marnier
2 cups heavy cream, whipped

1. In a bowl, combine the egg yolks, sugar, and gelatin. Stir in the hot milk. Put this mixture in a saucepan and, over medium heat, stirring constantly, cook until it coats a spoon. *Do not boil.* Strain through a fine sieve.

2. Stirring with a wooden spoon, add the Grand Marnier. Let the mixture cool to room temperature, stirring occasionally. Then gently fold in the whipped cream. Put the mixture in a large mold (or 8 small molds). Refrigerate for at least 2 hours.

3. Just before serving, lower the mold into hot water for half a minute. Then invert the mold onto a serving plate.

Note: Serve with Crème Anglaise (page 488) flavored with Grand Marnier; or with a fruit coulis.

Crème Caramel à la Julienne
d'Orange Confite

CARAMEL CUSTARD WITH ORANGE RIND

Note: This recipe calls for eight 6-ounce ramekins, which is how it is cooked and served at Lutèce. But you can also prepare it in 1 large soufflé dish.

Serves 8

The Orange Zest

2 oranges   3 tablespoons sugar

The Caramel

½ cup sugar

The Cream

6 eggs   3 cups milk
6 ounces (¾ cup) sugar   1 vanilla bean, cut in half

The Orange Zest

1. With a vegetable peeler, peel the orange part of the rind from the oranges, and cut the rind into very thin strips.

2. Put the strips in a saucepan and cover them with ½ cup of cold water. Bring the water to the boil, and cook for 5 minutes. Drain. Repeat, and drain again.

3. Put the rind in a small saucepan. Add the 3 tablespoons of sugar and ½ cup of water. Bring slowly to the boil, and cook slowly, stirring from time to time, until the rind is candied—about 1 to 1¼ hours. When the rind is candied and enveloped in heavy syrup, set the saucepan aside.

The Caramel

4. In a saucepan, dissolve the sugar in ½ cup of water. Over medium heat, cook, stirring, until the water is evaporated, and the sugar is lightly caramelized (light brown). Immediately, pour ½ of this caramel onto the bottoms of eight 6-ounce ramekins.

5. To the caramel that remains in the saucepan, add ½ cup of water. Bring to the boil, and cook, stirring, over medium heat for 4 to 5 minutes. Set aside.

The Cream

6. In a bowl, beat together the eggs and sugar until the mixture is lemony white.

7. Preheat the oven to 275°.

8. Put the milk and the vanilla bean in a saucepan, and bring to the boil. Whisk the hot milk into the egg-and-sugar mixture. Strain this mixture through a fine sieve, and pour it into the 8 ramekins.

9. Put the 8 ramekins in a pan that will hold them. Add enough hot

Crème Caramel à la Julienne d'Orange Confite (continued)

water to the pan so that the water reaches halfway up the sides of the ramekins. Put the pan of ramekins in the preheated oven, and bake for 35 minutes. (If prepared in 1 large soufflé dish, bake 10 minutes longer.)

10. Remove the ramekins from the oven and let them rest at room temperature for 3 to 4 hours.

Note: At this point, the Crème Caramel may be refrigerated overnight, but it is best when fresh.

11. When you are ready to serve them, invert the ramekins over plates. Pour the remaining caramel over the custards. Sprinkle the custards with the candied orange rind.

Crêpes à l'Alsacienne

RASPBERRY CRÊPES

Serves 4 (16 crêpes)

The Crêpes

2 eggs
2 tablespoons sugar
salt
1 cup all-purpose flour, sifted
1¼ cups milk, lukewarm

5 tablespoons (⅝ stick) unsalted butter, melted
1 tablespoon framboise (raspberry eau-de-vie)

The Raspberry Coulis

1½ cups raspberries

¾ cup confectioners' sugar

Note: Off season, when fresh raspberries are not available, 1 cup of raspberry preserves may be substituted for this coulis.

The Sauce and the Finished Crêpes

¼ pound (1 stick) unsalted
  butter
3 tablespoons sugar
¼ cup raspberry liqueur (preferred), or framboise (raspberry eau-de-vie)

½ cup sliced almonds, toasted
1 cup raspberries (see the following *Note*)

Note: Off season, when Crêpes à l'Alsacienne are prepared with preserves instead of raspberries, this cup of raspberries is omitted.

The Crêpes

1. In a bowl, beat the eggs with the 2 tablespoons of sugar and a pinch
of salt. Thoroughly stir in the flour, then the milk, mixing until the mixture is smooth. Then stir in 2 tablespoons of the melted butter. Strain this
mixture through a fine sieve, and let it rest at room temperature, in a bowl
covered with plastic wrap, for at least 1 hour.

2. Heat some of the remaining melted butter in a 5-inch crêpe pan or
skillet. Stir the tablespoon of framboise into the crêpe mixture. Ladle
enough of the crêpe mixture into the pan to form a crêpe. When the crêpe
is nicely browned on one side, turn it over and brown the other side. Put
the crêpe in a warm place, and make another crêpe the same way. Continue, adding a little butter to the pan when necessary, until you have 16
crêpes.

The Raspberry Coulis

3. In a blender, combine the 1½ cups of raspberries and the sugar.
Blend until pureed—about 2 to 2½ minutes.

The Sauce and the Finished Crêpes

4. Preheat the oven to 275°.

5. In a saucepan, over high heat, melt the butter. Add the 3 tablespoons of sugar. Cook, stirring, until the sugar is slightly caramelized. Add
the coulis, bring it to the boil, and cook, stirring with a wooden spoon,
until smooth—about 3 or 4 minutes. Stir in the raspberry liqueur (or
framboise). Add the almonds and cook, stirring, for a few minutes more.
The sauce is ready when it begins to thicken.

Crêpes à l'Alsacienne (continued)

6. Spread 1 tablespoon of the mixture on each crêpe. Fold each crêpe in half, then in half again, to form a quarter circle. Arrange 4 folded crêpes on each of 4 plates. Spoon the remaining sauce over the crêpes, and sprinkle the 1 cup of raspberries around them.

7. Put the plates in the preheated oven for 2 minutes. Serve hot.

Crêpes Normandes

APPLE CRÊPES

Serves 4 (16 crêpes)

2 eggs
¼ cup sugar
salt
1 cup all-purpose flour, sifted
1¼ cups milk, lukewarm
5 tablespoons (⅝ stick) unsalted
    butter, melted

2 apples, Golden Delicious
    preferred
juice of ½ lemon
1 tablespoon Calvados (or apple
    brandy, or applejack)
½ teaspoon powdered cinnamon

1. In a bowl, beat the eggs with 2 tablespoons of the sugar and a pinch of salt. Thoroughly stir in the flour. Then stir in the milk, stirring until the mixture is smooth. Then stir in 2 tablespoons of the melted butter. Strain this mixture (the batter) through a fine sieve. Let it rest at room temperature in a bowl covered with plastic wrap for at least 1 hour.

2. Peel and core the apples and cut them in thin slices. Toss them with the lemon juice to prevent discoloration.

3. In a crêpe pan or skillet about 5 inches in diameter, heat 1 tablespoon of the butter. Sauté the apples over high heat for 2 minutes. Let the apples cool. When the batter has rested at least 1 hour, add the apples to the batter.

4. Preheat the oven to 300°.

5. Heat some of the remaining butter in a 5- or 6-inch crêpe pan. Stir

the Calvados (or apple brandy, or applejack) into the batter. Ladle enough of the batter-and-apple mixture into the pan to form a crêpe. When the crêpe is nicely browned on one side, turn it over and brown the other side. Put the crêpe in a warm place, and make another crêpe the same way. Continue, adding a little melted butter when necessary, until you have 16 crêpes.

6. Put the crêpes on a buttered baking sheet, overlapping them a little. In a small bowl, mix together the remaining sugar and the cinnamon, and sprinkle this mixture over the crêpes. Put the baking sheet in the preheated oven for 2 to 3 minutes. Serve at once.

Gâteau de Poires
(ou Bananes) au Caramel

PEAR (OR BANANA) CAKE, WITH CARAMEL

Serves 8

The Caramel and the Pears

1½ cups sugar
3 tablespoons (⅜ stick) unsalted
    butter

½ cup heavy cream
6 medium pears—the pears
    must be ripe

The Cake Mixture

3 eggs
¼ cup (2 ounces) sugar
grated rind of 1 lemon
6 tablespoons all-purpose flour
1½ ounces crushed walnuts (or
    another nut)

¼ teaspoon baking powder
3 tablespoons (⅜ stick) unsalted
    butter, melted

Gâteau de Poires au Caramel (continued)

The Caramel and the Pears

1. Put the sugar and butter in a saucepan with 2 ounces of water. Over medium heat, bring to the boil, and cook, stirring, until caramelized. Add the cream, and continue cooking and stirring until smooth. Pour this caramel into a cake pan 8″ by 12″.

2. Peel and core the pears, cut them in ¼-inch slices, and arrange the slices on the caramel.

The Cake Mixture

3. In an electric mixer, mix the eggs and sugar until they double in volume. Remove the bowl from the mixer, and stir in the grated lemon rind, flour, nuts, and baking powder. *Do not overwork.* Then stir in the melted butter.

The Final Assembly and Baking

4. Preheat the oven to 350°.

5. Pour the cake mixture over the pears. Put the cake pan in the pre-heated oven, and bake for 35 minutes.

Note: Invert the cake onto a serving plate, and serve with Sauce Sabayon (page 488) made with pear eau-de-vie (poire) instead of Grand Marnier.

Note: When preparing this dish with bananas instead of pears, substitute 5 peeled ripe bananas, cut in ¼-inch slices, for the sliced pears. Serve with Sauce Sabayon (page 488) made with rum instead of Grand Marnier.

❧❧

Glace aux Oeufs

ICE CREAM

One night, two young women came into Lutèce, beautifully dressed up for dinner. They were very happy to be in Lutèce, and they looked very proud of themselves. With them they were carrying a sign (which they gave to me, and which I still have). The sign said TWO MUSICIANS FROM NEW ORLEANS NEED MONEY FOR DINNER AT LUTÈCE.

They were classical violinists, and they were in New York for a job, and one afternoon they played on the street, on Seventh Avenue, with this sign next to them, and with a violin case on the sidewalk in front of them, open. Many, many people put money in the violin case for this charitable purpose. In fact, the people put in so much money that these young women had more than enough to come to Lutèce and order the tasting menu, and with it very good wines. They had a great time.

I do not remember everything I made for them, but I am sure that at the end I served them the Lutèce version of America's favorite dessert—ice cream. *Yield: approximately 3 pints*

The Unflavored Ice Cream Mixture

1 quart milk
⅞ cup heavy cream

10 egg yolks
1¼ cups (10 ounces) sugar

Banana Ice Cream

3 bananas, peeled and pureed

1 ounce rum

Mix together the pureed bananas and rum. Add at the end of Step 3.

Caramel Ice Cream (See page 445)

Chestnut Ice Cream

6 ounces chestnut puree (purée de marrons—available in specialty stores)

1 ounce rum

Mix together the chestnut puree and rum. Add at the end of Step 3.

Chocolate Ice Cream

6 tablespoons unsweetened cocoa powder

Dissolve in the mixture at the end of Step 3.

Glace aux Oeufs (continued)

Coffee Ice Cream

1 ounce instant coffee powder

Dissolve in the mixture at the end of Step 3.

Liqueur-Flavored Ice Cream (may be prepared with any liqueur or eau-de-vie)

2 ounces liqueur (or eau-de-vie)

Add at the end of Step 3.

Vanilla Ice Cream

2 vanilla beans, cut in half lengthwise

Add the vanilla beans to the milk during Step 1. Remove them before passing mixture through a fine sieve, in Step 4.

Preparing the Flavored Ice Cream

1. In a saucepan, bring the milk to the boil. Add the cream. Bring to the boil again. (Do not cook after the liquid has reached the boil.)

2. In a bowl, whisk together the egg yolks and sugar until the mixture is a very pale lemon yellow, and a ribbon forms when the whisk is lifted from the mixture.

3. Pour the hot milk and cream into the eggs, and mix thoroughly. Add the flavoring (except for Vanilla Ice Cream).

4. Return the mixture to the saucepan. Over low heat, stir it with a wooden spoon until it thickens slightly and coats the spoon—about 5 minutes. *Do not boil.* (To be certain the mixture is ready: With a finger draw a thin path through the mixture on the surface of the spoon; the mixture is ready when the path will not close up.) Pass through a fine sieve. Refrigerate until cold, stirring once in a while.

5. Process in an ice cream maker until firm. Freeze until served.

Glace Caramel

CARAMEL ICE CREAM

The Glace Caramel we serve at Lutèce is a particularly rich and tasty ice cream. We serve a lot of it—by itself and, especially, as a garnish with other desserts. *Yield: approximately 2½ pints*

1¼ cups (10 ounces) sugar	1 vanilla bean, cut in half
1½ cups heavy cream	lengthwise
2¼ cups milk	12 egg yolks

1. Put the sugar in a heavy-bottomed saucepan. Over medium heat, melt the sugar and cook, constantly stirring with a wooden spoon, until the sugar caramelizes to a light brown. Still over heat, add the cream, and stir with the wooden spoon until the mixture is smooth.

2. Put the milk and the vanilla bean in a pan, and bring to the boil. Pour this hot milk, with the vanilla bean, into the caramel, and stir until the mixture is blended.

3. In a bowl, beat the egg yolks. Pour the caramel mixture into the egg yolks and mix thoroughly.

4. Return the mixture to the saucepan. Over low heat, stir it with a wooden spoon until it thickens slightly and coats the spoon—about 5 minutes. *Do not boil.* (To be certain the mixture is ready: With a finger draw a thin path through the mixture on the surface of the spoon; the mixture is ready when the path will not close up.) Pass through a fine sieve. Refrigerate until cold, stirring once in a while.

5. Process in an ice cream maker until firm. Freeze until served.

Kugelhopf

ALSATIAN CAKE

An Alsatian legend says that when the Three Magis returned from Bethlehem, a pastry chef by the name of Kügel, who was from the Alsatian village of Ribeauvillé, received them. To thank him, the Magis made a cake in a special mold, and called it Kugelhopf. Today this Alsatian cake is still made in that special earthen mold, though sometimes, nowadays, the mold is made of stainless steel.

Traditionally, Kugelhopf is eaten for breakfast, or at afternoon tea, or for dessert after Sunday dinner. In my family, we had it for breakfast on Sunday morning.

Every Saturday night, at midnight, when the family was asleep, my mother baked a Kugelhopf for the next morning. If she had baked it earlier, it would have been a little stale by breakfast time. If she had made it in the morning, it would have been too fresh. She made it at midnight so that when we had it in the morning it would be exactly right.

My grandfather and two of my uncles were all bakers. During their careers, they made tens of thousands of Kugelhopfs. This recipe for Kugelhopf came to me from my grandfather. I still make it his way.

Serves 6

½ cup raisins (white or black)
2 tablespoons kirsch (or hot water)
½ ounce fresh yeast (or 2 envelopes of dry yeast)
1 cup milk, lukewarm
2 tablespoons sugar
1 scant teaspoon salt
1 pound all-purpose flour, sifted

1 large egg (or 2 small eggs)
7 tablespoons (⅞ stick) unsalted butter, softened, plus butter for buttering the mold
8 to 10 almonds, shelled, inner skins removed
confectioners' sugar

1. In a small bowl, soak the raisins in the kirsch (or hot water). Set aside.

2. Put the yeast, ½ cup of the milk, 1 tablespoon of the sugar, the salt, and 2 tablespoons of the flour in another bowl. Work these ingredients together with your fingertips until they form a soft paste. Cover the bowl with a cloth, and let this paste rise in a warm place until it doubles in volume—about 15 to 20 minutes.

3. In another bowl, whisk together the remaining milk and sugar, and the egg (or eggs). Add the remaining flour, and knead these ingredients together—at first with the fingertips, and then, when a paste has been formed, by picking up the entire batch of paste, and smacking it vigorously down onto a work surface until it is smooth. The process takes about 5 to 6 minutes.

4. Work the 7 tablespoons of butter into the dough, and resume picking it up and smacking it down onto the work surface for about 4 more minutes—it should be very smooth and still soft.

5. Add to this dough the yeast mixture prepared in Step 2, and work the two together, again by repeatedly picking up the dough and smacking it down onto a work surface until smooth—about 2 or 3 minutes.

6. Drain the reserved raisins of any remaining liquid (there should be very little), and mix the raisins into the dough until they are evenly distributed.

7. Butter well an 8-cup Kugelhopf mold. Put an almond in each groove of the mold. Form the dough into a roll 12 inches long, bend it into a circle, and set it in the mold. Put the mold in a warm place, cover it with a cloth, and let the dough rise to the top of the mold—about 40 minutes to 1 hour.

8. Preheat the oven to 350°.

9. Put the mold in the preheated oven, and bake for 45 to 50 minutes, until the top is golden brown.

Note: When the Kugelhopf is ready, it sounds hollow when tapped with the finger. At this point, a needle inserted in the cake will come out dry.

10. Let the cake cool for about 4 minutes. Then invert it onto a wire rack. Let it cool for at least another 2 hours at room temperature. Dust the cake with confectioners' sugar before serving.

Note: As a dessert, Kugelhopf is served with Sauce Chocolat Amer (page 487).

Mille Feuilles à la Mousse
de Pistache Sauce Chocolat Amer

PISTACHIO NAPOLEON WITH CHOCOLATE SAUCE

Serves 6

The Pastry

¾ pound Feuilletage Spécial
(page 532)

sugar for sprinkling
the pastry

The Pistachio Mousse

2 cups heavy cream
2 tablespoons sugar
½ teaspoon vanilla extract

⅓ cup pistachio paste (available
in specialty shops)

The Final Assembly and the Sauce

confectioners' sugar for sprinkling the finished pastry

1 recipe Sauce Chocolat Amer
(page 487)

The Pastry

1. Roll out the Feuilletage Spécial so that it covers a baking sheet 12"
by 18". Put the rolled-out pastry on the sheet, and prick the pastry heavily with a fork. Refrigerate for 20 minutes.

2. Preheat the oven to 350°.

3. Bake the pastry in the preheated oven until half baked—about 15
minutes.

4. Lower the oven temperature to 325°.

5. Sprinkle sugar over the pastry. Return it to the oven, and bake until
the pastry is crisp and the sugar caramelized—about 15 minutes.

6. When the pastry is ready, let it cool. Cut it lengthwise in 3 equal
strips.

The Pistachio Mousse

7. In a well-chilled bowl, whip the cream until it begins to thicken. Beat in the sugar and vanilla extract. Continue beating until stiff. Fold in the pistachio paste.

The Final Assembly and the Sauce

8. Spread one of the strips of pastry with ½ of the pistachio mousse, and cover it with a second strip of pastry. Spread the second strip of pastry with the remainder of the pistachio mousse, and put the third strip of pastry on top. Refrigerate for at least 15 minutes—and then powder the top with confectioners' sugar—before serving. Serve sliced, with the Sauce Chocolat Amer.

~·~

Mille Feuilles au Chocolat

CHOCOLATE NAPOLEON

Serves 6

Proceed as for the Mille Feuilles à la Mousse de Pistache (page 448). Instead of the pistachio mousse, use ⅔ of a recipe of Mousse au Chocolat (page 451), mixed with 1½ cups heavy cream, whipped.

Note: As this is itself a chocolate dessert, it may be served with or without Sauce Chocolat Amer (page 487).

~·~

Mille Feuilles aux Poires

PEAR NAPOLEON

Like many dishes, this one occurred to me on a ski slope. When I finished skiing that Monday, I drove to New York. And the first thing I
did, I made the pear mousse. I served this Napoleon that day. And I still
serve it.   *Serves 6*

Proceed as for the Mille Feuilles à la Mousse de Pistache, but substitute the following pear mousse for the pistachio mousse.

The Pear Mousse

1 cup sugar
juice of 1 lemon
3 tablespoons (⅜ stick) unsalted
    butter

3 pears—the pears must be ripe
1 cup heavy cream

1. In a saucepan, combine 1 tablespoon of cold water, the sugar, lemon
juice, and butter. Bring to the boil, and cook over medium heat, stirring,
until the mixture caramelizes.

2. Peel and core the pears. Puree them in a food processor. Add the caramel to the processor, and continue processing until the mixture is smooth—about 1 minute.
Let cool to room temperature.

3. While the mixture cools, whip the
cream. When the caramel has cooled,
gently fold it into the whipped cream.
Do not overwork.

Note: Omit the chocolate sauce that is
served with the other napoleons.

Mousse au Chocolat

CHOCOLATE MOUSSE

When I came to this country, I found that chocolate mousse, along with maybe two or three other dishes, was what Americans thought of as French cooking. There is much more to French cooking than that, but it is true that even in France this is a popular dish, in restaurants and at home.

There are many ways to make chocolate mousse, but the big difference between the others and the one we make at Lutèce is that we cook the sugar to 275° before adding it to the eggs. The hot sugar cooks the eggs, and that is why the mousse will not collapse—it stays fluffy (which other chocolate mousses do not), so it can be stored.   *Serves 6 to 8*

4 ounces bitter chocolate, melted	1 small egg
2 egg whites	1 teaspoon instant coffee powder
¼ teaspoon cream of tartar	1 teaspoon rum
⅞ cup sugar	1½ tablespoons unsalted butter, melted
1 tablespoon light corn syrup	1½ cups heavy cream
2 egg yolks	

1. Melt the chocolate in a double boiler.

2. Whip the egg whites until they are foamy. Then whip in the cream of tartar.

3. In a small, heavy saucepan, dissolve ⅜ of a cup of the sugar and ½ tablespoon of the corn syrup in 2 tablespoons of water. Cook until the mixture reaches 275° on a candy thermometer. Very slowly pour this mixture into the whipped egg whites, and continue whipping until they are stiff and have cooled to room temperature. Refrigerate.

4. Whip together the egg yolks and the small egg.

5. In a small, heavy saucepan, dissolve the remaining sugar and corn syrup in 2 tablespoons of water. Cook until the mixture reaches 275° on a candy thermometer. Very slowly pour this mixture into the whipped egg

Mousse au Chocolat (continued)

yolks and egg, and continue whipping until they have cooled to room temperature.

6. Dissolve the instant coffee in the rum, and stir this, with the melted butter, into the mixture prepared in Step 5. Fold in the melted chocolate. Then gently fold in the whipped egg whites.

7. Whip the cream to soft peaks, and gently fold it in.

8. Spoon the mousse into a serving bowl. You may reserve a little to pipe a design on top. Refrigerate for at least 2 hours before serving.

Note: The mousse may be stored in the refrigerator for up to 2 days.

Mousse de Bananes

BANANA MOUSSE

Serves 6

6 bananas	½ cup sugar
juice of 1 lemon	1 cup heavy cream

1. Without peeling them, cut the bananas in half lengthwise. Remove the fruit without breaking the skins. Retain 6 of the half-banana skins. Puree the bananas by pushing them through a fine sieve. (The bananas may be pureed in a blender, but care must be taken not to overprocess them, or they will liquefy.)

2. In a bowl, mix the pureed bananas, lemon juice, and sugar. Refrigerate.

3. Whip the cream until it is stiff. Fold it into the banana mixture.

4. Fit a pastry bag with a ½-inch star tube, and fill it with the mousse. Pipe the mousse into the half-banana skins, using a rotating movement, to form a ridged, curled pattern.

Oranges (ou Pamplemousses) Glacées au Sabayon

ORANGES (OR GRAPEFRUITS)
IN GRAND MARNIER SABAYON

Serves 6

3 medium oranges (or 2 grape-
    fruits)
½ pound sugar
2 tablespoons grenadine syrup

1 tablespoon Grand Marnier
1 recipe Sauce Sabayon au
    Grand Marnier (page 488)

1. Peel the oranges (or grapefruits), then cut the segments out of the fruits, eliminating the membrane. Remove and discard the seeds. Save the juice that comes out of the fruit during this step, and strain it through a sieve. You should have at least ½ cup of juice.

2. In a saucepan, combine the juice with the sugar. Over medium heat, bring the juice to the boil, and cook until syrupy—about 10 minutes. Add the orange (or grapefruit) segments and grenadine syrup, and cook 5 minutes more. Add the Grand Marnier. Set aside to cool.

3. Preheat the broiler.

4. Pour the Sauce Sabayon into 6 shallow serving cups. Arrange the orange (or grapefruit) segments on the sabayon in a petal pattern. Put the dishes under the hot broiler for 1 to 2 minutes—until nicely glazed. Serve hot.

Poires au Cidre

PEARS POACHED IN CIDER

Serves 4

4 pears—must be ripe, Anjou
    pears preferred
1 lemon
3 cups cider
1½ cups sugar
1 clove
½ tablespoon (½ envelope) pow-
    dered gelatin

1 tablespoon Calvados
1 pint Sorbet aux Poires (page
    457), or pear ice cream, or
    Vanilla Ice Cream (page
    442)
8 leaves fresh mint (if available),
    cut in fine strips

1. Peel, core, and halve the pears. Cut the lemon in half, and rub the pears all over with an inner surface of the lemon to prevent browning.

2. Put the cider, sugar, and clove in a saucepan. Bring them to a light boil. Add the pears, and poach slowly until they are soft—about 15 minutes. With a slotted spoon, remove the pears from the pan.

3. Reduce the liquid that remains in the saucepan by ⅔.

4. Dissolve the gelatin in the Calvados. Add the Calvados to the liquid in the saucepan. Cook gently for 2 minutes. Set the pan aside and let the liquid cool. It will be a little gelatinous.

5. Arrange the Sorbet aux Poires (or ice cream) and the pear halves on 4 cold plates. Coat the ice cream and pears with the cooled liquid. Sprinkle with the mint (if used).

Poires au Calvados

BAKED PEARS WITH CALVADOS

Serves 4

4 pears—must be ripe
2 tablespoons (¼ stick) unsalted butter, plus butter for buttering the gratin dish
½ cup sugar
¼ cup Calvados

2 eggs
1 pinch powdered cinnamon
salt
1 tablespoon all-purpose flour
¾ cup heavy cream

1. Peel and core the pears. Cut them in half, lengthwise. Then cut each half in 4 lengthwise sections.

2. Melt the butter in a sauté pan over medium heat. Add the pears, sprinkle them with ½ the sugar, and sauté until the pears are lightly caramelized. Add ½ the Calvados and set it aflame.

3. Lightly butter a gratin dish, and empty the sauté pan into it.

4. Preheat the oven to 350°.

5. In a bowl, whisk together the eggs and the remaining sugar until the eggs are frothy and nearly white. Add the cinnamon, a pinch of salt, and the flour. Slowly stir in the cream, then the remaining Calvados. Pour this mixture over the pears.

6. Cook in the preheated oven for 35 minutes—until the tops are lightly golden brown. Serve warm.

Sorbet

SHERBET

Yields: approximately 1½ quarts

For the Syrup

2½ cups sugar

In a pot, stir together 3½ cups of water and the sugar. Bring to the boil, boil for 2 minutes, and cool.

Note: Use this syrup to prepare the following sherbets, except the Orange or Grapefruit Sherbet.

For a Lemon Sherbet

1 quart syrup (approximately
    1 recipe)
¾ cup lemon juice

rind of 1 lemon, ground fine

For a Cassis Sherbet

1 quart syrup (approximately 1
    recipe)
2 cups (1 pound) puree of cassis
    (frozen black currant puree)

2 tablespoons Crème de Cassis
    (liqueur)
1 tablespoon lemon juice

For a Peach Sherbet

1 quart syrup (approxi-
    mately 1 recipe)

2 cups (1 pound) puree of peach
    (frozen peach puree, or
    pureed fresh peaches)
2 tablespoons peach liqueur
1 tablespoon lemon juice

For a Melon Sherbet

1 quart syrup (approximately 1
    recipe)
2 cups (1 pound) puree of melon
    (from approximately a 1½-
    pound melon)

1 tablespoon lemon juice

For a Cucumber Sherbet

1 quart syrup (approximately 1
    recipe)
4 medium cucumbers, peeled,
    seeded, and pureed (approxi-
    mately 2 cups)

2 tablespoons lemon juice
1½ ounces gin

To Prepare Any of the Above Sherbets

Stir the ingredients together, refrigerate until cold, and process in an ice cream maker until firm. Store in the freezer until served.

For an Apple or Pear Sherbet

1 pound apples or pears, peeled
    and cored
1 cup apple juice
1 cup sugar

1 pint syrup (approximately ½
    recipe)
1 tablespoon lemon juice

To Prepare an Apple or Pear Sherbet

In a saucepan, combine the apples (or pears), apple juice, and sugar. Bring to the boil, and cook for 10 minutes. Puree in an electric mixer. Stir in the syrup and lemon juice. Refrigerate until cold, and process in an ice cream maker until firm. Store in the freezer until served.

For an Orange or Grapefruit Sherbet

1½ cups sugar
1 quart orange juice or grape-
    fruit juice

1 tablespoon lemon juice

Sorbet (continued)

To Prepare an Orange or Grapefruit Sherbet

By stirring, dissolve the sugar in the orange juice or grapefruit juice. Stir in the lemon juice. Refrigerate until cold, and process in an ice cream maker until firm. Store in the freezer until served.

Note: These sherbets may be stored, but it is best to serve them no more than 2 hours after they are made. If the sherbets freeze hard, permit them to thaw—in the refrigerator, or at room temperature, *but not by the application of heat*—and process again in an ice cream maker until firm; store again in the freezer until served.

Note: To prepare a Kirsch Sherbet (or a sherbet of any other liqueur or eau-de-vie), substitute ¾ cup of kirsch for the lemon juice and lemon rind in the recipe for Lemon Sherbet.

∾❧∾

Soufflé au Kirsch

KIRSCH SOUFFLÉ

Serves 6

4 tablespoons (½ stick) unsalted butter, plus butter for buttering the soufflé dish
½ cup all-purpose flour, sifted
1½ cups milk
¼ cup sugar, plus sugar for sugaring the soufflé dish
1 vanilla bean
4 egg yolks
¼ cup kirsch
6 egg whites
confectioners' sugar for sprinkling the cooked soufflé

1. In a saucepan, over medium heat, melt the butter. Stir in the flour, and cook, stirring, until the flour begins to brown very slightly. Set aside and let cool.
2. In another saucepan, stir together the milk, sugar, and vanilla bean.

Bring to the boil. Turn off the heat, and let the liquid stand for 10 minutes. Remove the vanilla bean.

3. Whisking constantly, pour the cooked milk over the butter-and-flour mixture. Continue whisking until smooth. Put this mixture over medium heat, bring it to the boil, and, whisking constantly, cook for 5 minutes. Remove it from the heat.

4. Whisk in the egg yolks. Let the mixture cool a little. Then stir in the kirsch.

5. In a bowl, beat the egg whites until stiff. Gently fold the egg whites into the mixture.

6. Preheat the oven to 375°.

7. Generously butter the inside of a 3-cup soufflé dish. Then sprinkle the inside of the dish generously with sugar. Invert the dish to remove any excess sugar.

8. Fill the soufflé dish to within ⅜ of an inch of the top with the mixture. Smooth the surface.

9. Bake in the preheated oven for 20 to 25 minutes—until the top is golden brown and rises to approximately 1½ inches above its mold.

Note: The soufflé may also be prepared in 6 individual 8-ounce soufflé dishes (approximately 4 inches wide and 2 inches high). In the smaller dishes, the baking time is about 12 minutes, and the soufflés rise to approximately 1 inch above their molds.

10. Sprinkle with confectioners' sugar, and serve at once.

Note: The soufflé may also be prepared with other eaux-de-vie or with liqueurs, such as poire, framboise, or Grand Marnier. At Lutèce, dessert soufflés are usually served with Crème Anglaise (page 488) or Sauce Chocolat Amer (page 487).

Soufflé Glacé aux Framboises

FROZEN SOUFFLÉ WITH RASPBERRIES

When I first made this Soufflé Glacé, I made it the classic French way, the way I was taught, and everybody liked it.

Then—it was in the 1960s—a food writer wrote about Lutèce. Mostly it was a good review, but the Soufflé Glacé got a bad review: too grainy.

"Too grainy," I said to myself. What do these writers know! What I was thinking included some strong language.

But the next day, I calmed down a little bit. I cut myself a portion of my Soufflé Glacé, and I ate it. I hated to admit it, but it was too grainy.

The old way to make Soufflé Glacé is with layers of genoise, a cake. The cake soaks up the raspberry syrup, and when you freeze it, it becomes—grainy. I decided to make it instead with layers of *fond de succès*, which is like a kind of macaroon (and which in this recipe we call "almond pastries"). It does not soak up the syrup. It stays crunchy. I made one just to try it, and I never made a Soufflé Glacé the old way again.

Since then we have served thousands—it seems like millions—of these Soufflés Glacés. At Lutèce, nothing we make is more popular than this dessert.

Serves 8

The Almond Pastries

oil for oiling the parchment paper
2 egg whites
⅔ cup blanched almonds, ground
½ tablespoon all-purpose flour
½ cup sugar

The Raspberry Mousse

3 cups fresh raspberries
juice of ½ lemon
3 egg whites
½ cup sugar
1 tablespoon light corn syrup
2 cups heavy cream

The Almond Pastries

1. Preheat the oven to 200°.

2. Line a baking sheet with parchment paper. With a pencil, and with an 8-inch soufflé dish as a guide, trace 2 circles exactly the diameter of the dish onto the parchment paper. Lightly oil the paper.

3. Fold another sheet of parchment paper in half lengthwise, and wrap it around the outside of the soufflé dish so that it extends 3 inches above the top, like a high collar. Tape the parchment paper securely in place with masking tape.

4. Beat the 2 egg whites until they form stiff peaks. Stir together the ground almonds, the flour, and the ½ cup of sugar, and gently fold them into the beaten egg whites. Put this mixture in a pastry bag fitted with a round ½-inch tip.

5. From the pastry bag, beginning at the center of each circle, and spiraling outward, squeeze the mixture onto the parchment paper to form two 8-inch disks about ½ inch thick. Bake these on the pastry sheet, in the preheated oven, until they are crisp—about 1½ hours. Let them cool on a rack.

Note: These almond pastries may be prepared in advance and stored. They must be kept at room temperature in airtight containers.

The Raspberry Mousse

6. Choose some perfect raspberries for a garnish and set them aside. Puree the other raspberries in a processor or blender until very smooth. Put 2 tablespoons of this puree, with seeds, in a measuring cup.

7. Strain the remaining puree into a mixing bowl, eliminating the seeds in the process. To the 2 tablespoons of puree in the measuring cup, add just enough of this strained puree to make ½ cup. Add the lemon juice. Set aside. Refrigerate the remaining strained puree.

8. Beat the 3 egg whites in an electric mixer until stiff.

9. In a small, heavy saucepan, combine the ½ cup of sugar, 3 tablespoons of water, and the corn syrup. Bring slowly to the boil over medium heat, stirring occasionally, and brushing down any sugar crystals from the sides of the pan with a brush dipped in cold water. Raise the heat slightly, and cook until the temperature of the syrup reaches 275° on a candy thermometer.

Soufflé Glacé aux Framboises (continued)

10. With the electric mixer at slow speed, pour the hot syrup into the beaten egg whites in a thin stream. When all the syrup has been incorporated, raise the mixer speed and mix until the mixture is cool. Fold the raspberry-and-lemon mixture into this mixture until nearly blended.

11. Whip the cream until stiff. With a spatula, gently fold the whipped cream into the mixture until blended. *Do not overmix.*

The Final Assembly

12. Spread a ¾-inch layer of the mousse on the bottom of the prepared soufflé dish. Peel the paper from one of the almond pastries, and set the pastry on top of that layer. Add another ¾-inch layer of the mousse, then the second pastry. Add the remaining mousse, smoothing the top gently with a spatula. (This last layer extends above the soufflé dish and is held in place by the paper collar.) Freeze for at least 3 hours.

13. To serve, carefully remove the paper collar. Smooth the exposed outside of the Soufflé with a metal spatula, if necessary. Using a knife blade or long metal spatula, score a shallow crisscross pattern in the top of the Soufflé. Garnish with the reserved raspberries. Serve in wedges, spooning a little of the chilled raspberry puree around each serving. Serve the rest of the puree separately as a sauce.

Note: The Soufflé may be prepared days in advance, and stored in the freezer until needed.

Soufflé Glacé au Citron

FROZEN LEMON SOUFFLÉ

Note: To prepare a Soufflé Glacé au Citron, a lemon mousse is substituted for the raspberry mousse in the Soufflé Glacé aux Framboises:

A. Use the following ingredients instead of those listed under *The Raspberry Mousse.*

B. Perform the following Steps 1 through 3 instead of Steps 6 through 11.

C. Omit the raspberry garnish and the raspberry puree from Step 13.

The Lemon Mousse

2 cups heavy cream
2 cups sugar
8 egg yolks

grated rind of 3 lemons
juice of 3 lemons

The Lemon Mousse

1. Whip the cream, and set it aside in a cool place.

2. Cook the 2 cups of sugar in 5 ounces of water until the sugar is dissolved and the temperature reaches 275° on a candy thermometer.

3. Meanwhile, beat the egg yolks. When they are light and fluffy, slowly pour in the hot syrup prepared in Step 2. Continue beating until the mixture is cold. Stir in the grated lemon rind and the lemon juice. Fold in the whipped cream. *Do not overwork.*

᭟᭟᭟

Tarte à la Crème aux Amandes

ALMOND TART

In 1965, when I was traveling with my wife on vacation in France, I visited for the first time the restaurant of Paul Bocuse, in Lyon. Bocuse and I had never met before. He is a great host, and when he heard I was a chef, he insisted we try almost everything he made that day.

That lunch lasted until 4:30 in the afternoon. At the end, he served me a cream tart that he said he had learned from Madame Brazier, who was the proprietor of the legendary restaurant Mère Brazier, nearby. It was a fabulous tart.

We wanted to drive back to Paris after lunch, but Bocuse absolutely insisted that we do no such thing, that we have dinner at Troisgros instead—which at that time was not yet world-famous. Troisgros is about one hour away. Bocuse himself called and made the reservation for us, and arranged for us to stay that night at the inn.

So we had dinner at Troisgros, and at the end of our second fantastic meal in one day, Jean Troisgros—whom I had also never met before—took us next door to his bistro. "Try this tart," he said, "something new." And he served us—the same fabulous tart! Of course, he also had learned it from Madame Brazier.

When I came back to New York, I decided I wanted to have this tart at Lutèce. But I changed it a little. I added almonds. And since then I have never stopped making it. We have it almost every week.

My customers have never stopped raving about this simple dessert.

Serves 6

unsalted butter for buttering the flan ring and pastry sheet	3 eggs
¾ pound Pâte à Brioche (page 534)	¾ cup sugar
	1 teaspoon vanilla extract
2 cups heavy cream	2 cups sliced almonds

1. Butter a 10-inch flan ring, and put it on a buttered pastry sheet.

2. Roll out the Pâte à Brioche to make a 13-inch circle. The pastry should be about 3/16 inch thick. Lay the circle of pastry in the flan ring, and press the pastry against the inside of the ring. Fold the excess dough over the edge of the ring, and neatly cut this excess away by running a rolling pin over the ring. Refrigerate the pastry, or put it in the freezer, while you prepare the cream—around 10 minutes.

3. Preheat the oven to 350°.

4. With a whisk, combine the cream, eggs, sugar, and vanilla extract. Then stir in the almonds.

5. Take the pastry from the refrigerator. Make sure the edges of the pastry are clinging to the flan ring. If not, press them against the ring again. Fill the pastry with the cream-and-almond mixture.

6. Put the filled pastry in the preheated oven. After 5 minutes reduce the oven temperature to 275°, and continue baking another 30 minutes.

Note: The cream should not boil during the baking. The tart should be golden brown on top and moist inside.

7. Remove the tart from the oven and let it rest for at least 25 minutes. Serve at room temperature.

Note: At Lutèce we usually serve the Almond Tart with Vanilla Ice Cream (page 442) or Caramel Ice Cream (page 445).

❧

Tarte à la Rhubarbe

RHUBARB TART

I was surprised to find when I came to America that rhubarb is not much used here. Where I come from, everybody loves it, and it is everywhere.

I grow rhubarb in my own garden, and I make this tart at home every year without fail. When rhubarb is in season, I also make it several times at Lutèce.

I think that what makes this Tarte à la Rhubarbe so good is the contrast between the sweet custard and the sour fruit.

The tart is best when it is still a little warm, so there is a nice contrast also between the warm tart and the cold vanilla ice cream, or lemon sherbet, that we garnish it with at Lutèce.   *Serves 6 to 8*

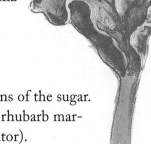

1 pound rhubarb, peeled and cut
    in ¾-inch pieces
½ cup sugar
¾ pound Pâte Brisée (page 537)
all-purpose flour for flouring the
    work surface
unsalted butter for
    buttering the pie pan

2 eggs
½ cup milk
½ cup heavy
    cream
3 drops vanilla
    extract

1. Put the rhubarb in a bowl. Add 1½ tablespoons of the sugar. Toss the rhubarb and the sugar together, and let the rhubarb marinate for 15 minutes (either in or out of the refrigerator).

2. On a floured surface, roll out the Pâte Brisée. Butter a 10-inch pie pan. Press the dough into the pie pan. Refrigerate for at least 30 minutes.

3. Preheat the oven to 400°.

Tarte à la Rhubarbe (continued)

4. Put the rhubarb in a colander to drain away the liquid it has given off.

5. Fill the pastry with the rhubarb and bake in the preheated oven for 20 minutes.

6. In a bowl, beat together the eggs and the remaining sugar. Whisk in the milk, cream, and vanilla. Pour this mixture over the rhubarb. Bake until the surface of the custard that forms on the tart is golden brown— about 20 minutes more.

꙾

Tarte au Chocolat

CHOCOLATE TART

Once a customer came back from Paris and told me about a wonderful chocolate tart he had there. He described it to me, and I tried to make it. I tried it a few different ways, but I was not successful.

Then one day I found a recipe for a chocolate tart in the *New York Times,* by Craig Claiborne. So I tried again, this time following Craig Claiborne's recipe. Again I was not successful. But in fairness to Mr. Claiborne, I think I was not careful enough—I think that maybe my oven was too hot or too cold or something like that.

But I kept trying. And finally I did come up with a beautiful chocolate tart.

This tart is not too hard to make, but in some things it is important to follow the recipe exactly. You should use only bittersweet chocolate (imported) that has a 42 percent butterfat content. In Step 7, the oven must be exactly 350°. And you have to bake for exactly seven minutes—not more, not less.

Serves 6

6 tablespoons (¾ stick) unsalted butter, softened, plus butter for buttering the pie pan	5 ounces bittersweet chocolate (42% butterfat content)
5 ounces Pâte Sablée (page 539)	2 egg yolks
	1 egg

2 tablespoons sugar
grated rind of 1 small orange

confectioners' sugar for sprinkling the tart

1. Butter an 8-inch pie pan. Roll out the Pâte Sablée and line the pie pan with it. Prick the pastry with a fork, and refrigerate it for 15 minutes.
2. Preheat the oven to 350°.
3. Line the pastry with parchment paper, and fill it with dried beans to weigh it down. Bake the pastry in the preheated oven until it is slightly browned—12 to 15 minutes. Remove the pastry from the oven, and remove the beans and parchment paper. (Leave the oven on.)
4. In a double boiler, melt the chocolate—heating it as little as possible—and *immediately* remove it from the heat.
5. In a mixer, whip the egg yolks, the egg, and the sugar until the mixture is very pale and falls from a whisk in a ribbon.
6. Remove the bowl from the mixer. With a wooden spatula, stir in the orange rind; then the 6 tablespoons of butter and the chocolate. Stir until blended.
7. Pour the filling into the pastry. Bake in the preheated oven *for exactly 7 minutes.* Sprinkle with confectioners' sugar before serving.

Note: At Lutèce we garnish this tart with Sauce Chocolat Amer (page 487) and Caramel Ice Cream (page 445).

Tarte à l'Orange

ORANGE TART

A food writer once asked me to make an orange tart—which I had never made before. This is what I came up with.   *Serves 6*

4 oranges
½ pound Pâte Sucrée (page 540)
2 cups Crème Bavarois au Grand
    Marnier (page 436), not
    refrigerated

Tarte à l'Orange (continued)

1. With a vegetable peeler, peel the outer portion of skin from 1 of the oranges. With a sharp knife cut this peel into *very* fine strips. Blanch in boiling water for 1 minute.

2. Remove the remainder of the skin from the first orange, and peel the other 3 oranges. Cut the orange segments out of all 4 oranges, eliminating the membrane. Remove and discard the seeds.

3. Preheat the oven to 375°.

4. Roll out the Pâte Sucrée to a circle ⅛ inch thick. Line a 9-inch pie plate with the pastry. Prick the bottom of the pastry all over with a fork. Line the pastry with parchment paper and fill it with dried beans or lentils. Bake the pastry in the preheated oven for 15 minutes.

5. Remove the pastry from the oven. Remove the beans (or lentils), and remove the parchment paper. Let the pastry cool.

6. Fill the pastry shell with the Crème Bavarois. Let it cool until stiff. Arrange the orange sections in a nice pattern on top. Sprinkle with the julienne of orange peel.

Tarte au Fromage

CHEESE CAKE

There were cheese cakes long ago. Even the Greeks and Romans made them. And they are in all the old Alsatian cookbooks. But for years and years, I never served cheese cake at Lutèce. Then a young American came to work for me as an extern. He had a family recipe for cheese cake, and when he made it for us, we all loved it.

It is an American cheese cake, but it is not so far from the old Alsatian ones. Even the lemon flavoring is the same. However, the pastry is different—in the old days a cheese cake crust was Pâte Brisée, but we use graham crackers (which did not exist in the old days). And Alsatian cheese cakes are made with French fromage blanc, but we make the Lutèce cake with American cream cheese.

One year I went to a big gastronomic fair in Alsace—in Colmar. Because cheese cake is both very American and also very Alsatian, I demonstrated this cake—made with cream cheese, and with a graham cracker crust, everything exactly the way we make it at Lutèce. It was a big hit.

Serves 8 to 10

1 pound cream cheese
3 eggs
1 cup sugar
1 teaspoon vanilla extract
1 pinch salt
grated rind of 1 lemon

1½ cups sour cream
½ cup crème fraîche
5 ounces (about 1½ cups) graham cracker crumbs
6 tablespoons (¾ stick) unsalted butter, melted

1. In a food processor, combine the cream cheese, eggs, sugar, vanilla extract, salt, and grated lemon peel. Process until smooth.

2. Remove the mixture from the food processor and put it in a bowl. With a spatula, stir in the sour cream and the crème fraîche.

3. In a bowl, thoroughly mix together the graham cracker crumbs and melted butter. Spread this mixture on the bottom of a 3-inch-high, 10-inch springform cake mold. Refrigerate for 10 minutes.

4. Preheat the oven to 275°.

5. Pour the filling over the graham cracker crust (it will not fill the mold). Set the mold in a shallow pan of hot water, and put it in the preheated oven for 1½ hours.

6. Refrigerate overnight. Serve at room temperature.

Note: At Lutèce, we often serve this cake with strawberries on top and with a strawberry coulis poured around the cake; or with raspberries; or with kiwi fruit.

Tarte aux Cerises Aigres

SOUR CHERRY TART

Serves 6 to 8

½ pound Pâte Brisée (page 537)
2 pounds fresh sour cherries, pitted
⅜ cup sugar, plus sugar for sprinkling the cherries and the tart

6 tablespoons heavy cream
1 egg
1 teaspoon kirsch (optional)

1. Preheat the oven to 375°.
2. Roll out the Pâte Brisée to a sheet ⅛ inch thick. Line a 9-inch pie pan with it. Put the cherries neatly in the unbaked shell. Sprinkle the cherries lightly with sugar, and bake the tart in the preheated oven for 15 minutes.
3. While the tart is baking, beat together the cream, egg, kirsch (if used), and ⅜ cup of sugar. Strain through a fine sieve.
4. After the first 15 minutes of baking, pour this mixture over the cherries. Bake 15 minutes more. Sprinkle with sugar before serving.

Note: This tart is best at room temperature.

Tarte aux Fraises au Bavarois

STRAWBERRY TART WITH BAVARIAN CREAM
(May Be Prepared with Kiwi Fruit)

Serves 8

The Pastry

½ pound Pâte Brisée (page 537)

The Bavarian Cream

4 egg yolks
½ cup sugar
1 cup milk
1 scant tablespoon (or 1 enve-
    lope) powdered gelatin

grated rind of 1 lemon
juice of 1 lemon
1 cup heavy cream, whipped

The Final Assembly

12 to 15 ripe strawberries (or
    4 kiwis)
¼ cup strawberry jelly, to which
    a little gelatin has been added,
    lukewarm

The Pastry

1. Preheat the oven to 375°.
2. Roll out the Pâte Brisée to a sheet ⅛ inch thick, and line a 9-inch pie pan with it. Line the pastry with parchment paper, fill it with dried beans or lentils, and put it in the preheated oven. Bake for 20 minutes. Remove the pastry from the oven, remove the beans and paper, and return it to the oven. Bake for about another 10 minutes—until it is slightly browned. Set aside and let cool.

The Bavarian Cream

3. In a bowl, beat the egg yolks with ½ of the sugar until the eggs are thick and fluffy.

Tarte aux Fraises au Bavarois (continued)

4. Put the milk, the remaining sugar, and the gelatin in a saucepan, and bring to the boil. Slowly pour this mixture into the beaten eggs, rapidly stirring all the ingredients as you pour. Return this mixture to the saucepan, and bring it *almost* to the boil.

5. Strain the mixture through a fine sieve into a bowl. Set the bowl over ice, and stir from time to time to speed the cooling. (Or refrigerate.)

6. When the mixture begins to thicken, add the lemon rind and lemon juice. Then thoroughly fold in the whipped cream.

The Final Assembly

7. Pour the mixture into the pastry shell, and refrigerate for 15 minutes.

8. Slice the strawberries (or the kiwis). Arrange the sliced fruit in a pattern on top of the cream. With a brush, coat the top of the tart with the strawberry jelly.

❦

Tarte aux Myrtilles

HUCKLEBERRY (OR BLUEBERRY) TART

The Vosges Mountains, where I come from, are covered with huckleberries—in French, "myrtilles."

When I was a child I picked buckets of them to make tarts and jam. Huckleberries are the only such berries we have in France—there are no blueberries. But, unfortunately, the French word "myrtille" has come to mean in English both "huckleberry" and "blueberry," even though these two berries are very different.

At Lutèce I must cook mostly blueberries, because the huckleberry season is short. But during the huckleberry season (for Lutèce, only September and October, because we are closed in August), I get great huckleberries from Oregon.

The tart is good with either berry, but whenever you can get them, use huckleberries—that is really the better way.

I give two versions of this tart. In Alsace, both are made, but the second one, Method II, is more common.   *Serves 6 to 8*

Method I

1¼ pounds huckleberries (or
    blueberries)
1 tablespoon kirsch
2 tablespoons sugar
flour for flouring the work
    surface
¾ pound Pâte Brisée (page 537)

unsalted butter for buttering the
    pie pan
½ cup cookie crumbs (or graham
    cracker crumbs)
1 tablespoon confectioners'
    sugar

1. Set 3 ounces of the berries aside.
2. Put the remaining berries in a bowl with the kirsch and the sugar. Toss these together.
3. Preheat the oven to 375°.
4. Flour a work surface, and roll out the Pâte Brisée. Butter a 10-inch pie pan. Press the dough into the pie pan, and refrigerate for 15 minutes.
5. Spread the cookie crumbs (or graham cracker crumbs) over the bottom of the pastry. Fill the pastry with the berries (*not* including the 3 ounces of reserved berries).
6. Bake for 25 minutes in the preheated oven.
7. Remove the tart from the oven, and sprinkle the reserved berries over the top. Press down on these berries a little to push them slightly into the surface of the tart. Let the tart cool to room temperature.
8. Sprinkle with the confectioners' sugar. Serve at room temperature. Do not refrigerate.

Method II

Additional Ingredients for Method II

2 eggs
¼ cup sugar
½ cup milk

½ cup heavy cream
3 drops vanilla extract

Tarte aux Myrtilles (continued)

1. Put all the berries in a bowl with the kirsch and the 2 tablespoons of sugar. Toss these together.

2. Preheat the oven to 375°.

3. Flour a work surface, and roll out the Pâte Brisée. Butter a 10-inch pie pan. Press the dough into the pie pan, and refrigerate for 15 minutes.

4. Spread the cookie crumbs (or graham cracker crumbs) over the bottom of the pastry. Fill the pastry with the berries.

5. Bake for 20 minutes in the preheated oven.

6. Lower the oven temperature to 325°.

7. In a bowl, beat together the eggs, the ¼ cup of sugar, the milk, cream, and vanilla extract. Pour this mixture over the berries.

8. Put the tart back in the oven, and bake for 15 minutes more. Remove the tart from the oven and let it cool to room temperature.

9. Sprinkle with the confectioners' sugar. Serve at room temperature. Do not refrigerate.

❧

Tarte aux Pommes à l'Alsacienne

ALSATIAN APPLE TART

Serves 6

½ pound Pâte Brisée (page 537)
4 apples, Golden Delicious pre-
    ferred
juice of ½ lemon
½ cup sugar

½ cup heavy cream
1 egg
1 teaspoon kirsch

1. Line a 9-inch pie pan with the Pâte Brisée.

2. Preheat the oven to 375°.

3. Peel and core the apples, and cut them in 8 slices each. Moisten the apple slices with the lemon juice, and arrange them on the pastry. Bake the tart in the preheated oven for 15 minutes.

4. While the tart is baking, mix together the sugar, cream, egg, and kirsch. Strain through a fine sieve, and pour over the tart after it has baked 15 minutes.

5. Return the tart to the oven for another 15 minutes. Serve at room temperature.

Note: At Lutèce we usually serve Vanilla Ice Cream (page 442) with this tart.

❧❧

Tarte aux Pommes Chaudes

HOT APPLE TART

This is some of the new French cooking that is still around. It is different from traditional French fruit tarts of this kind because it is prepared without cream or eggs, and because you make it at the last minute and serve it hot.

Simple as it is, it is a fabulous dessert.   *Serves 4*

½ pound Feuilletage Rapide (page 531)
5 medium apples, Golden Delicious preferred

juice of 1 lemon
6 tablespoons (¾ stick) unsalted butter, cut in thin slices
⅜ cup sugar

1. Roll out the Feuilletage Rapide, and put a 10-inch circle of the pastry on a pastry sheet. The pastry should be no more than ⅛ inch thick. Refrigerate.

2. Preheat the oven to 400°.

3. Peel and core the apples, and cut them in slices about 3⁄16 inch thick. Mix them with the lemon juice.

4. Arrange the apple slices in an overlapping circular pattern on the pastry. Leave a ½-inch border all around. Distribute the slices of butter over the apples. Sprinkle ½ of the sugar on top.

5. Bake the tart in the preheated oven for 10 minutes.

6. Remove the tart from the oven, and sprinkle the remainder of the sugar on top. Return the tart to the oven until the sugar is lightly caramelized—about 8 minutes. Serve hot.

❧❧

Tarte aux Pommes Rapées

GRATED-APPLE TART

Serves 6 to 8

flour for flouring the work
   surface
¾ pound Pâte Brisée (page 537)
unsalted butter for buttering the
   pie pan
4 cups grated apple (peeled and
   cored), grated with the
   largest holes of the grater (or
   use the grater attachment of
   a food processor)

juice of 1 lemon
¼ cup raisins (white raisins
   preferred)
2 tablespoons Calvados
2 eggs
1 egg yolk
⅔ cup sugar
1 cup heavy cream
confectioners' sugar for sprinkling the tart

1. Flour a work surface, and roll out the Pâte Brisée into a circle that will line a 10-inch pie pan. Butter the pie pan, press the pastry into it, and refrigerate for at least 30 minutes.

2. Toss the grated apple with the lemon juice. Set aside.

3. Put the raisins, Calvados, and 1 tablespoon of water in a small saucepan. Bring to the boil, and *immediately* remove the saucepan from the heat. Set aside.

4. Preheat the oven to 375°.

5. Break the eggs into a bowl, and add the egg yolk. Whisk in the sugar until it is dissolved. Stir in the cream. Add the apples and raisins, and mix thoroughly. Fill the pastry shell with this mixture, and bake the tart in the preheated oven for about 40 minutes—until the pastry is golden brown.

6. Serve lukewarm (or at room temperature), sprinkled with confectioners' sugar. *Do not refrigerate.*

Tarte Citron Mama

LEMON-ALMOND TART

Many years ago, when it was still a new restaurant, a man by the name of Michel Dreyfus used to come to Lutèce. He was the president of Dreyfus Ashby, the wine importers, and he helped us with our wine list. He was also a very good customer.

Once he told me that his family was originally from Spain, but because they were Jews they had to leave Spain many, many centuries ago, and they went to Switzerland. The woman of that family took with her to Switzerland the recipe for this tart. It was passed from the mothers to the daughters ever since, and it was always made on special family occasions. I told him that if he got the recipe, I would try to make it for him.

He wrote to his eighty-year-old sister in Switzerland, and she sent him the recipe. It was in German, but, because I am Alsatian, that was no problem. I tried the recipe, and it was a little shaky—but I figured it out. I must have got it right, because when I served it to Michel Dreyfus, it was just as if I brought back to him his childhood.

Eventually I taught Mr. Dreyfus how to make it for himself.

This tart is not like anything I had ever made before. We still serve it at Lutèce several times a year, and many people who have it, they ask for it again and again. Most of them have no idea where it comes from.

Serves 6

3 eggs, extra large, separated
1 cup sugar
grated peel of 1 lemon
1¾ cups almonds, ground fine
1 tablespoon all-purpose flour
2 egg whites

unsalted butter for buttering the
    pie plate
2 lemons, peeled, sliced thin,
    and seeded
confectioners' sugar for sprin-
    kling the tart

1. Preheat the oven to 350°.
2. Beat the 3 egg yolks and ¾ cup of the sugar until the mixture is very pale and falls from the whisk in a ribbon. Mix in the grated lemon peel.

Tarte Citron Mama (continued)

Mix in 1 cup of the ground almonds and the flour.

3. Beat 3 of the egg whites until stiff. Gently fold them into the batter.

4. Butter a 9-inch pie plate and pour in the batter. Bake in the preheated oven for about 30 minutes, or until the cake is lightly browned.

5. When the cake is ready, cover it with the lemon slices, overlapping them slightly.

6. Beat the remaining 2 egg whites until they reach soft peaks. Add the remaining ¼ cup of sugar in increments, beating after each addition. Gently fold in the remaining ground almonds, and spread this meringue over the lemon slices, using a spatula dipped in cold water.

7. Return the cake to the oven for 15 minutes. Serve at room temperature. Sprinkle with the confectioners' sugar just before serving.

Tarte aux Quetsches

PLUM TART

I n America, this very popular Alsatian dessert cannot be made exactly the way it is made in Alsace, because certain plums, called "quetsches" in France, are not grown here. The closest to them are the slightly small purple plums called Italian plums. But you can make this tart with any kind of plum. August and September, when plums are in season, is the best time.

Note: The recipe calls for Pâte Levée (page 538), but you can also use Pâte Brisée (page 537).

Serves 6 to 8

Method I

flour for flouring the work surface	3 pounds plums
½ recipe Pâte Levée (page 538)	½ cup sugar
unsalted butter for buttering the pie pan	1 scant teaspoon powdered cinnamon
½ cup cookie crumbs (or graham cracker crumbs)	

1. Flour a work surface, and roll out the Pâte Levée to a circle that will line a 10-inch pie pan. Butter the pie pan, and line it with the pastry. Prick the pastry with a fork. Spread the cookie crumbs over the bottom of the pastry.

2. With a sharp knife, cut the plums in half from the stem end to the opposite end, and remove the pits. Cut a ¼-inch incision into one end of each plum half, so that when the plum half is opened a little, the cut end forms 2 points.

3. Arrange the plum halves in concentric circles on the pastry, each piece with its cut end (the 2 points) up. (The plum halves are more or less standing on their uncut ends, and leaning against each other.)

Tarte aux Quetsches (continued)

4. Preheat the oven to 375°.

5. Put the tart in a warm place for 10 to 15 minutes, allowing the dough to rise a little. Sprinkle the tart with ¾ of the sugar.

6. Bake in the preheated oven for 30 minutes.

7. Mix together the remaining sugar and the powdered cinnamon. Just before serving, sprinkle this mixture over the tart.

Note: Do not refrigerate. Serve lukewarm.

Method II

Additional Ingredients for Method II

2 eggs
¼ cup sugar
½ cup milk

½ cup heavy cream
3 drops vanilla extract

1. Proceed as in Method I through Step 5.

2. Bake in the preheated oven for 20 minutes. Remove the tart from the oven.

3. Reduce the oven temperature to 325°.

4. In a bowl, beat together the eggs, the ¼ cup of sugar, the milk, cream, and vanilla extract. Pour this mixture over the plums.

5. Return the tart to the oven, and bake 15 minutes more.

6. Mix together the remaining 2 tablespoons of sugar and the powdered cinnamon. Just before serving, sprinkle this mixture over the tart.

Note: Do not refrigerate. Serve lukewarm.

Tarte Feuilletée aux Poires

PEAR TART

I t is important that this dish be prepared only with absolutely ripe pears.

Serves 6

The Pastry

6 ounces Feuilletage Rapide
   (page 531)

The Pears

4 cups sugar
juice of 1 lemon

2 pounds pears—must be ripe—
   peeled, cored, and cut in half

The Cream

3 egg yolks
2 tablespoons sugar
1 tablespoon flour

1 cup milk
1 tablespoon pear brandy

The Final Assembly

confectioners' sugar for sprinkling the tart

The Pastry

1. Roll out the Feuilletage Rapide to a 10-inch circle. It should be about ⅛ inch thick. Put the pastry on a pastry sheet. With a sharp knife, cut a shallow incision in the pastry ½ inch in from the edge and all the way around. Refrigerate for at least 30 minutes.

Note: The incision forms a circle ½ inch within the edge of the pastry. The cut should go halfway through the thickness of the pastry. *It must not go all the way through.*

The Pears

2. Preheat the oven to 300°.

Tarte Feuilletée aux Poires (continued)

3. In a saucepan, mix the sugar, lemon juice, and 1 quart of water. Bring to the boil. Add the pears, and bring to the boil again. Simmer until the pears are cooked—5 to 10 minutes, depending on the ripeness of the pears. Set aside, to let the pears cool in the syrup.

4. Remove the pastry from the refrigerator. Prick it heavily with a fork. Bake it on the pastry sheet in the preheated oven until it is nicely browned and dry—about 12 minutes. Remove from the oven. Set aside.

The Cream

5. In a bowl, whisk together the egg yolks and 1 tablespoon of the sugar, beating vigorously until the mixture is very pale yellow. (When the mixture is ready, a ribbon will form when the whisk is lifted from it.) Gently fold in the flour.

6. Put the milk and the remaining 1 tablespoon of sugar in a saucepan. Bring the milk to the boil, and stir it into the egg mixture. Pour the combined liquids back into the saucepan, and put them over heat. While mixing vigorously with a whisk, bring to the boil and boil for 1 minute. (At this point the liquid should be a smooth cream.) Whisk in the pear brandy.

The Final Assembly

7. Spread the cream over the baked pastry, taking care to keep it within the cut border.

8. Slice the pears, and arrange the slices on the cream. Sprinkle confectioners' sugar over the top. Caramelize the pears with a hot caramelizing iron—or by placing the pastry under the broiler. Serve at room temperature.

Note: If you caramelize under the broiler, protect the exposed edge of the pastry by wrapping it in aluminum foil, otherwise the exposed pastry will burn.

Tarte Lutèce

TART TATIN AS SERVED AT LUTÈCE

This is a Tart Tatin, but we call it Tarte Lutèce instead, because we do not make it the classic way. When you make a real Tatin, you cover the apples with the pastry, then bake the tart, and then you put it upside down on a plate. When you make it that way, you have to serve it at once, because otherwise it gets soggy.

But in a restaurant, you have to make the tart in advance, so I make it this way. It does not get soggy. Some people think this way is better. It is certainly better for Lutèce. *Serves 5 or 6*

6 ounces Pâte Brisée (page 537)
8 apples, Golden Delicious, or
    another baking apple
juice of 1 lemon
8 tablespoons (1 stick) unsalted
    butter
½ cup sugar
½ cup heavy cream

1. Preheat the oven to 350°.
2. Roll out the Pâte Brisée to a 9-inch circle, and bake it on a baking sheet in the preheated oven until it is light brown and cooked through.
3. Peel and core the apples and cut them into 8 sections each. Moisten them with the lemon juice to prevent them from turning brown.
4. Raise the oven temperature to 375°.
5. Put a large skillet or frying pan over high heat. Add the butter and sugar and stir until the mixture turns a golden caramel color. Add the heavy cream, and, still over high heat, continue cooking and stirring for another 2 minutes.
6. Add the apples. Make sure that each slice is coated with the caramel mixture. Cover the pan with aluminum foil or with a well-fitting lid, and put it in the oven for 10 minutes.

Tarte Lutèce (continued)

7. Remove the pan from the oven and arrange the apples on the pastry in a tightly assembled pattern of rings within rings.

8. Heat the caramel that remains in the pan for another 2 to 4 minutes, until it thickens. Pour this caramel over the apples. Serve hot.

Note: The tart may be prepared in advance and reheated the same day.

Vacherin Glacé au Pralin

ALSATIAN ICE CREAM CAKE

Serves 8 to 10

The 3 Meringues

8 egg whites
salt
1¼ cups sugar

oil for oiling the parchment paper

The Praline

½ cup sugar
¾ cup sliced almonds

oil for oiling the work surface

The Ice Cream

2 pints Liqueur-Flavored Ice Cream (page 442), using kirsch

The Whipped Cream

1 cup heavy cream, cold

¼ cup sugar

The 3 Meringues

1. Preheat the oven to 200°.

2. In a bowl, whip the egg whites, with a pinch of salt, until stiff. With a wooden spoon, mix in the sugar. Do not overwork. Put this mixture in a pastry bag fitted with a round ½-inch tip.

3. Draw with a pencil 3 circles, 8 or 9 inches in diameter, on a sheet of parchment paper. Lightly oil the paper, and put it on a pastry sheet.

4. Squeeze the mixture from the pastry bag onto the parchment paper, by making a small circle at the center of one circle, and spiraling outward, continuing in an ever-widening circle until you have covered the 8-inch or 9-inch disk with about a ½-inch thickness of the meringue. Repeat with the 2 remaining circles.

5. Bake the disks on the parchment paper, in the preheated oven, until they are dry—1½ to 2 hours. The meringues should not color more than very slightly. Cool them on a rack.

Note: These meringues may be prepared up to a week in advance, and stored at room temperature in an airtight box.

The Praline

6. Put the sugar in a saucepan with 2 tablespoons of water. Stir until the sugar is dissolved in the water. Over medium heat, cook, stirring constantly, until the mixture becomes a blond color—a very pale tan—and is completely smooth.

7. Add the almonds. Continue cooking, stirring, 1 minute more. Lightly oil a marble surface or pastry sheet. Pour the praline onto it. Let the praline cool until hard—about 10 minutes. Do not refrigerate.

8. Break the praline into pieces. In a mortar, crush the praline into small lumps (or crush it by rolling it with a rolling pin).

The Ice Cream

9. Stir ⅔ of the praline into the ice cream.

The Whipped Cream

10. In a bowl, whip the cream until it stands in stiff peaks. Do not overwork. Stir in the sugar.

Vacherin Glacé au Pralin (continued)

The Final Assembly

11. Set 1 of the meringues on a plate. Spread ½ the ice cream on the meringue. Set 1 of the remaining meringues on top. Spread this meringue with the remaining ice cream. Put the last meringue on top.

12. Coat the top and sides of the Vacherin with the whipped cream. With the tip of a knife, or any implement, cut a design in the top. Pat the remaining praline into the whipped cream on the top and sides of the Vacherin. Freeze until served.

Note: The Vacherin may be prepared hours in advance and frozen.

Note: At Lutèce the Vacherin is served with Sauce Chocolat Amer (page 487), but it may be served without a sauce.

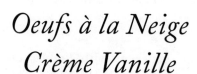

Oeufs à la Neige
Crème Vanille

FLOATING ISLANDS
WITH CRÈME ANGLAISE

This famous old dessert is still popular all over France, both in restaurants and at home. My mother made it often, usually as a treat for the children.

Serves 6

6 egg whites
1 small pinch salt
¾ cup sugar
1 recipe Crème Anglaise (page 488)
1 recipe caramel (page 437)
    OR

powdered chocolate, sweetened or unsweetened, for powdering the floating islands

1. Put the egg whites in a bowl, add the salt, and beat until stiff. Beat in the sugar.

2. Bring a large saucepan of water to the simmer. With a large spoon, spoon out portions of the beaten egg whites about the size and shape of small eggs, and slide these "eggs" onto the simmering water, where they will float. There should be about 12 eggs.

3. Cook the eggs in the simmering water for 1½ minutes. Then turn them with a slotted spoon so that they poach on both sides. (If necessary, poach in two batches.) Drain on a cloth or on paper towels until cool.

4. Spoon equal amounts of the Crème Anglaise into six small dessert dishes, and then place two eggs on the sauce in each dish. The eggs may also be floated on the Crème Anglaise in a large serving bowl.

5. Top the eggs with streaks of caramel, or with a little powdered chocolate.

Sauce Chocolat Amer

BITTER CHOCOLATE SAUCE

I learned to make this chocolate sauce in Switzerland, and we make it at Lutèce every day.

I have tried many chocolate sauces, but this is the simplest and the best-tasting. It is also a very beautiful deep, dark, polished brown.

Serves 6

¾ cup sugar
½ cup unsweetened cocoa

2 tablespoons (¼ stick) unsalted butter

1. In a saucepan—*not* over heat—whisk together the sugar, cocoa, and 1 cup of water.

2. Stirring constantly, put the saucepan over medium heat and bring the mixture to the boil. Still stirring with the whisk, continue to boil gently for 2 to 3 minutes.

Sauce Chocolat Amer (continued)

3. Whisk in the butter, and, still stirring, boil gently for 3 minutes more.

Note: The sauce may be served hot or cold. Also, it may be reheated.

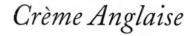

Crème Anglaise

VANILLA SAUCE

Yield: approximately 2 cups

½ cup sugar	2 cups milk
6 egg yolks	1 vanilla bean

1. In a bowl, beat together the sugar and egg yolks until the eggs turn very pale yellow.
2. In a saucepan, heat the milk and vanilla bean to the boiling point.
3. Prepare a double boiler. Put the sugar-and-egg-yolk mixture in the upper half over heat. Beat in the hot milk and then keep the mixture moving with a wooden spoon until it coats the spoon—about 5 minutes. *Do not boil.* Strain through a fine sieve.

Sauce Sabayon au Grand Marnier

GRAND MARNIER SABAYON

Yield: about 2 cups

2 eggs	1 cup heavy cream
1 egg yolk	1 tablespoon Grand Marnier
½ cup sugar	

1. In an electric mixer, beat the eggs and egg yolk until they are fluffy.

2. Cook the sugar with ¼ cup of water to 275° on a candy thermometer. With the mixer on, slowly pour the hot liquid into the beaten eggs, and continue mixing until the mixture has cooled.

3. Whip the cream. Fold it into the mixture. Stir in the Grand Marnier.

Holiday season dinner at Lutèce

Oeuf Surprise au Caviar (PAGE 119)

Soufflé aux Fruits de Mer (PAGE 161)

Dinde Farcie aux Marrons (PAGE 293)

Tarte Feuilletée aux Poires (PAGE 481)

Petits Fours et Mignardises
(SELECTED FROM THIS CHAPTER)

PETITS FOURS ET MIGNARDISES

AT NIGHT, AFTER DINNER, the waiters and the captains at Lutèce offer to all the tables trays of sweets (which we call in this book Petits Fours et Mignardises). The people have them after dessert with their coffee or with their brandy or just by themselves.

A few of the recipes for these sweets—the Pecan Diamonds, the Petits Fours de Noël, and the Truffes au Chocolat—are for things that we really serve only around Christmas time.

So this chapter of cookies and sweets begins with a menu for a festive Christmas dinner. You can have this dinner at Lutèce, or you can prepare it for your friends and your family at home. At either place, I suggest for after the dinner some of these Petits Fours et Mignardises.

Macarons au Chocolat et Amandes

ALMOND-CHOCOLATE MACAROONS

Yield: about 2 pounds of cookies

3 eggs
1½ cups sugar
¾ pound ground almonds

3 ounces bitter chocolate, grated
unsalted butter for buttering the
    parchment paper

Macarons au Chocolat et Amandes (continued)

1. In the bowl of an electric mixer, beat together the eggs and sugar at high speed until you have a pale-lemon mousse—about 5 minutes.
2. By hand, with a spatula, mix in the almonds and the chocolate.
3. Butter a sheet of parchment paper, and put it on a pastry sheet.
4. Using a teaspoon, put dots of the dough about 1 inch across on the parchment paper. Let them dry overnight, or for at least 4 hours, at room temperature.
5. Preheat the oven to 350°.
6. Bake in the preheated oven for 10 minutes.

Peau d'Orange (ou Pamplemousse) Confit

CANDIED CITRUS RIND

When you prepare Oranges (or Pamplemousses) Glacées (page 453), or any other citrus dessert, this is a good way to use the rind that otherwise you would throw away. For years, we discarded the rinds at Lutèce, but then I came up with this way of using them.

Every night at the restaurant, these Candied Citrus Rinds are served, together with petits fours and coffee, to our guests after dinner. The delicious sweets cost nothing. And everybody loves them. Often they are the very last thing the customers have before they leave.

One night, just as two customers were leaving, a waiter came up to me very excited. He said that he thought that these two people had taken a silver vase—one of the small silver vases in which there are roses on all the tables. Sometimes people take the roses, and we do not make a fuss about that, but normally they do not take the silver vase.

My wife was standing with me. "Are you sure?" she said. The waiter was not sure—except that the vase was no longer on the table. I did not know exactly what to do, we could not be sure they took it, and while we were talking about it and wondering what to do, these two people left, out the front door.

I thought to myself, if they have the vase, when they get outside they will take it out of a pocket or out of a purse and look at it. So I went to the front door and watched them (they did not know I was watching) while they walked away from the restaurant on 50th Street, toward Second Avenue. They walked side by side. There was nothing unusual about the way they walked. And they did not take anything out of a pocket or out of a purse.

Then they turned the corner onto Second Avenue. Very quickly I went to the corner to see what they would do now, when they thought they were out of sight. Sure enough, the woman, who all this time had in her hand the roses, reached in her pocket and took out the silver vase.

They were laughing. They enjoyed their joke so much that they were dancing on Second Avenue.

They did not see me coming. When I reached them, I grabbed the vase from her hand.

"What are you doing?" she said. She was very angry. "That's mine."

"No," I said, "it's mine."

"I'm going to call the police," she said.

"That's what I want you to do," I said.

I walked back to Lutèce with the silver vase. Nobody called the police.

Yield: approximately 60 pieces

3 medium oranges (or 2 grape-   1 cup sugar
    fruits)

1. With a sharp knife, cut away and discard a ⅓-inch top and a ⅓-inch bottom from each piece of fruit.

2. Working from top to bottom, cut the rind from the fruits in strips. Cut as close to the inner fruit as possible. The white pulp should remain attached to the colored portion of the rind, but none of the inner fruit should be attached to these strips. The strips should be about 3 to 4 inches long and about ⅓ of an inch wide.

Peau d'Orange Confit (continued)

3. Put the strips in a saucepan, and add ½ cup of cold water. Bring slowly to the boil, and boil for 3 minutes. Drain.

4. Repeat Step 3 three times. (These boilings remove the bitterness from the peel.)

5. After the 4 boilings, put the strips in a heavy-bottomed pot. Add ½ cup water and ¾ cup of the sugar. Mix well. Bring slowly to the boil, and cook very slowly, until the liquid becomes syrupy and the peels become translucent—about 1½ hours. The peels will be candied, and coated with syrup.

Note: At this point the strips may be stored in the syrup in the refrigerator, covered with plastic wrap, for weeks.

6. When you are ready to use them, pour off the excess syrup, and roll the sticks, one by one, in the remaining ¼ cup of sugar.

Pecan Diamonds

At Christmas time, every year, we make these diamonds for around three weeks during the holiday period, and we serve them with the regular petits four at dinner.

The recipe comes from the Culinary Institute of America, and we follow their recipe exactly.　　　　　　　　　*Yield: about 200 diamonds*

The Cookie Dough

10 tablespoons (1¼ sticks)
　　unsalted butter, softened
½ cup plus 1 tablespoon sugar
6 tablespoons (⅜ cup) solid
　　shortening

1 egg
½ teaspoon vanilla extract
3 cups all-purpose flour, sifted
1 teaspoon baking powder
½ teaspoon salt

The Filling

1 pound (4 sticks) unsalted
　　butter

1⅛ cups honey
½ cup sugar

2¼ cups (1 pound) light brown   ½ cup heavy cream
    sugar
8 cups chopped pecans (or
    walnuts)

The Cookie Dough

1. In a bowl, with a wooden spoon, make a paste of the butter, sugar, shortening, egg, and vanilla extract. Sift together the flour, baking powder, and salt. Add them to the paste, mixing to form a smooth dough. Wrap the dough in plastic wrap. Refrigerate overnight.

2. The next day, divide the cold dough into 3 equal parts. (While working with the first part, leave the other 2 parts in the refrigerator.)

3. Put the first ⅓ of the dough between 2 sheets of plastic wrap, and roll it out into a 5- by 12-inch rectangle, ⅛ inch thick. Remove the top sheet of plastic, and invert the dough onto a 12- by 16-inch baking sheet. (If the dough crumbles, push it together to patch it.)

4. Preheat the oven to 350°.

5. Repeat Step 3 with each of the 2 remaining portions of the dough. When all the dough is on the cookie sheet, prick it all over with a fork. Put the cookie sheet in the preheated oven, and bake for 10 minutes. Remove from the oven, and let cool. (Leave the oven on.)

The Filling

6. In a large saucepan, over medium heat, combine the butter, honey, sugar, and brown sugar. Bring to the boil, and boil for exactly 3 minutes. Remove from the heat. Let cool.

7. When the filling has cooled, fold in the pecans (or walnuts). Then fold in the heavy cream. Mix well.

The Final Assembly and Baking

8. Immediately spread the filling on the baked pastry. Return the cookie sheet to the oven, and bake for 35 minutes. Cool completely. Cut the sheet of filling-topped dough into small diamond-shaped cookies.

Petits Fours à l'Anise
(in Alsatian, Anisbretle)

ALSATIAN ANISE COOKIES

I have seen these only in Alsace, nowhere else. When you bake them, they rise a little—and the tops spread—so they look like small mushrooms.

These petits fours will keep for a long time in an airtight box. In Alsace every household has a box of Anisbretle always on hand to serve to unexpected visitors—with, of course, a glass of Alsatian white wine.

But my grandmother had her own way of serving them. When we were children, my brother and I used to visit her every few weeks. She would serve us these cookies, and with them, even though we were only small boys, a small glass of—port.   *Yield: about 1¼ pounds of cookies*

1 cup sugar	sifted, plus flour for flouring
3 eggs	the pastry sheet
1 tablespoon whole aniseeds	unsalted butter for buttering the
10 ounces all-purpose flour,	pastry sheet

1. Put the sugar and eggs in the bowl of an electric mixer. Mix for about 10 minutes at high speed, until a ribbon forms when a whisk is inserted and lifted from the mixture.

2. Add the aniseeds and beat for a few moments more, until the seeds are blended in.

3. By hand, with a spatula, gently fold in the flour. Put this dough in a pastry bag that is fitted with a round ½-inch nozzle.

4. Butter a pastry sheet, and dust it with flour. By pushing the dough out of the pastry bag and onto the pastry sheet, form the dough into circles about ¾ inch across. Let them dry overnight, or for at least 4 hours, at room temperature.

5. Preheat the oven to 275°.

6. Bake for about 10 minutes. *Do not let the cookies brown.*

Petits Fours au Beurre
(in Alsatian, Butterbretle)

ALSATIAN BUTTER COOKIES

These are very popular in Alsace, and I make them at Lutèce once in a while along with many other cookies and sweets that we serve after dinner with coffee.   *Yield: about 2½ pounds of cookies*

½ pound (2 sticks) unsalted
    butter
1 cup sugar
8 egg yolks
1 pound all-purpose flour, sifted,
    plus flour for flouring the
    work surface

1 pinch salt
1 egg beaten with a little cold
    water
crystallized sugar (coarse sugar)
    for sprinkling on the
    cookies

1. In a bowl, with a wooden spoon, work the butter until it is a soft paste. Add the sugar and work it into the softened butter for a few minutes.

2. Stir in the egg yolks, 2 at a time. Stir in the flour and salt, and mix with the wooden spoon until you have a smooth paste. Cover the bowl with plastic wrap and refrigerate for at least 1 hour or as long as overnight.

3. Preheat the oven to 325°.

4. On a floured work surface, roll out the paste to a sheet ⅛ inch thick. With cookie cutters cut the paste into various shapes. Combine the remaining paste into a ball, and again roll it out on the floured work surface to a sheet ⅛ inch thick. Cut again with cookie cutters. Repeat until all the paste is used up.

5. Put the cutouts on a pastry sheet, brush them with the beaten egg, and then sprinkle them with the crystallized sugar. Bake in the preheated oven until the cookies are golden brown—about 8 minutes.

Petits Fours au Vin

WHITE WINE COOKIES

Yield: about 1½ pounds of cookies

1 cup sugar
½ pound (2 sticks) unsalted
    butter, plus butter for
    buttering the pastry sheet
¾ cup white wine

1 scant teaspoon powdered
    cinnamon
½ pound all-purpose flour,
    sifted, plus flour for dusting
    the dough and work surface

1. With a whisk, or in the bowl of an electric mixer, beat together the sugar and butter until they form a pale-yellow mousse.

2. With a wooden spatula, mix in the wine and cinnamon. Still mixing by hand with the spatula, stir in the flour until you have a smooth paste.

3. Cover the bowl with plastic wrap. Refrigerate for at least 1 hour, or as long as overnight.

4. Remove the dough from the bowl and dust it with flour. On a floured work surface, roll out the dough to a sheet ⅛ inch thick. Cut the dough into sticks 3 inches long and ⅓ inch wide.

5. Arrange the sticks on a buttered pastry sheet, and let them rest for at least ½ hour—in the refrigerator, if you wish.

6. Preheat the oven to 350°.

7. Bake the cookies in the preheated oven until they are golden brown—about 10 minutes.

Petits Fours de Noël
(in Alsatian, Schwawebretle)

CHRISTMAS COOKIES

W hen I was young, every year, about three weeks before Christmas, all Alsatian housewives made these petits fours. That was the beginning of the Christmas season and of the feelings of the Christmas spirit.

Always, children helped their mothers to make the Christmas cookies. I did it when I was a child, and later my sister did it, and later my sister's children helped her. The little children climbed on the table where the dough was rolled out, and they stamped out the different shapes with the cookie cutters. *Yield: about 3 pounds of cookies*

½ pound (2 sticks) unsalted
    butter, plus butter for
    buttering the pastry sheet
1 cup sugar
½ teaspoon powdered cinnamon
3 ounces commercial candied
    orange rind, or Peau
    d'Orange Confit (page 492),
    chopped fine (optional)

8 ounces ground almonds
grated rind of 1 lemon
3 small eggs
1 pound all-purpose flour, sifted,
    plus flour for flouring the
    work surface and dusting the
    pastry sheet
1 egg beaten with a little cold
    water

1. In a bowl, with a wooden spoon, work the butter until it is a soft paste. Add the sugar and work it in for a few minutes until smooth.

2. Add the cinnamon, candied orange rind (if used), almonds, grated lemon rind, and the eggs, and mix thoroughly with a spatula. Add the flour and knead the mixture—on a floured surface, or in the bowl, with your fingers—until you have a smooth paste.

Petits Fours de Noël (continued)

3. Form the dough into a roll, and enclose it in plastic wrap. Let this rest in the refrigerator overnight, or up to 2 or 3 days.

4. On a floured work surface, roll out the dough to a sheet ⅛ inch thick. With cookie cutters cut the dough into various shapes. Combine the remaining dough into a ball, and again roll it out on the floured work surface to a sheet ⅛ inch thick. Cut again with cookie cutters. Repeat until all the dough is used up.

5. Preheat the oven to 300°.

6. Butter a pastry sheet, and dust it with flour. Arrange the cutouts on the pastry sheet. Brush them with the beaten egg. Bake in the preheated oven until they are golden brown—about 10 minutes.

Petits Fours Rapides

QUICK AFTER-DINNER ALMOND COOKIES

These petits fours are extremely easy to make, and because at Lutèce we make them every day, we serve them very fresh. But if you want to make them in advance, they will keep perfectly—as long as ten days—in an airtight box. *Yield: about 2 pounds of cookies*

6 eggs

1¼ cups sugar

1 teaspoon vanilla extract

10 ounces all-purpose flour,
    sifted, plus flour for dusting
    the pastry sheet

unsalted butter for buttering the
    pastry sheet

½ cup ground almonds

1. Put the eggs, sugar, and vanilla extract in the bowl of an electric mixer. Mix for about 10 minutes at a high speed, until a ribbon forms when a whisk is inserted and lifted from the mixture.

2. With a wooden spatula, gently stir in the flour.

3. Put the mixture in a pastry bag that has been fitted with a round nozzle about ¼ inch across.

4. Preheat the oven to 275°.

5. Butter a pastry sheet and dust it with flour. By pushing the mixture out of the pastry bag and onto the pastry sheet, form the mixture into both finger-length cookies as wide as the nozzle, and into circular cookies about 1 inch across. (The mixture will spread a little when it is put on the sheet, and again when it begins to bake.)

6. Sprinkle the lengths and circles of the mixture with the ground almonds. Bake in the preheated oven for 15 minutes.

❦

Truffes au Chocolat

CHOCOLATE TRUFFLES

Chocolate Truffles are strictly a Christmas sweet at Lutèce. We only make them for a few weeks around the holiday season, and we serve them with the petits fours after dinner.

During the Christmas season, many of the people who work in the Lutèce kitchen stay after hours and make these truffles to take home to their family and to give as presents to their friends.

Yield: about 50 truffles

3 ounces semisweet chocolate
1 tablespoon rum
2 egg yolks
¼ pound (1 stick) unsalted
    butter, softened

⅓ cup plus 1 tablespoon (3
    ounces) heavy cream
½ cup confectioners' sugar
½ cup unsweetened cocoa

1. Bring water to the boil in the bottom part of a double boiler. Put the top part of the double boiler over the bottom part, put the semisweet chocolate and the rum in the upper part, and melt the chocolate in the rum. When the chocolate has melted, remove the top part of the double boiler.

Truffes au Chocolat (continued)

2. Stir the egg yolks into the melted chocolate; then the butter; then the cream; then the confectioners' sugar. Finally, stir in ½ of the cocoa. Continue stirring until the mixture is smooth. Refrigerate for at least 3 hours.

3. With cold hands, form the mixture into small balls, and roll them in the remaining cocoa. Do not let your hands become warm while you are handling the truffles. Put each ball in a small paper cup ("bon-bon cup").

SAUCES, STOCKS, AND SUNDRY

Beurre Blanc

Serves 5 to 6

2 tablespoons chopped shallots   salt
½ cup vinegar   pepper, fresh ground
½ pound (2 sticks) unsalted
    butter, cut in small pieces

1. Put the shallots and vinegar in a small saucepan. Bring to the boil, and reduce the liquid by ¾. You should end up with 2 tablespoons of a sort of liquid puree.

2. Over medium heat, vigorously whisk in the butter, piece by piece. At the end, the sauce should be light and creamy. Add salt and pepper to taste. Strain through a fine sieve.

Note: This sauce should be prepared at the last minute and served immediately. Beurre Blanc cannot wait, and will separate while standing.

If it is necessary to make the sauce in advance, stir in 1 tablespoon of cream at the end of Step 1. Then go on to Step 2. With the cream added the sauce can be kept for 30 minutes.

Beurre d'Escargot

SNAIL BUTTER

Serves 6

½ pound (2 sticks) unsalted
    butter, at room temperature
1 ample tablespoon parsley
    chopped fine
1 scant tablespoon garlic
    chopped fine

1 tablespoon shallots chopped
    fine
½ tablespoon Pernod
    (preferred), or Ricard
1 teaspoon salt
¼ teaspoon pepper, fresh ground

In a bowl, mix together all the ingredients until they are thoroughly blended.

Note: Instead, you may combine the ingredients in a food processor for a few seconds, but *do not overwork them*—the snail butter should retain its texture.

Coulis de Tomates

PUREE OF TOMATOES

Note: This coulis may be prepared with red peppers, carrots, or celery. Omit the tomato paste and substitute the same weight of the other vegetable for the tomatoes.

Yield: 2 cups

¼ cup olive oil
1 medium onion, sliced
2 celery stalks, peeled, washed,
    and cut in small pieces
1 tablespoon tomato paste

2 pounds tomatoes, very ripe,
    cut in eighths
1 pinch sugar
2 garlic cloves, quartered, green
    germs removed

5 basil leaves
1 bouquet garni (page 55)

½ teaspoon salt
pepper, fresh ground

1. In a heavy-bottomed saucepan, heat the oil. Add the onion and celery, and sauté until barely browned—about 4 minutes. Add the tomato paste, and cook for 1 minute.

2. Add the tomatoes, sugar, garlic, basil, bouquet garni, salt, and pepper. Bring to the boil, cover, and cook gently, stirring occasionally, for 30 minutes. Discard the bouquet garni.

3. Put the contents of the saucepan in a blender. Puree until smooth—about 5 minutes. Strain through a fine sieve.

Note: The Coulis may be used either hot or cold.

Court Bouillon

This broth is mainly used for poaching fish.

Yield: about 2 quarts

½ cup white vinegar, tarragon
  vinegar preferred
1 leek, washed and sliced
4 stalks celery, peeled, washed,
  and sliced
1 medium onion, peeled and
  sliced
zest of ½ lemon
zest of ½ orange

1 tablespoon salt, preferably
  coarse salt
½ teaspoon cracked pepper
1 bay leaf
1 sprig thyme
2 garlic cloves, peeled, halved,
  green germs removed
1 cup dry white wine

1. Put all the ingredients except the wine in a large pot with 2 quarts of water. Bring to the boil, and simmer for 15 minutes.

2. Add the wine and simmer 5 minutes more. Do not strain.

Note: The Court Bouillon may be stored in the refrigerator for a few days.

Demi-Glace

This intense stock is always used as an ingredient for other sauces.

Yield: about 1½ quarts

2 pounds veal bones, cut in
    small pieces
2 carrots, trimmed, peeled,
    washed, and cut in ½-inch
    pieces
2 stalks celery, peeled, washed,
    and cut in ½-inch pieces
1 medium onion, peeled and cut
    in ½-inch pieces

1 bay leaf
1 sprig thyme
5 sprigs parsley
2 garlic cloves, unpeeled
1 tablespoon tomato puree
2 cups dry white wine

1. Preheat the oven to 450°.

2. In a roasting pan, roast the bones in the preheated oven until they are nicely browned—about 20 minutes. Add the carrots, celery, and onion to the roasting pan, and roast for 10 minutes more.

3. Put the bones and vegetables in a large pot. Pour off the grease from the roasting pan. Scrape up any browned material that adheres to the roasting pan and add it to pot.

4. Add the bay leaf, thyme, parsley, garlic, tomato puree, wine, and 3 quarts of water. Bring to the boil, and simmer, uncovered, for 3 to 4 hours, regularly skimming the grease and scum from the surface of the liquid. If the liquid reduces too much, add water. Strain through a fine sieve.

Note: The simmering time is 3 to 4 hours—the longer the liquid simmers, the more intense the Demi-Glace, and the lower the yield.

Fond Blanc de Canard

WHITE DUCKLING STOCK

Yield: approximately 2 cups

1 duckling carcass, plus the
  wings and the ends of the
  legs
1 medium onion, peeled and
  sliced
1 leek, washed and chopped

3 stalks celery, peeled, washed,
  and chopped
2 cloves
2 garlic cloves, unpeeled
1 bouquet garni (page 55)
½ teaspoon pepper, fresh ground

In a pot, cover the carcass, wings, and leg ends with cold water. Add
all the other ingredients. Bring to the boil, and cook, partially covered, for
2½ to 3 hours. Skim the fat and foam from the top of the liquid frequently.
Strain through a fine sieve.

Fond Brun de Canard

BROWN DUCKLING STOCK

Yield: 2½ to 3 cups

1 tablespoon peanut oil
1 duckling carcass (about 1
    pound of duckling bones)
½ pound vegetables (onions,
    carrots, and celery),
    trimmed, peeled, washed,
    and cut in ½-inch pieces

2 tablespoons Cognac
2 cups red wine
1 quart Fond de Veau (recipe
    follows), or water (see *Note*
    on page 58)

1. In a pot, heat the oil. Add the duckling carcass bones. Over high heat, brown them on all sides, turning them frequently, until they are well browned.

2. Add the vegetables, and brown for 5 minutes more.

3. Remove all oil and fat from the pot. Add the Cognac, and set it aflame.

4. When the flame subsides, add the wine. Bring to the boil, and cook over medium heat, uncovered, for 10 minutes.

5. Add the Fond de Veau (or water), bring to the boil, and cook slowly, partially covered, for 2 to 3 hours. Skim the grease from the top of the liquid frequently. Strain through a fine sieve.

❧

Fond de Veau, ou d'Agneau

VEAL STOCK, OR LAMB STOCK

Note: This recipe yields about 3 cups of stock, but you may double it if you wish, and store the extra stock in the refrigerator for up to 3 days. Or you may reduce the extra stock to ¼ its volume, store it in the refrigerator for up to 4 weeks, then dilute it when you need it. (See Glace de Veau, ou d'Agneau, below.)

Yield: about 3 cups

2 pounds veal (or lamb) bones, cut in small pieces
½ tablespoon peanut oil
½ cup chopped onions in ½-inch cubes
½ cup chopped carrots in ½-inch cubes
½ cup chopped celery in ½-inch cubes

1 ample tablespoon tomato puree
1 cup dry white wine
2 garlic cloves, unpeeled
1 bouquet garni (page 55)
1 teaspoon salt
scant ½ teaspoon cracked pepper

1. Preheat the oven to 400°.

2. Put the bones and oil in a roasting pan. Put the roasting pan in the preheated oven until the bones are nicely browned—about 18 minutes. Turn the bones from time to time while they are roasting.

3. When the bones are browned, add the onions, carrots, celery, and tomato puree, and stir everything together. Return the pan to the oven for 5 minutes more. The vegetables should barely brown, *but no more.* (If the vegetables brown too much, the Fond will be bitter.)

4. With a skimmer or slotted spoon, piece by piece, remove the solids from the roasting pan, and put them in a pot. Discard all fat from the roasting pan.

5. Add the wine to the roasting pan, and bring it to the boil on top of the stove. With a wooden spatula, scrape loose the solids that adhere to the pan. Add this liquid to the pot.

6. Add the garlic, bouquet garni, salt, pepper, and water to cover. Bring to the boil, skim the foam from the liquid, and cook gently, on top of the stove, partly covered, for about 4 hours. From time to time skim the grease from the surface of the liquid. Strain through a fine sieve.

Glace de Veau, ou d'Agneau

To avoid preparing a Fond de Veau, ou d'Agneau, every time a recipe calls for it, you may convert the Fond to Glace de Veau or Glace d'Agneau.

To produce the Glace, reduce the Fond by ¾. Then, when the Glace is

Glace de Veau, ou d'Agneau (continued)

cold, cover it with a little oil. It will keep for weeks in the refrigerator (a Fond will keep only for a few days).

Then, when a Fond is called for, dilute the Glace with water, 3 parts water to 1 part Glace.

Fond Blanc de Volaille

CHICKEN STOCK

Yield: approximately 2 quarts

2 pounds chicken backs and
  necks (or a 3-pound
  chicken)
2 leeks, washed and chopped
  coarse
2 carrots, peeled, washed, and
  chopped coarse

1 onion, peeled and sliced
2 stalks celery, washed and
  chopped coarse
2 garlic cloves, unpeeled
1 bouquet garni (page 55)
½ teaspoon pepper, fresh ground

1. In a pot, cover the chicken parts (or chicken) with 4 quarts of cold water. Add all the other ingredients.

2. Bring to the boil, and cook, partially covered, for 2½ to 3 hours. From time to time, skim the fat and foam from the top of the liquid.

3. Strain through a fine sieve. Let the stock cool, and remove all the fat that rises to the surface.

Note: If you prepare this stock with a whole chicken, you can, if you wish, remove the meat from the bones after the first hour of cooking (return the bones to the pot for the final hour or 2 of cooking). The meat may then be served cold with Vinaigrette (page 525), or it may be used in a salad.

Note: This stock may be kept in the refrigerator for several days, or in the freezer for 2 to 3 weeks.

Fumet de Poisson

FISH STOCK

Yield: about 1½ quarts

2 pounds fish bones and trimmings, washed

1 medium onion, peeled and
sliced

½ cup mushroom parings (peel
and stems), or chopped
mushrooms

1 leek, trimmed, washed, and
chopped fine

1 carrot, trimmed, peeled,
washed, and chopped fine

1 bouquet garni (page 55)

1 teaspoon salt

pepper, fresh ground

2 cups dry white wine

Put all the ingredients in a stockpot with 1½ quarts of water. Bring to
the boil, and boil slowly for 45 minutes. Skim the surface of the liquid regularly during the cooking. Strain through a fine sieve.

Gelée

JELLY FOR PÂTÉS AND TERRINES

Yield: approximately 1½ cups

1 carcass of duck, guinea hen,
   or chicken; or rabbit bones;
   or fish bones (for a fish
   jelly)
1 cup dry white wine
1 medium onion, peeled and
   cut in large cubes
1 medium carrot, trimmed,
   peeled, washed, and cut in
   large pieces

1 stalk celery, peeled, washed,
   and cut in large pieces
1 bouquet garni (page 55)
1 clove
salt
pepper, fresh ground
1 scant tablespoon (1 envelope)
   powdered gelatin diluted
   in ¼ cup water

1. Cut the carcass or bones in pieces, and put them in a pot. Add 3 cups of water. Bring to the boil and skim off the foam. Add all the other ingredients *except the gelatin*.

2. Bring the pot to the boil, and simmer, partially covered, for 45 minutes. The liquid should be reduced by ½.

3. Strain the liquid through a fine sieve into a saucepan, add the gelatin, bring the liquid to the boil, and simmer for 10 minutes.

4. Strain the liquid through a cloth.

Note: If you want a very clear jelly—for aspic—the liquid must be clarified, as follows:

In a bowl, beat the white of 1 egg until it foams, but *not* until stiff. Bring the liquid to the boil and then stir it into the beaten egg white. Put the liquid in a saucepan, and, stirring constantly, bring it to the boil again.

As soon as the liquid comes to the boil, set it aside, covered, and let it stand for 12 minutes. Strain the liquid through a sieve lined with a wet napkin.

Note: This is the recipe for how Gelée is made at Lutèce. But for home cooking, when there is no time to prepare a Gelée, a jelly made with commercial aspic jelly powder may be used.

～✥～

Mayonnaise

CLASSIC MAYONNAISE

Many people are afraid to make mayonnaise—which is too bad, because it is easy to make, and homemade mayonnaise is a thousand times better than commercial mayonnaise. There are even restaurants that use commercial mayonnaise, which to me is incomprehensible.

It is true that once in a while—very rarely—mayonnaise made by hand will separate. When it does, it is easy to correct—see the *Note* on page 516.

You can also make mayonnaise in a food processor. The oil does not have to be added slowly, and the mayonnaise will *never* separate—not even in the refrigerator.

To prepare Classic Mayonnaise with a food processor, put all the ingredients, except the oil, into the processor and blend for a few moments. With the processor still running, add the oil all at once, and process. The mayonnaise is ready when the ingredients are blended—a few moments more.   *Yield: about 2½ cups*

3 egg yolks
1 tablespoon tarragon vinegar
1 scant teaspoon Dijon mustard
½ teaspoon salt

white pepper, fresh ground
2 cups peanut oil, at room temperature

1. In a bowl that is at room temperature (*the bowl must not be cold*), whisk together the yolks, vinegar, mustard, salt, and pepper. Add the oil slowly, almost drop by drop, constantly whisking.

2. When all the oil is mixed in, adjust the seasoning. If the mayonnaise is too thick, correct by whisking in a little warm water.

Mayonnaise (continued)

Note: If the mayonnaise separates, combine 1 teaspoon of vinegar and 1 teaspoon of warm water in a bowl. Whisk the separated mayonnaise, very slowly, into the water and vinegar. The mayonnaise will bind again.

Caution: This recipe uses raw egg yolks, so there is a risk of salmonella contamination. Please use only farm-fresh eggs that have been kept refrigerated. This precaution notwithstanding, you prepare this recipe at your own risk.

Mayonnaise au Gingembre et Curry

MAYONNAISE WITH GINGER AND CURRY

This is an excellent sauce, easy to make, and very good with cold fish or vegetables. *Yield: about 3 cups*

1 apple (Golden Delicious, or
    another cooking apple)
½ tablespoon curry powder
2 tablespoons white wine, or
    water

1 teaspoon grated fresh ginger
1 recipe Mayonnaise (page 515)

1. Peel and core the apple, and cut it in ¼-inch cubes.
2. Dilute the curry powder in the wine (or water), bring to the boil in a small pan, and boil for 30 seconds.
3. Stir the apples and the ginger into the Mayonnaise. Then stir in the cooked curry and its liquid.

Sauce Béchamel

BASIC WHITE SAUCE

Today Sauce Béchamel almost has a bad name, because it is so often made badly. But in classic French cooking it is indispensable—if it is made the right way. It frightens me to think that in ten years no one will know how to make Béchamel.

Still, the recipes I give are not the way I (or any French chef) was taught to make this sauce. Here are two recipes for Sauce Béchamel. Neither one is the classic recipe, but I prefer them both to the old way because they make a Béchamel that is light.

Sometimes I use one of these methods, sometimes the other, and I cannot say why—it depends, really, on how I feel. Try one of them. Then, the next time, try the other. And see which one works best for you.

If you wish to make your Béchamel the classic way instead of the Lutèce way, substitute 3 cups of milk for the cream and water in Sauce Béchamel, Method II.

Method I

Yield: about 2 cups

2 tablespoons all-purpose flour	½ teaspoon salt
1 cup milk	pepper, fresh ground
2 tablespoons (¼ stick) unsalted butter	1 cup heavy cream
	1 egg yolk

1. Preheat the oven to its lowest setting.
2. Put the flour in a baking pan and put the pan in the preheated oven for 2 hours. After the 2 hours, sift the flour.

Note: Steps 1 and 2 are not absolutely necessary, but they make for a lighter Béchamel.

3. Heat the milk.

Sauce Béchamel (continued)

4. In a heavy-bottomed saucepan, melt the butter, and mix in the flour. Cook for 2 minutes, over medium heat, whisking constantly. Do not brown.

5. Remove the saucepan from the heat. Whisk in the hot milk, and continue whisking until the mixture is smooth and completely blended. Stir in the salt and pepper to taste.

6. Put the saucepan over medium heat, and, stirring constantly, bring it to the boil. When it comes to the boil, reduce the heat and continue cooking, still stirring constantly, for 8 minutes.

7. In a bowl, whisk together the cream and egg yolk. Add this mixture to the saucepan, and cook, stirring, for a few minutes more.

Method II

Yield: about 3 cups

1 cup heavy cream	1 scant teaspoon salt
3 tablespoons (⅜ stick) unsalted butter	white pepper
	1 pinch cayenne pepper
1½ ounces all-purpose flour	1 pinch grated nutmeg

1. Put the cream and 2 cups of water in a saucepan. Bring to the boil and keep hot.

2. Melt the butter in a saucepan. Stir in the flour, and cook slowly over low heat for 3 minutes. Do not brown. Remove the saucepan from the heat and stir in the hot liquid. Add the salt, pepper, cayenne, and nutmeg.

3. Return to high heat, bring to the boil, reduce the heat, and cook slowly for 20 minutes. Strain through a fine sieve.

Sauce Mornay

Many dishes described as "au gratin" are topped with Sauce Mornay and browned under the broiler.

If you want to prepare this Sauce Mornay, two short steps after Sauce Béchamel, and you have it: Stir 6 egg yolks into the Béchamel while it is still hot; then 4 ounces of grated Swiss cheese (Emmental or Gruyère).

❧✺❧

Sauce Gribiche

S auce Gribiche is served mostly with deep-fried fish, but also with tête de veau, hardboiled eggs, and, often, with roasted monkfish.

Yield: approximately 1½ cups

1 cup Mayonnaise (page 515)
1 hardboiled egg (page 119), chopped
½ teaspoon chopped fresh tarragon
1 tablespoon chopped

cornichons (small French pickles or gherkins)
½ tablespoon chopped capers
½ tablespoon chopped shallots
1 pinch cayenne pepper

With a wooden spatula, gently mix together all the ingredients.

Sauce Hollandaise

HOLLANDAISE SAUCE

Method I

Serves 5 to 6

½ pound (2 sticks) unsalted butter
1 scant tablespoon white vinegar
1 pinch white pepper, fresh ground

3 egg yolks
juice of ½ lemon
1 pinch cayenne pepper
salt

1. In a saucepan, melt the butter, but do not let it bubble. The butter should be warm, but not hot. Set aside and keep warm.

2. Put the vinegar, 1 tablespoon of water, and the pepper in a small

Sauce Hollandaise (continued)

saucepan. *The saucepan must not be of aluminum,* which would discolor the sauce. Bring to the boil, and cook until the liquid is reduced by half. Let cool.

3. Whisk together the egg yolks and 1 tablespoon of water. Then whisk the egg yolks and water into the reduced liquid. Put this saucepan into a pot of water that is hot, but not boiling (or use a double boiler if available).

4. Over low heat, so that the water in the bottom pot does not boil, vigorously whisk the egg mixture until it has the consistency of a smooth, heavy cream—about 8 minutes. Be certain to go into the corners of the saucepan with the whisk, so that the entire contents of the pan are incorporated into the mixture.

5. Remove the saucepan from the hot water and, away from heat, whisk for a few more minutes to cool the mixture somewhat. Little by little, whisk in the warm melted butter until all of it is absorbed, and the sauce is creamy.

Note: When adding the melted butter to the egg mixture, do not include the solids (if any) at the bottom of the melted butter.

6. Whisk in the lemon juice, then the cayenne pepper. Add salt to taste. (At this point, it is desirable, but not necessary, to strain the sauce through a fine sieve.)

Note: If, when you add the butter to the eggs, the sauce separates, do not panic. Heat 1 tablespoon of water in a saucepan. Whisk the separated sauce into the water. The sauce will recombine.

Note: This sauce may not be refrigerated and reused. But it may be kept warm, in a bain-marie of warm water, in a warm place, for up to 2 hours.

Method II

Today there is another method of making Sauce Hollandaise, *but you must be making at least twice as much as in Method I, by doubling the ingredients in Method I;* and you must have a hand blender—a very useful appliance.

This is now the only way we make Hollandaise at Lutèce.

Serves 10 to 12

1. In a saucepan, heat the butter until it is very hot, but not bubbling.

2. Put all the other ingredients in another saucepan. Add 2 tablespoons of water. With the hand blender inserted in these ingredients, and running, add the hot butter in a thin, steady stream. The sauce is ready in a few moments.

Note: This method makes a better Hollandaise—and one that almost never separates.

Note: This sauce may not be refrigerated and reused. But it may be kept warm, in a bain-marie of warm water, in a warm place, for up to 2 hours.

Sauce Choron

SAUCE BÉARNAISE
FLAVORED WITH TOMATO

Yield: 1½ cups

2 tablespoons tarragon vinegar
2 tablespoons dry white wine
1 tablespoon chopped shallots
1½ tablespoons chopped fresh tarragon (or tarragon preserved in vinegar)
1½ tablespoons chopped fresh chervil
scant ½ teaspoon salt
pepper, fresh ground
3 egg yolks

6 ounces (1½ sticks) unsalted butter
lemon juice
2 tablespoons tomato pulp, chopped fine, cooked in a saucepan for 1 to 2 minutes, and drained

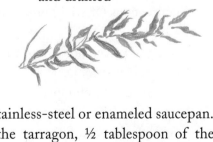

1. Put the vinegar and wine in a stainless-steel or enameled saucepan. Add the shallots, ½ tablespoon of the tarragon, ½ tablespoon of the chervil, the salt, and a pinch of pepper. Over high heat, reduce by ⅔. Let cool to lukewarm.

2. Beat in the egg yolks and 1 teaspoon of water. With the saucepan

Sauce Choron (continued)

on the edge of a low flame (or in a pan of warm water), whisk the sauce constantly until it begins to thicken.

3. When the sauce has begun to thicken, beat in the butter, a small piece at a time, adding another piece only after the previous piece is completely incorporated.

4. When all the butter is absorbed, add several drops of lemon juice. Strain the sauce through a fine sieve. Stir in the remaining tarragon and chervil.

5. Stir in the tomato.

Note: This sauce may not be refrigerated and reused. But it may be kept warm, in a bain-marie of warm water, in a warm place, for up to 2 hours.

Sauce Béarnaise

To prepare Sauce Béarnaise, eliminate Step 5.

Sauce Homard à la Crème

LOBSTER CREAM SAUCE

Serves 8

the shells of 2 lobsters	1 bay leaf
5 tablespoons (⅝ stick) unsalted butter	2 sprigs thyme
	2 sprigs tarragon
3 shallots, peeled and chopped	1 tablespoon Cognac
1 carrot, trimmed, peeled, washed, and chopped fine	1 cup dry white wine
	3 cups heavy cream
1 small leek (the white part only), chopped fine	salt
	pepper, fresh ground

1. Crush the lobster shells. In a saucepan, melt the butter. Add the shells, and brown them over high heat.

2. Add the shallots, carrot, leek, bay leaf, thyme, and tarragon, and sauté over medium heat for 2 minutes. *Do not brown.*

3. Add the Cognac, and set it aflame. When the flame subsides, add the wine, and cook over medium heat for 10 minutes. Add the cream and salt and pepper to taste, and cook over low heat for 20 minutes more. Strain through a fine sieve. Add more salt and pepper if necessary.

Sauce Périgourdine

Serves 8 to 10

¾ cup port

½ cup Cognac

¼ cup truffle juice from a
    canned black truffle

2 ounces black truffle, chopped

2 cups Demi-Glace (page 508)

4 tablespoons (½ stick) unsalted
    butter

salt

pepper, fresh ground

1. In a saucepan, reduce the port and Cognac by ¼.

2. Add the truffle juice, truffle, and Demi-Glace. Bring to the boil, and simmer for 10 to 20 minutes.

3. Stir in the butter. Add salt and pepper to taste. Simmer 10 minutes more.

Sauce Raifort

HORSERADISH SAUCE

Sauce Raifort is easy to make, and it is far better than any commercially prepared horseradish.

Many sauces called Sauce Raifort use a rich sauce, often Béchamel, as a base. But to me this version, which is the simplest, the most tangy, and the most natural, is also the best.

This sauce goes well with boiled meats, smoked trout, any cold fish. If you want a milder version—for example, to serve with a mild cold fish— the sauce may be blended with Mayonnaise (page 515).   *Serves 6*

½ pound fresh horseradish
6 ounces white bread, crust
    removed, cut in pieces
1 cup Fond Blanc de Volaille
    (page 512), or beef stock
1 teaspoon Dijon mustard

1 tablespoon vinegar
1 tablespoon peanut oil
1 pinch sugar
salt
white pepper, fresh ground

1. Peel the horseradish and grate it fine—with a hand grater, or through the fine holes of the grater attachment of a food processor.
2. Put the pieces of bread in a bowl. In a pot, bring the Fond Blanc de Volaille (or beef stock) to the boil, and pour it over the bread. Soak the bread in the stock for 5 minutes.
3. Put the horseradish, bread, stock, mustard, vinegar, oil, and sugar in a food processor. Add salt and pepper to taste. Process for about 30 seconds.

Sauce Vin Rouge

RED WINE SAUCE

Serves 4 to 6

4 tablespoons (½ stick) unsalted
    butter
½ teaspoon sugar
2 small carrots, trimmed, peeled,
    washed, and cut in ¼-inch
    cubes
1 celery stalk, peeled, washed,
    and cut in ¼-inch cubes
4 shallots (or ½ onion), peeled
    and chopped

1 garlic clove, peeled, halved,
    green germ removed
1 tablespoon all-purpose flour
2 cups red wine
¼ cup Fond de Veau (page 510),
    or water (see *Note* on page
    58)
1 bouquet garni (page 55)
salt
pepper, fresh ground

1. Preheat the oven to 300°.

2. In an ovenproof saucepan, melt 2 tablespoons of the butter. Add the sugar. Cook for about 1 minute, to caramelize the sugar lightly.

3. Add the carrots, celery, shallots (or onion), and garlic, and sauté gently for 4 to 5 minutes.

4. Stir in the flour. Put the saucepan, uncovered, in the preheated oven for 5 minutes. Stir occasionally during the 5 minutes.

5. Remove the saucepan from the oven. Add the wine and the Fond de Veau (or water). Bring to the boil on top of the stove. Add the bouquet garni, salt, and pepper. Cook gently for 30 minutes, uncovered.

6. Strain through a fine sieve into another saucepan. Over heat, stir in the remaining 2 tablespoons of butter. Add salt and pepper if needed.

Vinaigrette

BASIC VINAIGRETTE

Yield: 1 cup

1 ample tablespoon chopped
    onion
2 teaspoons Dijon mustard
¼ cup vinegar, tarragon vinegar
    preferred
½ teaspoon salt

⅛ teaspoon pepper, fresh ground
2 drops Tabasco sauce
¼ cup olive oil
½ cup peanut oil (or another
    salad oil)

1. In a bowl, crush the chopped onion to a puree with a fork. Add the mustard, vinegar, salt, pepper, and Tabasco, and whisk until blended.

2. Beat in the oils gradually. Taste, and adjust the seasoning.

Note: This vinaigrette may be prepared in advance. But if it is, omit the onion. Just before serving, add the onion. Then thoroughly mix again.

Confiture

FRUIT PRESERVES

I do not make confiture at Lutèce, but I do make it often at home. I include it in this book because during the season I find so much joy in making confiture for my family. And what a pleasure, in the middle of the winter, to open a jar of preserves and to be reminded by this perfume of the spring and summer.

Once in a while I have made as many as thirty jars of raspberry preserves. I have made as much as two bushels of peaches into preserves. Cooking is love and joy, and making confiture is for me an important part of it.

Most commercial fruit preserves are made with pectin, and I have tried it that way. But with no success. My mother taught me how to make these fruit preserves—with no pectin—and that is the way that works the best for me.

I make preserves of strawberries, rhubarb, peaches, plums, etc. All these fruits grow in the Catskill Mountains, where I have my house.

Most of the time, I combine two fruits—for example, strawberries with rhubarb, or peaches with plums. Sometimes I add a julienne of orange or grapefruit rind, or vanilla beans, ginger, cinnamon, mint, raisins, etc. All these things are a matter of taste—and there is really no limit to what may be added. I basically follow one recipe, and vary the fruit and flavorings. I vary the amount of sugar according to what I think is right for the fruits I am using. *Yield: 4 pounds*

4 pounds (net weight) fruit (peeled and pitted, if necessary)
3 pounds sugar

juice of 2 lemons
flavorings of your choice (rind, spices, dried fruits, herbs, etc.)

1. In a bowl, mix the fruit, sugar, and lemon juice. Refrigerate overnight.

2. Put the contents of the bowl in a colander to drain. Keep the juice

that drains from the colander, and put it in a large pot. Bring the pot to the boil. With a skimmer, skim the foam from the surface of the liquid.

3. Add the flavorings, and cook until the liquid becomes a fairly thick syrup—about 30 to 40 minutes. Stir once in a while with a wooden spoon during the cooking to prevent burning at the bottom of the pot.

4. Add the fruits to the pot. Return to the boil, and cook until the liquid thickens slightly—about 35 minutes.

Note: To test for consistency, put a very small amount of the hot liquid on a plate, and let it cool to room temperature. It is ready when it has thickened to the consistency you want, but bear in mind that the confiture will thicken a little more when stored.

5. Transfer immediately to very clean jars. Cover the jars with plastic wrap, and seal them with their lids.

Note: Store the jars upside down, and wait at least 2 to 3 weeks before opening them; during this time the preserves will thicken. Confiture may be stored at room temperature for months.

Mousseline de Poisson

MOUSSELINE OF FISH

Note: This mousseline may be prepared with pike, sole, bass, whiting, or tilefish.

Yield: approximately 2 cups

½ pound fish fillets
1 large egg
1 scant teaspoon salt

pepper, fresh ground
1 cup heavy cream

Put the fish fillets, egg, salt, pepper, and cream in a food processor. Process until smooth—about 1½ to 2 minutes.

Quatre Épices

MIXED SPICES

This spice mixture is used for pâtés, terrines, foie gras. It can be found in stores ready mixed. Or you can make it yourself, and store it in a tightly closed jar—which is what we do at Lutèce.

Yield: approximately 4 tablespoons

1 tablespoon dried thyme
1 tablespoon bay leaf, crumbled, long stem removed (if present)
1 tablespoon dried sage
½ teaspoon coriander
5 cloves
1 tablespoon black or white peppercorns

1. Put all the ingredients in a chopper-mixer or in a blender. Chop or blend until you have a thoroughly mixed powder.
2. Pour through a sieve, and store in a tightly closed jar.

BASIC PASTRIES
AND BREAD

BASIC PASTRIES

Feuilletage Rapide

FAST PUFF PASTRY

Note: This recipe calls for the quick-dissolving flour called Wondra. All-purpose flour may be used instead, but quick-dissolving flour works better.

Yield: about 2¼ pounds

1 pound quick-dissolving flour (Wondra)

flour for flouring the work surface and the pastry (about ½ cup)

1 pound (4 sticks) unsalted butter, very cold, cut in 1-inch pieces

1 teaspoon baking powder

½ teaspoon salt

1 cup water, ice cold

1. Put all the ingredients in a large bowl (except the flour for flouring the work surface and the pastry). Mix them together with your hands for about 30 seconds (or for a few seconds in an electric mixer), just enough for the ingredients to gather into a ball. The butter must still be in pieces.

2. Sprinkle a work surface with flour—enough flour so that the dough

Feuilletage Rapide (continued)

does not stick. Roll the dough into a rectangle 18 inches by 8 inches. Sprinkle generously with flour, to coat all the pieces of butter and prevent sticking to the rolling pin.

3. Brush any excess flour from the surface of the dough, and fold it in half, then in half again, into a rectangle 4 inches by 9 inches. Lightly flour the top of the pastry. Turn the rectangle clockwise a quarter turn so that a narrow side is toward you, and again roll out the pastry to a rectangle 18 inches by 8 inches.

4. Repeat Step 3. Then repeat it again. If the dough is too stiff for the second repeat, wait 15 minutes.

5. Fold the dough in thirds, and wrap it in plastic wrap. Refrigerate for 15 minutes.

6. Repeat Step 3. Then repeat it again. Wrap the dough in plastic wrap. Refrigerate for at least 30 minutes.

Note: This pastry may be kept in the freezer for up to 2 weeks. If the pastry has been frozen, defrost it slowly, in the refrigerator, for 2 to 3 hours before using.

❧

Feuilletage Spécial

SPECIAL PUFF PASTRY

My recipe is different from the classic puff pastry. By increasing the amount of butter, and by increasing the number of turns of the dough, I get exceptionally flaky pastry. At Lutèce, when I prepare dishes that call for very, very light puff pastry—napoleons, for example—this is what I use.

Note: This recipe calls for quick-dissolving flour, but it may also be prepared with regular all-purpose flour, sifted. ⸱

Yield: almost 3 pounds

1 pound quick-dissolving flour
(Wondra), very cold, in the
freezer for at least 2 hours
before using
1 pound, 3 ounces (4¾ sticks)
unsalted butter, at room
temperature

1 cup water, ice cold
1 scant teaspoon salt
½ teaspoon baking powder
flour for flouring the work
surface and the pastry (about
3 ounces)

1. Mound the 1 pound of flour on a work surface. Form a well in the flour. In the well place 3 ounces (¾ stick) of the butter, the water, salt, and baking powder. Combine with the fingers until thoroughly mixed into a dough. *Do not overwork.*

2. Flour the work surface, and roll the dough into a rectangle 5 inches by 5 inches. Wrap the dough in plastic wrap. Refrigerate for at least 30 minutes.

3. Work the remaining 1 pound of butter with your fingers—or tap it with the rolling pin on the work surface—until it is pliable. (This will require only very little working of the butter.) Form the butter into a 6-inch square. Refrigerate the butter for the short time until it is needed.

4. Lightly flour the work surface. Roll the dough into a 12-inch square. Put the square of butter at the center of the square of dough. Each corner of the square of butter should point to the center of 1 side of the square of dough. (The sides of the square of butter *must not be parallel* to the sides of the square of dough.)

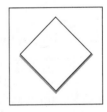

5. Fold each corner of the square of dough over the butter, so that the corners of the dough meet at the center. The folded corners of dough should overlap slightly, the dough completely encasing the butter.

6. Lightly flour the work surface again. And lightly flour the pastry. With a rolling pin, gently pound the folded dough down.

7. Roll the dough into a rectangle 10 inches by 20 inches. Brush all excess flour from the dough, and fold it in thirds—as a letter is folded—into a rectangle approximately 10 inches by 7 inches. Turn the folded pastry a quarter turn clockwise so that a 7-inch side is toward you. Again lightly flour the top of the pastry. Again roll out the pastry to a rectangle 10 inches by 20 inches. Brush all excess flour from the dough again, and

Feuilletage Spécial (continued)

again fold it in thirds. Wrap in plastic wrap. Refrigerate for at least 30 minutes.

8. Repeat Step 7 three times. Roll out the pastry twice each time; fold it twice each time. Refrigerate for at least 30 minutes after the first 2 of these repeats of Step 7. Refrigerate for at least 2 hours after the third repeat (if possible overnight) before using.

Note: This pastry may be kept in the freezer for up to 2 weeks. If the pastry has been frozen, defrost it slowly, in the refrigerator, for 2 to 3 hours before using.

Pâte à Brioche

BRIOCHE PASTRY

Yield: about 2 pounds

½ ounce fresh yeast (or 1 envelope active dry yeast)
¼ cup water (or milk), lukewarm
1 pound all-purpose flour, sifted
1 scant teaspoon salt

1 teaspoon sugar
6 eggs
½ pound (2 sticks) unsalted butter, softened

1. Put the yeast in the bowl of an electric mixer (or in a mixing bowl). Add the lukewarm water (or milk), and blend the yeast and the liquid.

2. Add ¼ of the flour and stir it in well. Cover the bowl with a cloth, set it in a warm place, and let it double in volume—about 10 to 15 minutes, depending on the temperature of the room.

3. Add the salt, sugar, the remaining flour, and 4 of the eggs. Mix in the electric mixer, at medium speed, until the dough starts to pull away from the sides of the bowl—about 4 minutes (about 8 minutes by hand).

4. Add the remaining 2 eggs, one at a time, mixing the first egg in thoroughly before adding the second.

5. Add the butter. Mix with the electric mixer at low speed for about

1 minute, or mix by hand. Cover the bowl with a cloth, and set it in a warm place until it doubles in volume—about 1 to 1½ hours.

6. Punch the dough a few times to make it collapse. Refrigerate for 3 hours (or enclose it in plastic wrap and refrigerate overnight).

Note: To make an even finer brioche, increase the butter to ¾ pound. (This dough will be a little more difficult to handle.)

Note: To prepare a loaf of Brioche bread, put the dough in a buttered bread pan that has been lined with buttered parchment paper. Let the dough rise in a warm place until it has doubled in size—about 20 minutes. Bake in a preheated 325° oven for 25 minutes.

~◦≫◦~

Pâte à Choux

CREAM-PUFF PASTRY

Yield: approximately 8 servings

3 tablespoons (⅜ stick) unsalted butter	¼ teaspoon sugar
	1 cup all-purpose flour, sifted
¼ teaspoon salt	4 large eggs

1. Put 1 cup of water, the butter, salt, and sugar in a heavy-bottomed saucepan. Bring to the boil.
2. Remove the saucepan from the heat. Add all the flour at once, and mix well with a wooden spoon.
3. Put the saucepan over medium heat, and cook, constantly stirring with the wooden spoon, until the mixture is fairly dry—about 3 minutes.
4. Remove the saucepan from the heat. Add 1 egg, and stir it in until the mixture is very smooth. Repeat with the remaining eggs, one at a time. At the end, the paste should be very smooth.

~◦≫◦~

Pâte à Frire (Pâte à Beignet)

PASTRY FOR FRITTERS

Serves 4 (approximately 12 beignets)

1 pinch sugar
1 pinch salt
1 egg yolk
¾ cup beer

1¼ cups all-purpose flour, sifted
1 tablespoon peanut oil
2 egg whites

1. In a bowl, stir together the sugar, salt, egg yolk, and beer.
2. Put the flour in another bowl, and form a well in it. Pour the liquid into the well, and whisk the liquid and flour together until smooth—the paste will be quite loose.
3. Distribute the oil over the top of the paste (to prevent the top from crusting). Cover the bowl with plastic wrap, and put it in a warm place—preferably warmer than room temperature—for at least ½ hour.
4. When you are ready to use the paste, beat the egg whites until stiff, and gently fold them into the paste.

Pâte à Pâté

PASTRY FOR PÂTÉS

Pâte à Pâté is used only for pâtés. The effect of the hot lard and hot water is to make the pastry very stable—more stable than other pastries—and easier to cut without breaking it.

Yield: approximately 1½ pounds

1 pound all-purpose flour, sifted
¼ pound lard

1 teaspoon salt
½ cup water, heated to 150°

1. Put the flour in a mixing bowl or on a work surface. Form a well in the flour.

2. In a skillet, melt the lard and heat it beyond the melting point—*but do not let it smoke.* Pour the lard in the well. Add the salt.

3. Work the flour and the lard together with your fingertips until the combination has a sandy consistency.

4. Form a well in the combined flour and lard. Pour the heated water into the well, and knead—first with your fingers, then with your hands—until a dough is formed.

5. When the dough can be formed into a ball, wrap it in plastic wrap. Refrigerate at least 2 hours before using—preferably overnight.

❦

Pâte Brisée

PASTRY FOR PIES OR TARTS

Pâte Brisée is the pastry we use for the Tarte Lutèce—and for a number of other tarts for which we have to have a flaky pastry.

Note: This pastry may be prepared in a food processor, but when Pâte Brisée is prepared this way, *extreme care must be taken not to overwork the dough. Stop processing as soon as the dough forms a ball.*

Yield: approximately ¾ pound of pastry, enough for a 10-inch tart

1¼ cups all-purpose flour, sifted	1 egg
¼ teaspoon salt	1 tablespoon cold water
¼ pound (1 stick) unsalted butter, cut in small pieces	

1. Put the flour on a table or in a mixing bowl, and form a well in it. Put the salt and the butter in the well. With the fingertips, blend the flour, the salt, and the butter until you have a crumbly dough.

2. Add the egg, then the water. Knead again with your fingertips until the dough forms easily into a ball in your fingers. *Do not overwork.*

3. Wrap the ball in plastic wrap. Refrigerate for at least 1 hour. (Pâte Brisée may be refrigerated overnight.)

❦

Pâte Levée

RAISED PASTRY

This pastry is used for dessert tarts, in place of Pâte Brisée, where a softer, less flaky and less crunchy pastry is wanted—the texture is a little like that of brioche.   *Yield: about 2 pounds*

½ ounce fresh yeast (or 1 enve-
    lope active dry yeast)
1 cup milk, lukewarm
1 pound all-purpose flour, sifted
1 scant teaspoon salt

½ cup sugar
1 large egg
¼ pound (1 stick) unsalted
    butter, softened

1. In a small bowl, dissolve the yeast in ⅓ of the milk. Stir in 3 table-spoons of the flour to make a soft paste. Cover the bowl and let it rest in a warm place until the volume doubles—about 10 to 15 minutes.

2. Put the remaining flour in a bowl, and form a well in the flour. Put the salt, sugar, egg, and the remaining milk in the well, and mix. Add the contents of the small bowl, and mix thoroughly with a spoon until a soft, sticky dough forms—about 5 minutes. (This mixing may also be done in an electric mixer set at slow speed.)

3. Add the butter, and, in the bowl, knead the dough by hand until it no longer sticks to the bowl or to your fingers. Cover the bowl and let it rest in a warm place until the volume of the dough doubles—about 15 to 20 minutes.

4. Punch the dough a few times to make it collapse. Refrigerate for at least 3 hours, or (preferably) enclose the dough in plastic wrap and refrigerate overnight.

Pâte Sablée

PASTRY FOR TARTS

If you have a food processor, this is a remarkably easy pastry to make. It comes out perfect every time. You can use the processor's special blade for making dough, but if you do not have the special blade, you will get a good result with the regular blade.

Pâte Sablée can be used in fruit tarts, in place of Pâte Brisée, or whenever you want a crumbly pastry instead of a flaky one.

Yield: about ¾ pound of pastry, enough for a 10-inch tart

1¼ cups all-purpose flour, sifted
¼ pound (1 stick) unsalted but-
    ter, cut in small pieces

1 tablespoon sugar
¾ teaspoon salt
¼ cup water, ice cold

1. Put the flour, butter, sugar, and salt in a food processor, and process for 10 seconds—no longer.

2. Add the ¼ cup ice water to the processor. Process for 10 seconds more—the dough will just begin to form into a ball.

3. Wrap the ball in plastic wrap. Refrigerate for at least 1 hour. (The Pâte Sablée may be refrigerated overnight.)

Pâte Sucrée

This is an extremely easy pastry to make for those who have a food processor. It is basically a Pâte Brisée with sugar, and is used only for sweet dessert tarts.   *Yield: about 1 pound*

1½ cups all-purpose flour, sifted
⅓ cup sugar
½ teaspoon salt
¼ pound (1 stick) unsalted
    butter, cut in small pieces

1 egg
1 tablespoon water, ice cold

1. Put the flour, sugar, salt, and butter in a food processor. Process for 20 seconds. Add the egg and water. Process until you have a smooth ball—about 1 minute.
2. Wrap the pastry in plastic wrap. Refrigerate for at least 2 hours.

Ravioli Dough

Yield: about ½ pound

1 cup all-purpose flour, sifted
1 egg yolk
1 tablespoon peanut oil

¼ cup very cold water, but not
    ice cold
1 pinch salt

1. Put all ingredients in the bowl of a food processor. Process quickly—15 to 20 seconds—until the dough forms a ball.
2. Wrap the dough in plastic wrap. Refrigerate for at least 1 hour.

BREAD

Pain de Campagne

COUNTRY BREAD

Yield: 1 large round loaf, approximately 1½ pounds

⅔ ounce fresh baker's yeast
    (preferred), or 1½ envelopes
    active dry yeast
½ cup lukewarm water
1½ pounds all-purpose flour,
    sifted, plus flour for flouring
    the top of the loaf

2 scant teaspoons salt
oil for oiling the baking sheet

1. In a bowl, dissolve the yeast in the ½ cup of warm water. Add ½ cup of the flour, and mix until smooth.

2. Cover the bowl with a cloth or with plastic wrap, and put it in a warm place. Let the mixture rise until it doubles in volume—about 25 to 30 minutes.

3. Put the remaining flour in the bowl of an electric mixer. Add the salt and the risen mixture. Mix in 1½ cups of water. Using the hook attachment, mix at slow speed until the dough is smooth, and starts to pull away from the sides of the bowl—about 8 minutes.

4. Remove the bowl from the mixer, cover it with a cloth or with plas-

Pain de Campagne (continued)

tic wrap, put it in a warm place, and let the dough rise until it doubles in volume—about 40 minutes.

5. Punch the dough down. Knead it briefly in the bowl with your fingers. Shape it into a large round loaf. Lightly oil a pastry sheet, and put the loaf on the sheet. With a knife, cut a cross in the surface of the loaf. Put the loaf in a warm place, covered, until it doubles in size again.

6. Preheat the oven to 400°.

7. Brush the top of the loaf very lightly with water, and sprinkle it lightly with flour. Put the loaf in the preheated oven, and bake for 40 to 50 minutes. The bread is ready when it is browned and nicely crusted, and when tapping it produces a hollow sound.

Note: The bread must be cooled on a rack before using.

Pumpernickel Raisin Bread

Yield: 1 loaf, approximately 1½ pounds

½ ounce fresh baker's yeast, or 1 envelope active dry yeast
1 cup lukewarm water
½ cup espresso (or strong dark coffee)
3 tablespoons molasses
1 teaspoon unsweetened cocoa

1 pound whole wheat flour, sifted
3 ounces rye flour, sifted
½ teaspoon salt
2 ounces (⅜ cup) raisins
oil for oiling the loaf pan

1. In the bowl of an electric mixer, dissolve the yeast in the lukewarm water. Add the espresso (or coffee), molasses, cocoa, and ¼ of the whole wheat flour. Using the hook attachment, mix at low speed until blended.

2. Remove the bowl from the mixer, cover it with a cloth or with plastic wrap, put it in a warm place, and let the dough rise for 20 minutes.

3. Return the bowl to the mixer. Add the rye flour, the remaining whole wheat flour, and salt to the bowl. Using the hook attachment, mix

until the paste is smooth and the dough pulls away from the sides of the bowl—about 8 minutes.

4. Add the raisins, and mix them in, which should take about 1 minute. Remove the bowl from the mixer, cover it with a cloth or with plastic wrap, and let the dough rise in a warm place until it doubles in volume.

5. Preheat the oven to 400°.

6. Knead the dough briefly. Put the dough in an oiled metal loaf pan approximately 12 inches by 5 inches by 4 inches. Cover it with a cloth or with plastic wrap, and let it rise in a warm place until it doubles in size.

7. Bake in the preheated oven for 40 minutes.

Note: The bread must be cooled on a rack before serving.

Pumpernickel Walnut Bread

To make Pumpernickel Walnut Bread, substitute shelled walnuts, broken in pieces, for the raisins.

~∗~

Pâte à Pain Ordinaire

BASIC BREAD DOUGH

This is not the bread we serve at Lutèce, but it is good as an everyday bread, and it is the right bread for certain special purposes—Jambon en Croûte, Pissaladière, Pizza, and so on.

To prepare this recipe as loaf bread, see Steps 6 through 8.

Yield: 1 loaf, approximately 1¼ pounds

⅓ ounce fresh baker's yeast, or ⅔ envelope active dry yeast

1¼ cups water, lukewarm

1 teaspoon sugar

1 pound all-purpose flour, sifted, plus flour for flouring your hands

1 teaspoon salt

Pâte à Pain Ordinaire (continued)

1. In a bowl, dissolve the yeast in the water, then add the sugar.

2. Mound the flour on a work surface, and form a well in it. Put the salt in the well. Little by little, incorporate the dissolved yeast and sugar into the flour, kneading with your fingers at first, and at the end with your hands, until you have a smooth paste—about 5 to 8 minutes of kneading altogether.

3. Form the dough into a ball. Put it in a bowl, cover the bowl with a damp cloth, and let the dough rise in a warm place for about 1½ to 2 hours.

4. Flour your hands, and knead the dough again to deflate it—1 to 2 minutes. Form the dough into a ball again. With a knife, cut 2 incisions about ½ inch deep in the form of a cross into the top of the ball.

5. Put the dough in a bowl again, cover it with a damp towel, and let the dough rise in a warm place for about 2 hours.

Note: The dough may be used right away, but it is better to refrigerate it for a while before using.

To Prepare as Bread

6. Preheat the oven to 400°.

7. The dough may be formed into a loaf or into a baguette. Dust the dough lightly with flour, put it in a lightly greased baking pan, let it rise to at least double its volume, and bake in the preheated oven until the crust is golden brown and the bread is baked through—about 50 minutes to 1 hour.

Note: For better bread, throw a tablespoon of water into the oven—to create steam—2 or 3 times during the first 10 minutes of baking.

8. When the bread has baked, remove it from the oven and let it cool on a rack. Do not serve until it has been out of the oven at least 2 hours.

Whole Wheat Bread

This recipe was given to me by a pastry chef who retired to the community in the Catskill Mountains where I have my weekend house. I used to visit him often. One time, he served me this bread. It was delicious, so of course I asked him for the recipe.

At Lutèce we serve it just with certain dishes, such as smoked salmon and gravlax.   *Yield: 1 loaf, approximately 2 pounds*

1 ounce fresh yeast, or ⅔ envelope active dry yeast
½ tablespoon brown sugar
¾ tablespoon molasses
¼ cup warm water (a little
   warmer than room
   temperature)

½ pound rye flour, sifted
½ pound unbleached flour, sifted
½ pound whole wheat flour,
   sifted
2 teaspoons salt
unsalted butter for buttering the
   molds

1. In a bowl, mix together the yeast, sugar, molasses, and water.

2. In another bowl, thoroughly mix the 3 flours together, and then put the flours in a food processor. Add the salt. Add 1½ cups of cold water. Using the plastic blade (the dough blade) of the processor, process for about 10 seconds.

3. Add to the processor the yeast-sugar-molasses mixture, and process until the dough forms into a ball—about 10 seconds.

4. Preheat the oven to 325°.

5. Butter the inside of a 3-quart bread mold approximately 12 inches by 5 inches by 4 inches high. Put the dough in the mold—the mold should be about half full. Put the mold in a warm place, covered with a cloth, and let the dough rise until the mold is a little more than full.

6. Bake the bread in the preheated oven for 40 minutes. Then turn the loaf onto a rack to cool at room temperature.

Pain de Noix

WALNUT BREAD

Yield: 1 loaf, approximately 1½ pounds

⅔ ounce fresh baker's yeast (preferred), or 1½ envelopes active dry yeast
1 cup milk, lukewarm
1 egg, beaten
½ tablespoon sugar

2 cups all-purpose flour, sifted
1 cup chopped walnuts
½ teaspoon salt
unsalted butter for buttering the loaf pan

1. In a bowl, dissolve the yeast in the milk. Stir in the beaten egg. Add the sugar, flour, walnuts, and salt. Stir the dough vigorously with a wooden spoon for about 10 minutes.

2. Put this mixture in a buttered loaf pan, approximately 7 inches by 3 inches. Put the loaf pan in a warm place, cover it with a cloth or with plastic wrap, and let the dough rise for 30 minutes.

3. Preheat the oven to 300°.

4. Bake in the preheated oven until golden brown—about 35 minutes.

Soft Rolls

For our regular bread at Lutèce we serve hard rolls that we buy from an excellent baker. But when we have time, we serve soft rolls also, which we make ourselves.

These rolls are very easy to make at home.   *Yield: 30 rolls*

1½ ounces fresh baker's yeast, or 3 envelopes active dry yeast
1¼ cups water, lukewarm

1 pound, 6 ounces all-purpose flour, sifted
1 tablespoon salt

¼ cup sugar
scant ½ cup powdered milk,
    sifted
1 egg
oil for oiling the pastry sheet

1 egg beaten with a little cold
    water
1½ teaspoons celery seeds,
    crushed

1. In the bowl of an electric mixer, mix the yeast and water. Add the flour, salt, sugar, powdered milk, and the *unbeaten* egg. Using the hook of the mixer (not the whipper) mix at medium speed until you have a smooth dough—about 10 minutes.

2. Cover the dough with a cloth or with plastic wrap, and let it rise in a warm place (approximately 80°) until it doubles in size—about 1 hour.

3. Punch the dough a few times so that it collapses. Let the dough rest for 20 minutes.

4. Oil a pastry sheet. Divide the dough into 30 equal ball-shaped parts. Put these balls on the pastry sheet at 2-inch intervals. Brush each of the balls with the beaten egg, and sprinkle each of them with crushed celery seeds.

5. Preheat the oven to 350°.

6. Cover the balls with a cloth or with plastic wrap, and let them rise in a warm place (approximately 80°) until they double in size.

7. Bake in the preheated oven for about 7 minutes.

Note: It is not practical to prepare fewer than 30 of these rolls. If 30 are more than you want, the extra ones may be wrapped in plastic wrap and frozen until needed.

Index

A NOTE ABOUT THE AUTHORS

André Soltner was born in Thann, Alsace, in 1932. At the age of fifteen, he decided to become a chef. He trained in the French provinces and then in the Swiss Alps, before working in Paris at the restaurant Chez Hansi. In 1961, the founder of Lutèce, André Surmain, lured Soltner to New York to be its first chef. He eventually became a partner in the restaurant, and in 1972 its sole owner. After more than three decades at Lutèce, Soltner sold the restaurant in 1994, but he remains a part owner. In 1968, his talents were commended with the highest distinction, the title Meilleur Ouvrier de France.

Seymour Britchky has been writing about food, wine, and New York restaurants for twenty-five years.

A NOTE ON THE TYPE

This book was set in a modern adaptation of a type designed by the
first William Caslon (1692–1766). The Caslon face, an artistic, easily
read type, has enjoyed more than two centuries of popularity in the
United States. It is of interest to note that the first copies of the Dec-
laration of Independence and the first paper currency distributed to
the citizens of the newborn nation were printed in this typeface.

Composed by North Market Street Graphics,
Lancaster, Pennsylvania
Printed and bound by Quebecor Printing Martinsburg,
Martinsburg, West Virginia
Designed by Virginia Tan